ArtScroll History Series®

Rabbi Nosson Scherman / Rabbi Meir Zlotowitz

General Editors

Reb Shraga

by
Yonoson Rosenblum
Based on Rabbi Aharon Sorasky's *Shelucha Derachmana*

Published by
Mesorah Publications, ltd

Feivel

The Life and Times of
Rabbi Shraga Feivel Mendlowitz
the Architect of Torah in America

FIRST EDITION
First Impression … June 2001
Second Impression … December 2001

Published and Distributed by
MESORAH PUBLICATIONS, LTD.
4401 Second Avenue / Brooklyn, N.Y 11232

Distributed in Europe by
LEHMANNS
Unit E, Viking Industrial Park
Rolling Mill Road
Jarow, Tyne & Wear, NE32 3DP
England

Distributed in Australia and New Zealand by
GOLDS WORLDS OF JUDAICA
3-13 William Street
Balaclava, Melbourne 3183
Victoria, Australia

Distributed in Israel by
SIFRIATI / A. GITLER — BOOKS
6 Hayarkon Street
Bnei Brak 51127

Distributed in South Africa by
KOLLEL BOOKSHOP
Shop 8A Norwood Hypermarket
Norwood 2196, Johannesburg, South Africa

ARTSCROLL HISTORY SERIES®
REB SHRAGA FEIVEL
© *Copyright 2001, by* MESORAH PUBLICATIONS, Ltd.
4401 Second Avenue / Brooklyn, N.Y. 11232 / (718) 921-9000 / www.artscroll.com

Typography by CompuScribe at ArtScroll Studios, Ltd.
Printed in the United States of America by Noble Book Press Corp.
Bound by Sefercraft, Quality Bookbinders, Ltd., Brooklyn N.Y. 11232

We remember

Mr. Marvin Berlin

משה בן זאב וואלף

5 Nissan 5769 ❖ *March 26, 1999*

We salute his wife

Mrs. Alice Berlin

for sponsoring the Hebrew Edition
and supporting the

Reb Shraga Feivel Book

Table of Contents

Publisher's Preface

R EB SHRAGA FEIVEL MENDLOWITZ LEFT THE SCENE IN 1948, more than half a century ago, at the fairly young age of 62. His career in Mesivta Torah Vodaath spanned only twenty-five years, yet virtually every major *gadol* of his era proclaimed him unreservedly as the premier architect of Torah in American history. As this magnificent biography shows, that appellation is not the least bit exaggerated.

He insisted on being addressed as "Mister" Mendlowitz, and those who had the temerity or foolishness to call him "Rabbi" — a title he richly earned — were either ignored or rebuked. But, as the Talmud says of such historic but untitled greats as Hillel and Shammai, their very names meant more than the loftiest titles. The same applies to Mister Mendlowitz; the name Reb Shraga Feivel is more august than pages of titles and superlatives. The burgeoning Torah world of today is his legacy, as this volume shows simply by relating the bare facts of his life, aspirations, and achievements.

Our generation has much to learn from him. In his time, he

fought hopelessness; in our time he would have fought compla-
cency. His motif was that a Jew must always strive to increase the
glory of Heaven, bring his fellow Jews close to Torah, never be content with his own accomplishments, infuse his life with joy in
serving G-d, and try to find and blend the finest strands of the various Jewish communities and traditions. Those goals never change,
although the challenges to them change from generation to generation. Every reader will find lessons for life in this book — as well as
a role model in how to fulfill them.

To chronicle and explain such a great man requires an outstanding biographer. The Jewish public is indebted, therefore, to RABBI
YONOSON ROSENBLUM, whose biographies of Rabbi Yaakov
Kamenetsky and Elimelech (Mike) Tress have set a high standard —
a standard he maintains here in *Reb Shraga Feivel.* This is a book that
can be read on more than one level. It is a biography, a textbook in
allegiance to the Torah and its Giver, and a guidebook in how to educate a generation, as well as individual students.

We are grateful to RABBI SHMUEL MENDLOWITZ and RABBI AVRAHAM
ABBA FREEDMAN for choosing us to produce this book. Although it is
based in great measure on the Hebrew *Shelucha D'Rachmana,* by the
distinguished journalist and author RABBI AHARON SORASKY, this biography is essentially a new work.

Many people contributed time and effort to help make this volume possible, some of whom Rabbi Rosenblum has mentioned in
his own acknowledgments. We would be remiss, however, if we did
not express our own appreciation to RABBI MENDLOWITZ and RABBI
FREEDMAN for their help and confidence. Rabbi Freedman has made
it a primary mission of his life to bring the message of Reb Shraga
Feivel to new generations; in his own person he embodies much of
it. RABBI NESANEL QUINN, himself one of the premier *mechanchim* in
the history of American yeshivos, gave of himself unstintingly.
Graciously and meticulously, he reviewed the manuscript several
times, always adding valuable comments and observations. We are
grateful to him beyond words. The source notes of the book indicate
the many *talmidim* of Reb Shraga Feivel who shared memories and
insights with Rabbi Sorasky and Rabbi Rosenblum. RABBI MOSHE

KOLODNY, director of the Agudath Israel Archives, contributed his customary cooperation and vast erudition. We thank them all.

In particular we express our profound appreciation to SIDNEY GREENWALD and RABBI MENDEL RAPAPORT, who wisely and patiently facilitated the publication of the book. We and the public are grateful to them both. In addition, Reb Sidney, as a close and still buoyant *talmid* of Reb Shraga Feivel, added his personal insights to the book. GARY TORGOW, too, expended time and effort to bring this work to fruition.

Finally, we are grateful to our staff members, whose skill and dedication are evident on every page. ELI KROEN sets a high standard of graphic excellence. AVRAHAM KAY, MRS. ESTY FRANKEL, and ESTHER SCHWARTZ did the graphics and layout, and MRS. MINDY STERN and MRS. FAIGIE WEINBAUM proofread. With his usual efficiency and devotion, AVROHOM BIDERMAN directed the process that turned manuscript, galleys, photos, and comments into a book.

Someone commented, "This is not a 'book,' it's a '*sefer*.'" True. We hope that this *sefer* acquaints a new generation and reminds an older generation of one of the greatest Torah figures of the 20th century, and thereby gives new impetus to his efforts to stamp the glory of Torah on the New World.

Rabbi Meir Zlotowitz / Rabbi Nosson Scherman
Sivan 5761 / June 2001

Photo Acknowledgments

We are grateful to the following people who supplied photographs:

Rabbi and Mrs. Norman Eller, the Leiman family, Rabbi Shmuel Mendlowitz, Mrs. Dinah Pirutinsky, Rabbi Y. Y. Rotenberg, and Mrs. Hindy Silberberg.

Acknowledgments

AS WE PREPARE TO GO TO PRESS WITH THIS BIOGRAPHY of Reb Shraga Feivel Mendlowitz זצ"ל, my primary emotion is a profound sense of sadness for the loss of two figures to whom this book would have meant so much and who did not live to see it in print: RABBI ALEXANDER SENDER LINCHNER, Reb Shraga Feivel Mendlowitz's son-in-law; and DR. JOSEPH KAMINETSKY, who was tapped by Reb Shraga Feivel to be the national director of Torah Umesorah, and who oversaw the flowering of the day-school movement in his nearly four decades heading the organization.

My only consolation is that both Rabbi Linchner and Dr. Kaminetsky reviewed the entire manuscript before their passings and expressed their warmest approval.

I first spent any substantial amount of time with Rabbi Linchner in the winter of 1995. He was already 86 years old and suffering from pneumonia. Neither of us had any idea whether he would survive the winter. But survive he did. Not only did he survive, he returned to running the vast Boys Town facility in Jerusalem, which he had built from scratch in fulfillment of Reb Shraga Feivel's deathbed injunction to "do something for *Eretz Yisrael*."

Over the next two years, Rabbi Linchner and I became extremely close, speaking on the phone almost every day. More than forty years his junior, I felt like an old man in his presence. He had more plans in a day than most people have in a lifetime. By the end of his morning swim, he had usually hatched four or five new initiatives. He was an enthusiast to the end. I never came into his study without finding a pile of heavily underlined books at his side. When a new biography of Rabbi Samson Raphael Hirsch appeared, he sent the author, whom he did not know, his entire collection of Rabbi Hirsch's works in the original German as a token of his appreciation. Despite repeated trips to the hospital and frequently being in great pain during the two years I was privileged to know him, Rabbi Linchner remained, to the last, the most absolutely alive person I ever knew.

Dr. Joseph Kaminetsky, more than any other person, made Reb Shraga Feivel's vision of a day school in every Jewish community a reality. Travel bag draped over his shoulder, he set off on journey after journey by bus or train across America. A fiery speaker capable of infusing others with his enthusiasm, he had supreme confidence in the power of Torah — unembellished and unadorned — to sell itself, if children were only exposed to it.

I knew Dr. Kaminetsky only as an old man. It was hard for me to make the connection between the dynamic speaker on the old tapes and the elderly gentleman with a perpetual half-smile etched on his lips, despite the pain that was his constant companion. Yet even in those years of physical decline, I witnessed a greatness that served as a lasting proof of his love of Torah and of the inspiration he had received from Reb Shraga Feivel.

Every morning, I watched him laboriously make his way from his ground floor apartment to be among the first to arrive at the shul next door for the 6:30 a.m. *minyan*. No one who saw him struggling to and fro — half an hour each way — will ever be able to justify his own absence or lateness for *minyan* again. By 8:30 a.m. he was already on his way back to the *kollel* where he learned with men a half a century or more younger than he. Even when his face was black and blue from another nocturnal fall, his constant refrain was, "I want to go learn." In the last week of his life, he was still being carried down the stairs to the *kollel* in a wheelchair.

But for RABBI AVRAHAM ABBA FREEDMAN, neither this book nor the classic Hebrew biography of Reb Shraga Feivel, *Shlucha D'Rachmana*, would ever have been written. He secured the funding for the research and writing of both books, and was the driving force behind the project, never letting either author forget the supreme importance of bringing the image of Reb Shraga Feivel to life.

From the moment that Reb Shraga Feivel sent Rabbi Freedman and his close friend Rabbi Shalom Goldstein to Detroit as young men to spread *Yiddishkeit*, it is fair to say that Rabbi Freedman never stopped thinking about his revered *rebbi* and that his guide throughout life has been a single question: "What would my *rebbi* have done?" No obstacle or humiliation ever deterred Rabbi Freedman in his efforts to spread Torah, which continue unabated, well into his eighth decade. He had been given a mission by Reb Shraga Feivel and he would fulfill it. The cost to himself was irrelevant. For Rabbi Freedman, Reb Shraga Feivel was quite simply the greatest figure of this century, and no biography, this one included, could ever do him justice.

If this book would not have been written but for Rabbi Freedman, it would never have been published but for REB SIDNEY GREENWALD. Only Reb Sidney himself will ever know the full extent of his contribution. The manuscript languished for nearly four years before Reb Sidney and a group of close *talmidim* of Reb Shraga Feivel decided that the lessons that Reb Shraga Feivel still has to teach our generation, more than half a century since his passing, were simply too important to allow any further delay.

RABBI AHARON SORASKY'S research for the Hebrew classic *Shlucha D'Rachmana* served as the basis for this volume as well. Though nearly fifty additional interviews were conducted in preparation for this English biography, Rabbi Sorasky's volume remains indispensable.

RABBI NESANEL QUINN, the long-time *menahel* of Mesivta Torah Vodaath, was in Reb Shraga Feivel's first class in the Mesivta. First as a *talmid* and later as a member of the *hanhalah*, he was close to Reb Shraga Feivel for the entirety of the latter's public career. He has reviewed the entire book at least three times, and his imprint — both in terms of what was included and what was left out — is felt on every page.

RABBI NOSSON SCHERMAN, one of the premier writers in the Torah world today, generously lent his talents to reviewing and editing the entire manuscript. His contribution to the final product cannot be overstated.

Rabbi Scherman and RABBI MEIR ZLOTOWITZ are treasured mentors, dear friends, and esteemed colleagues. Over a decade ago, they welcomed me to the ArtScroll family, and since then everything I have achieved has been inextricably bound to their warm support. This book is a product of their friendship.

Everything that I write is a small repayment to my parents, PAUL AND MIRIAM ROSENBLUM שיחיו, whose boundless love and unstinting generosity has been the basic fact of my existence since I first gained consciousness. May they and my father-in-law, MR. ROBERT BLOCK שיחי׳, be granted many more years of health and happiness and be *zocheh* to see their children and grandchildren fully involved in Torah and mitzvos.

My wife JUDITH is a full partner in everything that I do, and without her nothing would be possible. Truly "all that is mine is hers," above all, the wonderful children she has borne and for whom she serves as the best possible model of every *middah tovah*.

As always, my final and deepest debt of gratitude is to the *Ribbono Shel Olam* for having showered me with blessings without end and for having entrusted me to portray Reb Shraga Feivel Mendlowitz to a generation that never knew him but which desperately needs to hear his message. In his vision, his insistence that a *mechanech* (educator) is a public servant, who must be above any personal interest, and in his resolve to arm his students with the fullest breadth of Torah thought in order that they be prepared to confront the challenges of modernity, Reb Shraga Feivel continues to speak to us with astonishing contemporaneity.

Yonoson Rosenblum

Introduction

He Let in the Light

SITTING ON THE GROUNDS OF BAIS MEDRASH ELYON IN Monsey one day, surrounded by his students, Reb Shraga Feivel Mendlowitz turned to one of them and asked him to lift up a nearby rock firmly embedded in the ground. Underneath was a swarm of insects suddenly exposed to the light of day. That sight provided Reb Shraga with a powerful metaphor to describe the mission he envisioned for himself and which he sought to pass on to his students:

Were It Not for Him

> Look at all these bugs. Until this moment, they knew only a dark and dreary world. By lifting up the rock, you have suddenly revealed to them a world filled with light and beauty. You've revealed to them the sun and the moon, the smell of fresh air and blue skies. That is our task as well: to roll the heavy stones off souls that are veiled from the spirituality that is present everywhere in the world. When we have re-

moved the boulders, we can call upon all those dwelling in darkness, "Lift up your eyes to the Heavens, behold your Creator, know your *Yiddishkeit.*"[1]

More than any other single person, Reb Shraga Feivel caused the light of Torah to shine in America. In the words of Rabbi Moshe Feinstein, he was nothing less than "the father of all [American] *bnei Torah* in this generation and in all the generations to come."[2] Echoing Reb Moshe's assessment, the Satmar Rebbe once commented, "Reb Shraga Feivel planted the first seed of Torah in America, and from that seed grew everything that followed."[3]

In a quarter-century, he built Mesivta Torah Vodaath, the first major yeshivah of its kind in America; almost single-handedly brought into existence the day school movement, in which nearly 200,000 Jewish children are presently enrolled; established Bais Medrash Elyon, which was in its time America's premier postgraduate yeshivah and *kollel;* founded the first summer learning camp for yeshivah students; and played a role in the formation of other major yeshivos in America. No wonder that Rabbi Aharon Kotler was heard to remark at his *levayah* (funeral), "It will take 1,000 communal workers to replace him."

But most important of all, he formed the souls of thousands of *talmidim* who passed through the portals of Mesivta Torah Vodaath in his lifetime. Of him it could truly be said that his *sefarim* were written on the hearts of his *talmidim* (students).[4]

The Talmud (*Bava Basra* 21a) says of Rabbi Yehoshua ben Gamla,

---

1. Rabbi Yitzchak Chinn, "Ohr Shraga — The Light of Reb Shraga Feivel," Jewish *Observer,* September 1983, p. 4. [Hereinafter cited as Chinn, "Ohr Shraga."]

2. From a letter sent by Rabbi Feinstein to a twenty-fourth *yahrzeit* gathering of Reb Shraga Feivel's *talmidim.*

3. Yosef Binyamin Wulliger.
   The Satmar Rebbe often said that his task of creating institutions in Williamsburg was made much easier by Reb Shraga Feivel's pioneering efforts in building Torah Vodaath. *Sidney Greenwald.*

4. When asked why he had never authored any *sefarim* (religious works), the Rizhiner Rebbe is said to have replied, "I do my writing on the hearts of my *talmidim.*"

who instituted, during the time of the Second Temple, the first system of public education, "Without him Torah would have been forgotten from Israel." In modern times, the same could be said of Rabbi Chaim of Volozhin, who founded the first modern yeshivah, at a time when Torah learning in Lithuania was at a low ebb; of Rabbi Samson Raphael Hirsch, who stemmed, if he could not completely stop, the flood tide toward Reform in Germany, with the development of the *Torah im Derech Eretz* concept and schools; and, in our own century, of Sarah Schenirer, the Cracow seamstress who founded the Bais Yaakov educational system for girls and thereby ensured that there would be new generations of Jewish women raised with traditional Torah values.

To this list must be added the name of Reb Shraga Feivel Mendlowitz, who initiated advanced Torah learning in America at a time when even the most observant and learned Jews were convinced — sadly, it is true — that such an achievement was impossible in the "*treifeh* soil" of the New World.

MORE THAN FIVE MILLION JEWS WERE LIVING IN THE UNITED States when Reb Shraga Feivel first set foot on its shores in 1913.

The Challenge Among those who had preceded him were many hundreds of *talmidei chachamim* and rabbis of stature, and hundreds of thousands of G-d-fearing Jews. Yet no one had succeeded in slowing the flood of assimilation of American Jewry. America remained "a land that devour[ed] its inhabitants." The overriding concern of the devout Jews was to avoid sinking into the morass. But even if they saved themselves, pitifully few were able to save their own children.

Orthodox Jews then had none of their present self-confidence. Their heads were bare at work — even if they owned their own businesses. "In those days, when you went to the doctor's office you took off your head-covering; when you went to the library, you took off your head-covering; when you went to college, you took off your head-covering," remembers Elias Karp.

Never had any Jewish community confronted such powerful assimilationist forces as those facing American Jewry. Two and a half million Yiddish-speaking Jews arrived in America in the first decades of the 20th century, yet within two generations, Yiddish was dead as a spoken language outside of a few chassidic enclaves. Children of those immigrants saw no reason to preserve a language that separated them from other Americans, whose customs and observances they hoped to emulate.[5] The demise of Yiddish is a fair measure of how strong were the forces of assimilation that swept up first- and second-generation Americans.

America presented an unprecedented puzzle that had to be solved if anything was to be saved of Judaism as it had existed in Europe. The materialism of American society, the relative ease with which newcomers integrated into a land of immigrants, the desire of Jewish parents that nothing should stand in the way of their children's success in their adopted country were all pieces of the puzzle. Because the puzzle was new, so too would the solution have to be new. No European approach could be transplanted intact to America — not that of Lithuania nor of Pressburg nor of Galicia — nor even of Frankfurt. A new formula drawing upon all the spiritual resources that had developed in Europe over nearly two millennia was needed.

Reb Shraga Feivel never stopped re-examining the old and exploring the new, seeking better and better ways to recreate in America the vibrant Jewish life of Europe. He came closer and closer to that goal, but he always wanted more. Asked whether he was satisfied with what he had achieved in America, he replied, "If I were the type of person to be satisfied, I would not have achieved even this much."

But if the task was not his to complete, neither did he leave it for a single moment. Rabbi Simchah Wasserman once used the comparison between Noach and Avraham to explain why Reb Shraga Feivel succeeded where so many others had failed, or were so sure

---

5. Ruth Wisse, "Is Yiddish Back From the Dead?" *New Republic*, May 27, 1996, p. 17.

Even the few Yiddish-speaking communities that exist today are not evidence of counter-assimilationist trends in the first half of the century. Those communities are almost exclusively a product of the immigration after World War II.

of failure that they did not make the attempt.[6] Even though Noach succeeded in preserving his own spirituality in a generation of ubiquitous depravity and moral degeneration, he did not save a single soul outside of his immediate family. Avraham Avinu, on the other hand, spread knowledge of G-d wherever he was and brought many under the canopy of the *Shechinah*.

Noach viewed the generation of the Flood as impervious to rebuke or improvement; he could not envision a reality different from the one he saw before him. Avraham Avinu, on the other hand, would not accept the existing situation as immutable. He set about to create an upheaval in human existence as it was then known.

American Jews at the time of Reb Shraga Feivel's arrival were in desperate need of another Avraham Avinu, of someone who refused to accept the status quo and who could envision and labor for a transformed America. Reb Shraga Feivel was that Avraham Avinu. As he told the Klausenburger Rebbe the first time they met, "Here [in America] you have to be a revolutionary and battle the status quo."

Through the sheer force of his determination and the power of his vision, he wrought a revolution in America. The Talmud's (*Taanis* 23a) description of Choni HaMe'agel applies to him as well: He brought light to a generation dwelling in darkness; he uplifted a generation sunk [in the mire]; he redeemed a generation bent under the weight of its own sins; he saved a contaminated generation. Reb Shraga Feivel proved that the materialism of America need not stand in the way of producing uncompromising Torah Jews and erudite, idealistic *talmidei chachamim*.

What was the essence of this man who inspired a Torah revolution?

---

6. I am indebted to Rabbi Pesach Segal of Jerusalem for his transcription of Rabbi Wasserman's remarks at a *yahrzeit* gathering in honor of Reb Shraga Feivel, 3 Elul 5748 (1998).

WE ALL INSTINCTIVELY RECOGNIZE THAT SOME SOULS ARE greater than others, that they seem to be hewn from directly beneath

A Genius of the Neshamah the Divine throne, so to speak. But such truly great souls are rare indeed. As Rabbi Shimon bar Yochai said, "I have seen the *bnei aliyah* [illustrious personalities], and they are few" (*Succah* 45b).

Whoever met Reb Shraga Feivel recognized that he possessed a sublime soul. He was, said Rabbi Reuven Grozovsky, "a *gaon* of the *neshamah*" — a genius in matters of the soul.[7] He was not only a brilliant scholar, he was creative in matters of the spirit. In fact, the spiritual side of his existence completely dominated the physical.

The Ponevezher Rav hinted at the dominance of the hidden, spiritual side of Reb Shraga Feivel when, in a play on the latter's insistence that he be given no title other than "Mister," the Rav dubbed him "*Nistar* (the Hidden) Mendlowitz." The title was fitting, for his essence, his soul, remained masked and only slightly revealed in his actions. Even Reb Shraga Feivel's closest *talmidim* knew that they were permitted to glimpse no more than a small fraction of his essence. "Your thoughts are private property," he told his students. "Do not make them public property."[8]

The pleasures of the physical world, whether money or honor, held no attraction for him. His pleasure was in intellectual and emotional holiness. His joy was to see the progressive advancement of Torah observance by the masses or even by a simple individual. His happiness did not depend on anything in the physical world. His poetic soul knew the joy of awareness of its Creator. He once confided that although he suffered a variety of afflictions in his life, he could recall only one half-hour of depression. It happened in May 1933, when a doctor told him that he was infected with advanced tuberculosis and, since there was no medical cure for the malady, he had only five or six weeks to live. After half an hour of depression, he decided that there was much to be accomplished even in those

---

7. Rabbi Alexander Gross and Dr. Joseph Kaminetsky, "Shraga Mendlowitz," in *Men of the Spirit*, Leo Jung ed. [Kymson Publishing Co., New York, 1964], p. 553. [Hereinafter cited as Gross and Kaminetsky].

8. Rabbi Elias Schwartz, *V'shee-non-tom*, Vol. II, p. 286.

few weeks, so there was no reason to dwell on his plight. He lived — and accomplished — for another twenty-five years. He was capable of the most intense joy: the joy of a soul aware of its Creator.

"*Der grester glick fun leben iz leben alein* — The greatest joy in life is life itself," he would say. After the sheer experience of existence itself, all else is anticlimactic.[9] He loved life because it gave him the opportunity to serve G-d and appreciate His universe. His responsiveness to the world of nature revealed his constant awareness of G-d's presence — everywhere and at all times. He was literally intoxicated with that awareness.

Hashem proclaims through the prophet, "I will give you a new heart, and put a new spirit within you; I will remove the heart of stone from your flesh and give you a heart of flesh" (*Yechezkel* 36:26). In place of a stony heart, deaf to Hashem's call, we will receive a soft heart that erects no barriers between us and Him. Reb Shraga Feivel already possessed such a heart of flesh, one that always responded to the rush of emotions coursing through it. The emotions of his soul would not be constrained by social convention. He could not prevent himself from breaking down and sobbing before his students — nor did he try.

At the intellectual level, we know that our love of Hashem must be qualitatively different and infinitely more powerful than our love for anything in the physical world. Yet we find that the first remains abstract, while love of our children and financial success, for instance, is the most concrete thing in our lives. With Reb Shraga Feivel it was not like that. The spiritual realm was as tangible and real for him as the physical world is for most people. He mourned the *galus HaShechinah* (the Exile of the Divine Presence caused by people's abandonment of faith) with the same intensity that others mourn a lost child.

His own children sensed that he loved his *talmidim* as much as he loved them, not because he loved his children less than other parents love theirs, but because his love of every Jewish soul was so great that there was no room for distinction. "A real *rebbi* has as

---

9. Gross and Kaminetsky, p. 569.

much love for his *talmidim* as for his children," he once told his son.[10]

Because the soul is above the dimensions of time and space that delineate the physical world, it is perpetually constrained by the limitations of the body. The greater the soul, the greater that sense of constraint.[11] The mission of the soul in this world is to sublimate the body and thereby infuse the physical domain with Heavenliness. The restless energy that propelled Reb Shraga Feivel all his life was but one manifestation of a soul yearning to break free. No achievement ever satisfied him. And that dissatisfaction spurred him to yet greater action.

The extraordinary vision that allowed him to picture a Jewish world very different from the one before him is another aspect of his soul's struggle to break free of temporal reality. His soul soared above time. Someone who considered Reb Shraga Feivel an impractical dreamer once criticized him as not being a man of the 20th century. "You're right," replied Reb Shraga Feivel calmly. "I am a man of the 21st century."

A Nefesh Klali

THE SOUL OF MOSHE RABBEINU, *CHAZAL* TELL US, ENCOMPASSED the souls of all the Jews who stood at Sinai. There will never be another Moshe Rabbeinu, but in every generation there are Jews who possess a soul resembling the *nefesh klali* (all-embracing soul) of Moshe Rabbeinu. Reb Shraga Feivel was one of these. In his heart was love and understanding for young and old, learned and ignorant, observant or nonobservant, brilliant or dull.

How is such a soul identified? Reb Shraga Feivel himself provided the clue with his interpretation of the verse, כֹּל הַנְּשָׁמָה תְּהַלֵּל

---

10. Rabbi Shmuel Mendlowitz.

11. The description of the soul as constantly seeking to break free of bounds of space and time is drawn from Rabbi Yitzchak Hutner's *Pachad Yitzchak, Pesach, Maamar* 1. Reb Shraga Feivel himself once wrote to a student whose wedding he was unable to attend because of illness, "My soul, unconstrained by distance and above all time and space, the true 'I,' which is joined to you with all its might, will have a large share in your *simchah* (celebration)."

הֹ-יָ, *Let all the soul praise G–d"* (*Tehillim* 150:6). This verse, he explained, can be interpreted in two ways. The word כל can mean that the *entire* soul will praise Hashem or that *all* the souls in the world will praise Him. Reb Shraga Feivel taught that both these explanations are really one. Anyone who serves and glorifies Hashem with the entirety of his soul will succeed in influencing others to do so, as well.

The key to this complete service of Hashem is selfless dedication to the service of G-d. The Torah describes Moshe Rabbeinu as the most humble man who ever lived. His humility consisted of the obliteration of his own ego, of any sense of personal interest apart from the interests of Hashem and His Torah. Because he had no sense of himself as an isolated individual, Moshe Rabbeinu was able to encompass within his soul the souls of all *Klal Yisrael*.

A similar negation of self was, according to Rabbi Simchah Wasserman, at the heart of Reb Shraga Feivel's teaching. We find ourselves in a world of overwhelming beauty, he said, but too frequently our sense of ourselves looms so large that it blocks out the majesty of the world; when not self-centered, a person can see the world, but a selfish disposition impedes spiritual accomplishment. "Hashem," he once said, "creates something from nothing. Our task is to take something — our sense of self — and transform it into nothing."[12]

In all his endeavors for the glory of G–d, for the spread and intensification of Torah study, for helping individuals as well as the nation, there was a complete absence of self-interest. Even his own personal growth took second place to his duty to serve G-d and bring others closer to Him. After all his brilliant successes he remained the same humble Mr. Mendlowitz. Rabbi Yaakov Kamenetsky said this of Reb Shraga Feivel:

> I have been privileged to know many great men in my life, but I never found another one like him, totally free of any

---

12. Rabbi Shmuel Mendlowiz.

personal *negiah* (self-interest) to the last degree . . . Certainly, I knew others of whom there could be no thought of being influenced by honor, or money, or favors, but nevertheless there was perhaps a slight trace of being influenced by some personal spiritual consideration . . . With Reb Shraga Feivel there was not even that. Everything he did was for Hashem alone, free from any trace of even any spiritual *negiah*, no matter how slight.

When his own *roshei yeshivah* and board of directors pleaded with him to stop his practice of helping other yeshivos by sending them some of the best students of Torah Vodaath, Reb Shraga Feivel replied, "My purpose is to produce soldiers for the A-mighty. What do I care whether they are deployed to the East or the West."[13] "Whoever speaks of **my** *rebbi*, **my** *derech* (approach)," he said, "has no *rebbi* and no *derech*; all he has guiding him is himself."[14]

The expansiveness of his soul enabled him to communicate with Jews from every background. Speaking only Yiddish, he nevertheless became the primary influence on thousands of boys whose first language was English. A product of the most restrictive of Hungarian yeshivos, he somehow found a common language with American boys torn between the study of Torah and the lure of acceptance and prosperity. Just as Rabbi Yochanan transformed Reish Lakish from the head of brigands to the greatest of Torah scholars, so too could Reb Shraga Feivel influence a student to give up his dreams of athletic fame, material success, or professional recognition, and instead toil to become a *rosh yeshivah*.

He met his students in the realm of the soul, the place where all barriers between Jews break down, for the spiritual realm is characterized by unity. Reb Shraga Feivel lived as if there were no lines of demarcation between himself and others. The suffering of a fellow Jew was not a momentary pinprick; it affected him just as if it were

---

13. Gross and Kaminetsky, p. 568.
14. Sidney Greenwald.

his own. During the Holocaust, he lived in constant anguish. Of even rarer nobility was his capacity to share completely another Jew's joy.

He was alive to every facet of genuine Torah expression. "Some souls," he used to say, "drink from *Tanya*. Others from the Ramchal. Still others from Rabbi Samson Raphael Hirsch. I drink from all of them, though at any given time, I might drink from one in particular."[15] He had the genius to draw from every strand of authentic Jewish thought, to place those various strands in relation to one another, and to see each of them as simply another path to knowledge and service of the Divine. Who else could have used the works of Rabbi Samson Raphael Hirsch to explain a difficult passage in a classic chassidic work such as *Tanya*, or vice versa.

". . . The Tree of Life was in the center of the Garden" (*Bereishis* 2:9). "That means," Reb Shraga Feivel taught, "that no matter how far apart the various ideas you learn may seem to be, they are all different approaches to the *Eitz HaChaim* (the Tree of Life), different paths to reach the A-mighty. No one of them has an exclusive right to the A-mighty's favor."[16] As long as the Tree is in the center, it can be approached from every direction. "*Der sechel iz elastish* — The mind is elastic," he reminded his students. "It can be stretched from one extreme to another if you are intellectually honest with yourselves."[17]

But, though an openness of heart and mind toward finding a path to Divine service was a trademark of his *talmidim*, he was not content that his students remain merely eclectic. He insisted that the strands of their personal *hashkafah* (outlook) must be taken from authentic, traditional, classic sources. In the new world of America, where there was an ingathering of many Torah traditions, they could gather the best that had been produced in previous generations, and Reb Shraga Feivel encouraged his students to exercise

---

15. Rabbi Mannes Mandel.

16. Gross and Kaminetsky, pp. 565-66.

17. Chinn, "Ohr Shraga," p. 8.

that freedom. Never stop "gathering," he urged them.

He himself had done the same thing. Though he was the student of some of the greatest Hungarian *roshei yeshivah* of his day, he was made in none of their images. From an early age, his intellectual searching took him far beyond the curriculum of his day — a fact that landed him in trouble on more than one occasion. He fashioned his own views from the primary sources — from *Chovos HaLevavos* and *Kuzari*, from Rabbi Moshe Chaim Luzzatto and Rabbi Samson Raphael Hirsch, from the *Tanya*, Reb Tzaddok of Lublin, and the *Sfas Emes*.

He pressed his students to do the same. Not surprisingly, those students often seem very different from one another. It is said of the *talmidim* of the Baal Shem Tov that each, as it were, took away a single spark given off by his pipe, and the same can be said of Reb Shraga Feivel's *talmidim*. His own breadth and the variety of the sparks he gave off are reflected in the differences of his *talmidim* one from another.

This, then, was Reb Shraga Feivel Mendlowitz. Profound thinker, man of the spirit, lover of Hashem, His Torah and His people — a man of whom Rabbi Meir Shapiro exclaimed, "*Halevai*, I should be seated next to him in *Gan Eden*." Dreamer, visionary, builder of Torah institutions and builder of souls, the one who, in the words of the Ponevezher Rav, "put Torah on its feet in all of America." What follows is his story.

Chapter 1

Youth

REB SHRAGA FEIVEL MENDLOWITZ BEGAN LIFE HUMBLY enough in 1886 in the small Hungarian village of Vilag, near the present-day border between Hungary and Poland. His **Childhood** father Moshe was a Sanzer chassid, who earned his livelihood as a tanner. The Mendlowitz clan claimed no distinguished lineage on either side.

Though the Mendlowitz household was marked by no signs of external distinction, Reb Moshe and his wife Sima Tcheba created within their home an atmosphere of simple faith and *chesed*. Once a group of visitors arrived unannounced in Vilag on Erev Shabbos, and all found lodging that night in the Mendlowitz's three-room home. The entire Mendlowitz family spent the night on the floor on makeshift bedding. On this and other such occasions, Reb Moshe would scold any child who was reluctant to relinquish his or her bed as lacking *ahavas Yisrael*, or love of Jews, and of ignoring the mitzvah of welcoming guests.[1]

---

1. Rabbi Yisrael Spinner.

As a young boy, Shraga Feivel was the source of great concern to his parents because he did not utter a single word until he was 5. At that age, his mother's tears and prayers were finally answered, and he began to talk.[2] As soon as he was able to speak, Reb Moshe took his son to the local *melamed* to learn the *aleph-beis*.[3]

It was soon clear that Shraga Feivel was blessed not only with a quick grasp but an unusually sensitive soul. As he herded the family geese through Vilag's unpaved streets, he would recite *Tehillim* (Psalms) by heart.[4] His lively imagination was set aflame by his *rebbi's* stories. When he was 8 years old, his *rebbi* mentioned Rabbi Shimon bar Yochai's statement that "if *Klal Yisrael* were to observe Shabbos two weeks in succession they would be redeemed immediately" (*Shabbos* 118b). He resolved that when he was old enough, he would rent a horse and wagon and convince all Jews to observe the same two Sabbaths. Such were the dreams of his childhood.[5]

Another time, his *rebbi* told the class that the ten tribes of Israel had been exiled to a place beyond the River Sambatyon and would return at the time of the Redemption. Again the young boy began hatching plans for organizing an expedition to locate the River Sambatyon and find the missing tribes of Israel.

At the age of 10, Shraga Feivel suffered a terrible tragedy with the death of his mother in a fire that destroyed the family home on Yom Kippur.[6] Shraga Feivel's father eventually took a second wife named Toibe, and moved his family from Vilag to Humenne. Shraga Feivel and his siblings were particularly fortunate in their father's choice of a second wife, as Toibe showered her husband's young children with love and raised them as if they were her own.

---

2. Mrs. Shulamis Schiff, Reb Shraga Feivel's daughter.

3. Reb Shraga Feivel always remained grateful to his first *rebbi*. Years later, an old man came into the *beis medrash* of Mesivta Torah Vodaath, and Reb Shraga Feivel hurried to honor him. "This is my first *rebbi*," he told his students, "he taught me *aleph-beis, and* thereby gave me the foundation stones for learning the entire Torah." *Rabbi Alexander Sender Linchner, Reb Shraga Feivel's son-in-law.*

4. Rabbi Yisrael Spinner.

5. Rabbi Nesanel Quinn.

6. Students in Torah Vodaath recall the feeling with which he would learn Mishnayos in the *beis medrash* on the evening of Yom Kippur for the benefit of his mother's *neshamah* (soul).

WHEN SHRAGA FEIVEL WAS 12, THE *CHEDER* IN HUMENNE PRO-
nounced itself unable to teach him anything more, and his father
Chust sent him to Mezo-Laboretz[7] to study under Reb Aharon,
the local *dayan*, who maintained a small yeshivah in his
house. Shraga Feivel remained with Reb Aharon for three years. At
that point, he embarked on sojourns through the leading yeshivos
of Hungary. In succession he learned in Chust, under Rabbi Moshe
Greenwald, author of *Arugas HaBosem*; in Unsdorf under Rabbi
Shmuel Rosenberg, author of *Be'er Shmuel*; and in Pressburg under
Rabbi Simchah Bunim Schreiber, the grandson of the Chasam
Sofer.

The first of Shraga Feivel's great *rebbis* was Rabbi Moshe
Greenwald, the Arugas HaBosem. Until 1887, the Arugas
HaBosem had served as *rav* and *av beis din* in Humenne, where he
also maintained a small yeshivah. The awe with which the Jews of
Humenne remembered their former *rav* was likely the major reason that Shraga Feivel chose to go to Chust to begin his advanced
studies.

The Arugas HaBosem was one of a group of the leading students
of the Ksav Sofer who had taken on chassidic ways, and the

---

7. Rabbi Zvi Elimelech of Dinov, author of *Bnei Yissas'char,* had previously served as
rav of the town.

yeshivah in Chust in his day was steeped in Chassidus.[8] Reb Shraga Feivel attributed the Chassidic *varmkeit* (warmth) he instilled in Torah Vodaath to his years in Chust. "If only you had been in Chust ... ," he would say wistfully.[9]

The Arugas HaBosem stressed the importance of always striving to find "the truth of the Torah." In *Hachanah D'Rabbah*, a small volume written a few days before his passing, he set forth his philosophy of learning and expressed misgivings about the intricate *pilpulim* favored in some yeshivos. He acknowledged that *pilpul* can be a useful tool in clarifying the underlying logic of the halachah and allowing the advanced student to compare different situations to determine whether they are governed by the same halachic principles. Yet he advised extreme caution in the use of *pilpul* lest it lead to nothing more than exercises in mental gymnastics. He concluded his final epistle:

> To those of my beloved students favored by Hashem to teach students [of their own], please do not waste too much time in [teaching them] *pilpul*, but rather strive to give them a wide knowledge of Torah and a breadth of concepts . . . in the Gemara and *poskim* (halachic decisors) . . . Accustom yourselves to looking deeply into every subject and to acquiring a clear understanding of underlying principles of the halachah so that you can derive one halachah from another and compare one halachah to another in a true fashion.

Shraga Feivel soon acquired the title "Feivel *Masmid* (the diligent one)" among his fellow students. His own thirst for in-depth understanding found ready encouragement from the *rosh yeshivah*. The Arugas HaBosem numbered Shraga Feivel among his favorite *talmidim* and appointed him to tutor his son Levi Yitzchak. At the

---

8. Reb Shraga Feivel said of the Arugas HaBosem, "Every day I saw a new person *shteiging* (advancing) in *davening*." Interestingly, Rabbi Yitzchak Schneider, the assistant *menahel* of the Mesivta in the '40s, once said the same of Reb Shraga Feivel. Asked to describe him, Rabbi Schneider replied, "How can you describe someone who is different every day?" *Rabbi Avraham Abba Freedman.*

9. Rabbi Eliyahu Yehoshua Geldzhaler.

beginning of *shiur*, the Arugas HaBosem would ask, "Is the *bachur* from Mezo-Laboretz here yet?"[10]

Each of the top students in the yeshivah was assigned a particular mitzvah in which he was to become expert, and to the surprise of all, the 16-year-old Shraga Feivel was assigned *mikvaos* (ritual baths), an extremely difficult topic. Shraga Feivel set out to acquire a thorough knowledge of this highly complex area, which requires knowledge not only of an intricate Mishnaic tractate and its laws, but a practical understanding of the engineering involved in the construction of *mikvaos*. When Rabbi Greenwald was preparing *Arugas HaBosem* for print, he gave Shraga Feivel a preliminary draft of the section on *mikvaos* and subsequently changed a number of passages because of Shraga Feivel's comments.[11]

THE NEXT STATION ON SHRAGA FEIVEL'S JOURNEY WAS UNSDORF, a picturesque village in the Carpathian Mountains. The 17-year-old

Unsdorf Shraga Feivel had already completed most of *Shas* and was eager to hear the *shiurim* of Rabbi Shmuel Rosenberg, who was known in the Hungarian yeshivah world as "the *rebbi* of the *roshei yeshivah*" and whose students included virtually every major teacher of Torah in the Hungarian yeshivah world of the following generation.

For the rest of his life Shraga Feivel considered the Unsdorfer Rav his *rav muvhak* (primary teacher). Many years after he left Unsdorf, Reb Shraga Feivel was walking deep in thought and stepped into the street. Suddenly his *rebbi* appeared to him and commanded him to stop. Startled by the vision, he stepped back — and narrowly avoided being struck by a passing car. The miracle highlights the place the Unsdorfer Rav held in Reb Shraga Feivel's thoughts.[12]

Rabbi Rosenberg's *talmidim* both loved and revered him. In the

---

10. Reported by Rabbi Avraham Shalom Katz, the Riskaver Rav and author of *Orchos Mishpatim*, who was a fellow student in the *shiur*.

11. Rabbi Hershel Mashinsky.

12. Rabbi Shmuel Mendlowitz.
 Reb Shraga Feivel named his third son Shmuel after the Unsdorfer Rav.

introduction to his major work, *Be'er Shmuel,* he writes that only someone who combines the qualities of "the left hand pushes away while the right hand draws near" was qualified to be a *rav* and guide *talmidim.* Reb Shraga Feivel's *talmidim,* in later years, had no difficulty finding the parallels between his descriptions of his *rav muvhak* and Reb Shraga Feivel himself. "Three things my master and teacher from Unsdorf despised — money, honor, and excess indulgence in food," he said, and the same was true of him.[13]

The Unsdorfer Rav served as Reb Shraga Feivel's model for the devotion of a *rebbi* to his students. In his introduction to *Be'er Shmuel,* Rabbi Rosenberg wrote:

> If the *rav's* primary purpose in teaching students is some form of personal fulfillment, there will be little benefit to the student. If, however, the *rav* gives no thought to himself, but only to forming his students ... from such a *rav* will the students have great benefit ...
>
> Did I not learn with you many tractates that I myself had already learned countless times? For me personally, there are many new *sugyos* that I should have been learning in depth, as well as studying the works of the Arizal for the perfection of my soul. But I have ignored my own spiritual needs in order to learn with you those things that will be to your benefit.

Reb Shraga Feivel told his own students many stories of the Be'er Shmuel's concern for his students. The first *seder* (study period) was from 2 a.m. to 7 a.m., and the *Rav* tested the students every week. If dissatisfied with their progress, he cried out in grief, "Woe to me. I'm at fault . . . for the students' desire is to learn."[14] He was once overheard telling a *talmid* who was not concentrating on his studies, "What more can I do for you? Haven't I already fasted many times in order that Heaven should give you a desire to learn? Haven't I prayed at the graves of *tzaddikim* that your eyes be opened to

---

13. Rabbi Yisrael Spinner.
14. Rabbi Shmuel Mendlowitz.

Torah?" When Reb Shraga Feivel told these stories to his students, he would exclaim, "My master and teacher did all that was in his power for his *talmidim,* until the very limit of his strength, and I haven't done even this." His pain as he said these words, remembers Rabbi Yaakov Leshinsky, was worth more than ten *mussar shmuessen* (lectures on ethics).

In Unsdorf, every *shiur* began with ten minutes of study of the classic early *mussar* work, *Chovos HaLevavos.* It was not unusual, Reb Shraga Feivel would tell his students in later years, for the Unsdorfer Rav to bring him to tears during those ten minutes.[15]

Above all, Reb Shraga Feivel learned from his *rebbi* that a teacher must form bonds of love with his students. Referring to *Chazal's* dictum that a person learns best in the areas of the Torah to which his heart is drawn, the Unsdorfer Rav extended this to mean that one can learn best with a *rebbi* whom he loves. So strongly did he make the *talmidim* feel that he was a father to them that they also became like brothers to one another. Whenever Unsdorf students met, even after the passage of many years, those meetings were invariably marked by the hugging associated with family gatherings.[16]

Though both the Arugas HaBosem and the Be'er Shmuel were leading disciples of the Ksav Sofer, their approaches to learning and teaching were very different: The Arugas HaBosem was a majestic figure, while the Be'er Shmuel was the picture of humility. Nevertheless, Shraga Feivel was able to absorb and grow from contrasting styles in learning and *avodas Hashem* (Divine service). From an early age, receptivity to a broad range of influences was one of his outstanding traits.

AT 18, SHRAGA FEIVEL RECEIVED *SEMICHAH* FROM THE BE'ER Shmuel. He had already covered most of the major topics in the
Pressburg Talmud, and was once again overcome with the desire to experience another approach to Torah.[17] He traveled to Pressburg, where the Chasam Sofer had founded the mother of all Hungarian yeshivos, to hear *shiurim* from Rabbi

---

15. Gross and Kaminetsky, p. 556.

16. Avraham Fuchs, *The Hungarian Yeshivos* [Jerusalem, 1979], p. 116.

17. Rabbi Shmuel Mendlowitz.

Simchah Bunim Schreiber, author of the *Shevet Sofer.* Rabbi Schreiber was famed for his sharpness, and only the deepest of thinkers could penetrate his meaning.

In Pressburg too, Shraga Feivel's depth in learning was soon noted. According to his childhood friend Rabbi Binyamin Felsenberg, who studied with him in Chust, Unsdorf, and Pressburg, Reb Shraga Feivel was viewed in each of these yeshivos as one of the leading *lamdanim* (profound scholars), and it was assumed that he would one day be recognized as a *gaon* (Torah genius).[18]

Little is known of Reb Shraga's time in Pressburg; he talked about that period far less than about the years in Unsdorf and Chust. Two stories, however, have come down to us, and both foreshadow the man to come. One day two brothers, who were descendants of the Chasam Sofer, arrived in Pressburg, dressed and coiffed in the modern style. The Shevet Sofer was anxious to accept them in the yeshivah, but he could not admit them looking as they did. He entrusted them to Reb Shraga Feivel's care. From morning until night, Reb Shraga Feivel discussed with them all aspects of Jewish faith. After two weeks, these talks had the desired effect, and the two brothers had removed their pompadours. More importantly, they began to learn in earnest.[19]

On another occasion, Reb Shraga Feivel found himself the object of criticism when he was seen studying Rabbi Samson Raphael Hirsch's works. Because Rabbi Hirsch wrote in the German vernacular, his works still occasioned suspicion within the deeply conservative Hungarian yeshivah world of the day. Reb Shraga Feivel was summoned to appear before the yeshivah administration. At his "trial," he enlisted the assistance of an old Jew living in

---

18. After their years learning together, Rabbi Felsenberg and Reb Shraga Feivel lost touch with one another. Somehow, however, Reb Shraga Feivel learned that Rabbi Felsenberg, by then a respected *talmid chacham,* was living in Vienna. When the Nazis entered Vienna, he immediately wrote Rabbi Felsenberg, urging him to bring his family to America, and offering to do everything possible to secure the necessary papers.

In his reply to his old friend, Rabbi Felsenberg expressed his joy upon receiving Reb Shraga Feivel's letter, because he had been told that same day that there was little chance for him to secure the necessary visas since he had no friends or relatives in America.

19. Rabbi Shmuel Mendlowitz.

Pressburg, who testified that thirty years earlier, when his first wife's mental disability forced him to seek permission from one hundred rabbis to take a second wife, the Divrei Chaim of Sanz had advised him to travel to Frankfurt-am-Main to obtain the signature of Rabbi Hirsch, telling him, "What I am to Galicia, he is to Germany."[20]

The reading of Hirsch was just one more example of an independent streak that had already embroiled Reb Shraga Feivel in controversy. One *bein hazemanim* (intersession), when he was in Humenne, his practice of learning *Nach* created something of a local controversy.[21] He was also criticized for teaching Torah to his younger sister.[22]

There was a public outcry against Shraga Feivel. As a consequence, when a leading *rebbe* visited the town, Reb Moshe Mendlowitz was subjected to intense pressure to take his son to the *rebbe* for his opinion. Reb Moshe succumbed to the pressure. After a conversation of more than an hour,

Rabbi Samson Raphael Hirsch

the *rebbe* pronounced his verdict: "Reb Moshe, your son is an *adam gadol* (literally: a great man), an *adam shalem* (literally: an all-around man), to whom you should give every honor, including standing up when he enters the room."[23]

---

20. Berl Belsky.

21. The study of *Tanach* was then frowned upon by Hungarian *chassidim* since *Tanach* had long since become the favorite text of *maskilim,* the so-called "enlightened ones," to the exclusion of the Talmud. The Unsdorfer Rav, however, did not entertain these suspicions about *Tanach,* and always made a point of quoting the full chapter whenever a verse from *Nach* appeared in the Gemara under study. He thus demonstrated that the study of *Nach* was worthy of serious study.

22. Rabbi Avraham Abba Freedman.

23. This story was related in a letter to the editor to *The Jewish Observer,* March 1984, p. 40. The writer heard it personally from Reb Shraga Feivel's younger half-sister, Freidel Kaufman.

Chapter 2

An Eye to the Future

THE 22-YEAR-OLD SHRAGA FEIVEL MARRIED BLUMA Rachel Shaller, his stepmother Toibe's younger sister, on Rosh Chodesh Elul 5669 (1909). Over their thirty-nine years of marriage, Bluma Rachel was her husband's closest friend. She supported all his undertakings, even when these resulted in greatly increased strains on her and on the family's always meager budget.

Marriage

Only because of her complete dedication to the household was Reb Shraga Feivel able to immerse himself in his various endeavors. In their early years of marriage, she supported the family by running a small clothing store, and later she was left alone to care for two small children for more than six years, while he was in the United States. He went originally to see if it was possible for him to bring Torah to the American wasteland, but while he was there, World War I broke out and he was stranded for four years, unable to return to his family. Yet no matter how strained the family's circumstances, she bore it all stoically and was always able to find

R' Shimon HaLevi Shaller,
the father-in-law of Reb Shraga Feivel

something to give to those less fortunate than herself.

The young couple was married in the bride's hometown of Riminov. There Reb Shraga Feivel once again found himself at the center of controversy. There was general tumult at the wedding when the groom steadfastly refused to wear a *shtreimel*, despite his father-in-law's request that he do so and the pressure of local chassidim. "I will not put it on and then remove it," he insisted, "and I am not yet ready to wear one always."[1] Already then, he had the ambition to bring Torah to America, and he was convinced that he would be more successful if he wore modern attire.

After the marriage, Reb Shraga Feivel and his new bride moved to Humenne. There the first two Mendlowitz children, Moshe Yitzchak and Bas Sheva, were born. (Another five were subsequently born in America.[2]) In Humenne, Reb Shraga Feivel learned all day long; the family's meager income came exclusively from Bluma Rachel's small clothing store.

---

1. Gross and Kaminetsky, p. 556.
   Some have seen in Reb Shraga Feivel's words a premonition that his future lay far away from Hungary, in a place where the wearing of a *shtreimel* was then almost unknown and might have hindered his work.

2. Moshe Yitzchak ל"ז married Dina Friedman ע"ה and Bas Sheva married Rabbi Alexander Sender Linchner ל"ז, the founder of Boys Town in Jerusalem. The Mendlowitz children born in America were: Rivkah ל"ז, who married Rabbi Yitzchak Karpf, a *rosh yeshivah* in Torah Vodaath and Bais Shraga; Channah, whose husband Rabbi Berel Greenbaum ל"ז, was the principal of Yeshivah of Spring Valley for many years; Avraham Mordechai ל"ז; Shmuel, founder and *menahel* of Yeshivas Bais Shraga in Monsey; and Shulamis, the wife of Rabbi Yehoshua Schiff, *rosh yeshivah* of, Mesifta Bais Shraga.

WHILE MOST OF REB SHRAGA FEIVEL'S DAY WAS DEVOTED TO THE study of Gemara and *Shulchan Aruch*, there is much to suggest an

Charting a Course

emerging sense of his life's task of drawing young Jews close to their faith and Torah. During this period, he began to delve deeply into both classic and contemporary works of Jewish thought. Much of his vast knowledge of classical Jewish thought had its roots in his four years in Humenne. Indicative of the breadth of his reading is that he spent one-third of his dowry to purchase Zev Yavetz's *Toldos Am Yisrael*, the first comprehensive Jewish history in harmony with our *mesorah*.[3]

Having concluded that a comprehensive grounding in traditional Jewish thought was an indispensable weapon in his upcoming battle, Reb Shraga Feivel did not study the classic texts in isolation. His analytic mind probed the differences in terminology and presentation between the various presentations of Torah Judaism, which sometimes obscured the much larger areas of agreement.

For the impending battle, Rabbi Samson Raphael Hirsch became the model. Rabbi Hirsch's success in arresting the rush to Reform in Germany served as an example of what one man could do. Rabbi Hirsch's ability to speak the language of modern man — the product of the Enlightenment and the scientific worldview — while remaining entirely rooted in classic Jewish sources and thought, was something Reb Shraga Feivel explicitly sought to emulate. Rabbi Hirsch had not been intimidated by 19th-century thought or the rapid advance of science in his day, and neither would Reb Shraga Feivel shy away from the challenges of the 20th century. Having identified Rabbi Hirsch as one of the exemplars of what he hoped to achieve in life, Reb Shraga Feivel pored over his vast corpus of writings.

Reb Shraga Feivel frequently told his wife that every person in this world senses an obligation to fulfill the specific task for which he was created. That sense of calling may have no logical explanation and be

---

3. When Rabbi Yitzchak Isaac Halevi's *Doros HaRishonim*, a detailed refutation of the works of secular Jewish historians, subsequently appeared, Reb Shraga Feivel was filled with excitement. He profoundly identified with the viewpoint of Rabbi Halevi and considered his works crucial for a pure Torah *hashkafah*.

incapable of verbal expression, but it nevertheless gives a person no rest. Just as the animals instinctively do that for which they were created, even though they have no appreciation of the consequences of their actions, so too, man is instinctively driven to fulfill his task. It happens in history that a person without any great intrinsic merit of his own is nevertheless chosen as Hashem's instrument for revolutionary change. That being the case, there is no reason for pride, even if one is summoned by Providence for a crucial task.[4]

One of his favorite Midrashim expressed this sense that every person has a specific mission from Hashem, which he is not free to shirk: "And G-d declared to the prophets: 'Do not delude yourselves that should you refuse to do My bidding . . . there is no one else. I will fulfill My purpose in Creation even if it must be accomplished by a mere gnat, a lowly snake, or a croaking frog!'"[5]

In years to come, he would tell his students, "Make no mistake about me. What am I and what is distinctive about me? But sometimes *HaKadosh Baruch Hu* uses a frog, or even a gnat, as his agent. So assume that I am no more than a frog or a gnat; nevertheless it is incumbent upon you to listen to me as an agent of *HaKadosh Baruch Hu*."[6] In spite of his genuine humility, when the occasion demanded it, he rose up forcefully to advance the cause of Torah and faith in the A-mighty.

The first concrete outgrowth of the years of preparation in Humenne was a plan to open a yeshivah for younger boys in Germany. Reb Shraga Feivel was eager to see whether the fire of Chassidus could be wedded to the discipline and self-restraint that distinguish German Jews.

The plan was never realized. He proceeded so far as to travel to a major German city — either Hamburg or Frankfurt-am-Main. Soon after his arrival, he was approached in shul by the *gabbai* and offered a contribution from the community's charity fund. Reb Shraga Feivel

---

4. Gross and Kaminetsky, p. 559.

5. Ibid.

6. Rabbi Moshe Yechezkel Samuels.

rejected the offer, to which the *gabbai* remarked mockingly, "Can it be? An *Ostjude* (Eastern European Jew) who does not accept handouts?"[7]

In the course of his travels in Germany, Reb Shraga Feivel decided that although he could have established a yeshivah there, to do so in the United States was a more important goal.[8]

---

7. Rabbi Eliyahu Yehoshua Geldzahler.

8. Rabbi Avraham Abba Freedman.

Chapter 3

America

REB SHRAGA FEIVEL'S PLAN TO EVENTUALLY ESTABLISH a yeshivah in the United States was accelerated by the imminent threat of conscription into the Austro-Hungarian army, which, for a chassidic Jew, would have meant severe privation or worse. The Great War that would cost millions of young men their lives was less than a year away. In 1913, at the age of 27, he left for America. The haste with which he was forced to depart gave Reb Shraga Feivel no chance to take his wife and two young children with him, and the family parted with the idea that they would soon be reunited in America. Had he determined that there was a good chance to found a yeshivah, he would have sent for them immediately. In reality, however, the separation was to last six years, for most of which time communications between the United States and Hungary were severed because of the war.

Reb Shraga Feivel chose to go to America as a continuation of his initial plan to establish a yeshivah, but in America rather than Germany. His dream was to plant Torah in the United States and

Reb Shraga Feivel in 1913

then go on to *Eretz Yisrael*, the land of his longing. An old friend from his days in Humenne asked him shortly before his departure, "How could someone of whom Reb Aharon [the *dayan* in Humenne] always said, '*Feivel, du bist a gaon* — Feivel, you are a genius,' go to America?" Reb Shraga Feivel replied cryptically that he was going to America to look for Torah, a response that provoked derisive laughter from his friend.[1]

Before he left Hungary, he visited Rebbe Yeshayeleh of Keristier to receive his blessing. After blessing him, Rebbe Yeshayaleh made a number of predictions about what Providence had in store for him in America. Each one of these predictions, Reb Shraga Feivel said later, came true.[2]

In September 1913, Reb Shraga Feivel's ship docked in Philadelphia harbor, and he set foot on American soil. The most immediate problem confronting him was how to earn a livelihood. Before leaving Hungary, he had learned *shechitah* (ritual slaughter) and received a *kabbalah* (certification), but his first job as a *shochet* (ritual slaughterer) on the Lower East Side lasted less than an hour. After slaughtering his first seventeen chickens, he realized that he

1. This story was related by Y.M. Moskowitz in a letter to the *Jewish Morning Journal* shortly after Reb Shraga Feivel's *petirah*. The writer was a close relative of the friend in the story.

2. Rabbi Shmuel Mendlowitz.

was unsuited to being a *shochet,* and he put down his *chalaf* (knife for ritual slaughter) forever. His mission in life was to give life rather than take it.[3]

His next stop was Bridgeport, Connecticut, where he was a *melamed* (teacher) for a short time. He often spoke fondly of his time in Bridgeport and the satisfaction he had in the progress of his young students, but for reasons not altogether clear, that stop, too, was a short one. One probable reason is that he saw no possibility of building a yeshivah in Bridgeport.[4]

FINALLY, REB SHRAGA FEIVEL SETTLED ON SCRANTON, Pennsylvania, as the likeliest place for him to found a traditional

Scranton yeshivah. Most of the Jews of Scranton came from Hungary, and an uncle and sister had already preceded him there. The community was searching for a G-d-fearing *melamed* to teach the older boys, and Reb Shraga Feivel was hired for the position. He was overjoyed to be greeted in Scranton by a group of Jews who resembled those he had left behind in Hungary. In particular, he was impressed by the *deveikus* (sense of closeness to God) in *davening* of an old Zhidichov chassid whom he met shortly after his arrival.[5]

In Scranton, he rented a room with a Jewish family, with whom he also ate. Because of his concerns about kashrus, his diet was extremely limited. The limited diet and the undercooked fare he was regularly served permanently robbed him of his previous good health and strength, and he developed ulcers that plagued him for the rest of his life.[6] So severe was the pain that, as he taught, he had to keep in front of him two prohibitions: "Do not become angry" and "Do not strike a fellow Jew," lest his suffering cause him to lose patience and hit a student.[7]

In Scranton, Reb Shraga Feivel never mentioned his *semichah* from the Unsdorfer Rav. Just before his first Pesach there, however,

3. Rabbi Nesanel Quinn.

4. Ibid.

5. Rabbi Hershel Mashinsky.

6. Mrs. Bas Sheva Linchner, Reb Shraga Feivel's daughter.

7. Rabbi Moshe Wolfson.

his hostess was cleaning his room and discovered it. When Reb Shraga Feivel found out what had happened, he promptly tore up his *semichah*. Later, concerned that someone might find the pieces and tape them together, he retrieved them and burned them.[8] For the rest of his life, he refused to answer to any form of address other than "Mister." If addressed as "rabbi" or "*rav*," he did not respond; and when responding to a telephone caller, he would say, "No one lives here by the name of Rav Mendlowitz."[9]

There are many explanations for his insistence on the title "Mister." No doubt his own natural modesty and the awe with which he viewed his own teachers made him reluctant to appropriate the title "*rav*" for himself. But equally important, he was a caustic critic of much of the American rabbinate of his day — increasingly so the longer he remained in America — and for him the title "rabbi" had a largely irreverent connotation.[10] Finally, he felt that he would have more influence among American youth without the title rabbi attached to his name.[11]

Reb Shraga Feivel used the years in Scranton to deepen his own Torah knowledge. Often learning through the night, he went through tractate after tractate of Gemara. Free time during the day was often spent pondering the deepest works of Jewish thought. On a visit to Scranton many years later, he pointed out a majestic oak tree on the outskirts of town to a group of his students and told them, "In the shade of that tree, I spent many, many days going through the entirety of *Tanya*." He used to say that the mark of a thinker was not

---

8. Heard from Avrohom Gross by his nephew Rabbi Yehoshua Leiman.

9. On one of Rabbi Yitzchak Isaac Sher's visits to America on behalf of Slabodka Yeshivah, Reb Shraga Feivel went to hear a *mussar shmuess* from Rabbi Sher. After the *shmuess*, the two men were introduced, and Rabbi Sher commented excitedly, "You are Rav Mendlowitz about whom I have heard so much?" Reb Shraga Feivel immediately replied, "You're mistaken, I'm only Mister Mendlowitz."

Rabbi Sher was not fazed, however, and told Reb Shraga Feivel, "Be 'Mister,' if you wish, but I have heard that you have done more to ensure that Torah will not be forgotten than many great rabbis." Gross and Kaminetsky, p. 558.

10. Rabbi Moshe Aharon Stern.

11. Rabbi Nesanel Quinn.

the ability to think about ten things in an hour, but the ability to think about one thing for ten hours,[12] and Scranton provided an opportunity for him to spend many such hours deep in thought.

THE EARLY DAYS OF REB SHRAGA FEIVEL'S CAREER AS A TEACHER in the Scranton Talmud Torah were difficult ones. He was assigned

Melamed to teach a class of about forty teenagers, who learned for three hours after public school. His students had scant knowledge of Jewish subjects, whether *Chumash* or Talmud, and were quite a rowdy bunch. Their *limudei kodesh* (Hebrew studies) began only in the middle of the afternoon, after a long day in school, and at a time when they would have greatly preferred to be outside playing ball with their friends. In addition, the boys had a sense of themselves as being more worldly and sophisticated than their "ignorant" *melamed*, who knew little English. That sense of superiority was fully reflected in the lack of respect shown to their *rebbi*, which made it impossible to maintain any discipline or to deliver a properly prepared lesson. Every day of his first three weeks in Scranton, Reb Shraga Feivel tendered his resignation at the end of the day, and every day the president of the community refused to accept his resignation and begged him to try it for just a little while longer.

One day Reb Shraga Feivel came up with a stratagem. He invited four of the class ringleaders to talk with him privately. What he said to them is unknown, but from that day on his relationship with the four ringleaders changed completely. They were so impressed with him that they turned serious about learning and the rest of the class followed their lead. After that, Reb Shraga Feivel's teaching proceeded smoothly and effectively — and the students enjoyed it.

Soon the boys were coming to class eager to listen and learn, despite their fatigue from the school day. Even at that early stage in his career as a *mechanech* (educator), Reb Shraga Feivel was blessed with the ability to explain the material with remarkable clarity.

---

12. Yonah Zev Herskowitz.

What he taught remained with his students not as mere information but as part of their being. By nature he was introverted and quiet, but when he started teaching, a sudden transformation came over him, and he spoke with great animation and passion. Many of his students in Scranton attested years later that much of what they heard from him remained as clearly etched in their minds as on the day they heard it.[13]

A student from Scranton once told Rabbi Shmuel Mendlowitz, "I had many great teachers in my life, including famous professors, but I never had another one who had your father's ability to arouse a class emotionally. He had the ability to inflame a class . . . Our classes in *Tanach* were something alive . . . All the *Yiddishkeit* that remains with me today, I owe to him."[14]

DESPITE HIS OWN RELATIVE SUCCESS WITH HIS STUDENTS, REB Shraga Feivel was under no illusion that a few hours of learning af-

Plan for the Future
ter school could substitute for a proper yeshivah education, and he decided to found such a yeshivah in Scranton. He knew he could count on the support of a number of families in the community for this undertaking, in particular, his close friend Rabbi David Eisenberger.[15]

The immediate reaction to his project, however, was complete apathy. Some parents argued that a yeshivah would destroy their

---

13. Gross and Kaminetsky, p. 558.

14. Chinn, "Ohr Shraga," p. 5.
    A student from those years, who afterward lost contact with Reb Shraga Feivel for many years, recalls that the day before his wedding Reb Shraga Feivel paid him a surprise visit and spoke to him at length about the importance of *taharas hamishpachah* (the laws of family purity) and *shemiras Shabbos*. Reb Shraga Feivel did not leave until he had extracted from his former student a promise to observe both these mitzvos. In subsequent years, the student found Shabbos a severe test since Saturday was his most profitable business day. Nevertheless, whenever he felt that the temptation to remain open on Shabbos was too great to withstand, he would remember his promise to Reb Shraga Feivel.

15. Rabbi Eisenberger was, like Rabbi Shraga Feivel, a native of Hungary. Before emigrating to the United States, he took the precaution of learning *shechitah* in order to have food in his own home that he felt comfortable eating. In Scranton, he tutored boys privately in his house, and on Thursdays he would drive around to the various little towns near Scranton to slaughter chickens for the Jews living there.

children's only chance to earn a decent livelihood. Fear of Heaven, they claimed, could be absorbed at home, and Torah learning could take place in the hours spent in Talmud Torah after school. Others objected to the suggestion of combining in one framework both religious and secular studies — something which had been unknown in the yeshivos of Hungary. Yet a third group of parents raised perhaps the most telling objection: Where will the money come from? To Reb Shraga Feivel's great dismay, even the distinguished local rabbis were not enthusiastic. Their reaction was one of surprise that an apparently intelligent man like Reb Shraga Feivel did not recognize the impossibility of establishing the sort of yeshivah he envisioned.

Reb Shraga Feivel was deeply pained by the indifference with which his plan was received in Scranton. Above all, he could not understand how parents who were G-d-fearing Jews did not see what was happening before their very eyes. Did they not realize that it was almost impossible to remain religious without a yeshivah education? Nor could he make peace with the attitude of many rabbis: "This is America. What can be done?"

Despite the coolness of the response, Reb Shraga Feivel nevertheless concluded that there was no fundamental barrier to the establishment of a yeshivah in America. Certainly there were enough *talmidei chachamim* already in America to staff a yeshivah. The greatest obstacle, then, was money. Reb Shraga Feivel decided to start a business. As a successful businessman, he was sure, he would be able to support the yeshivah with his own earnings and with funds that he would raise from his associates. He would choose a principal and teachers from among the many qualified *talmidei chachamim* in the country.[16]

All these plans, however, were temporarily put aside when, with the end of World War I, it once again became possible to travel to Europe. Reb Shraga Feivel's first concern was to bring his wife and children to America.

---

16. Rabbi Nesanel Quinn.

Reunited AT THE VERSAILLES CONFERENCE OF 1919, THE VICTORIOUS ALLIES established a new order for Europe, designed to cripple Germany and her Hapsburg allies. To that end, the Austro-Hungarian Empire was divided up into smaller nations. That division had immediate consequences for Reb Shraga Feivel: Humenne was made part of the newly created Czechoslovakia. As a result, he was now free to return to Europe, and he promptly did so.

He arrived home to find that his wife and children had endured indescribable suffering in the course of the war. In particular, his wife's health had deteriorated greatly in the wake of a long series of diseases. Surveying the devastation all around him, he immediately decided to bring his family, including his stepmother and half brothers and sisters, back to America.[17]

As soon as the necessary arrangements were made, the entire family set sail aboard the appropriately named *S.S. Hope*. En route he told his children, "We are on our way from *galus* to *Eretz Yisrael*, but along the way we have to make a temporary stop in America." During the entire journey, he talked in poetic language of the magical beauty and special qualities of *Eretz Yisrael*.[18]

Upon returning to Scranton, Reb Shraga Feivel was confronted with the difficult task of supporting a large family. His first venture was selling plots of land in *Eretz Yisrael*.[19] Neither that nor a variety of other ventures — selling rope and twine, a grocery store — proved successful, and after a year in Scranton, he moved his family in 1921 to the Williamsburg section of Brooklyn, which was just beginning to attract religious families.

In New York, Reb Shraga Feivel was finally ready to implement

---

17. Besides his stepmother, he brought his half brother Reuven and his half sisters, Frieda (Kaufman) and Masha (Sontag). As a grocer in Williamsburg, Reuven was famous for his generosity in extending credit throughout the Depression and his willingness to ignore the debts of families that could not pay.

18. Mrs. Bas Sheva Linchner.
   According to Rabbi Nesanel Quinn, Reb Shraga Feivel always intended to live in *Eretz Yisrael*, after first establishing a beachhead for Torah in America. In 1937, after Mesivta Torah Vodaath was well established, he planned to make *aliyah* with his family, but the plans were never realized.

19. Mrs. Bas Sheva Linchner.

the plan he had conceived in Scranton of starting a business to support a yeshivah. He set up a factory on the Lower East Side to manufacture kosher ice cream and opened a store to sell the ice cream and other milk products. There was no kosher rennet then available, and he had to find alternative means of causing the ice cream to jell. He had only indifferent success in this respect, and most of the ice cream melted long before the purchaser could bring it home.[20] Not surprisingly, the dairy business proved a financial disaster, and Reb Shraga Feivel lost not only all his own money, but went heavily into debt.[21]

Nevertheless, with his move to New York, the stage was now set for Reb Shraga Feivel's emergence into the public arena.

---

20. Ibid.

21. According to at least one report, part of Reb Shraga Feivel's difficulty in business was that he often forgot that to make money one must sell the product. Youngsters visited the factory to learn with him, and he would shower them with treats from among the factory's products. His wife once commented, "Of course, he didn't make money. When others put in milk powder he put in cream." *Rabbi Shmuel Mendlowitz.*

Chapter 4

In a Place Where
There Is No Man …

Shortly after his arrival in Williamsburg, Reb Shraga Feivel wrote inquiries to the Gerrer Rebbe, Rabbi Avraham Mordechai Alter, and to the Rogatchover Gaon, Rabbi Yosef Rosen.[1] His question: Should he dedicate himself to strengthening religious observance and spreading Torah in America or would it be preferable to focus on his own spiritual development? Their replies were virtually identical and left no room for doubt. He was obligated to do whatever was in his power to save his fellow Jews in America from spiritual oblivion.

IN THE WINTER OF 1922-23, REB SHRAGA FEIVEL ORGANIZED A small group of like-minded young men to plan a newspaper to combat what he and his confederates viewed as the **Dos Yiddishe** poison of the contemporary Yiddish press, then **Licht** dominated by highly ideological writers committed to Socialism or Zionism.

---

1. With these letters, he established a lifelong practice of consulting with leading Torah sages prior to embarking on any major undertaking.

| *The Gerrer Rebbe,* | *The Rogatchover Gaon,* |
| *Rabbi Avraham Mordechai Alter* | *Rabbi Yosef Rosen* |

So important was this project in Reb Shraga Feivel's view that he borrowed $10,000 — the equivalent of eight years' average salary in

those days — to invest in it. The great *chazzan* Yossele Rosenblatt was the other major investor and contributed $25,000 of his own money. Both spent years repaying the debts piled up by the paper, *Dos Yiddishe Licht* (*The Light of Israel*).[2]

Dos Yiddishe Licht drew on the talents of a number of writers, including Rabbi Leo Jung, who wrote weekly articles in English.

---

2. Reb Shraga Feivel struggled for many years to pay back the money he had borrowed. Yossele Rosenblatt had to go on tour for a year to recoup his losses.

Rabbi Leo Jung

Reb Shraga Feivel was one of the most prolific. Under the name Shraga Feivish Mendlowitz, he published a series of impassioned pleas for improved kashrus supervision and for observance of other major mitzvos. He published other articles under pseudonyms or anonymously.

The lead editorial in the first edition, published Shevat 5683 (February 1923), proclaimed the paper's goal of casting the light of Torah and *emunah* (faith) on the situation in America. The editors expressed their conviction that American Jews, like their ancestors in Egypt, had reached the forty-ninth level of impurity and time was running out for American Jewry. They concluded by expressing their intent to bring before American Jews every major world event for examination through "the lenses of traditional Judaism, which alone allows for the proper appreciation of events."

This last line strongly suggests that the author was none other than Reb Shraga Feivel, who was wont, in later years, to tell his students, "Put on the glasses of Torah, look at the world through the lenses of Judaism, for then you will see before you the world and events in an entirely different perspective." *Dos Yiddishe Licht* was comparable in style to much of the emerging Agudah press in Europe. It was aggressive with respect to the major issues facing American Jewry, but, at the same time, preserved a delicacy of expression not typical of the Yiddish press of the time. It appealed to the mind, as well as the emotions, of American Jews. Above all, it sought to arouse American Jews from their lethargy and to prevent them from making a comfortable peace with American society, the peace of the spiritual graveyard.

DURING THE SAME PERIOD, REB SHRAGA FEIVEL WAS ALSO ACTIVE in the formation of a religious organization named *Kesher Chizuk Hadas*, which aspired to make a drastic improvement in Jewish communal life, especially in the area of kashrus supervision.

Kesher Chizuk Hadas

The chaotic state of kashrus supervision in America was one of the first things that struck any visitor from Europe. Rabbi Yaakov David Wilovsky of Slutsk (the *Ridbaz*) was one of the first great European scholars to come to America. He eventually had to flee for his life — literally — from Chicago, as a consequence of his efforts to impose some supervision on kashrus in that city. In the introduction to his *Nimukei Ridbaz*, he painted a vivid picture of the sad situation in America at the turn of the century:

Rabbi Yaakov David Wilovsky of Slutsk (the Ridbaz)

In America, Jews have gathered from all four corners of the globe, and, as a consequence, no one knows anyone else or what he was in his native city. Many who were outcasts in their native lands because of their evil deeds come to America and give public sermons that any priest, *lehavdil*, could also give in his church. They take a crown for themselves and are called "rabbis."

Similarly, well-known evildoers in their hometowns come here and disguise themselves as "butchers," and sell what is, according to them, "kosher" meat. These "rabbis" and "butchers" have joined forces. The "butchers" pay a fee for the certification of the "rabbis," and the two of them together feed *treifos* to Jews . . . The *shochet* is himself generally drawn from that class of frivolous people that attends the theater, even on Shabbos . . .

Everywhere you go there are signs proclaiming "kosher meat" so that you would soon gain the impression that there is no non-kosher meat to be had in the whole country. Because the stomachs of Jews have become defiled with every form of prohibited food, *Rachmana litzlan*, the spirit of Judaism has dried up in their midst and they are overcome by a lust for every abominable thing.

Such was the situation that Reb Shraga Feivel set out to rectify. In an editorial in *Dos Yiddishe Licht* announcing the formation of *Kesher Chizuk Hadas*, Reb Shraga Feivel stressed that many of the problems confronting American Jewry, and especially that of kashrus supervision, could not be addressed by Jews acting individually but would require collective action.[3] Two weeks later, Rosh Chodesh Nissan 5683 (1923), at the founding meeting of *Kesher Chizuk Hadas*, Reb Shraga was elected secretary of the fledgling organization.

The consensus of those present was that kashrus was the first issue to which the new organization should address itself. Over the next two months, smaller gatherings were held in neighborhoods throughout the New York metropolitan area in order to enlist new members. At one of these meetings, Reb Shraga Feivel reported on the organization's activities to date and announced that a number of meatpackers had agreed to place their plants under the supervision of *Kesher Chizuk Hadas*.

The subject of kashrus was one to which Reb Shraga Feivel had already addressed himself in *Dos Yiddishe Licht*. "For How Long?" one of his few signed articles, was a stinging attack on the American rabbinate and the Orthodox community for their failure to confront the widespread fraud in kashrus supervision.[4]

Reb Shraga Feivel began with a quotation from *Yirmiyahu* (20:9) that fully captured the turbulence within himself: "Then I said: I will not make mention of Him, nor speak any more in His Name. But His word was in my heart like a burning fire within my bones, and I am weary with containing myself, and I cannot." Reb Shraga Feivel knew that, like Yirmiyahu, his words would cause him to be denounced, and many would be eager to see him stumble (see *Yirmiyahu* 20:10). That may be why he chose to sign this particular article: He may have considered it inappropriate to criticize others under the cover of anonymity.

The Yiddish press, he charged, contained advertisements attack-

---

3. *Dos Yiddishe Licht,* Issue 5, p. 13.

4. Ibid., Issue 3, p. 3.

ing butchers openly selling avowedly non-kosher meat, but a conspiracy of silence governed the much more insidious problem of butchers selling so-called kosher meat under the *hashgachah* of unqualified "rabbis." He rejected the excuse that such criticism would breed disrespect for all rabbis:

> The honor of rabbis is also dear to me. But the honor of the Torah, which is today relegated to the rubbish heap, and of the truth, which is trampled underfoot, are far more dear. And especially where the issue is one of *chillul Hashem* (desecration of the Divine Name), there is no place for concern with the honor of rabbis.

He acknowledged that some would consider it *"chutzpah"* for one who claimed no rabbinic title to accuse rabbis of permitting nonkosher meat to be sold under their supervision or of turning a blind eye to such activities by others. Nevertheless, he could not restrain himself after personal appeals to a number of rabbis proved fruitless.

In his opinion, the rabbinic leaders had been derelict in not weeding out from their ranks impostors and others for whom the lure of the dollar had proven stronger than their *yiras Shamayim*. In an article written just before Pesach of 1923, entitled "The Lifesaving Operation," he again addressed himself to the leaders of the American rabbinate.[5] With reference to advertisements taken out by leading rabbinic organizations in the Yiddish press stating that one could not rely on the kashrus supervision in certain butcher shops, he asked:

> Why do you warn the public and not the "rabbis" themselves, who wittingly or unwittingly place their *hechsher* on *treifeh* products? Why do you not publicize the names of these "rabbis" who dispense their *"hechsherim"* on every form of forbidden product?
>
> If the honor of Torah is so precious in your eyes, then it is incumbent upon you to weed out the worthless from the good, and to place any rabbi whose behavior brings about a

---

5. Ibid., Issue 6, p. 3.

chillul Hashem — be he the greatest of Torah scholars — completely outside the camp [of G–d-fearing Jews].

The inability, or unwillingness, of the American rabbinate to organize itself into a cohesive, effective body was a further subject of his criticism. In an article entitled "For How Long?" he wrote: I accuse important rabbis, the leaders and shepherds of the flock. Because of their jealousy of one another . . . if one says "forbidden" the other must say "permitted" and when one says "pure" the other must say "impure." The result, he concluded, is that they have prevented the imposition of any proper order on kashrus supervision.

> In "Who Is to Lead?" he posed the question: Why do we have four rabbinical organizations when one would suffice and be more effective? . . . There are no serious differences between them, no differences of principle, no disputes over any of the fundamentals of religion, nor even over the most insignificant *minhag* (custom).[6] The only issue dividing the organizations from one another, is, as in the days of Rechavam and Yerovam: Who will be the leader? Torah scholars are supposed to bring peace in the world, so why do you not make peace among yourselves?

Nor did he spare Orthodox laymen the sting of his lash. The apathy of the Orthodox public was anathema to him. For the epigram of an article entitled "Wake Up! Why Do You Sleep," he chose King David's lamentation over Avner: "Your hands were not bound, nor your feet in fetters. As a man falls before villains have you fallen" (*II Shmuel* 3:34). He described the course of Jewish history from the time of Avraham — "one man against the entire world" — as a continuous struggle to realize Hashem's ideals in the world. In that battle, he pointed out, there is not one example of retreat and certainly not of failure to mount a vigorous struggle for the honor of God. That being the case, he wondered, how could American Orthodoxy stand

---

6. Ibid., Issue 14, p. 3.

idle while blasphemy and scorn are directed at G–d, the Torah is trampled upon, and the holidays and Sabbaths are desecrated. "Where is your pride? Where is your spirit?" he demanded to know.[7]

Elsewhere he accused the Orthodox population of having "sunken into the sleep of Choni HaMe'agel and [being] blind to what is going on all around it":

> You have recently begun to establish Talmud Torahs and yeshivos to give your children a Jewish education . . . but don't you realize that those fattened on *treifos* and *neveilos* can never become Jews with Jewish *middos* (character traits)? Don't you know that *neveilos* and *treifos* contaminate the Jewish heart?
>
> Your ancestors allowed themselves to be burned and slaughtered in order to preserve our holy Torah. From you no such sacrifice is demanded. For a pittance, the situation could be improved dramatically. Yet you sleep on.

REB SHRAGA DID NOT CONTENT HIMSELF WITH ARTICLES ADdressed to immediate day-to-day issues. The times demanded, he

Battle in the Realm of Ideas felt, the use of modern means of communication to create a literature that was Jewish at its core and which was specifically designed to do battle with all those seeking to lure Jews from their ancestral faith.

Just as Rabbi Samson Raphael Hirsch had done in Germany in his day, he sought to make it possible for a religious Jew to proudly proclaim his adherence to traditional Judaism without being labeled a hopeless reactionary. He sallied forth to battle against both kinds of materialism — the unabashed pursuit of money and the "scientific materialism" of the Marxists who proclaimed religion to be "the opiate of the masses."

One of Reb Shraga Feivel's first efforts contrasting Torah *hashkafah* and modern thought was "Hellenism and Judaism."[8] He began the article with a series of dichotomies between Greek and

---

7. Ibid., Issue 4, p. 4.
8. Ibid., Issue 18, p. 2.

Jewish thought: Judaism stresses the soul, while Greek thought places the highest value on the intellect; in Jewish thought the perfection of one's *middos* is the ultimate test of a man, in Greek thought it is the development of his mind; Judaism's primary concern is with the person's conduct, Greece's with the person's thought; Judaism emphasizes purity, Greece beauty — regardless of its vulgarity; Jewish culture arouses man to holiness, Greek culture to self-gratification; Judaism is derived from a Divine Torah given at Sinai to the entire Jewish people, while Greek culture is the product of human intelligence.

At root these two worldviews are irreconcilable, Reb Shraga Feivel wrote. All efforts to harmonize them — from Philo of Alexandria to the Rambam — have ended in failure. The first confrontation between these two cultures took place more than 2,000 years ago when the Chashmonaim revolted against Antiochus and his Seleucid dynasty. "Where will we find today," Reb Shraga Feivel asked, "such great men of spirit who will use all their abilities to once again cast out the idols as our ancestors did? What is lacking today," he charged, "is the burning fire which formerly characterized our people."

In the words of Rabbi Leo Jung, Greece taught the holiness of beauty; Jews taught the beauty of holiness.

In the second installment of the article, Reb Shraga Feivel turned to the contrast between the Greek emphasis on external form and beauty and Judaism's focus on the internal spirit that is hidden from view. The Greek stress on external form, he noted, had entered into the study houses and synagogues of America. This occasionally shows itself in a stress on decorum during prayer, at the expense of the feeling and cleaving to Hashem that was formerly the hallmark of Jewish prayer. While our Sages had found a place for the "beauty of Yefes" within the "tents of Shem," they had never permitted that pursuit of beauty to become more important than holiness.[9]

Another topic to which Reb Shraga Feivel turned his attention

---

9. Yefes is the son of Noach from whom Greece descends. The name itself implies beauty. The Jewish people, whose destiny is to dwell in the tents of Torah, are the descendants of Noach's son Shem.

was Shabbos.[10] He did not content himself with harangues directed at those who had succumbed to economic pressure to work on Shabbos. Rather than stressing the seriousness of the transgression involved, he focused instead on the positive: the beauty of Shabbos and its lifegiving qualities to those who observe it. He defined Shabbos as rest not only for the body but for the soul — a day when the soul can best free itself from the shackles of the *yetzer hara* (evil inclination), a day of not just *menuchah* (rest) but of *kedushah* (holiness).

Just as Pesach is called the "time of our freedom" in the context of the yearly calendar, so Shabbos is "the time of our freedom" in the context of the weekly calendar. That freedom takes two forms: at the physical level, freedom from external pressures; at the spiritual level, release from the grasp of our materialistic desires. The latter aspect — attaining freedom from the *yetzer hara* so that one can begin to define himself as a refined human being — is far more difficult, said Reb Shraga Feivel, than attaining one's physical freedom. When Hashem told the Jews leaving Egypt that they would be His servants, He meant that they would no longer be servants to their *yetzer hara*.

Even though modern man has succeeded in freeing himself from servitude to others, he remains a slave to his own instinct for self-gratification. As his mastery over nature grows, he comes more and more to worship himself and bow down to "the work of his hands, formed by his own fingers" (*Yeshayahu* 60:21). By providing man with respite from the involvement with his physical needs, Shabbos allows him to concentrate entirely on the spiritual "I" that is at his core. He can take stock of himself and reflect on his place and task within the entire created universe. The moment a person frees himself from the narrow confines of his physical existence, he immediately sees before him the entire universe operating according to eternal laws in perfect harmony.

Reb Shraga Feivel concluded with a plea to his fellow Jews to recognize the redemptive power of Shabbos and to experience its

---

10. *Dos Yiddishe Licht,* Issue 8 (1923), p. 2.

ability to nourish and enliven the soul as well as recharge the body.

Reb Shraga Feivel was fond of repeating the statement of *Chazal:* "Why is Avraham called אֹהֲבִי (he who loves Me, i.e., God) (*Yeshayahu* 41:8)? Because he generated the love of *HaKadosh Baruch Hu* in his many followers." Reb Shraga Feivel set himself a similar task in his own generation. The first stage of his ambitious mission was the years spent clarifying and refining his own thinking; the second stage giving expression to those thoughts in writing; and the third, and by far most fruitful, would be instilling those ideas in the coming generation of American Jews.

Chapter 5

Yeshivah Torah Vodaath:
A Miracle

T
O ANYONE UNINFORMED ABOUT THE TRAGIC PAUCITY of Torah education in America in 1918, it is impossible to fully appreciate the significance of the founding of Yeshivah Torah Vodaath that year. Although it did not signal an end to the general apathy of first-generation immigrants to their children's slide away from mitzvah observance, it was nevertheless a major counterattack against the firmly rooted conviction of the Jewish establishment, as well as the masses, that unadulterated Torah education in America was unattainable.

FOR THE VAST MAJORITY OF THE NEARLY 300,000 SCHOOL-AGE Jewish children in 1918, public-school education was the only edu-

Early Jewish Education

cation they knew. According to one survey that year, less than one-quarter of New York City's Jewish youngsters had any Jewish education, and that included many who were in schools associated with the various

Socialist or Bundist groups.[1] For those who received some kind of religious instruction, the typical venue was an afternoon Talmud Torah, where boys spent an hour or two after public school, learning to read Hebrew and preparing for their bar mitzvahs. There, in an atmosphere of apathy, a poorly paid *melamed* to whom English was a second language confronted boys who preferred to be outdoors playing stickball.

After a brief and unhappy sojourn in America, Rabbi Yaakov David Wilovsky of Slutsk (the *Ridbaz*) penned a bitter portrait of Jewish life in America. He described compulsory-education laws, which forced Jewish boys and girls to spend their days together with non-Jewish children, as the single greatest cause for the lowly state of American Jewish life. Even where parents attempted to give their children some type of after-school learning, he wrote in his introduction to *Nimukei Ridbaz* (his commentary on *Chumash*), the children paid scant attention to the *melamed* because all their energies were taken up with their work in public school. As a consequence, by the age of 13 or 14, most boys could not even *daven* properly, and even fewer were accustomed to saying the requisite blessings prior to eating, if they were aware of the blessings at all.

The only ray of hope the *Ridbaz* saw in this bleak scene was that compulsory-education laws also permitted the establishment of religious schools. But it was an opportunity that religious parents

Rabbi Yosef Stern

were notoriously slow to seize. Less than one percent of Jewish boys of elementary-school age attended the few "yeshivos" that then existed. For girls there was no elementary-school education of any kind, other than a few afternoon Talmud Torahs.

Historians have generally assigned the title the "first yeshivah" to Eitz Chaim, founded in 1886 by Rabbi Yosef Stern, a

---

1. Irving Howe, *The World of Our Fathers*, p. 202.

former student of the Chofetz Chaim. The founding protocols called for the "yeshivah to be run solely according to our holy Torah," and to employ "only G-d-fearing individuals, who are learned in the Torah and are not lax with respect to even the least of the mitzvos of the Torah." Eitz Chaim eventually merged with Yeshivas Rabbeinu Yitzchak Elchonon, which had opened its doors ten years later. In the years following the founding of Eitz Chaim, a handful of other yeshivos were established.[2] The most successful of these institutions, Yeshivas Rabbeinu Jacob Joseph, founded by Rabbi Shmuel Yitzchak Andron, opened its doors on the Lower East Side early in 1899. By 1910 it had 500 students.[3]

Rabbi Jacob Joseph,
the first Chief Rabbi of New York

Rabbi Shmuel Yitzchak Andron

---

2. Yeshivah D'Harlem was founded in what was then a largely Jewish neighborhood in the early years of the century. It was followed by Talmud Torah R' Yisrael Salanter, established in the Brownsville section of Brooklyn in 1906. Six boys made up the first class of this Talmud Torah, which would one day become Yeshivas Rabbi Chaim Berlin. Tifereth Jerusalem opened on the Lower East Side in 1907 as an afternoon Talmud Torah. In 1923, Rabbi Chaim Yechezkel Moseson, formerly *menahel* of Torah Vodaath, changed it to a full-day elementary school.

3. The yeshivah was named after the first Chief Rabbi of New York, one of Rabbi Yisrael Salanter's outstanding *talmidim*, who died in 1902 broken by his experiences in the New World.

These few institutions were far from adequate to reach more than a tiny fraction of New York's school-age Jewish population. Nor did the title of "yeshivah" recall the yeshivos of Europe. While R.J.J. and Eitz Chaim were fine institutions, most "yeshivos" were nothing more than schools for boys up to the age of bar mitzvah, in which five hours of daily religious instruction were offered. The requirement of a full curriculum of secular studies and the fact that Jewish education rarely extended past the age of bar mitzvah made it impossible to offer more than the barest rudiments of Mishnah and Gemara. Even those parents who wanted to provide their children a Torah education like the one they had known in Europe were confronted with many obstacles. There was a dearth of qualified teachers, and many of these institutions were forced to employ teachers whose own religious commitment was questionable.

The closest contact the vast majority of American Jews had with yeshivos in the classic sense were the visits — increasingly frequent with the passage of time — of leading *roshei yeshivah* from Europe, who were forced to travel abroad to raise funds for their institutions. Whatever residual guilt American Jews felt as a result of their failure to provide their own children with a traditional Jewish education was assuaged by contributions to the great Torah centers of Europe. The collections for European yeshivos also tended to reinforce the widespread view that Torah was for the *alter heim* (the Old Country), while making money was the proper goal of life in America.

LIKE MANY REVOLUTIONARY EVENTS, THE FOUNDING OF TORAH Vodaath had consequences far beyond anything anticipated, or capable of being anticipated, at the time.[4] When **Binyamin** Binyamin Wilhelm set out in 1917 to create a yeshivah **Wilhelm** in Williamsburg, he was responding primarily to two conflicting demands: his wife's desire to escape the teeming Lower East Side for a larger apartment in Williamsburg in which to raise the growing Wilhelm clan, and his own insistence that his sons at-

4. The following account of the founding of Torah Vodaath is based almost entirely on Binyamin Wilhelm's written reminiscences, supplemented in a few places by an interview with his daughter, Mrs. Chanah Belsky.

tend yeshivah. Wilhelm's determination to provide his sons with a proper Torah education resulted in a transformation of the face of American Jewry.

Wilhelm had fled his native Poland for the United States in 1907 to avoid the Russian army. Prior to setting out for America, he was in contact with some friends who had already emigrated to America and who were members of *Adas Bnei Yisrael*, a fraternal organization of young immigrants organized for the purpose of strengthening one another in *Yiddishkeit*. These friends encouraged him to come, and after his arrival *Adas Bnei Yisrael* became the center of his social life.

R' Binyamin Wilhelm

Four years after his arrival, the young Radomsker chassid married Bertha Weberman, whose father Moshe Weberman owned a Lower East Side delicatessen, known for the reliability of its kashrus.[5] When her friends teased the vivacious American-born Bertha about marrying a "greenhorn," she replied, "My father says if I want to be happy I should marry him."

By 1917 the Wilhelm family had outgrown its apartment on the Lower East Side, and Bertha cast her eye across the Williamsburg Bridge to Williamsburg. Williamsburg, however, lacked a yeshivah of any kind. The oldest Wilhelm child, Yehoshua, was already 4, and

---

5. The Webermans were one of the few families whose *Yiddishkeit* was not adversely affected by life in America. Moshe Weberman used to give treats to little boys who came into the delicatessen wearing *tzitzis*. He once saw a father get a glass of water for a teenage son while the two were sitting at a table and waiting to be served. He hurried over to the table, took the glass of water and poured it into the sink, explaining to the astounded father and son, "In my restaurant, the son brings the water for the father, not the father for the son."

Binyamin Wilhelm was hesitant about moving to a neighborhood without a yeshivah.

One day, as Wilhelm was contemplating his wife's desire to move, Leibel Dershowitz, a friend who already lived in Williamsburg, walked into Wilhelm's paper and twine store at 18 Norfolk Street. Wilhelm shared his misgivings about Williamsburg, and Dershowitz replied that the only solution was for him to move to Williamsburg and establish a yeshivah himself.

In his memoirs, Wilhelm recalled:

> I was then a young man, not yet 30, filled with vigor. Without giving much thought to the difficulties awaiting me, I answered, "Good. I'll try. If Hashem helps, and I succeed, so much the better . . . and if not, I'll return to the Lower East Side where there is already Yeshivas Rabbeinu Jacob Joseph."

A Lonely Crusade

JUST BEFORE SHAVUOS OF 1917, THE WILHELM FAMILY MOVED TO Williamsburg, and Binyamin Wilhelm's efforts to start a yeshivah commenced. The nearby Beis Aharon *shtiebel* on Ross Street was full of devout chassidim and men of substantial Torah learning, and it was there that Wilhelm decided to begin. To his dismay, he soon found that even the most religious and learned Jews had long since despaired of providing their children with a serious Jewish education. It was not unusual in those days, even in *shomer Shabbos* homes, for father and children to leave their apartments together Shabbos morning, with the father going to the *mikveh* and his sons and daughters going to work; or for a mother to give the children a few pennies for the cinema after the Shabbos *cholent* and *kugel*, excusing herself with the comment, "They're still children, and they need a little enjoyment."[6]

Many of those with whom Wilhelm spoke in Beis Aharon, and thousands like them, had come to America without their families, leaving their wives and children behind while they tried to gain an

---

6. Berl Belsky.

economic toehold in the new land. By the time they were able to bring their families over, the children had grown up without paternal discipline and were ripe to be indoctrinated into the American social mores and values.

Against this background, the standard response to Wilhelm's efforts to whip up enthusiasm for a yeshivah was: "Do you seriously think that you can make 'American boys' into *lamdanim, talmidei chachamim, tzaddikim*? We also thought like you when our children were younger, but the passing years have taught us better. There is nothing to be done. This is America, and the situation is hopeless." Reb Binyamin began to feel that people were nodding pityingly in his direction, as if to say, "Look at this dreamer making a fool of himself." A conversation with one of the most distinguished of Beis Aharon's members was typical of those he had in the *shtiebel:*

> "What is all this noise all day long — yeshivah, yeshivah? Do you think you will succeed in convincing even one parent to take his children out of public school?"
>
> "Yes, you!" Wilhelm shot back. "You are going to take your children from public school and put them into yeshivah."
>
> "And let's say you convince me, how are you going to convince his mother to let him be turned into a *chenyok* (misfit)?"
>
> "The yeshivah will not turn him into a *chenyok*, but into someone who will find favor with both G-d and man."
>
> "And his sister who is already studying to be a teacher, how are you going to convince her to let her brother be turned into a benchwarmer in a yeshivah?"

Wilhelm walked from one *beis medrash* to another trying to stir up interest in a yeshivah. In one, he asked the president of the congregation for permission to speak. The man looked at him in wonderment, before surmising out loud, "Oh, you must be a Hebrew teacher, who wants a yeshivah so you'll have a job." The man then showed him the palm of his hand and told him, "You have as much chance of founding a yeshivah here as I have of growing hair on the palm of my hand."

The only enthusiastic support for Wilhelm's efforts came from old friends from *Adas Bnei Yisrael* who had preceded him to Williamsburg. He and his friends spent the entire summer organizing meetings to publicize the idea of a yeshivah. Most of these meetings attracted no more than three or four participants, and at some, Wilhelm found himself "alone with the *Ribbono Shel Olam*." At the end of the summer, the organizers decided to schedule a large fund-raising meeting for the night of Hoshana Rabbah in Beis Aharon, since most of the members would, in any event, be there to recite the night's *Tikkun*. That meeting proved to be the first major success. Aharon Siegel, for whom the Beis Aharon was named, pledged $1,000 (a very large sum in those days) and a number of other significant pledges were received.

Based on the success of the Hoshana Rabbah meeting, Wilhelm decided to schedule a *melaveh malkah* for the next *Motza'ei Shabbos*. That night his wife was due to go into labor, and she asked her husband as he was walking out the door how he could leave her at such a time. He tried to calm her by telling her, "From my going tonight there will be a yeshivah . . . and you will be watched by *HaKadosh Baruch Hu*." A number of prominent Williamsburg *rabbanim* came to the meeting, including Rabbi Zev Gold, later president of World Mizrachi, who was elected president of the new yeshivah.[7] In addition, several more significant pledges were received.

One aspect of the meeting, however, did not go according to Wilhelm's plans. Those who had promised substantial sums, including Rabbi Gold, began to talk of collecting large amounts of money in order to put up a building prior to opening a yeshivah. For Wilhelm,

---

7. Rabbi Gold's influence was felt in the choice of name for the new yeshivah. Torah Vodaath was the name of an earlier school established in 1896 in Lida by Rabbi Yitzchak Yaakov Reines, a founder of Mizrachi. Rabbi Reines sought to combine secular studies, Jewish studies, and traditional Gemara learning. The Torah Vodaath of Lida failed after seven years.

who had undertaken the whole project primarily for the sake of providing his son with a traditional Jewish education, the idea of waiting until such a large sum could be collected was out of the question.

Wilhelm's continued insistence on opening a yeshivah immediately made him *persona non grata* with the other members of the board, and they began to "forget" to invite him to meetings. But he always found out when and where the meetings were scheduled and continued to press his case. At last he wore down the resistance of the others, and they agreed to place plans for a large building on the back burner and to start on a smaller scale. For $8,000, a small house was purchased at the corner of Marcy Avenue and Keap Street.

Around Pesach of 1918, the yeshivah held its first banquet, and the summer was devoted to convincing parents to register their children for the coming school year. By the end of the summer, fifty children of all ages were enrolled. That Yom Kippur, Wilhelm kept his *davening* short, and walked from *shtiebel* to *shtiebel* trying to gather students. His efforts bore fruit, and by Chol HaMoed Succos, ninety boys were registered.

At that point, Wilhelm again found himself in conflict with his fellow board members. To save costs they wanted each teacher to be responsible for two classes and for the principal to teach as well. Wilhelm, however, insisted that no teacher be responsible for more than one class and that the principal and other administrative personnel be free to devote themselves exclusively to their administrative tasks. Once again his unyielding insistence paid off, and his view prevailed.

Torah Vodaath opened its doors the day after Succos 1918 with classes from kindergarten through sixth grade. The timing of its opening was propitious, since it coincided with the arrival in America

Yeshiva Torah Vodaath at 206 Wilson Street

just after World War I of many religious immigrants who had not yet despaired of raising their children as Jews.

Under its first principal, Rabbi Mordechai Eliyahu Finkelstein, the yeshivah immediately flourished. Rabbi Finkelstein combined a number of important qualities: He was learned, a chassid (like most of the parents), and possessed a secular education. Most importantly, he was able to attract some teachers who were both learned and observant.

Though the yeshivah grew rapidly, Wilhelm and those closest to him were still not completely satisfied with either the quality or quantity of the Torah studies. In 1920, Rabbi Chaim Yechezkel Moseson, who had been the principal of Yeshivas Chaim Berlin in Brownsville, came to Torah Vodaath with a mandate to upgrade the standard of Torah studies. Meanwhile the yeshivah continued to grow. By late 1920, there was no choice but to purchase three adjacent houses on Wilson Street to accommodate the growing student body and create room for further expansion.

Reb Shraga Feivel Comes to Torah Vodaath

BINYAMIN WILHELM, HIS BROTHER-IN-LAW BEN ZION Weberman, and Abraham Lewin met Reb Shraga Feivel shortly after his move to Williamsburg in 1921.[8] They knew that he had been a *melamed* in Scranton, and on a number of occasions suggested that he join the staff of Torah Vodaath. Reb Shraga Feivel, however, consistently rejected all their entreaties. He was not eager to earn a livelihood from teaching Torah,[9] and still entertained the hope of earning enough money in business to open a yeshivah of his own. Not until 1923 did he abandon that dream and agree to consider a position as a *rebbi* in Torah Vodaath.

Nearly sixty years later, Wilhelm still recalled with amusement Reb Shraga Feivel's first meeting with Rabbi Moseson and the rest of the staff. The teachers showed no signs of being particularly

---

8. Reb Shraga Feivel and Binyamin Wilhelm were the closest of friends and confidants for the rest of Reb Shraga Feivel's life. For many years, the Wilhelm and Mendlowitz families spent their summer vacations together in Far Rockaway. *Mrs. Chanah Belsky.*

9. "Do not make the Torah . . . a spade with which to dig" (*Pirkei Avos* 4:7).

impressed with their new colleague, and many of them wondered openly whether someone who had no formal training as a pedagogue and who had not learned in any of the famous Lithuanian yeshivos was even suited for the staff. Nevertheless, Wilhelm, Weberman, and Lewin had great confidence in him, and he was hired as *rebbi* of the eighth-grade class, the senior class in the school.

Within weeks of the opening of the school year, Rabbi Moseson left Torah Vodaath for Tifereth Jerusalem on the Lower East Side,[10] leaving Torah Vodaath without a principal. While Wilhelm and Weberman were convinced that Reb Shraga Feivel was the perfect

person for the vacant position, the Board of Trustees and the teaching staff remained far more skeptical. The businessmen on the board could not get used to the idea of a *melamed* with a beard and *peyos* as the principal, and the teachers, many of whom had received a more *"maskilish"* ("enlightened") education in Europe,[11] were similarly unenthusiastic. But when Abraham Lewin, the most influential board member, came around to the Wilhelm-Weberman position, the matter was clinched.

The board was particularly struck by one difference between

Mr. Abraham Lewin

10. Rabbi Moseson was given the task of turning what had until then been an afternoon Talmud Torah into a yeshivah for boys up until high-school age. In 1932, Rabbi Joseph Adler left Torah Vodaath to create Mesivta Tifereth Jerusalem for high-school-age boys and older. Upon his arrival in America in 1937, Rabbi Moshe Feinstein became the *rosh yeshivah*.

11. Prior to Reb Shraga Feivel's arrival at Torah Vodaath, there were school assemblies every Friday at which the Zionist flag was displayed. *Elias Karp*. In part this may reflect the influence of Rabbi Zev Gold, the first president of the Board of Directors and one of the leaders of the Mizrachi movement in America. And in part it reflects the Lithuanian origins of much of the staff. Both *Haskalah* and Zionism had made greater inroads in Lithuania than they had in Reb Shraga Feivel's native Hungary.

Reb Shraga Feivel and all the other candidates. Each of the other candidates insisted on a written contract specifying in detail the terms and conditions of employment. Reb Shraga Feivel, on the other hand, refused to negotiate salary or the other conditions of employment. "If, with Hashem's help, I succeed, I know I can depend on you with respect to my salary and the like," he told them. "And if I see I am not suited for the task, I won't wait for you to tell me. I'll quit first."[12]

The new principal had the threefold task of selling himself to the teaching staff, the students, and the parents. The teachers, who at first referred to him somewhat derogatorily as the "*melamed* from Mezo-Laboretz," soon recognized that he was a natural pedagogue and that even in those subjects in which the *maskilim* concentrated — *Tanach*, Hebrew grammar, and Jewish history — he was more knowledgeable than they. "He knew more history than the historians, more grammar than the grammarians, and more Chassidus than many *rebbes*," recalls Elias Karp, one of his first students.

He ruled not by giving orders but by infusing the teachers with his own enthusiasm. Teachers who had been teaching for years were amazed at how much more material they could suddenly cover and by their own powers of creativity in the classroom. When Reb Shraga Feivel became founding principal of the Mesivta in 1926, the elementary school *rebbeim* found themselves unable to complete the same lesson plans they had used in his three years as principal of the elementary school. Without his daily spark, the fire grew smaller.

Reb Shraga Feivel also spared no effort to add new *rebbeim* imbued with his own deep faith. One of those whom he brought to Torah Vodaath was his good friend Rabbi David Eisenberger. Reb Shraga Feivel brushed aside Rabbi Eisenberger's protests that he lacked classroom experience. "I know you better than you know yourself. And I am convinced that you are suited for it," he told his

12. Gross and Kaminetsky, p. 560.

friend. Time proved Reb Shraga Feivel correct, and Rabbi Eisenberger developed into one of the *rebbeim* with the deepest influence on students.

Several times a week, Reb Shraga taught a *shiur* at night for the Board of Directors and other parents. One of his primary goals was to win them over to his educational goals and make them realize that bar mitzvah should be the beginning, not the end, of a Jewish boy's education. His natural, unabashed love of Torah was infectious. As the parents saw how their children advanced each week, they could not help but be infected with some of Reb Shraga Feivel's enthusiasm. Word that a sliver of *ruchnius* (spirituality) had sprung up in Williamsburg spread, and a variety of temporary classrooms — in shuls and *batei medrash* — had to be found to accommodate the growing student body.

Whatever his success as principal of the elementary school, had Reb Shraga Feivel remained in that position it is doubtful that he or Torah Vodaath would be more than a historical footnote today. All that was achieved in the elementary-school years would soon have been dissipated in public high school and beyond. The forces pulling boys away from traditional Jewish observance were simply too powerful to be withstood with an eighth-grade Jewish education.

The stage was set for the creation of the Mesivta.

Chapter 6
The Mesivta — Another Miracle

W ITH THE OPENING OF MESIVTA TORAH VODAATH for boys above bar mitzvah age in the fall of 1926, Reb Shraga Feivel sparked a revolution in Torah education in America. He raised the clarion call that it is incumbent upon every Jew — and especially his children — to be steeped in knowledge of the Talmud to the full extent of his ability.[1] Mesivta Torah Vodaath would, in time, be recognized as the progenitor of all advanced yeshivah learning in America.

The only form of post-bar mitzvah religious education known at the time was Yeshivas Rabbeinu Yitzchak Elchonon, which was designed to produce rabbis. Studying for the rabbinate was sufficiently career oriented to satisfy parents whose primary concern was that their children not know the same life in the sweatshops and factories that they did. What was unknown, however, was Torah studies without a spe-

---

1. The name Mesivta was carefully chosen to distinguish the new institution from a "yeshivah," which in the existing American parlance referred to a religious school up to the eighth grade.

cific career goal in mind.[2] A critical editorial in the Yiddish-language *Morning Journal* shortly after the announcement of the opening of the Mesivta captures the lack of understanding of the purpose of the new institution. "Just as the Reform have a single rabbinical seminary in Cincinnati, and the Conservative have the Schechter Seminary in New York, so should Yeshivas Rabbeinu Yitzchak Elchonon suffice [to produce Orthodox rabbis]," opined the anonymous author.

The extent of Reb Shraga Feivel's innovation is evident from the difficulty he had selling the idea of the Mesivta even to the religious public of the time — to everyone from his own Board of Directors to parents of would-be students. Certainly no one dreamed at the time that the Mesivta would go on to produce generations of graduates, ranging from internationally renowned *talmidei chachamim* to religious *baalebatim* in the thousands.

---

2. Prior to the establishment of Mesivta Torah Vodaath, it was assumed that parents would agree to intensive Torah learning for their children only as part of their professional training for a rabbinical career. Rabbi Simchah Wasserman captured the vast difference between Torah learning as a prelude to a profession and Torah learning for its own sake with a story about Rabbi Yisrael Salanter.

Reb Yisrael was once offered a position as head of a government-sponsored rabbinic seminary in Vilna. To avoid the pressure placed upon him to accept the position, he fled to Kovno. Soon after his arrival in Kovno, he was approached by a religious doctor, who challenged his decision not to assume the leadership of the rabbinic seminary. The doctor pointed out that a *talmid chacham* of Reb Yisrael's stature could have completely transformed the nature of the state-supported rabbinate. In response, Reb Yisrael explained that the very idea of learning Torah for a career ensured that nothing good could come out of the seminary.

Traditionally, said Reb Yisrael, Jews had learned Torah without any other purpose than fulfilling the mitzvah of learning Torah. Those who achieved a high level of scholarship often became *baalei horaah* (halachic decisors) out of a sense of responsibility to the Jewish community, which depends on halachic guidance for its very existence. But the years spent in Torah learning prior to that were never perceived as career training.

Reb Yisrael then pointed out to the doctor the difference between a *rav* and professionals of any kind. The *rav's* primary concern must be with the poorest members of the community. If a rich man brings a chicken with a question on one of its lungs, the *rav* need not spend too much time before declaring the chicken *treif*. But if a poor man presents the same *she'eilah* (question), the *rav* must use all his expertise to search for a *heter*. By contrast, he told the doctor, "You went to medical school to earn a good living, and as a consequence your primary concern is necessarily with the richest members of the community. If a poor man awakens you in the middle of the night with a complaint, you tell him to come to the office the next morning. But if a rich man sends his servant to your door, you leap from bed and rush to him, no matter how trivial his complaint from a medical standpoint."

Reb Shraga Feivel's ability to perceive a need that others did not was a reflection of his unique vision of Jewish life in America. He was at once more optimistic and more pessimistic about the future of American Jewry than were his contemporaries. On the one hand, he defied the conventional wisdom that in America it was impossible to raise children with the fear of Heaven, and without the need to compromise. At the same time, he saw more clearly than most just how far American Jews would sink without any grounding in Torah. The prevalent attitude was to try to save whatever could be saved through a series of strategic retreats and compromises. Reb Shraga Feivel not only rejected such compromises on principle, he saw that they would not work in practice and in the end nothing would be saved.

IT IS EVIDENT THAT REB SHRAGA FEIVEL WAS THINKING ABOUT the creation of a yeshivah for high-school-age boys and beyond al-

An Idea Whose Time Had Come most from the first moment he stepped into Torah Vodaath. The schedule for the elementary school was 9 a.m. to 3 p.m. for religious studies, and then an hour break. General studies ran from 4 p.m. to 7 p.m. In each of his three years as principal of the yeshivah, Reb Shraga Feivel convinced a number of eighth graders to continue their studies in the yeshivah after graduation. At 2:30 p.m., they would cross the Williamsburg Bridge to the high-school division of Yeshivas Rabbeinu Yitzchak Elchonon on the Lower East Side for their secular courses.

In September 1923, Reb Shraga Feivel appointed Rabbi Joseph Adler as the eighth-grade Gemara *rebbi*. He was very successful and for the next three years, he advanced with his class. To teach *Chumash, Navi*, and halachah after lunch, Reb Shraga Feivel engaged another master teacher, Rabbi Feivel Weiler. In September 1925, Reb Shraga Feivel assigned Rabbi Weiler to a full-time class, and taught the above subjects to the tenth grade himself. His probable motive was to influence the boys to become the forerunners of a mesivta of advanced learning. In addition, he initiated *mishmar* (late-night learning) sessions on Thursday night. The first hour was for Talmud review, followed by a period of free discussion. Reb

Shraga Feivel encouraged the *talmidim* to suggest subjects and problems for discussion. Rabbi Nesanel Quinn recalls how Reb Shraga Feivel introduced these *mishmar* sessions. He asked the boys to come to the Mesivta in the evening. They were greeted by him and Mr. Abraham Lewin, one of the active board members. Reb Shraga Feivel delivered a Torah thought and Mr. Lewin distributed refreshments. This small beginning gradually evolved into long learning sessions that extended past midnight.

Rabbi Nesanel Quinn

Reb Shraga Feivel squeezed in classes with that small group of pioneers on Thursday nights and at many other times. Together they succeeded in completing almost all of *Tanach*. Whatever he taught was with passion. Even Hebrew grammar was filled with his enthusiasm for *lashon hakodesh* (the holy tongue), not a dry class in philology.[3]

Despite their grueling day, Reb Shraga Feivel pushed the boys to excel in their secular studies. He was careful not to leave parents any excuse to remove their sons from the Mesivta on the grounds that they were not obtaining a proper secular education. Simultaneously, Reb Shraga Feivel kept adding to their Torah studies.[4] Despite the

---

3. Elias Karp.

4. In later years, the more advanced students would gather in Reb Shraga Feivel's office around midnight on Thursday night. One of the students would present a *chaburah*, an original Torah presentation, in the presence of Reb Shraga Feivel and the *rosh yeshivah*, Rabbi David Leibowitz. When he was done, a lively discussion would ensue. Then Reb Shraga Feivel and Reb David would speak. *Rabbi Nesanel Quinn.*

post-midnight classes, the boys were expected to be in the *beis medrash* precisely on time the next morning. In the doorway, they could count on finding Reb Shraga Feivel with his ever-present pocket watch in hand.

In those days, recalls Rabbi Quinn, it was easier to push students: "I don't remember any of my classmates ever complaining that we were overworked . . . Almost all our parents worked long hours for scant pay, and we understood that working hard is the natural way of life." With their Torah studies and night school, the boys were kept too busy to be distracted by the siren song of American society. "We fulfilled Pharaoh's command to the Egyptian overseers — 'Make heavier the burden so that they cease paying attention to false ideas' (*Shemos* 5:9)," says Rabbi Quinn.

Almost the only free time that most boys had was the long Saturday night during the winter. Reb Shraga Feivel soon laid claim to that time as well. When one of the *bachurim* confessed to him that Saturday night was movie night, he invited the boys to his home instead. "No learning. We'll just sit and talk," he assured them. And he was good to his word. The boys were encouraged to ask about whatever was on their minds. Only at the end of the evening would Reb Shraga Feivel say, "*Ober un gornisht pahst nit* — No Torah study at all just isn't proper," and he would spend a few minutes with them studying a mitzvah in *Sefer HaChinuch*.[5]

A Visit to New Haven

BEFORE HE OPENED THE MESIVTA, REB SHRAGA FEIVEL WANTED his students to experience a real *beis medrash* on the European model, so he took them on Lag B'Omer up to New Haven, Connecticut, where Rabbi Yehudah Heschel Levenberg, the *rav* of the city, had founded the first advanced yeshivah in America in 1922.[6] The Torah Vodaath students spent a whole day soaking up the atmosphere of the

---

5. Berl Belsky; Chinn, "Ohr Shraga," p. 7.

6. Moshe Mintz, who had been Reb Shraga Feivel's closest student in Scranton, was a student in New Haven. Moshe Mintz married Rabbi Levenberg's daughter Brachah, and it was likely he who first brought Reb Shraga Feivel and Rabbi Levenberg together. Later Reb Shraga Feivel was to attribute much of his interest in the works of Rabbi Moshe Chaim Luzzatto (*Ramchal*) to Rabbi Levenberg.

yeshivah and it made an indelible impression on them.

Rabbi Levenberg was one of the shining lights in the Slabodka Yeshivah of his time, and a spellbinding orator; at the age of 19, he was chosen to eulogize Rabbi Zvi Hirsch Spektor, the *rav* of Kovno. The Alter (Elder) of Slabodka, Rabbi Nosson Tzvi Finkel, the head of that great yeshivah, was a master educator and judge of people. Impressed with Rabbi Levenberg's oratorical skills, refined character, and distinguished personality, the Alter sent him to America to found a *mussar*-oriented yeshivah, on the model of Slabodka.

There is a tradition from Rabbi Samson of Ostropolia that to introduce Torah to a new country, one must be ready to sacrifice everything, even his life. Like Reb Shraga Feivel, Rabbi Levenberg was such a

Rabbi Nosson Tzvi Finkel, the Alter of Slabodka

person. The major part of his income as chief rabbi of New Haven went to maintain the yeshivah. There was only paltry support from American Jewry because of the almost universal conviction that such a Torah institution had no place in America. Nevertheless, Rabbi Levenberg succeeded in producing many outstanding personalities, whose contributions still flourish. Among his thirty or so students were Rabbi Baruch Kaplan, who, with his great rebbetzin, created the Bais Yaakov movement in America; Rabbi Alexander Sender Linchner, architect of Boys Town Jerusalem; Rabbi Chaim Pinchas

Mr. Charles Batt

Rabbi Chaim Pinchas Scheinberg

Rabbi Alexander Linchner

Scheinberg, *rosh yeshivah* of Torah Ore in Jerusalem; and Rabbi Schachne Zohn, head of the Kollel Kodashim in Jerusalem. Charles Batt, a distinguished and influential lay leader, was one of the community activists who were Rabbi Levenberg's students.[7]

Rabbi Levenberg was even reduced to collecting tomatoes from Jewish farmers in the area to feed the *talmidim.* On his deathbed, he told Rabbi Sender Linchner:

> Do you know what *mesiras nefesh* is? You probably think of *mesiras nefesh* as being burned at the stake to sanctify

---

7. This was in 1924 or 1925. *Rabbi Alexander Linchner.*

Hashem's Name. That is *mesiras haguf* (sacrifice of the body). I could have stayed in Slabodka and spent my life going through *Shas* many times. And instead I came to America and spent my days collecting tomatoes from the Jewish farmers around New Haven so the boys would have something to eat. That is *mesiras hanefesh.*

Rabbi Levenberg's inability to keep the New Haven Yeshivah open for more than a few years is but one example of the way that America destroyed great Torah scholars in those years.

RABBI NESANEL QUINN RECALLS THE EARLY DAYS WHEN REB Shraga Feivel decided to found the Mesivta/High School department, and brought his ambitious plan to the Board of Directors. He explained his firm conviction that it was imperative to produce genuine *talmidei chachamim* if uncompromising Torah observance was to survive. Although the board agreed with him in principle, they refused to accept the financial burden of maintaining both a mesivta and a high school. They contended that as it was they were barely able to maintain Torah Vodaath, and they could not undertake new obligations. Reb Shraga Feivel argued that the A-mighty wants us to act and create the institution first, and then the funds will come, somehow. But the directors lacked that degree of *bitachon* (trust). Almost unanimously, they voted not to open a mesivta.

A Mesivta Comes Into Being

Reb Shraga Feivel was stunned.

But there was a ray of hope. He had three stalwart supporters on the board: Binyamin Wilhelm, the founder of Torah Vodaath; his brother-in-law, Benzion Weberman, an attorney; and Abraham Lewin, a textile merchant and vice president of the school and also of the Hebrew National Orphan Home. They were ready to help Reb Shraga Feivel achieve his goal, despite the opposition of their colleagues.

Mr. Lewin was friendly with local members of the Republican Congress Club, which had recently left its Williamsburg quarters for a new location. Lewin offered his friends $35,000 for the vacant building — a bargain price — and the club accepted. He came to the Torah Vodaath Board of Directors with his windfall opportunity, but they refused to buy the building for a mesivta. Undaunted, Lewin borrowed $15,000 from Mr. Daniel Reisman and bought the building in his own name.

A real-estate broker offered Lewin an immediate profit of $15,000 on the building. Mr. Lewin had to be sorely tempted, because he had lost his business shortly before then, and he was deeply in debt. Fifteen thousand dollars in 1926 was the equivalent of about a quarter-million dollars today, but Lewin passed the test. He had purchased the building for the Mesivta Torah Vodaath, and a mesivta building it would remain. In September 1926, the Mesivta opened with four classes of pioneering teenagers, and a *beis medrash* with eleven *talmidim*, imported from the yeshivah in New Haven. That building was at 505 Bedford Avenue. In later years, when the main quarters of the Mesivta moved to 141 South Third Street, the original building was used for the seventh and eighth grades and was known as the "Old Mesivta."

After a time, the Board of Directors of Torah Vodaath agreed to assume title to the building, but the courage and sacrifice of Abraham Lewin remain an example of the idealism and dedication of the handful of people who built Torah in America.

There was opposition in principle to Reb Shraga Feivel's plan to open a mesivta. In an editorial, the *Jewish Morning Journal* asserted that it was not in the interest of the Jewish community to have another yeshivah, since the Yeshivah Rabbeinu Yitzchak Elchonon was adequate to fill the need of training Orthodox rabbis. Not surprisingly, the administration of that yeshivah agreed.

Also opposed was the Religious Zionists of America, then known as the Mizrachi, because Reb Shraga Feivel was known for his disenchantment with that organization's policy of compromise at the expense of Torah.

An effort was made to abort the proposed new mesivta by enticing the students of Torah Vodaath to transfer to Yeshivah Rabbeinu Yitzchak Elchonon. The *talmidim* were in a dilemma — which school should they choose? Abraham Lewin came to Torah Vodaath and

*R' Binyamin Wilhelm leading the parade for
the Chanukas HaBayis of the Mesivta*

*The parade for the Chanukas HaBayis of the Mesivta building. R' Shraga Feivel is in the fore-
ground. In the background (right to left): Rabbi Baruch Kaplan, Rabbi Schachne Zohn, Rabbi
Gedaliah Schorr, and Rabbi Nesanel Quinn*

Parade for the Chanukas HaBayis of the Mesivta building

The first Mesivta building, on Bedford Avenue

The Mesivta building on South Third Street

Students in the yeshivah

A classroom

The lunchroom

A classroom in the Mesivta

The Beis HaMedrash

The Mesivta library

spoke to the boys for half an hour, urging them not to desert the yeshivah after it had done so much for them. His emotional plea deepened the quandary, and a heated, but inconclusive, discussion ensued after he left the room.

Shortly after, Reb Shraga Feivel entered the room. His first words were, "I want you to do what is better for you, not what is better for the yeshivah." In short order, he then explained what they could expect in his proposed mesivta.

His words carried the day. Not a single *talmid* left Torah Vodaath.[8]

CONSISTENT WITH HIS PRINCIPLE OF "NO COMPROMISE," REB Shraga Feivel did not allow secular studies in the Mesivta building,

Adding Secular Studies

because, historically, secular studies had not been incorporated into a yeshivah curriculum. The high school was conducted in outside, rented quarters.

Not wishing to rely on his own decision, however, he addressed the question to four European *gedolim*: Rabbi Chaim Ozer Grodzenski of Vilna, Rabbi Baruch Ber Leibowitz of Kamenitz, Rabbi Yosef Rosen, the Rogatchover Gaon of Dvinsk, and Rabbi Elchonon Wasserman of Baranovitch.

(Left to right) Rabbi Baruch Ber Leibowitz of Kamenitz, Rabbi Aharon Kotler

Reb Baruch Ber's response was negative, based on the precedent of the great Volozhin Yeshivah. The other three expressed hesitation to answer, based on their inadequate knowledge of the circumstances in America. However, citing the critical need for traditional yeshivos there,

---

8. Rabbi Nesanel Quinn.

they felt that since a high-school education was required by law in the United States, Torah Vodaath should incorporate general studies into its curriculum. They added that, if at all possible, classrooms used for *limudei kodesh* (sacred studies) should not be used for general studies. Reb Shraga Feivel followed the decision of the majority, and the high school entered the Mesivta building for the next year.

Rabbi Chaim Ozer Grodzenski of Vilna

FOR THE POSITION OF FIRST *ROSH YESHIVAH* OF THE MESIVTA, Reb Shraga Feivel chose Rabbi Moshe Rosen, who was already well

The First Roshei Yeshivah known in the yeshivah world as the author of *Nezer HaKodesh*, a series of works on *Seder Kodashim*. In his *haskamah* (letter of approbation) to *Nezer HaKodesh*, Rabbi Baruch Ber Leibowitz, the Kamenitz *Rosh Yeshivah*, wrote, "I thank Hashem for His great kindness to our brothers in America in that He sent them faithful shepherds and *geonim* to light the way for them in Torah."

Prior to coming to America just after World War I, Rabbi Rosen had served for years as the *rav* of Chavaidan. There he had enjoyed a particularly close friendship with the Chazon Ish, who lived in Chavaidan for several years after his marriage. Together they started a yeshivah for younger *bachurim*.[9] With the choice of Rabbi Rosen, Reb Shraga Feivel served notice that he was aiming for a very high standard of learning.

---

9. As a *rav* in Lithuania, Rabbi Rosen was a confidant of Rabbi Meir Simchah of Dvinsk (the *Ohr Samayach*); the Slabodka Rosh Yeshivah, Rabbi Moshe Mordechai Epstein; and the leader of the generation, Rabbi Chaim Ozer Grodzenski of Vilna.

Upon his arrival in America, Rabbi Rosen settled in the Brownsville section of Brooklyn, where he served as the rabbi of one of the largest shuls.

Rabbi Moshe Rosen,
the first rosh yeshivah of the Mesivta

Rabbi Shlomo Poliachek,
the Meicheter Iluy

Rabbi Rosen gave a *shiur klali*, a weekly lecture to all the older students, and learned daily with a group of eleven advanced students. The daily *daf shiur* for the other students was given by Rabbi Moshe Don Sheinkopf, an outstanding product of Slabodka, who had previously taught in Rabbi Levenberg's yeshivah in New Haven. At a time when "parasite" and "benchwarmer" were the common descriptions of a *yeshivah bachur*, the sense of being part of a spiritual elite, with which Rabbi Sheinkopf imbued his students, was a needed antidote. He stressed that the *talmidim* should be careful in their dress and in their speech, in keeping with the Slabodka emphasis on *gadlus haadam* (the dignity of man).[10]

After one year in the Mesivta, Rabbi Sheinkopf left to become a rabbi in Waterbury, Connecticut, and Rabbi Rosen left shortly thereafter when his group of older *talmidim* disbanded. The most fateful decision in the early years of the yeshivah now confronted Reb Shraga Feivel: the selection of an appropriate *rosh yeshivah* to build American boys into *talmidei chachamim*. Reb Shraga Feivel trained his sights on two of the greatest European *talmidei chachamim* who were willing to accept such a position: Rabbi Shlomo Poliachek, uni-

---

10. Rabbi Nesanel Quinn.

sally known as the Meicheter Iluy, and Rabbi Simchah Soloveitchik, the younger brother of Rabbi Chaim Soloveitchik. At that time, the Meicheter was *rosh yeshivah* at Yeshivas Rabbeinu Yitzchak Elchonon, but was anxious to leave when the institution opened a college.

The Kovno Rav, Rabbi Avraham Dov Kahana Shapira, however, mentioned a third candidate, who was younger and less well known than the other two: Rabbi David Leibowitz, one of the shining lights of the famous Kovno Kollel and the great-nephew of the Chofetz Chaim. Reb David was then in America raising funds for the Kovno Kollel, as members of the *kollel* were expected to do after six years of learning. The Kovno Rav told Reb Shraga Feivel, "If you are primarily interested in making the yeshivah famous, then you should choose the Meicheter Iluy, but if you are considering who would be most suited for the boys in the Mesivta, who are not yet at a level to appreciate the Meicheter, take Reb David." True to his unwavering policy of doing what was best for his *talmidim*, Reb Shraga Feivel did not hesitate to engage Reb David.

The choice was immediately vindicated. Reb David devoted himself to the *talmidim*, and over the next seven years fashioned a number of them into advanced Torah scholars. In an appreciation written shortly after his passing, Rabbi Avraham Pam, one of his closest *talmidim*, captured something of his impact on his students:

Rabbi Avraham Pam

His weekly *shiur* was never a lecture but an impassioned plea for a proposed solution to the complexities he found in the halachah in question . . .

He would take a single thought and toy with it for an hour, analyzing it, dramatizing it, expanding it, at the risk of distortion, reexamining it again and again, at the risk of tedium — ever fearful that the point was not yet fully appreciated, ever straining to exhaust the beauty of the concept. He was particularly fond of Midrashim relating to personality traits — to *middos* . . .

To be a *lamdan* — was an ideal he constantly glorified. To acquire a Torah outlook — was the greatest of achievements. To be a *maven* (connoisseur) of Talmud — was a source of justifiable pride. To be a *marbitz Torah* (a teacher of Torah) was the crowning achievement of a *talmid chacham*.[11]

REB SHRAGA FEIVEL HAD NO EUROPEAN MODELS TO GUIDE HIM in the Mesivta. The most obvious difference between the Mesivta

Lithuanian Learning With Chassidic Bren

and its European predecessors was, of course, that the Mesivta was forced to provide a secular education — equivalent to that provided in public high schools — to have any hope of surviving. Under the best of circumstances, it was difficult to assure parents that their children were not going to be consigned to a life of poverty by virtue of their Torah studies. A yeshivah that did not offer quality secular education could not have attracted any students.

Nor would the secular education for many of the Mesivta's graduates end in high school. College was then perceived by Orthodox and non-Orthodox parents alike as the ticket out of the privation in which most first-generation immigrants lived. Even those who spent their entire day in the *beis medrash* were likely to attend college in the evening.[12] Reb Shraga Feivel, on the other hand, was firmly opposed to college attendance, because the professors and instructors sought to impose on their students a worldview that was contrary to the Torah.

---

11. "With All Thy Heart and All Thy Soul," *Orthodox Youth*, February 1942, p. 4.

12. Elias Karp.

A group of talmidim in the Mesivta in the 1930's

Reb Shraga Feivel self-consciously set out to create a new type of *bachur* in the melting pot of America, one who would, like Reb Shraga Feivel himself, draw from all that was best of the many strands of European Jewish life. America, he said, would produce a new Jew, combining within himself the best elements of Europe: the Lithuanian intellectual acuity, the *bren* (warmth) of Chassidus, the organizational abilities of German Jewry, and the appreciation of *hiddur mitzvah* (beautification of the mitzvah) of the Hungarians. Above all, the American Jew would be characterized by his *temimus* (sincerity), a trait that was much more a part of American culture than of Europe.[13] From the beginning, the style of Gemara learning in the Mesivta adhered as closely as possible to that of the great Lithuanian yeshivos. Though he was anxious to bring great chassidic Torah scholars to the Mesivta, he did not succeed in doing so, and the Mesivta[14] *roshei yeshivah* were, with few

13. Rabbi Ephraim Wolf.

14. Reb Shraga Feivel invited Rabbi Menachem Ziemba of Warsaw to teach in the Mesivta and worked hard to procure an immigration visa for him. Though the visa eventually came, it was already too late to save Rabbi Ziemba from the Warsaw Ghetto, where he was shot during Pesach, 1943. Another invitation was sent to the Tchebiner Rav, Rabbi Dov Berish Weidenfeld, who went to *Eretz Yisrael* instead. Reb Shraga Feivel also recruited Rabbi Yaakov Flanzgraben, a Sochatchover chassid who was a stellar *rebbi* in Yeshivah Rabbi Shlomo Kluger on the Lower East Side, but Reb Yankele preferred to remain where he was.

Rabbi Elya Chazan

exceptions, among the finest products of the Lithuanian yeshivos — Rabbi Moshe Rosen, Rabbi David Leibowitz, Rabbi Yaakov Kantrowitz, Rabbi Shlomo Heiman, Rabbi Reuven Grozovsky, Rabbi Yaakov Kamenetsky, Rabbi Elya Chazan, Rabbi Simchah Sheps, Rabbi Zelik Epstein, and Rabbi Aharon Yeshayah Shapiro, to name but a few.

Upon his arrival in America, Rabbi Aharon Kotler expressed his amazement that Reb Shraga Feivel, a product of the great Hungarian yeshivos, should have chosen his *maggidei shiur* exclusively from the ranks of the Lithuanian yeshivos. But Reb Shraga Feivel apparently felt that the analytical style of the Lithuanian yeshivos was best suited to the modern American *bachur* — i.e., that if American boys could be shown the

Rabbi Dov Berish Weidenfeld, the Tchebiner Rav

Rabbi Aharon Kotler

analytical rigor of Reb Chaim Brisker at an early age, they would be less subject to the lures of all those secular fields in which human thought seemed to be progressing toward ever greater rigor and precision.[15]

But if the Gemara learning was patterned on Lithuania, the atmosphere was chassidic. With singing and dancing, Reb Shraga Feivel captured the boys' hearts and insured that their feelings for *Yiddishkeit* did not remain only in their heads. Reb Aharon remarked with classic understatement, "The synthesis [of Lithuanian learning and chassidic *bren*] is not one I myself would have thought of."[16]

Unprecedented perhaps. But it was a synthesis that planted Torah in America.

---

15. Rabbi Yaakov Kamenetsky's attitude toward the so-called "Brisker *derech*," which had swept the Lithuanian yeshivos in the latter decades of the 19th century, was close to that of Reb Shraga Feivel's. Though Reb Yaakov was himself critical of the overemphasis on *lomdus* (profound analysis) at an early age, he nevertheless saw in the revolution in the method of learning in the Lithuanian yeshivos the workings of *Hashgachah* (Divine Providence). In modern times, said Reb Yaakov, it was necessary to give students the sheer intellectual pleasure and joy of learning in order to combat the many outside influences that compete for their attention. Students who had experienced the excitement of learning in depth, he felt, would find themselves less attracted to secular studies.

16. Rabbi Moshe Aharon Stern.

Chapter 7

Instilling Yiddishkeit

THE EASIER PART OF REB SHRAGA FEIVEL'S TASK WAS conveying the knowledge of Judaism that can be gained from books. Far more difficult was instilling in his students the same emotional attachment to their *Yiddishkeit* that had been absorbed automatically by Jewish youngsters in the relatively isolated Jewish communities of Eastern Europe. He wanted his students to yearn for the beauty of Jewish life, to feel the inner warmth of Chassidus, to recognize that it was not enough to study Torah and even to become a *talmid chacham* — one must commit oneself to become a model for others and to spread Torah wherever possible. The greatest obstacle to be overcome by American youth, he would say, is that they lacked examples of an old-time *"ehrlicher Yid"* and had never experienced how the Shabbos Queen should be received properly. He confounded the skeptics by succeeding to an extraordinary degree.

America and Europe were separated by far more than the Atlantic Ocean. Many of the immigrants came from towns and villages almost unchanged from what they had been a hundred years earlier. Their children, by contrast, were born and raised in the world's fastest-paced society. Even in the most close-knit immigrant families, there was a certain estrangement of parents and children. Children rightly saw themselves as growing up in a world vastly different from that in which their parents had been raised, and this inevitably lessened parental authority.

The Atlantic crossing thus marked a break in the orderly transmission of values and wisdom from one generation to another that had once characterized Eastern European Jewish life. As a result, the Mesivta not only had to teach the traditional yeshivah curriculum, it had to inculcate the values and emotions that had once been transmitted in the home. Reb Shraga Feivel and the *rebbeim* served as both teachers and parents.

That transmission of values was further complicated by the wide gulf separating American boys from the typical European *yeshivah bachur*. Feelings that developed organically in a society steeped in Jewishness could not simply be transplanted into boys raised in a very different society. Talking to a *bachur* — who arrived in America from the Mirrer Yeshivah just before the war — about another student in the Mesivta, Reb Shraga Feivel said, "*Halevai*, I should have his *yiras Shamayim*, but he still is a religious American."[1] The organic connection to Torah and mitzvos was not something that could be learned, he felt; it had to be absorbed heart to heart, *neshamah* to *neshamah*, with deep emotion.

American boys were not rooted in an American Jewish community (which was itself in rapid transition) in the same way that their parents or grandparents had been in the seemingly timeless *shtetls* of Europe. As much as these boys were Jews, they were also Americans. The unprecedented openness of American society ensured that. Because American society was so accessible, the *yetzer*

---

1. Rabbi Yaakov Leshinsky.

hara to accept its mores and emulate its practices was increasingly strong, even among religious Jews.[2]

REB SHRAGA FEIVEL'S GOALS CONTINUALLY EVOLVED OVER THE years, based on the needs of the period. The first stage in his long-

Producing Frum Baalebatim
range plan for the transformation of American Jewry was the creation of a large group of Orthodox *baalebatim* (laymen); he was realistic enough to know that not every student in the Mesivta would grow up to be a *lamdan* (an erudite, analytical scholar) or a chassid.

There were many times when he convinced boys who shared the typical American's love of sports to give up stickball on Shabbos. "I built a yeshivah to teach boys to put on *tefillin*, keep Shabbos, and eat kosher food," he used to say. For many his only aspiration was that they remain religious. He once told a student about to leave the Mesivta, "I have no idea where life will take you. But one thing I know for sure: You will never be able to fully enjoy any *aveirah* (transgression). Your conscience will give you no rest. And that is the result of the classes in *hashkafah* you heard in the Mesivta."[3]

Characteristically, an alumnus whose business required him to travel widely, and often endure considerable hardship in finding kosher food, decided that, for a change, he would go to a non-kosher restaurant and pick out permissible dishes from the menu. As he approached the restaurant, he had a vision of Reb Shraga Feivel blocking the entrance. He went back to his fare of fresh fruit and vegetables.[4]

The next stage was to make sure that those *baalebatim* had an ap-

---

2. The Vilna Gaon divides the various forms of the *yetzer hara* into three categories: physical desires; the various distortions of man's spiritual side — e.g., the desire for honor and for dominion over others; and the temptation to throw off the Divine yoke. To these he adds a fourth *yetzer hara,* which he describes as worse than the other three: the desire to mix with the nations of the world and become indistinguishable from them. This is the most dangerous of all because it involves the loss of the sense of wrong, and with it all incentive to struggle against the first three forms of the *yetzer hara.*

3. Elimelech Terebelo.

4. Rabbi Nesanel Quinn.

preciation for the importance of a Torah education and a sense of commitment to the *klal* (community). His approach was similar to that of Rabbi Meir Shapiro, *rav* of Lublin and founder of Yeshivas Chachmei Lublin, who once remarked that even if only one of the five hundred boys in his yeshivah developed into a great Torah scholar, he would be content if the other 499 were at a level to appreciate a great Torah scholar. Reb Shraga Feivel did not view the major problem of American Jewish life as the absence of *talmidei chachamim* of stature. In the '20s and '30s, there were already in America many noted European scholars: The problem was that they had no audi-

Rabbi Meir Shapiro

ence and patrons; Reb Shraga Feivel set out to provide them.

The pitiful situation of these European-trained scholars was summed up in one of his characteristically pithy, witty remarks, "Why be a *rav* and have the businessmen tell you what to do? Become a businessman and tell the *rav* what to do."[5] Orthodox rabbis, he would say, were completely subject to the whims of their presidents, many of whom were often unlearned, arrogant, and autocratic. Often the most active, and therefore the most influential, people in the shul were the members of the Ladies Auxiliary.[6]

Rather than viewing the rabbinate as an opportunity for transforming American Jewry, Reb Shraga Feivel saw it primarily as a trap for the unwary, and in its early years the Mesivta had no *semichah* (ordination) program. Without a core of learned *baalebatim*

---

5. Rabbi Ephraim Wolf.
6. Jack Klausner.

capable of appreciating a real *rav*, there was, in Reb Shraga Feivel's opinion, little value in directing his *talmidim* in that direction. He later asked Reb Elchonon Wasserman whether, in light of the pitfalls of the rabbinate, he could encourage his students to become rabbis. Reb Elchonon did not disagree with Reb Shraga Feivel's analysis of the dangers involved and the need to warn students interested in becoming a rabbi,[7] but he did point out that the production of up-right rabbis was essential for American Jewry, and it was therefore the Mesivta's duty to produce *rabbanim*.[8]

TWO OF THE HALACHIC ISSUES FOR WHICH REB SHRAGA FEIVEL turned to *gedolei Yisrael* for guidance in the early years of the

Two She'eilos

Mesivta serve to highlight the difference between American *bachurim*, raised in a society whose influ-ence was pervasive, and their European counterparts. The first question revolved around American styles of dress and grooming, which differed radically from those that had prevailed in Europe, and Reb Shraga Feivel wrote to Reb Elchonon Wasserman for guidance on where to draw the line on longish hair with pompadours in front. The halachic issues, replied Reb Elchonon, were already covered in the *Mishnah Berurah*, which discusses the issue of whether long hair prevents the *tefillin* from resting on the head in the proper place.[9]

Yet despite the possible halachic problems involved, Reb Elchonon counseled against taking too firm a stand on the matter, for fear that such an approach might cause boys to leave the Mesivta and go to public school. Rather than taking any fixed public stand, he advised Reb Shraga Feivel to speak privately to those boys upon

---

7. Reb Elchonon told his son Rabbi Simchah Wasserman when he came to America that he could be whatever he wanted to be except a rabbi. A rabbi, Reb Elchonon explained, has to flatter too many non-observant people.

8. Rabbi Nesanel Quinn.

As the Mesivta produced more students who attained an advanced level of learn-ing, a number of them did seek careers in the rabbinate and Reb Shraga Feivel instituted a *semichah* program for them, including a homiletics class given by Rabbi Zelig Fortman, a former *chavrusa* of Rabbi Moshe Feinstein. After Rabbi Fortman passed away, the class was continued by his son-in-law, Rabbi Moshe Sherer.

9. See *Mishnah Berurah* 26:15.

whom he had the most influence.

The second halachic question concerned a much different issue, that of boys whose sincerity was leading them too far. Sometimes when *bachurim* became fully caught up in their *Yiddishkeit*, they could tend toward extreme behavior. The lure of American society was so powerful that they felt the need to cut themselves off from it in radical ways. This was the case with a zealous group of *bachurim* in the Mesivta, known as the *malachim* (literally: angels).

The *malachim* were under the influence of Rabbi Chaim Avraham Dov Levin, known as the *Malach*, who arrived in America just after World War I and settled in the Bronx, where he was rabbi of Congregation Nusach Ari. In his person, he combined Lithuanian scholarship — having been a leading student of Reb Chaim Brisker — with a total immersion in Chassidus, particularly *Tanya*. The combination naturally appealed to Reb Shraga Feivel, who was attempting to give his students both these approaches, and he encouraged students to see such a personality.[10] Reb Shraga Feivel counseled Rabbi Levin as to what guidance to give the Torah Vodaath students. From May 1934 until September 1935, however, Reb Shraga Feivel was in Liberty, New York recovering from tuberculosis, and during that time Rabbi Levin introduced the students to practices that were unacceptable to their absent mentor.

Without Reb Shraga Feivel's watchful presence, many in this group fell completely under the sway of Rabbi Levin's magnetic personality. Imitating their master, they eschewed American dress, and took to wearing long black jackets and a very long *tallis katan* over their shirts, with the *tzitzis* showing below their jacket hems. This was at odds with Reb Shraga Feivel's preference for הַצְנֵעַ לֶכֶת (modest conduct), as opposed to ostentatious displays of piety.

---

10. Reb Shraga Feivel himself studied *Tanya* with the *Malach* in order to check the interpretations he had arrived at in his years of private study against the received traditions in the Lubavitch community. *Rabbi Shmuel Mendlowitz.*

According to Rabbi Ephraim Wolf, Rabbi Yitzchak Hutner also joined these study sessions with the *Malach.*

Though it had been Reb Shraga Feivel who initially encouraged the connection with Rabbi Levin, the *malachim* came to pose a serious problem for the Mesivta. Many of the *rebbeim* came to feel that they were having a disruptive effect on the Mesivta, acting basically as they pleased or in accord with the instructions of their *rebbe*.

There was no question of the idealism and commitment of the *malachim*, a commitment proven by their continuation as a distinct group in Williamsburg, and later in Monsey, for over three generations. But their approach of ostentatious separation from all the manifestations of American Jewish life was far from Reb Shraga Feivel's. He was fond of quoting the Gemara (*Niddah* 30b): "Even if the whole world says that you are a *tzaddik*, remain in your own eyes an evildoer." To make oneself known as a *tzaddik*, he suspected, betrayed a certain lack of "walking humbly," and especially when everything about one's external appearance called attention to that *tzidkus*.

Reb Shraga Feivel did not distance the *malachim*; he made great efforts to convince them that their conduct was not the Jewish way. His *talmidim*, however, took the initiative in defending his honor.

Eventually, the *malachim* declared openly that they refused to accept guidance from Reb Shraga Feivel and some spoke to him disrespectfully. That was more than his students would tolerate. Some of the older *talmidim* prevented the *malachim* from entering the Mesivta. Finally the *malachim* left Torah Vodaath and founded their own yeshivah, which they named Nesivos Olam.

Reb Shraga Feivel was critical of his *talmidim*. He had preferred to continue his patient efforts. He consulted with Rabbi Yehoshua Baumel, author of *Teshuvos Emek Halachah*, as to whether it had been proper to distance the *malachim* and, in effect, to force them out of the Mesivta. Rabbi Baumel fully supported the decision. He noted that even the *Tanna* Rabbi Yirmiyah was ejected from the *beis medrash* for annoying his teachers with his questions.[11] He also noted that the *Mahari Bruna* in his *teshuvos* had already decried the practice of young students walking in public with their *tzitzis* on the outside as appropriating "a crown of *perishus* (separation from mundanity) not befitting them."

---

11. See *Bava Basra* 23b and Rashi *ad loc.*

IN EASTERN EUROPE, A JEW KNEW NOT ONLY WHO HE WAS BUT also who he was not. The line of demarcation between Jews and

Between Jew and Gentile

gentiles was sharply drawn. Where the only gentiles with whom many Jews came into contact were illiterate, drunken peasants, the recitation of the morning blessing, "… Who did not make me a gentile," had been easy. But in America, where there were many examples of cultured, refined gentiles, the distinction between Jew and gentile was necessarily blurred. Here the task was to reveal the richness of the Jewish soul. The rich German culture with its abundance of moralists, philosophers, poets, and literary giants did not deter their statesmen, judicial personalities, medical men, and industrialists from committing monstrosities against defenseless men, women, and children.

An underlying theme of everything Reb Shraga Feivel taught was the question: What is a Jew? How does he think, feel, act, learn, pray? Reb Shraga Feivel impressed upon his *talmidim* the words of the Talmud that Jews are endowed with a hereditary instinct to be רַחְמָנִים בַּיְשָׁנִים וְגוֹמְלֵי חֲסָדִים, *people of compassion, shame, and kind deeds*. He added that the Torah, Written and Oral, is more than a source of knowledge. It also edifies, sublimates, and instills holiness in the soul. And he never ceased to exhort his students to live up to this challenge.[12]

In the non-Jewish world, Reb Shraga Feivel explained to his students, a person who is distinguished in any area is honored regardless of his behavior in other areas. Thus, a great mathematician is honored by all, no matter how degraded his private life; a leading philanthropist can expect to have his business ethics largely ignored; and a talented artist will be forgiven any depravity. Not so among us. Of all the recognized and respected thousands of Torah leaders over the generations, you will not find one who was lacking in good character, without compassion, or who succumbed to unbridled physical desires.

---

12. It is said in the name of the Chofetz Chaim that when a Jew makes the blessing every morning שֶׁלֹּא עָשַׂנִי גּוֹי, he should examine himself to make sure that he is, in fact, a Jew in his essence, and that his character has not been influenced by the corrosive norms of modern society.

A JEW, REB SHRAGA FEIVEL ALWAYS STRESSED, IS DEFINED BY HIS emotional responses no less than his book knowledge. One can

Acquiring a Jewish Heart
know the entire Talmud, but if he turns to the works of Shakespeare for spiritual sustenance, is apathetic to the needs of others, or is deficient in the *kedushah* (holiness) that refines conduct, he has not yet acquired a Jewish heart. It was that Jewish heart he sought to give his students.

Reb Shraga Feivel encouraged students to develop their emotional responses. Rabbi Elias Schwartz will never forget the day he arrived late to the Mesivta and Reb Shraga Feivel berated him for his tardiness. That morning Schwartz found himself too upset by his *rebbi's* rebuke to learn, and he went up to Reb Shraga Feivel's office to speak to him. When Reb Shraga Feivel saw how upset his student was, he made a play on the verse in *Eichah* and Schwartz's Hebrew name, Eli. Instead of אוּלַי יֵשׁ תִּקְוָה, *Perhaps there is hope* (*Eichah* 3:29), he said, "Read the verse: אֵלִי יֵשׁ תִּקְוָה, *There is hope for Eli*." He then circled his desk and embraced Schwartz, telling him,

Rabbi Elias Schwartz

"If you really have such a heart, you'll be a *groisser mentch* (a great man)."[13]

He taught his students to see the world through spiritual lenses. Once he found out that the Torah Vodaath Ladies Auxiliary had been raising money through card parties. "You probably think," he explained to his students, "that money raised in this fashion will buy bricks like any other bricks, and with them we can build a building for Torah like any other building. But if you could put on spiritual glasses and view the building made out of those bricks,

---

13. Rabbi Elias Schwartz.

you would see that it is filled with holes where those bricks were placed." The bottom line: Torah cannot be built on *falshe zachen* (false things).

On another occasion, two of Torah Vodaath's major supporters proposed a benefit performance of Broadway-style entertainment to raise money for the yeshivah. They confidently expected to raise thousands of dollars in this fashion. Reb Shraga Feivel, however, rejected out of hand the idea of raising money for a yeshivah from a theater performance, and thereby further encouraging the adulation of secular culture. The end could not justify the means.

He made the boys feel that the performance of mitzvos is the greatest joy, not an imposed burden. He once said that those who experience mitzvos primarily as restrictions are comparable to the wicked Bilaam. "Even if Balak would give me a houseful of silver and gold," Bilaam told the messengers of Balak, "I could not transgress the *word* of Hashem." "The word of Hashem he would not transgress," said Reb Shraga Feivel, "but the *desire* of Hashem he did not seek to fulfill." If a Jew is preoccupied only with avoiding Hashem's explicit prohibitions, without a feeling of wanting to perform His every desire, then he is no better than Bilaam. The Jew's task, he said, is not merely to ask what is forbidden and what is permitted, but to discern Hashem's will and make it his own.[14]

He once spoke in class about Jews who spend Shabbos playing chess. He did not tell his students that chess is forbidden, but he pointed out that anyone who thinks of Shabbos primarily as a day for playing chess perceives Shabbos as merely a day of rest. He does not understand that Shabbos was given for spiritual rejoicing. Reb Shraga Feivel gave his students a completely different sense of Shabbos. We are commanded not only to guard (לִשְׁמוֹר) Shabbos by avoiding any of the prohibited activities, he pointed out, but to make (לַעֲשׂוֹת) Shabbos. The latter requires us to recognize that

_____

14. Rabbi Moshe Aharon Stern.

Shabbos is not only a day of rest but a day of *kedushah* (moral refinement). To fully experience that *kedushah*, however, demands preparation and effort. That effort is hinted at in the command "to *make* Shabbos." Shabbos itself, he taught, infuses every Jew with an added capacity to praise Hashem, as we say in the blessings before *Krias Shema* on Shabbos morning, "The seventh day praises [Hashem] and says, 'It is good to give thanks to Hashem.' Therefore do all His creatures glorify and bless the L-rd."[15]

In those days there were few Jews in America who ate only hand-made *shemurah matzah* for Pesach. The *Poilisher Shtiebel* on the East Side ran the only bakery in America producing such matzos, and it was able to satisfy the entire demand with only a few workers. In the Mesivta's first year, Reb Shraga Feivel purchased a packet of six hand matzos for each boy in the highest class. Thinking back at the delighted surprise with which they received their precious packets, Rabbi Nesanel Quinn remarked, "Who could receive a free package of matzos from his *rebbi* one year and not continue to purchase such matzos himself in future years?"

Just as he taught his students not to view mitzvos as a checklist of do's and don't's, but as the means of drawing close to Hashem, so he showed them that the Torah is not a body of information external to themselves. Rather, any true Torah study must transform the student. In this vein, he gave an interesting twist to the words of Hillel (*Pirkei Avos* 4:7): "He who exploits the crown [of Torah for personal benefit] shall fade away. From this you derive that whoever seeks personal benefit from the words of the Torah removes his life from this world." In Reb Shraga Feivel's version, Hillel's intent was quite different: Whoever truly experiences the spiritual joy of Torah is completely removed from the world, in the sense that he is not attracted by the pleasures of the world. He is transformed into a better person.[16]

---

15. Quoted by the Chiddushei HaRim in the name of Rabbi Avraham Yehoshua Heschel of Apt, the *Oheiv Yisrael.*

16. A play on the Hebrew חלף which usually indicates some kind of exchange, in this case a transformation of oneself.

"Why do we seek guidance from Torah authorities whenever we have a serious problem, even when the issue would not seem to be a halachic question?" he asked the *talmidim*. The answer: Because one who has studied Torah in depth transforms his own understanding into the understanding of the Torah. He used to bring a proof for this point from *Chovos HaLevavos*. For every point that the author makes, he attempts to bring a proof from the Torah itself and from logic. At first glance, Reb Shraga Feivel noted, this procedure seems strange, for if there is a proof from the Torah why does the author need a supplemental logical proof? But if we examine the logical proofs of the *Chovos HaLevavos*, we are struck by the fact that they are far from the logic of the ordinary man in the street. His logic is the logic of the Torah, and that comes only from being steeped in Torah learning.

Learning by Example

THE MOST EFFECTIVE LEARNING IS LEARNING BY EXAMPLE. AS Reb Shraga Feivel put it, "*Middos* are caught, not taught." Telling someone, "Control your temper," "Don't yell," and the like will rarely have any impact, but if he is around those who are models of proper behavior and character, their *middos* will rub off on him. This process of absorbing good *middos* from one's teachers is what Reb Shraga Feivel referred to as coming to yeshivah not to learn Torah, but to "learn *from* Torah."[17] To study Torah and not be refined by it, he said, is like erecting a building but not living in it.

He once asked why Rabbi Shimon prefaces his statement, "I have found nothing better for oneself than silence" (*Pirkei Avos* 1:17), by describing how he was raised among the Sages. Reb Shraga Feivel answered that Rabbi Shimon is teaching us that in addition to the Torah one learns from a *talmid chacham*, one can learn both halachah and proper behavior by observing their every action, for a true *talmid chacham* is a living *Sefer Torah*. It was precisely that type of example that he felt American boys were so lacking. Serving as a model for the students, he felt, was as important a part of their task as classroom instruction.

---

17. Rabbi Elias Schwartz.

He himself served as the principal example. Introverted by nature, still he could not fully contain himself when teaching, or prevent his powerful emotions from spilling over into public view. He deliberately let the *talmidim* see the turbulence of his soul so that they would learn how a Jew thinks and feels.

One day he was teaching *Tehillim* 84, whose subject is the Jew's eternal pining for return to Jerusalem and the Temple that once stood there: "My soul yearns, indeed it pines for the courtyards of Hashem" (84:3). When he reached the verse, "Even the sparrow finds a home, and the swallow its nest" (84:4), the tears ran down his cheeks, as he lamented, "Everything has its place except for the *Shechinah* (the Divine Presence), which remains in exile." The contrast between the wild bird and the homeless Jew, between the ever-present nest and the absent *Beis HaMikdash*, was too much for him. He could not continue.[18]

For his *talmidim* who witnessed this, *galus HaShechinah* (the exile of the Divine Presence) ceased to be an abstraction. They had never seen an adult male cry in this way, and certainly not over what was for them only an abstract idea. For the first time they had a taste of how Jews over the centuries have longed for *Eretz Yisrael* and poured out their tears in *Tikkun Chatzos* (the midnight prayer for the restoration of the *Beis HaMikdash* and the Divine Presence) over the exile of the *Shechinah*. Any doubts the *talmidim* might have harbored about whether they were still in *galus* in America were washed away by Reb Shraga Feivel's tears.

---

18. Rabbi Eliyahu Yehoshua Geldzhaler; Chinn, "Ohr Shraga," p. 9.

Chapter 8

With Neginah and Rikud

D RY WORDS WILL NOT HAVE THE SAME IMPACT AS words spoken with pathos; the tone makes an enormous difference. Reb Shraga Feivel always spoke with dramatic emotion, and when he sang the impact was even greater. *Neginah*, song, is the language of the soul. To develop powerful Jewish feelings, Reb Shraga Feivel stressed the chassidic emphasis on such things as the joy of a mitzvah, loyal friendships, and rejoicing on Shabbos and Yom Tov. Emotional and joyous singing and dancing helped achieve this goal. A welcome side effect was that the magnetic glow of these activities counteracted the corrosive attraction of popular literature and entertainment. He was always teaching new *niggunim* (songs). One Simchas Torah, he took aside a group of *talmidim* and sang with them a new *niggun* to *Hu yiftach libeinu* (He will open up our hearts). Suddenly he unbuttoned his vest and pointed at his heart. "It is not enough that Hashem open our hearts," he said, "*we* have to open them first."

As Reb Shraga Feivel danced with his students at Rabbi Gedaliah Schorr's wedding, one of the *gedolim* present remarked, "That Jew

Rabbi Gedaliah Schorr in the 1940's

has done more with his dancing than most others have done with all their *derashos* (sermons)." In the last year of his life, as he and a group of *talmidim* were singing "*V'al kein nekaveh* (Therefore we put our hope in You, Hashem)," Reb Shraga Feivel said, "With this *niggun,* I built Torah Vodaath."[1]

The dancing and singing in the Mesivta on Simchas Torah was the highlight of the recruiting trips in which boys from as far away as Baltimore and Detroit were brought to the Mesivta. The walls of the *beis medrash* reverberated and the floor shook from the force of the dancing and singing. That enthusiasm was often the crucial impetus impelling boys to leave home and come to the Mesivta.[2]

Reb Shraga Feivel rarely missed an opportunity to draw the boys into a circle of dancers. As the circle went round and round, even shy students gradually lost their inhibitions and were caught up in the experience.[3] Boys who were otherwise awed by Reb Shraga Feivel felt the barriers between them breaking down in the hours spent dancing together.

A year and a half before his *petirah,* when he was in very poor health, he did not desist from leading the *talmidim* in Bais Medrash Elyon in fervent dancing on Shavuos. When his son-in-law Rabbi Sender Linchner, fearing that the strenuous activity would bring on another heart attack, tried to stop him, he pushed him away, telling him, "Please don't stop me. Didn't I build the Mesivta with singing and dancing? And so will it continue. Let the heart burst, but let the boys learn to dance."[4]

---

1. Rabbi Eliyahu Yehoshua Geldzhaler.
2. Chinn, "Ohr Shraga," p. 7.
3. Rabbi Shubert Spero.
4. Gross and Kaminetsky, p. 567.

Reb Shraga Feivel singing a song of deveikus at the wedding of his son-in-law Sheah Schiff, who is seated to his left. To his right is his mechutan, Reb Berish Lampert.

The singing and dancing could go on for hours at a time without anyone tiring or stopping to eat or drink. Reb Shraga Feivel was capable of singing one *niggun*, even one line, for an hour or more. "You can't jump from *niggun* to *niggun*," he told his students. "You must wring the last bit of juice out of a *niggun*, as you squeeze juice from a lemon."[5] The words of the *niggunim* were often straight from the prayers — "*Kad'sheinu bemitzvosecha* (Sanctify us with Your mitzvos)"; "*Vetaher libeinu* (Purify our heart)"; "*Tzam'ah l'cha nafshi* (My soul thirsts for You)"; "*Baruch Elokeinu sheb'ra'anu lichvodo* (Blessed is our God Who created us for His glory)"; "*Atah vechartanu* (You have chosen us)" — but through the constant repetition in joyful song, their meaning penetrated ever deeper into the hearts of the *talmidim*.

The dancing was not mere acrobatics, no working off of excess teenage energy. Even on Simchas Torah, the mood was both joyful and

---

5. Chinn, "Ohr Shraga," p. 8.

emotional, yet also serious and meditative. There was no conversation during the *Hakafos*. Reb Shraga Feivel told his students that Simchas Torah is not Purim, and described how in Ropshitz, the chassidim learned *Reishis Chochmah,* a classic *mussar* work, between the *Hakafos*.

Reb Shraga Feivel had a clear vision of what he wanted to achieve with the singing and dancing.[6] The day before a Yom Tov, he carefully selected the songs for the desired emotional effect.[7] He began with a march and then would swing into emotional songs of praise to Hashem, followed by songs seeking His assistance in acquiring Torah knowledge and purity of *middos*. He would conclude with songs of yearning and longing for Mashiach. When he sang *Od Yishama* (Let there be heard in the cities of Judah and Jerusalem), tears would roll down his cheeks. The deepest ideas penetrated best amid the warmth and emotional arousal of the dancing. His voice as he led his *talmidim* in singing, "*Im Ani Kan, Hakol Kan* (If I am here, all is here)"(see *Succah* 53a), still rings in their ears. First he would call out, "*Bachurim, tantzt Rashi's pshat* — Boys, dance to Rashi's explanation" (that "I" refers to G-d — i.e., if the *Shechinah* is present, then we all belong here). Then he would urge, "*Bachurim, tantzt Tosafos' pshat* — Dance to the explanation of *Tosafos*" (that "I" refers to *Klal Yisrael* — i.e., if we, the Jewish people, remain attached to the *Shechinah*, then the *Shechinah* will rest upon the *Beis HaMikdash)*.[8]

The highlight of the week for boys in the Mesivta was *shalosh seudos*, the third Shabbos meal. Boys who had grown up on the typical *shalosh seudos* of the *shtieblach* — a few *niggunim*, a few comments on the weekly *sidrah*, and some herring on challah — were amazed to discover that the final hour of Shabbos is the most precious of all, the one whose inspiration is felt throughout the week.

The singing consisted of beautiful, haunting melodies, both with and without words. At the head of the table sat Reb Shraga Feivel enveloped in thought, his eyes closed, the *talmidim* seated around long tables, barely able to see him in the waning light. Never was his

---

6. Rabbi Yaakov Greenwald.

7. Rabbi Avraham Abba Freedman.

8. Chinn, "Ohr Shraga," p. 8.

influence greater than in those last moments of Shabbos. "We felt as if we were in *Gan Eden*," remembers Rabbi Hershel Mashinsky. "We hoped it would never end."

Over the years the Mesivta was blessed with many musically gifted students — Mannes Mandel, Yonah Zev Herskowitz, Moshe Yitzchak and Shmuel Mendlowitz, Shlomo Horowitz, Shlomo Twersky, Mendel Rokeach, the Rosengarten brothers, the Flam brothers, Hertzl Shechter, and others — and never was the singing more beautiful than at *shalosh seudos*. Ben Zion Shenker, Moshe Wolfson, and Shmuel Mendlowitz brought back new *niggunim* from the *tisch* of the Modzhitzer Rebbe,[9] and these too entered the *shalosh seudas* repertoire.

Reb Shraga Feivel did not speak at *shalosh seudos* — the hour was like *Shemoneh Esrei*, he used to say. When asked once why he did not take advantage of the mood of spiritual arousal to deliver inspiring words, he responded that the *zemiros* themselves were the most powerful words of *mussar* and would have the most lasting impact. His students agreed. "My heart is filled with pity," says Rabbi Moshe Wolfson, the present *Mashgiach* of Mesivta Torah Vodaath, "for anyone who was not privileged to sit opposite our *rebbi* at *shalosh seudos*. His *shalosh seudos* was like a *mikveh* in which one immersed his entire soul."

Rabbi Shlomo Heiman, a product of the leading Lithuanian yeshivos, was once asked why Torah Vodaath had no daily *mussar seder*, as was common in the Lithuanian yeshivos. He replied, "The *shalosh seudos* with Reb Shraga Feivel has as much power to scorch off impurities from the soul and instill love of Hashem as the study of *mussar*."[10]

Marking the Calendar

IN THE 20'S AND 30'S IN AMERICA, THE SHOW OF STRONG EMOTIONS by boys, and certainly by men, was considered something akin to a breach of etiquette. Holidays and joyous occasions, remembers Rabbi Nesanel Quinn, were celebrated in a perfunctory way. Reb Shraga Feivel changed all that; he revealed a new world filled with rejoicing in the mitzvos.

---

9. The Modzhitzer Rebbe, Rabbi Shaul Yedidyah Taub, himself once came to the *shalosh seudos*. Afterwards he and Reb Shraga Feivel spent an hour together discussing the works of Reb Tzadok HaKohen of Lublin. *Rabbi Hershel Mashinsky.*

10. Rabbi Eliyahu Yehoshua Geldzhaler.

The first Purim in the Mesivta, the boys were singing *niggunim* near midnight, when Reb Shraga Feivel appeared, together with Moshe Mintz, his closest *talmid* from Scranton.[11] The two of them led the boys in dancing and singing of an intensity as yet unknown to American-born *bachurim*. After two or three hours, Reb Shraga Feivel stood up and began singing *Od Yishama*, the prophetic verse from *Yeshayahu* that foretells the future rejoicing that will saturate the cities and streets of *Eretz Yisrael*. As he sang, the tears coursed down his face. At first, the boys were too startled to appreciate what was happening before them: They had never before seen a man in his 40's sobbing and had no idea why he was crying or how they should respond. Every moment was like an eternity to them. Only later would they learn that at the end of every joyous occasion and Yom Tov, Reb Shraga Feivel was filled with the same intense longing for *Eretz Yisrael*.[12]

The next day, on Purim, the *talmidim* joined Reb Shraga Feivel in his home after completing their own Purim meals. His mood was one of "rejoicing with awe," a living example of what *Chazal* meant when they said that Yom Kippur is a day like Purim.[13] Though Reb Shraga Feivel offered those with a talent for *grammen* or Purim Torah a chance to display their wares, there was not a trace of light-headedness. Before long, he would begin singing one of his *deveikus niggunim* (songs of cleaving to Hashem). Those present withdrew deeper and deeper into their own thoughts, as Reb Shraga Feivel's voice, which itself seemed to demand some form of spiritual arousal, cut through the air.

The hours flew by. The eyes of the *talmidim* remained fixed on their teacher at the head of the table, his face aflame. It was late at night when the *talmidim* left to return to their own homes, each having received sustenance for his soul that would last for a lifetime. "The dancing of *Rabbeinu* on Purim, when he sang *HaAderes VeHaEmunah*," remembers Elias Karp, "is the moment most deeply engraved in my soul."

---

11. Rabbi Mintz once told Rabbi Sender Linchner, his roommate in New Haven Yeshivah, that he and Reb Shraga Feivel learned six tractates together in Scranton.

12. Rabbi Nesanel Quinn.

13. A play on the phonetic similarity of כפורים and פורים: Hence יום כפורים is described as a יום כְּפורים, *a day like Purim*.

On Pesach night, his *talmidim* would begin to knock on his door after the conclusion of their own *Sedarim,* around midnight. On the last day of Pesach, Reb Shraga Feivel would gather with his students one more time at the yeshivah. For hours on end, they would dance energetically, all the while singing only a few *niggunim* over and over, such as *"Kad'sheinu b'mitzvosecha* (Sanctify us with Your commandments)" and *"Baruch Elokeinu sheb'ra'anu lichvodo* (Blessed is our God Who created us for His glory)."[14] He moved from one boy to another, urging each in turn to sing solo and give physical expression to his deepest emotions. *"Leibidik,"* "Open your hearts," "Sing to Hashem a new song," he would call out. On the last night of Pesach, during one of the early years of the Mesivta, long past nightfall, Reb Shraga Feivel put his arm around an old *chassid,* Reb Asher Zelig Podolsky, and sang *Od Yishama.* At the sight of his weeping, there was not a boy who did not feel chills running up and down his spine.[15]

In 1928, Reb Shraga Feivel borrowed money and rented a farmhouse in the Catskills for the thirty-four *talmidim* of the *beis hamedrash.* That was before the days of yeshivah summer camps. From him, American boys gained a glimpse of what the destruction of the *Beis HaMidkash* means. On Tishah B'Av, he himself led the *Kinnos* of the day. Though few of the boys could understand the difficult Hebrew of the *Kinnos,* his sobbing and the feeling in his voice was itself a *peirush* (explanation). The boys felt as if the Temple were burning before him and that all the suffering of *Klal Yisrael* throughout the generations was being relived in his heart.

---

14. Rabbi Arnold Wolf.

Before that dancing began, there were *divrei Torah* interspersed with the sweet melodies of Rebbe Isaac of Kahliv. In discussing the mitzvah of relating the Exodus from Egypt, Reb Shraga Feivel asked: Why does the verse (*Shemos* 10:2) first tell us that Hashem wrought all the miracles in Egypt "in order that you shall tell it to your son and your son's son" and then conclude, "and know that I am Hashem"? Why the shift in focus from the command of transmitting to succeeding generations to one's personal knowledge? This teaches us, said Reb Shraga Feivel, that the reciting of the *Haggadah* to our children must also effect a change within the father who is telling the story.

15. Rabbi Nesanel Quinn.

Reb Shraga Feivel put each holiday into individual perspective and in its proper relation to the others. One Shavuos, for instance, he told a diligent *talmid* who did not join in the dancing that whoever does not express joy over his accomplishments will not adequately repent on Yom Kippur for his shortcomings.[16]

By teaching his *talmidim* the essence of each holiday, Reb Shraga Feivel showed them the form their *avodah* (Divine service) should take for that day. On Rosh Hashanah, he emphasized above all that the essence of the day is recognizing Hashem as the King over all Creation, including ourselves. One year the students were amazed when he gathered them together after Minchah of Rosh Hashanah for an hour of slow singing and restrained dancing to *"V'al kein nekaveh* (And therefore we put our hope in You)." When they were done, he said, "You saved my Rosh Hashanah for me."[17] At the same time, he did not neglect the somber aspect of Rosh Hashanah as the Day of Judgment. After Mussaf one year, a student lingered in the *beis medrash* for a few minutes and as he passed Reb Shraga Feivel's *shtender*, the boy touched the handkerchief that had been left on it. The handkerchief was drenched with tears.[18] Prior to Yom Kippur, he reminded the boys that *Chazal* tell us that if we open our hearts to Hashem the breadth of a needle's point, He will enlarge the opening and make it as wide as the entrance to a large hall — but our own opening must be like that of a needle; no matter how small it must pierce through completely.[19]

---

16. Rabbi Alexander Sender Linchner.

17. Ibid.

18. Ibid.

One year, Reb Shraga Feivel published in *Dos Yiddishe Licht* a collection of Breslov insights on Rosh Hashanah, all of which emphasized the fear that should grip a Jew. According to one, for instance, we should imagine ourselves being buffeted by a fierce wind as we hang by a slender thread far above the ground. In a moment, the thread might snap, causing us to plummet to a certain death. At that moment, we would certainly cry out to the *Ribbono Shel Olam* to save us, and each word of our prayer on Rosh Hashanah should resemble that cry of terror. On Rosh Hashanah we should firmly reaffirm that the A-mighty keeps us alive, and that our aberrations can cause life to be withheld from us.

19. Rabbi Shmuel Mendlowitz.

Reb Shraga Feivel had a unique ability to take the most profound ideas and make them accessible. A *talmid* once asked him to explain, as they were sitting together in the *succah*, what the Arizal meant when he wrote that the *gematria* (numerical value) of *succah*, 91, is equal to the *gematria* of the two sacred Names of God י-ה-ו-ה plus א-ד-נ-י. The *Shem Havayah* (the four-letter Name beginning *yud kei*), he responded, refers to the fact that Hashem is above space and time; He is at once past, present, and future. The name א-ד-נ-י refers to G–d as Master of the world, as He reveals Himself in the Creation. The *succah* hints at both these aspects. For in the *succah*, one must be able to see the stars, i.e., perceive a small portion of G–d's greatness as He manifests it through nature. At the same time, the *s'chach*, which covers the *succah*, must obscure more than it reveals — an allusion to our inability to apprehend Hashem, as He transcends space and time.

Just as Reb Shraga Feivel's first Purim with his *talmidim* in the Mesivta was forever ingrained in their hearts, so was his last Purim in Bais Medrash Elyon. He joined their Purim meal in the middle. The *talmidim* were singing exuberantly and enjoying one another's *grammen*. Reb Shraga Feivel signaled that he wished to speak to them. His subject was the teaching cited in *Yalkut Shimoni*, that with the coming of Mashiach, all the holidays will cease, and only Purim will still be observed. This is puzzling, he said, because no part of the Torah will ever be suspended!

Reb Shraga Feivel explained that we view the universe as an organism that functions according to set natural laws, and the hand of God is not visible except through miracles that override the laws of nature, miracles such as those that accompanied the Exodus from Egypt and the Revelation at Sinai. Those miracles are commemorated by the festivals. But Purim is different. The miracle of Purim was not at all obvious; it could easily be interpreted as a series of royal intrigues pitted against the wisdom of Mordechai and the faith of Esther. Only the teachings of the Sages show us that the drama of Esther and Achashveirosh, of Mordechai and Haman, was as much a miracle as the Splitting of the Sea, except that it was hidden.

The influence of Mashiach will be such that we will recognize the A-mighty in everyday nature as well as in open miracles. What is more, we will perceive clearly that the natural is as miraculous as the supernatural.

Thus, while all the festivals will surely be observed, as the Torah prescribes, the "miracles" that they commemorate will no longer be regarded as more extraordinary than everyday "normal" events. In other words, the lesson of Purim, that everything is G–d given and directed, will be the primary lesson of our lives, and it will prevail over our present perception of the festivals as the primary manifestations of G–d's providence.

Reb Shraga Feivel interpreted the verse קוֹל ה' בַּכֹּחַ, קוֹל ה' בֶּהָדָר, *The voice of Hashem comes in power, the voice of Hashem comes in majesty* (*Psalms* 29:4), as follows: "Through every force and all the beauty of nature, the voice of the A-mighty proclaims, 'There is a Creator!'"[20]

---

20. Rabbi Nesanel Quinn.

Chapter 9

In the Classroom

COMBINING LITHUANIAN-STYLE LEARNING WITH CHASsidic fervor was Reb Shraga Feivel's first major innovation in the Mesivta. The second was the emphasis he placed on *shiurim* in Jewish thought and *Tanach*.[1] This emphasis on *Tanach* in addition to Gemara distinguished Torah Vodaath from most other yeshivos, before or since.[2]

---

1. He often noted that a *talmid chacham* is required to know all twenty-four books of *Tanach* (see *Rashi* to *Shemos* 31:18), and pushed his *talmidim* to just *"daven"* *(read)* five chapters a day, even superficially. They would thereby aquire a strong familiarity with the text and then develop their understanding. *Rabbi Avraham Abba Freedman.*

He himself had a complete command of *Tanach,* and once expressed the hope that he would one day have the time to write his own commentary. When the first volume of Rabbi Chaim Dov Rabinowitz's *Daas Soferim* appeared in 1942, Reb Shraga Feivel telegraphed the author that the generation was in dire need of such a commentary and offered to raise money for the publication of future volumes. *Rabbi Hershel Mashinsky.*

2. He strongly urged the more advanced students to cover much ground in the afternoon session, as had been common in the Hungarian yeshivos of his youth. He expected them to learn at least a hundred *blatt* (folios) in the afternoon session of the winter semester. *Rabbi Elias Schwartz.*

Reb Shraga Feivel gave a novel interpretation to the injunction in *Pirkei Avos* (1:1): הַעֲמִידוּ תַלְמִידִים הַרְבֵּה, *Develop many disciples*, to mean, "Raise your students very high." And he did. He exposed his students to the finest outpourings of the Jewish soul over the ages. "I want you to be able to swim like ducks in the classic Jewish texts," he told them.[3]

Boys in the Mesivta learned *Chumash* and *Nach*, studied *siddur* (the prayer book) so that the words of their *davening* would be alive for them, covered the mitzvos applicable after the Destruction of the *Beis HaMikdash*, and delved into many of the classics of Jewish thought. Reb Shraga Feivel taught each of these subjects himself. Among the texts he taught repeatedly over two decades in the Mesivta were *mussar* classics such as *Shaarei Teshuvah* and *Kitzur Sefer Chareidim*; major works of medieval Jewish thought such as *Shemoneh Perakim, Kuzari*, and *Chovos HaLevavos*; and, among the works of later Jewish thinkers, *Mesillas Yesharim, Derech Hashem*, and *Daas Tevunos* by Rabbi Moshe Chaim Luzzatto,[4] and *Tanya*, the classic chassidic work by Rabbi Shneur Zalman of Liadi.[5] He also introduced some of the more advanced students to leading chassidic thinkers such as Rabbi Tzaddok HaKohen of Lublin, the Tzemach Tzedek, and the Sfas Emes.[6]

In the course of his classes, he gave the students broad knowledge

---

3. Gross and Kaminetsky, p. 566.

4. He once told Rabbi Yaakov Greenwald that he had learned the Ramchal's major works thirteen times.

5. Reb Shraga Feivel sought the opinion of the Munkaczer Rebbe on whether it was appropriate to teach *Tanya* to young American *bachurim*. The Rebbe expressed his wholehearted approval in a letter found among Reb Shraga Feivel's papers, describing the words of *Tanya* as "salve to the eyes, which purify the heart and soul." Provided that the teacher was capable of teaching such a deep work at a level appropriate to his students, the Munkaczer Rebbe wrote, the *Tanya* could do much to instill deep *emunah* (faith) in the students.

6. No student learned all of these texts with Reb Shraga Feivel, but he taught all of them repeatedly over two decades in the Mesivta, and his *shiurim* constituted a major part of the Torah Vodaath experience for most of the students in those years.

The number of *shiurim* he gave in any particular period varied, though rarely did he teach less than seven or eight classes a week. The *shiurim* were primarily confined to the late afternoon and *Motza'ei Shabbos*. In later years he taught a *Tanach shiur* from 9 to 9:30 a.m. That *shiur* was one of the few at which attendance was compulsory.

of *lashon hakodesh* and Jewish history.[7] Ignorance of Jewish history irked Reb Shraga Feivel. To someone who asked whether the prophets lived during the First or Second Temple, he replied tartly, "Tell me which came first."[8] Those who were ready for it studied Jewish history from Rabbi Yitzchak Isaac Halevi's *Doros HaRishonim.*[9]

In the *shtetls* of Eastern Europe, there had been less need to inculcate the basics of *emunah* (faith) and a complete Jewish worldview: Those were absorbed as a matter of course in an environment that was almost exclusively Jewish. Not so in America where isolation was impossible and the broader American society impinged daily on every boy's consciousness in countless ways. Here it was necessary to give the boys everything: the fundamentals of faith, a powerful emotional attachment to their *Yiddishkeit,* a spiritual arousal that would save them from the pull of the street, a sense of themselves in the panorama of Jewish history,[10] and a conviction that the Torah provides answers to the problems of the age.

Reb Shraga Feivel's goal, above all, was to create a "complete Jew," for only such a Jew would be sufficiently protected against the broader social forces around him. Many boys who chose the Mesivta would have to confront negative pressures at home and from friends. They might have to stand alone in a world in which there was a stampede for scientific and other forms of secular knowledge, and in which it was assumed that only a college education could guarantee a comfortable living.[11] To do so would require

---

7. In the first years of the Mesivta, he gave a number of separate lectures on Jewish history. In all the programs Reb Shraga Feivel developed in the 40's for future teachers, courses in Jewish history were an integral part of the curriculum.

8. Chinn, "Ohr Shraga," p. 5.

9. Interview with Rabbi Shmuel Prero.

10. He used to tell his students: "We are now studying the Torah that was given to us in the desert, and which was expounded in the Oral Torah by scholars living in Babylonia. The Ramban, who wrote commentaries on both the Written and Oral Torah, lived in Spain, and Rashi in France. The Maharsha who concentrates mainly on *Tosafos* lived in Poland, and we who drink from the water of all of them live in Williamsburg, where we study the same Torah that was given at Sinai."

11. Elias Karp.

the richest of spiritual and intellectual resources.

Reb Shraga Feivel knew that few of his students would remain sheltered in a *beis medrash* for the rest of their lives, and he sought to prepare them for the challenges they would face once they left yeshivah, especially in that era when few positions were available to uncompromising *bnei Torah*. Though he knew that the particulars of the texts he taught would be lost with the passage of time, he was confident that his *talmidim* would retain the general principles, and that the emotional impact of his *shiurim* would remain.

That is not to say, however, that he would have viewed a thorough grounding in classical Jewish thought as no longer necessary for a generation of widespread *kollel* learning. He did not simply teach these works as an antidote to the times; they were his lifeblood. The issues with which he dealt — e.g., fear and love of Hashem, the prosperity of the wicked and the suffering of the righteous, the nature of Jewish distinctiveness — were timeless ones. The specific mix of texts chosen today might be different, but Reb Shraga Feivel would still have considered a thorough grounding in the basics of Jewish faith and thought a prerequisite for a full life as a Jew.[12]

Different souls, he recognized, are aroused in different ways, and he did not assume that an exclusive diet of Gemara learning is always a sufficient bulwark against the siren song of the surrounding society. Even the love of learning was not necessarily sufficient. He quoted, from time to time, the Maharal's introduction to *Tiferes Yisrael*, in which the Maharal writes that there are those for whom the love of learning replaces the love of the Creator, rather than bringing them close to their Creator. To fulfill this need, Reb Shraga

---

12. By discussing the eternal issues of Jewish belief in a systematic fashion, he was able to show his students that their questions had been considered by the greatest Jewish thinkers for thousands of years. Where these issues are not addressed as part of a Jew's basic education, he feared, the result would be Orthodox adults living with doubts — some niggling, some serious — and without even any awareness that there are answers to their questions.

The apprehension that many religious Jews today feel in trying to draw nonreligious Jews closer to their heritage has been attributed in part to their own lack of sufficient grounding in traditional Jewish *hashkafah* and consequent fears that they will not be able to answer the questions they are likely to be asked.

Feivel chose to teach the classic *mussar* works to implant *yiras Shamayim* and noble character in the *talmidim*.

REB SHRAGA FEIVEL'S *SHIURIM* PLACED BEFORE HIS *TALMIDIM* A heretofore undreamed-of panorama, as he revealed to them the

Opening New Vistas

breadth and depth of the Jewish worldview. "He opened my eyes for the first time in my life," remembers one of his first students, Elias Karp, "to the vast horizons of *Yiddishkeit*." "Watching him cry over the verse (*Yeshayahu* 41:14), 'Fear not, O worm Jacob ...,' " recalls another student, "helped me understand for the first time the situation of the Jew in the world."[13]

Ostensibly the *shiur* consisted of Reb Shraga Feivel reading from and translating the text he was expounding. He deliberately sought to minimize his own additions to the material under discussion.[14] It was not only his modesty that dictated this approach; he had a carefully thought-out pedagogic purpose. The authority of the classic texts removed his words from the realm of personal opinion that the boys would feel free to accept or reject, as they saw fit.

Only as they grew older did the students realize how much he added to the works they were learning. Two of the outstanding *bachurim* in the yeshivah stopped attending the afternoon *hashkafah shiurim*, which they considered too elementary for them. Reb Shraga Feivel was loathe to compel their attendance — although his associate, Rabbi Schneider, did insist that they attend — but he did invite them to his office to learn *Derech Hashem* with him. They learned only a paragraph together, but that was enough for the two students to grasp how much of the depth of the Ramchal's words they had missed, and they once again began attending Reb Shraga Feivel's classes faithfully.[15]

The seemingly simple form of the classes hid Reb Shraga Feivel's intricate weave. "I have never met another person who possessed

---

13. Rabbi Shubert Spero.

14. Only rarely did he give any hint of how hard he had worked to explicate the text in such a seemingly simple fashion. He once asked the class after a *shiur* on *Tanya*, "Do you think that I shook that interpretation out of my sleeve? It took me twenty years to arrive at that explanation." *Rabbi Moshe Yechezkel Samuels*.

15. Rabbi Nesanel Quinn.

his overwhelming knowledge in every area," recalls Elias Karp. "When he taught *Tanach*, for instance, he brought to it his expertise in grammar, history, *paytanus* (liturgical poetry), and Jewish philosophy. And all in one seamless web." A single class might blend together *Moreh Nevuchim*, Rabbi Samson Raphael Hirsch, *Sfas Emes*, and *Tanya*.[16] There was hardly a *Chumash* or *Nach shiur* without a citation from Rabbi Hirsch.[17] By combining in one class thinkers with contrasting approaches, Reb Shraga Feivel demonstrated that the apparent differences are primarily ones of vocabulary and expression, not of substance.[18] Thus it was no accident that when he wanted to demonstrate the superiority of *talmud Torah* over all other mitzvos, he turned to a chassidic work like *Tanya* for the proof.[19]

Whenever applicable, a *shiur* would be put into the context of world and Jewish history.[20] *Tanya* comments that the sources of evil — known as the *klipos*, i.e., "barriers," or "husks," that stand between man and God — are identified by the prophet Yechezkel in his first vision (1:4). Reb Shraga Feivel explained these *klipos* as follows: The "great cloud" refers to all forms of ignorance and intellectual foginess; the "flaming fire" to one's physical desires and passions; and the "storm wind" to the winds of revolutionary thought. This passage in *Tanya* prompted Reb Shraga Feivel to examine the revolutionary ideas to which many of his students had been, or soon would be, exposed to in modern society. The fourth barrier, he said, is the pursuit of gluttonous self-gratification.[21]

ONE OF THE MESSAGES THAT REB SHRAGA FEIVEL CONVEYED TO his students in many forms over the years was that everything one

Pedagogue Par Excellence

does in life requires forethought. Nowhere was Reb Shraga Feivel's emphasis on preparation more evident than in his teaching. He

---

16. Rabbi Yaakov Greenwald.
17. Rabbi Avraham Abba Freedman.
18. In his classes on *Tanya*, for instance, he sought to minimize the differences in the chassidic and misnagdic approaches. *Gershon Kranzler.*
19. Sidney Greenwald.
20. Elias Karp.
21. Sidney Greenwald.

felt keenly the awesome responsibility of teaching Torah, and he never gave a *shiur* without having prepared carefully in advance, no matter how many times he had taught the subject matter before. The Rambam's dictum that one should never speak publicly without having rehearsed what one wants to say was his guide.

One day he had to attend to an urgent matter during the hour that he had set aside for preparing his *shiur*, and as a consequence, he refused to teach that day. He could easily have taught without preparation, he assured his *talmidim*, and they might even have found the *shiur* more interesting than usual: When one is not prepared the adrenaline flows and many new ideas flash into one's head. But that, he said, is not teaching. True teaching requires that the *rebbi* know exactly what he wants to convey. Students who peeked into his *sefarim* found them copiously annotated and the particular passages he wanted to teach meticulously marked off.[22]

A major aspect of his preparation was carefully calibrating the *shiur* for the intended audience. The *Tanya shiur* given in later years in Bais Medrash Elyon, for instance, bore little resemblance to that given to much younger boys in the Mesivta. Advanced students were summarily dismissed from *shiurim* aimed at younger boys. (Occasionally an advanced student like Yosef Levitan would attempt to hide behind a younger boy when Reb Shraga Feivel commanded, *"Lomdim arois* — Scholars out."[23]) Even such an august personality as Rabbi Eliyahu Eliezer Dessler was denied permission to attend

Rabbi Eliyahu Eliezer Dessler

22. Jack Klausner.
23. Chinn, *"Ohr Shraga,"* p. 11.

Rabbi Avraham Pam

a *shiur*, because, Reb Shraga Feivel explained, his *shiurim* were always limited to his *talmidim*.[24]

Reb Shraga Feivel's refusal to speak in *public* was in part connected to his perception of the role of a teacher. True teaching — the kind that leaves a lasting impact — depends on the emotional bond between the teacher and the student and on the teacher's understanding of the student and his needs. That kind of relationship cannot exist in a public forum where most of the audience consists of strangers.[25] Rabbi Avraham Pam conjectures that Reb Shraga Feivel feared that if he began to deliver public lectures, it would detract from his concentration on the yeshivah.

He gave a great deal of thought to what texts each student needed. Many of the *shiurim* were semiprivate for a select group of students who, he felt, would benefit from a particular work. As much as he loved *Tanya*, for instance, he could still tell a *talmid* from a strong Lithuanian background, like Rabbi Elya Svei, "*Tanya* is not for you. Your *sefer* is *Nefesh HaChaim*."[26]

---

24. On Rabbi Dessler's first visit to the United States, Reb Shraga Feivel invited him to speak on *Tanya* in Bais Medrash Elyon. When Rabbi Dessler learned that Reb Shraga Feivel was then giving classes in *Shaar HaYichud* (the Gate of Divine Unity) in *Tanya*, he expressed an interest in attending. Reb Shraga Feivel flatly refused. *Rabbi Eliyahu Yehoshua Geldzhaler* (who later married Rabbi Dessler's daughter).

25. Rabbi Shmuel Mendlowitz.

26. That is not to say that he never taught *Tanya* to boys from nonchassidic backgrounds. Rabbi Yaakov Leshinsky, who came to Torah Vodaath from the Mirrer Yeshivah in Europe, was one of those in Reb Shraga Feivel's *Tanya shiur* in Bais Medrash Elyon. Reb Shraga Feivel did not, however, try to force a particular *sefer* on anyone. He taught such a broad range of works that every student was bound to find one that spoke to him personally.

His success as a teacher was a reflection of the degree to which he had made everything he taught part of himself. In his one public address — to a group of Pirchei Agudath Israel youth leaders[27] — he stressed that it is impossible to convey to students any aspect of Torah that is not alive within oneself. "He was fully identified with every word he taught," remembers Rabbi Nesanel Quinn. "When he taught us from *Tanya* about the level of a *'perfect tzaddik,'* we saw this spiritual level in him before our eyes. When he read from the prophecy of Yeshayah it was like hearing the *navi* (prophet) speak himself." Another *talmid* from the early days relates how he used to listen to Reb Shraga Feivel recite *Tehillim* before *davening* in the morning. "What he taught us in class and the way he said *Tehillim* were one."[28] As he spoke, his face often turned red and the veins protruded from his temples.

He worked hard to find the distinctive mood and character of each thinker whose works he taught. One day the key could not be found for the bookcase in which the copies of the *Kuzari* were stored. One of the students suggested that Reb Shraga Feivel teach *Tanach* instead, but he rejected the suggestion. He had placed himself in the frame of mind for the *Kuzari*, he explained, and could not just switch over to *Tanach*.

REB SHRAGA FEIVEL WAS CAREFUL TO MAKE SURE THAT EVEN the deepest texts did not remain on an abstract, intellectual plane

Lessons for Life alone. He was a master at finding parables to illustrate the ideas under discussion, and those parables had the effect of making ancient texts speak to modern American boys. Once he was discussing the *Kuzari's* treatment of prophecy. According to Rabbi Yehudah HaLevi, prophecy is always available but only some people have the proper receptacles to receive it. This, said Reb Shraga Feivel, may be compared to radio

---

27. This speech was delivered at the request of Sidney Greenwald, who was then national director of Pirchei Agudath Israel. Reb Shraga Feivel was persuaded only by the fact that the Pirchei leaders were then at the forefront of efforts to bring public school boys into yeshivos.

28. Yonah Zev Herskowitz.

signals. The signals are being constantly broadcast, but without a radio one cannot pick them up.[29]

He was not interested primarily in a subtle *derher* (perceptive insight), but in a simple understanding of the text from which his demands on the students flowed naturally. Almost every class ended with an implicit demand for some form of personal growth, and, at times, for a greater contribution to *Klal Yisrael*.[30]

He had no desire to be remembered for beautifully polished *shiurim* faithfully recorded in his students' notebooks, and stored on a shelf. His goal was much greater: that the words enter the deepest recesses of his students' hearts and leave them forever changed. One night Yitzchak Chinn was sitting in the *beis medrash* writing over his notes from Reb Shraga Feivel's *shiurim* when he suddenly felt the table pushed into his stomach. Looking up in surprise, he saw Reb Shraga Feivel standing there. "Yitzchak, *kasveim al luach libecha*, Write them on the tablets of your heart."[31]

How well he succeeded in engraving his words on their hearts can be discerned from the following story. Rabbi Nesanel Quinn was in Los Angeles on a fund-raising trip for the Mesivta, and someone recommended that he visit a certain prospective donor. The address was not in an affluent section of the city, and Rabbi Quinn knocked on the door of a modest house, without any great expectations. To his surprise, however, he received a very generous gift. The *baalebos* told Rabbi Quinn that he had grown up in Williamsburg, but as a boy had no enthusiasm for learning Torah. A student in Torah Vodaath stopped him on the street and convinced him to learn with him ten or fifteen minutes a day after public school. One day he happened to enter the *beis medrash* during a *Tehillim shiur*, at one of those moments when Reb Shraga Feivel was moved to emotional tears. Those tears, he told Rabbi Quinn, had changed his life forever and helped him become an observant Jew.

---

29. Rabbi Elias Schwartz.

30. Rabbi Shubert Spero.

31. Chinn, *"Ohr Shraga,"* p. 11. Dr. Jerry Fink reports an almost identical incident involving himself.

One set of *shiurim* was explicitly designed to be of immediate practical application: those on the mitzvos. Reb Shraga Feivel often asked younger students in the Mesivta to name for him all the mitzvos still applicable in *galus* (exile). Inevitably they succeeded in identifying only a small percentage of the mitzvos. He would comment critically, "If you don't even know the names of the mitzvos in which you are obligated, how can you expect to keep them?" To remedy their lack of knowledge, he gave classes in the mitzvos based on the third section of *Shaarei Teshuvah,* or *Sefer HaChinuch,* or, most frequently, *Kitzur Sefer Chareidim* by Rabbi Elazar Azkari.[32]

The *shiurim* in mitzvos had a twofold purpose: to familiarize the students with the details of the mitzvos and to teach them some of the underlying ideas connected to each mitzvah. One day he spent a full hour on the prohibition against building a private house higher than a *beis haknesses* (synagogue). Though the *shiur* explored in depth the parameters of the prohibition as set forth in the halachic literature, the main idea that Reb Shraga Feivel wanted to instill was the centrality of a *beis haknesses* in Jewish life and the awe that one must feel for it.

The effect of these *shiurim* was often immediate. In those days, most of the boys bought their *tefillin* from stores on the Lower East Side, and many of them were of questionable kashrus. As soon as they heard Reb Shraga Feivel's class on *tefillin,* many of the students went to have their *tefillin* checked by a reliable *sofer,* and most of them decided to buy new pairs. Rabbi Moshe Aharon Stern remembers dozens of students in the Mesivta spending an entire summer doing odd jobs in order to purchase better *tefillin.*

In those days, even many who wore a *tallis katan* often wore one smaller than that prescribed by the *Shulchan Aruch.*[33] After Reb Shraga Feivel went through all the details of the commandment, a number of boys went on an intensive search for *tallisos ketanos* of the proper measure, with *tzitzis* woven *lishmah* (for the sake of the mitzvah).

---

32. One of the many publishing projects that Reb Shraga Feivel encouraged was *Sefer Mitzvos HaKatzar* of the Chofetz Chaim, which covers all the mitzvos applicable today in a concise fashion.

33. Yonah Zev Herskowitz.

When an individual boy's behavior was unacceptable, Reb Shraga Feivel preferred to speak to him privately; he would never humiliate a *talmid*. He would discuss the boy's conduct with him and try to convince him that it was improper and, most important, show him how to act. This method of reproof was required by the Torah, he said, which commands הוֹכֵחַ תּוֹכִיחַ, *you shall reprove* (*Vayikra* 19:17). The Torah uses the word *hochachah*, which implies discussion and convincing, rather than harshness and hurt.

Reb Shraga Feivel could be exceedingly outspoken when the need arose, and he did not hesitate to discuss any subject that he felt was of importance to his students. Mixed dances were still the norm in many Orthodox synagogues, and Reb Shraga Feivel fought against this trend with all his might.

In the Mesivta itself, he did not mince words with the boys or engage in abstract philosophical discussions on the issue of boys and girls socializing. Rather he gathered together the older boys in the Mesivta and learned together with them the relevant sections of *Shulchan Aruch Even HaEzer*.[34] By teaching the class as a straightforward halachah *shiur*, he insured that the full gravity of the topic would be grasped. In the course of that lengthy *shiur*, he laid out all the varying opinions of the Rishonim, and explained the underlying differences between them, but the bottom line was not intellectual stimulation. At the end of the *shiur*, there was no room for doubt in the minds of the *talmidim* that what was under discussion was not mere *middas chassidus* (commendable, but optional, piety), but a most serious transgression.[35]

Reb Shraga Feivel taught a similar *shiur* on the subject of forbidden reading matter. His starting point was the first Mishnah in the final chapter of Tractate *Sanhedrin*, which discusses those who have no place in the World to Come. In this category Rabbi Akiva includes those who read *sefarim chitzonim* (literally: outside books). With his students, Reb Shraga Feivel would explore at length the definition of *sefarim chitzonim*.

---

34. Chapters 21-23.

35. Rabbi Eliyahu Yehoshua Geldzhaler.

He did not hesitate to share with the *talmidim* his own experience with respect to forbidden reading matter. As a young boy, he recounted, he had submitted to the entreaties of local *maskilim* and secretly read one of their books. "For weeks after that," Reb Shraga Feivel recalled, "I looked askance at the face of a *frum* Jew."

Chapter 10

Opening Up the Siddur

FEW *SHIURIM* LEFT SO LONG LASTING A MARK ON REB
Shraga Feivel's students as those on the *siddur* (prayer book),
Making in which he went through most of the *siddur*
Each Word word by word. Without an understanding of
the words one is saying, he stressed, one's
Count prayer is a mere physical act, lacking soul, not
the service of the heart of which our Sages speak.[1] So important did

---

1. To emphasize the importance of each word of Torah, he frequently played on the
double meaning of the word תֵּבָה, [Noah's] *Ark* and *word. Chazal* give two interpretations of the צֹהַר that Noach was commanded to place at the top of the Ark — צֹהַר
תַּעֲשֶׂה לַתֵּבָה: either it refers to a window or to a precious gem that gave off light. Reb
Shraga Feivel related both explanations to prayer. If *tzohar* refers to a window, then the
command can be understood homiletically to imply the obligation to look deeply into
the hidden meaning of each word (תֵּבָה), as if through a well-lit window. And if it
means a precious gem, we are commanded to make every word of our prayer a precious gem giving off rays of light.

In a similar wordplay, the Baal Shem Tov commented on Hashem's command to Noach
to enter the Ark: בֹּא אַתָּה וְכָל בֵּיתְךָ אֶל הַתֵּבָה (*Bereishis* 7:1). A Jew must put his whole being
into every word of his prayer. Reb Shraga Feivel added that just as the Ark was the means
by which Noach was saved from the Flood, so each word of prayer is a bastion through
which a Jew can save himself from the floods of secularism and physical drives.

he consider an intimate knowledge of the *siddur* that he personally tested *semichah* candidates on difficult passages in the Psalms.[2]

His goal was to give his *talmidim* the tools to make their daily *davening* a conversation with G-d. *Shemoneh Esrei*, he emphasized, is meant to be a personal plea to Hashem, not a formulaic petition contained in the *siddur*. But a Jew lacking a basic understanding of the words of the prayers, as well as the depth of meaning hidden within those words, is limited in his entreaties to G-d according to the needs of the moment and his individual spiritual state.[3] He could be particularly caustic when discussing those who pray by rote, with no sense of what they are saying. He said, "A long *Shemoneh Esrei* is not necessarily a good *Shemoneh Esrei*." He once remarked, "Of the many hours we spent *davening*, how many were really with proper *kavannah* (meditation and intent)? So why did it take so long?" He was also critical of those who raised their voices in prayer, saying that unless a person prays with a significant degree of *penimius* (inner meaning), demonstrative prayer is artificial.

His *shiurim* forced the *talmidim* to think for the first time about every word in the *siddur*. Why, he asked, do we begin every blessing addressing G-d as "*You* — אַתָּה," and then switch to the third person — "Our G-d, King of the universe, Who has sanctified us with His mitzvos"? His answer was based on the *Rashba*.[4] We begin a blessing with the recognition that Hashem is the Source of all existence, and this recognition causes us to feel His closeness, as if we were addressing Him face to face. But even as we feel Hashem's proximity, we realize that though we see His creations, we know nothing of His essence; therefore we switch to the third person.

The connection of the first words on our lips in the morning,

---

2. Before a student was allowed to be tested on *Yoreh Deah,* he was first examined by Reb Shraga Feivel on the *siddur* or *Tehillim* (Psalms), from which much of the *siddur* is derived. *Aryeh Leib Kramer* and *Sidney Greenwald.*

3. Reb Shraga Feivel's explanations of the words were not designed to fix the meaning of the prayers. He was critical of any routinization in *davening.* He could not understand people whose davening is exactly the same length and intonation, day in and day out.

4. See *Teshuvos HaRashba* V:52.

"*Modeh ani lefanecha,* I give thanks before You," to the last ones at night took on rich new meaning in Reb Shraga Feivel's classes. The entirety of the *Chovos HaLevavos'* discussion of *hakaras hatov* (recognition of another's beneficence toward us), he said, is contained within *Modeh Ani,* in which we acknowledge that we exist at this moment only because Hashem keeps us alive. At the same time, we also thank Hashem for the "*ani,*" the unique self that connects the person who went to sleep the night before with the one who awakened this morning.[5]

Even commonly repeated phrases took on new depths of meaning. "... His majesty appears over Israel (עַל יִשְׂרָאֵל גַּאֲוָתוֹ), His invincible might is in the heavens (וְעֻזּוֹ בַּשְּׁחָקִים)," he taught, refers first to Hashem's revelation through the history of the Jewish people and then to His revelation through the wonders of nature. When we sing, "How happy are we, how good is our portion (חֶלְקֵנוּ), how sweet our destiny (גּוֹרָלֵנוּ)," we are giving thanks not only for the Divine soul that we share in common with every other Jew — חֵלֶק אֱלוֹקַּ מִמַּעַל, *the portion from G-d above* — but also for the destiny that distinguishes us from every other Jew and which dictates our specific task in life (גּוֹרָלֵנוּ).

The Power of Prayer

REB SHRAGA FEIVEL DID NOT CONFINE HIMSELF TO EXPLICATING the words of the *siddur.* He wanted to give his students a sense of the incomparable sweetness of prayer, an understanding of why those moments of the day spent in prayer are, in the words of Avraham ben HaRambam, the most precious of which a human being is capable. The Gemara (*Shabbos* 10a) relates that Rava once saw Rav Hamnuna praying at great

---

5. Rabbi Shubert Spero.
   To convey the richness of *Modeh Ani,* he told a story about Rabbi Avraham Yehoshua Heschel of Apt, known after his work Oheiv Yisrael. A Jew once entered the shul for his morning prayers together with the Oheiv Yisrael. The man completed a chapter of Mishnayos, *davened,* and learned a *blatt* (folio) of Gemara. When he was done, he found the Oheiv Yisrael still immersed in his preparations for *davening.* Later he asked the Oheiv Yisrael what could have taken him so long, and the latter replied, "As soon as I started *Modeh Ani,* I began thinking: Who is this 'I' and Who is this 'You' before Whom I stand, and I was thrown into such a rhapsody that it took me hours to calm myself." *Rabbi Eliezer Schnell.*

length and asked why he was giving up eternal life (חַיֵּי עוֹלָם), i.e., Torah study, for that which is only transitory (חַיֵּי שָׁעָה). In what sense is prayer transitory, wondered Reb Shraga Feivel, since elsewhere the Gemara (*Berachos* 6b) describes the power of prayer as standing at the most exalted heights? And if it brings a person to repentance and to a deeper experience of his relationship with God, how can it be considered of temporal importance?

When a person prays properly, he answered, he is lifted above the physical world. A tree ceases to be merely a tree for him, and a stone a stone. All become part of a symphony of song to the Creator. But such an ecstatic experience cannot be sustained for long. That is why Rava refers to it as momentary life — חַיֵּי שָׁעָה. Torah, on the other hand, returns us to this world and guides us in how to sanctify it, and it is in this sense that Rava described Torah as חַיֵּי עוֹלָם — life of the world.[6]

Reb Shraga Feivel emphasized the special quality of prayer with a congregation. Even the petitions of those who are less worthy, he noted, are elevated when offered together with those of great merit. This may be compared to a village that was preparing to receive the king. Each villager was to contribute a jewel for a diadem to be presented to the king. One poor man, however, was unable to furnish a jewel and instead offered a round, translucent pebble of no particular value. While others scoffed at his gift, the village wise man spoke up: "If we were each to present our jewels to the king separately, surely the one who presented a stone would be jailed for ridiculing the king. But if the pebble is part of a crown in which all the jewels cast their luster together, then this stone will also find its place."[7]

Reb Shraga Feivel set prayer in the context of other forms of Divine service and the different aspects of prayer in relation to one another. Torah, for instance, is Hashem speaking to *Klal Yisrael*; prayer is our speaking to Hashem. But before we can expect Hashem to listen to us when we speak to Him, we must first listen

---

6. The term עוֹלָם as used by Rava is normally understood as meaning "forever" or "eternal"; Reb Shraga Feivel, however, interpreted it according to its other meaning of "world."

7. Rabbi Elias Schwartz, *Delving Within*, pp. 116-17.

to Him when He speaks to us. Otherwise our prayer is unworthy.

Even within the prayers, we find many different facets. The Hebrew root of *tefillah*, פלל, connotes both reflection and judgment, and both of these, said Reb Shraga Feivel, should be part of our *davening*. Prayer is an opportunity to reflect on the universe, the wonders of Creation, and Hashem's purpose in bringing the world into existence; but it is also an opportunity to submit ourselves, the miniature universe, to scrutiny and self-judgment.

The Book of Psalms uses different terms to describe prayer: תְּפִלָּה לְעָנִי , *A prayer of a pauper*; תְּפִלָּה לְמֹשֶׁה, *A prayer of Moshe*; and תְּפִלָּה לְדָוִד, *A prayer of David*. Each of these three aspects of prayer may be present every day, but the mix among them will constantly vary.

The first type of prayer is like that of a poor man who goes door-to-door begging for scraps of bread, or of a mother pleading for the health of a critically ill child. It is the prayer of a broken and contrite heart. The prayer of Moshe is the achievement of a higher level of clarity and understanding of the world and one's place in it. And finally, the prayer of David is the outpouring of emotion that comes from an overwhelming thirst for closeness to God.

ABOVE ALL, REB SHRAGA FEIVEL TAUGHT HIS STUDENTS HOW TO *daven* through personal example. He also encouraged the *rebbeim* to

Reb Shraga Feivel's Own Davening

daven with the *bachurim* in the morning. "Just as we learn Tractate *Bava Kamma* in the Mesivta, so do we have to learn the tractates of *yiras Shamayim* (fear of Heaven) and *ahavas Hashem* (love of G–d)," he used to say, and he viewed it as no less incumbent upon the *rebbeim* to teach the latter two "tractates."[8]

The most important part of *davening*, he taught, is the preparation.[9] Without a proper frame of mind, prayer is impossible. Prayer, תְּפִלָּה, is related to the Hebrew root, תָּפֵל, *unimportant*, which refers to an object's loss of identity in relation to something greater than it. Thus prayer must be preceded by a feeling of one's complete re-

---

8. Rabbi Shmuel Mendlowitz.
9. Rabbi Avraham Abba Freedman.

liance on Hashem and feelings of cleaving and submission to Him.

Reb Shraga Feivel was invariably one of the first in the *beis medrash* in the morning. Rabbi Moshe Aharon Stern, the late *Mashgiach* of Yeshivas Kamenitz in Jerusalem, remembers hiding from view as he observed Reb Shraga Feivel readying himself for *davening*. He began by repeating for almost fifteen minutes, "לְעוֹלָם יְהֵא אָדָם יָרֵא שָׁמַיִם בְּסֵתֶר וּבַגָּלוּי ... מָה אֲנַחְנוּ, מֶה חַיֵּינוּ, מֶה חַסְדֵּנוּ *Let a person fear Heaven both in private and in public ... What are we, what is our life, what are our deeds?"* Then he

Rabbi Moshe Aharon Stern

continued ten or fifteen times, "Are not the great men of strength as nothing before You and men of renown as if they never existed?" From that one experience of overhearing Reb Shraga Feivel preparing for *davening*, Rabbi Stern traces a complete transformation of his own approach to *davening*.

A second prerequisite for successful prayer, said Reb Shraga Feivel, is a heart overflowing with love for one's fellow Jews.[10] He would quote the Arizal that before *davening* a Jew should vocally accept the commandment to "love your fellow as you love yourself," so that one's prayer should be for everyone.

He was very demanding of himself — never did he feel his *avodah* (service) was good enough. But with others he was more solicitous. To someone who felt that his *davening* was shallow he offered consolations, saying, "אַתָּה שׁוֹמֵעַ תְּפִלַּת כָּל פֶּה, The A-mighty hears the prayer uttered *by the mouth* — even if it is lacking in thought."

In the Mesivta, Reb Shraga Feivel placed great emphasis on proper decorum. Conversation, even where halachically permitted,

---

10. Rabbi Nesanel Quinn.

was not allowed. To a parent who repeatedly spoke between one *aliyah* and the next, Reb Shraga Feivel advised that he find another place to *daven*.

He personally chose the *baalei tefillah* even on the weekdays, because a good *chazzan* arouses the emotions of the congregation. To qualify as a *chazzan* in Mesivta, a *talmid* had to pronounce the words correctly, possess a clear and melodious voice, and he had to *daven* with feeling.[11]

Reb Shraga Feivel's own *davening* was a model of self-restraint. Each word was pronounced clearly, but his *Shemoneh Esrei* was not prolonged in any way. He shared the Kotzker Rebbe's skepticism about a person's ability to concentrate throughout a lengthy *Shemoneh Esrei*. He once described a certain *rosh yeshivah* as an *ehrlicher* (honest) Jew, and cited as proof the fact that he did not *daven* a long *Shemoneh Esrei*.[12] One Rosh Hashanah, he asked Rabbi Mannes Mandel, the *shaliach tzibbur*, after *davening*, "Of all the many hours we spent *davening*, how many were really with *kavannah* (intention)? So why did it take so long?"[13]

Only on Shabbos did he permit himself a long *Shemoneh Esrei*. He began *davening* long before the rest of the congregation, yet did not finish the *Shemoneh Esrei* until the *Sefer Torah* was being removed from the *Aron Kodesh*.[14] (He never permitted the *shaliach tzibbur* to wait for him to finish *Shemoneh Esrei* before starting his repetition.)

He had the same aversion to any external physical displays in *davening*. Those who raise their voices excessively in the Rosh Hashanah *davening* were, in his opinion, descendants of the prophets of *Baal* who confronted Eliyahu HaNavi on Mount Carmel.[15] Overhearing someone crying out loudly in his *davening*, he remarked with a smile, "To permit oneself to use so much *chitzonius*

---

11. Ibid.
12. Rabbi Heshy Leiman.
13. Chinn, "Ohr Shraga," p. 10.
14. Rabbi Moshe Wolfson.
15. See *Berachos* 24b.

(external display) one would need very deep resources of *penimius* (inner devotion). Where can one obtain such *penimius*?"[16]

Though it might take an astute observer to notice the inner turmoil roiling beneath the surface as Reb Shraga Feivel *davened*, no student doubted the seriousness with which he approached it. "I still quake when I think of a *bachur* sitting near me who repeatedly spoke during *davening*," wrote Rabbi Yitzchak Chinn. "*Arois! Ven du vest veren a baalebos vest du redden* — Get out! When you are a *baalebos* you can speak," Reb Shraga Feivel ordered.[17] Once he was *davening* in a *minyan* of *baalebatim* who talked continuously. After *Aleinu*, he admonished the congregation with the words of the prophet Yirmiyahu הַמְעָרַת פָּרִצִים הָיָה הַבַּיִת הַזֶּה אֲשֶׁר נִקְרָא שְׁמִי עָלָיו בְּעֵינֵיכֶם " :(7:11), *Has this Temple, upon which My Name is proclaimed, become a cave of criminals in your eyes?"*

---

16. Rabbi Nesanel Quinn.
17. Chinn, "Ohr Shraga," p. 10.

Chapter 11

The Roshei Yeshivah

AS WITH ANY MAJOR INNOVATION, REB SHRAGA Feivel's attempt to meld Lithuanian learning with chassidic spirit did not proceed without **Rabbi David** difficulties. The most significant of **Leibowitz's** these turned out to be the divergent **Departure** visions of Reb Shraga Feivel and the *rosh yeshivah* of Torah Vodaath, Rabbi David Leibowitz. Reb David had been one of the leading members of the Slabodka (later Slabodka-Kovno) Kollel,[1] and in 1933 he decided to leave the Mesivta with the goal of establishing a yeshivah patterned as closely as possible on the model of Slabodka.

---

1. Several of the members of that *kollel* who went on to become leaders of Torah Jewry in America attributed much of their own development to Reb David: Rabbi Yaakov Kamenetsky described himself as having been a *talmid/chaver* (student/study partner) of Reb David; Rabbi Yaakov Yitzchak Ruderman, over ten years younger than Reb David, credited him with much of his development as a *lamdan*. *Rabbi Yitzchak Brandriss, "Torah, Slabodka, and Harbatzas Torah: The Vision of Rabbi David Leibowitz," The Jewish Observer, December 1991.*

142 / REB SHRAGA FEIVEL

Reb David had personally molded the learning of every advanced student in the Mesivta, and all felt great loyalty to him. Of the advanced students only a handful of Reb Shraga Feivel's first *talmidim* remained behind. Elias Karp, who was a member of the Mesivta's first class, told Reb David, "Mister Mendlowitz took us from the gutter and made *mentchen* out of us. He's our whole life. Without him we have nobody, and we can't leave him."

But whether *talmidim* went with Reb David or stayed behind

Rabbi David Leibowitz

in the Mesivta, they were painfully torn by Reb David's departure. Even those who remained had learned with Reb David for seven years and knew that they owed their entire foundation in Talmudic learning to him. They would continue to view him as their *rav muvhak* (primary teacher) for the rest of their lives. At least one felt so torn by the dispute that he could neither remain in the Mesivta nor follow Reb David, and went to learn in Europe.[2]

Though the differences between Reb Shraga Feivel and Reb David proved too great to be reconciled within one institution, what they shared was ultimately much more important than what divided them. They were both optimistic that a vibrant, uncompromising Torah Judaism could be created in America at a time when virtually no one else shared that view. Reb David told Rabbi Yaakov Kamenetsky, shortly after the latter's arrival in America, "There is no money here. But if you want *ruchnius* (spiritual accomplishment), you can grab it by the fistfuls." He continued, "If you want to enjoy this world, go back to Slabodka, but if you want

---

2. Rabbi Alexander Linchner.

Rabbi Yaakov Kamenetsky

Rabbi Yaakov Kantrowitz

to earn the World to Come, build Torah in America." Reb David was prepared to sacrifice himself totally for the achievement of that goal. After he established Yeshivas Chofetz Chaim, there were times when he had to borrow money to buy food for his next meal.

Both Reb Shraga Feivel and Reb David recognized the other's views as *l'shem Shamayim* (for the sake of Heaven), and for that reason their dispute was never personal. Reb Shraga Feivel was never heard to say a negative word about Reb David, nor would he permit others to do so. And just as the Mishnah assures us that something of lasting value will be the result of any dispute for the sake of Heaven, so was the permanent legacy of their disagreement — the creation of Yeshivas Chofetz Chaim, which has had such a substantial impact on the development of Torah Jewry in America.

THE TURMOIL SURROUNDING REB DAVID'S DEPARTURE AND THE mounting responsibilities of running the growing Mesivta eventu-

Retreat to Liberty

ally took their toll on Reb Shraga Feivel's health. Nor were matters helped when Reb David's immediate successor, Rabbi Yaakov Kantrowitz, one of the greatest of the surviving *talmidim* of the Volozhin Yeshivah and author of *Tzilusa D'Shmait'sa*, was severely injured in a fall — less than a year after coming to the Mesivta — and was unable to continue as *rosh yeshivah.*

Reb Shraga Feivel continued working until he was barely able to move, and only then did he consult a doctor. The doctor diagnosed him as having an advanced case of tuberculosis and told him that he had no more than four or five weeks to live. Upon hearing that news, Reb Shraga Feivel fell into what he would later describe as the only depression of his life, albeit one that lasted for only half an hour. When that half-hour had passed, he said to himself, "Why should I listen to the doctor? Don't I have a merciful Father in Heaven?"

Though he was indeed spared, he was confined to bed and forced to recuperate in Liberty, New York, in the Catskills, where the mountain air was considered therapeutic for his lungs. He was there from May 1934 until September 1935, and during that time, his closest student, Rabbi Nesanel Quinn, continued to run the Mesivta along the lines Reb Shraga Feivel had laid down.

Even while physically removed from his beloved Mesivta, Reb Shraga Feivel's thoughts were never far from it. When Binyamin Wilhelm came to visit him in Liberty, Reb Shraga Feivel refrained from talking about himself and would talk only about the Mesivta. He insisted on going into great detail about every aspect of the Mesivta's operation.To close friends who wrote inquiring about his condition, he responded with typical modesty, "With respect to my physical condition, I am pleased to be able to inform you that I'm growing stronger all the time, בע"ה, but my spiritual state is constantly declining."

Despite his frustration at the enforced inactivity, Reb Shraga Feivel did not allow the time to go to waste. In later years, whenever he had to encourage students suffering from physically debilitating illness, he would offer his year and a half in Liberty as proof that a disease of the body need not interfere with the working of one's mind.[3] In Liberty, Reb Shraga Feivel took on a long list of resolutions for the future if he merited to return to the leadership of Torah

---

3. Elimelech Terebelo.

Vodaath. That list was unfortunately lost with the passage of time, but among the resolutions that various family members recall are: (1) to *daven* out loud in order to have more influence on the *davening* of the *talmidim* in the Mesivta; (2) to spend even more time than before considering how to help each *talmid* reach his full potential; (3) to wage an ongoing battle against all forms of luxury; and (4) to establish a *bikkur cholim* society.

EVEN FROM HIS SICKBED, REB SHRAGA FEIVEL CONTINUED HIS search for a *rosh yeshivah* steeped in the classic Lithuanian mode of

Search for a New Rosh Yeshivah

learning. As he reflected on the development of the Mesivta to date, he became more convinced than ever that only the combination of Lithuanian learning with chassidic spiritual arousal — a brew entirely of his own making — could answer the needs of American *bachurim*.

Rabbi Chaim Ozer Grodzenski of Vilna (C) with Rabbi Baruch Ber Leibowitz (L) and Rabbi Shimon Shkop of Grodno (R)

In his search for a *rosh yeshivah*, Reb Shraga Feivel enlisted the help of the leader of the generation, Rabbi Chaim Ozer Grodzenski of Vilna. In letters to Reb Chaim Ozer, he noted that Torah Vodaath was the anchor of all the *Yiddishkeit* developing in America and the best hope for the future of American Jewish youth. Reb Chaim Ozer also recognized the crucial importance of the position of *rosh yeshivah* of the Mesivta and did everything he could to help find an appropriate replacement for Rabbi David Leibowitz.

When Reb Shraga Feivel suggested, however, that Reb Chaim Ozer prevail upon his brother-in-law, Rabbi Elchonon

Wasserman, to assume the position, Reb Chaim Ozer balked. He wrote to Reb Shraga Feivel that it was pointless to pursue that avenue since Reb Elchonon was totally bound up with his yeshivah in Baranovitch and would under no circumstances consider leaving it. Still Reb Shraga Feivel did not give up and approached Reb Elchonon directly. Reb Elchonon's response left no room for further entreaties:

Rabbi Elchonon Wasserman

With this I inform you of the *daas Torah* [with respect to your request]. I am not permitted to fulfill your request, for *Chazal* tell us, "Do not destroy one *beis knesses* until you have built another *beis knesses*" (*Bava Basra* 3b). Concerning the matter under discussion, the destruction is certain but the building is in abundant doubt ... especially inasmuch as the yeshivos in America combine *limudei kodesh* with secular learning, something not in accord with the tradition we have received from our ancestors ...

After the failure to convince Reb Elchonon, Rabbi Aryeh Leib Rudensky proposed the name of his brother-in-law, Rabbi Shlomo Heiman, then serving as the *rosh yeshivah* of Yeshivas Rameilles in Vilna and as a member of Reb Chaim Ozer's *beis din*. Since Reb Shlomo had served for many years as a *maggid shiur* in Baranovitch, Reb Shraga Feivel again wrote to Reb Elchonon seeking his opinion about

Rabbi Shlomo Heiman

the suggestion. Reb Elchonon replied that "the crown would certainly fit" Reb Shlomo, but expressed doubts as to whether it was permissible for Reb Shlomo to leave Yeshivas Rameilles, since he was irreplaceable.

Reb Shraga Feivel wrote next to Reb Chaim Ozer seeking his opinion on the suggestion and his help in bringing matters to a satisfactory conclusion if he approved. He thereby placed Reb Chaim Ozer in an awkward position, since Yeshivas Rameilles was under his supervision, and the loss of Reb Shlomo would be a very damaging blow to the yeshivah. Reb Chaim Ozer replied:

> … [Reb Shlomo] is truly one of the greatest of the *roshei yeshivah* today, a *gaon* in Torah, blessed with broad knowledge and depth of understanding. He brings forth *chiddushei Torah* that are logical and sweet, reflecting the clarity of the piercing intellect for which he is noted, and is not attracted to excessive *pilpul* … Aside from his greatness in Torah, he is a true *y'rei Shamayim*, greatly beloved by his *talmidim* and crowned with excellence of *middos*, giving pleasure to both his Creator and his fellow beings. His *talmidim* follow him with their entire souls.
>
> I cannot hide the truth that his departure from Yeshivas Rameilles would be very painful for me, and we will not easily find a replacement for him, but what can I do, I must tell you the truth.

Reb Chaim Ozer did not stop there. He ruled that the importance of saving the coming generation in America was such that Reb Shlomo should accept the offer.[4] Upon hearing Reb Chaim Ozer's opinion, Reb Shlomo Heiman gave up his position as *rosh yeshivah* in Vilna and left behind the Lithuanian milieu in which he had spent his entire life.

---

4. Reb Shlomo had been in contact with Reb David Leibowitz, whom he knew from Lithuania, and was concerned that he, too, might not find his place in Torah Vodaath. Reb Chaim Ozer assured him, "[Torah Vodaath] wasn't for Reb David; it will be fine for you." *Rabbi Eliyahu Yehoshua Geldzhaler.*

WITH THE ARRIVAL OF REB SHLOMO IN 1935, TORAH VODAATH'S position as the premier yeshivah in America was secure. Reb

Rabbi Shlomo Heiman

Shlomo had been the outstanding *talmid* of Rabbi Baruch Ber Leibowitz's yeshivah in Slabodka, Knesses Beis Yitzchak. In a letter to the Board of Directors of Torah Vodaath, Reb Baruch Ber expressed what Reb Shlomo meant to him. "All my mother's birth pains were justified if I have merited to shape one student like Reb Shlomo," he wrote.

Rabbi Reuven Grozovsky

Reb Shlomo was distinguished by his love of Torah and depth of understanding. As a draftee into the Russian Army in World War I, he reviewed *Kesubos* from beginning to end while in a trench on the frontline. Rabbi Reuven Grozovsky, his successor as *rosh yeshivah* at Torah Vodaath, used to say that Reb Shlomo had in his head a scale on which he weighed every *sevara* (logical principle used to explain the Gemara), not just to decide whether it was true or not, but also to determine its relative strength in comparison to countervailing *sevaros*.[5]

Reb Shlomo's career as a *maggid shiur* began during World War I, when Knesses Beis Yitzchak was forced to flee from Slabodka to Kremenchug, deep into White Russia. When Kremenchug itself was threatened by the Bolsheviks, he accepted the Chofetz Chaim's offer to become a *maggid shiur* in the latter's yeshivah, also in wartime exile, which was then located in Smilovitch under the direction of Reb Elchonon Wasserman. After the war, Reb Shlomo joined Reb Elchonon in Baranovitch, where he gave the *shiur* below Reb Elchonon's. Every night as he returned to the yeshivah for *Maariv*, he was surrounded by his students eager to discuss that day's *shiur*.

---

5. According to Rabbi Simchah Wasserman, Reb Shlomo's greatness lay not in what he said but in what he did not say. He was absolutely incapable of saying anything that was not straight and sound.

Never did he leave his *talmidim* until each one had had an opportunity to ask whatever he wanted. If a student expressed an insight into the Gemara, Reb Shlomo would praise his *chiddush* (novel idea) effusively, often improving the *chiddush* in the process, and repeat it in the *talmid's* name to other *talmidim* and *rebbeim*.

In *shiur*, his method was to actively involve the *talmidim* in the search for solutions. To encourage their participation, he often began with expressions of his own perplexity: "I don't know *pshut*"; "I can't understand what the Rambam means here." When they heard that he was leaving for America, former students joked that he should forgo such introductions in America, where the students would likely take his expressions of confusion seriously.

Reb Shlomo was pleasantly surprised by what he found in America. In his first letter to Reb Chaim Ozer, he could not conceal his surprise to find students of such a high standard. He had not dreamed that such advanced students existed in America.[6]

Reb Shraga Feivel referred to Reb Shlomo as the "prince among our *roshei yeshivah*." His *talmidim* revered him as they loved him. The bond between them was soul to soul. Reb Shlomo developed in them depth of thought … and more. Their love for learning was so strong that it was unthinkable for them to leave the yeshivah even part time and enroll in college.

Despite their very different backgrounds, Reb Shraga Feivel and Reb Shlomo became extremely close, and were constantly seen in consultation with one another. When Reb Shraga Feivel was informed in the middle of a *shiur* one day that Reb Shlomo had been diagnosed with cancer, he was so badly shaken that he could not continue the class. And upon Reb Shlomo's return to the Mesivta after surgery, Reb Shraga Feivel stood listening to his *shiur* like any other *bachur* in the yeshivah.

Reb Shlomo passed away in Kislev of 5705 (1944), still in his early 50's. The day after Tishah B'Av that year, Reb Shraga Feivel complained to one of his *talmidim* that he was still suffering greatly from the previ-

_____
6. Rabbi Nesanel Quinn.

ous day's fast. Due to the condition of his heart and lungs, Reb Shraga Feivel confided, he was not allowed to fast. "All the years that the *rosh yeshivah*, Reb Shlomo *zt"l*, was alive, he always warned me that I was forbidden to fast and made sure that I didn't," said Reb Shraga Feivel. "But now that he is gone, there is no one to order me not to fast."

Reb Shlomo's Successors

DURING REB SHLOMO'S FINAL ILLNESS, REB SHRAGA FEIVEL RE-cruited two of the greatest of Reb Shlomo's contemporaries from Europe: Rabbi Reuven Grozovsky and Rabbi Yaakov Kamenetsky. With the addition of Reb Reuven and Reb Yaakov to its staff, Torah Vodaath continued to offer its *talmidim* the finest examples of the Lithuanian *derech* of the time. Rabbi Reuven was already recognized as one of the *gedolei hador* in Europe, where he was a *rosh yeshivah* in

the Kamenitz Yeshivah, founded and led by his father-in-law, Rabbi Baruch Ber Leibowitz. After Reb Shlomo's passing, Reb Reuven took over the *shiur klali* (*shiur* to the entire *beis medrash*), and Reb Yaakov gave the daily *blatt shiur* to the most advanced students in the yeshivah.

Rabbi Shraga Feivel (on the right) with Rabbi Reuven Grozovsky at the chuppah of a talmid

In the opinion of Reb Yaakov, Reb Reuven was the outstanding *mechanech* (teacher of Torah) of his generation, and gave to his *talmidim* not just the answers to specific difficulties in the Gemara, but an entire approach to learning.[7] Moreover, said Reb Yaakov, he

---

7. Reb Reuven and Reb Yaakov were boyhood friends in Minsk, where Reb Reuven's father served as a *dayan*. It was Reb Reuven who was responsible for bringing Reb Yaakov and Rabbi Aharon Kotler to the Slabodka Yeshivah.

Many of Reb Reuven's *shiurim* were collected by his son-in-law, Rabbi Don Ungarisher, after his passing and published in several volumes under the title *Chiddushei Reb Reuven*.

carefully chose what he would include in a *shiur*, based on the maturity and level of learning of the *talmidim*. It was his practice to deliver the *shiur* in a slightly simplified presentation to the youngest group in the *beis medrash*, and later in the day to the entire *beis medrash*, with more complexity. With the formation of the Mesivta's advanced division, Bais Medrash Elyon, he would deliver the *shiur* there with much enhanced content. Above all, he taught his students the need for scrupulous honesty in unraveling the Gemara's difficulties. Shortly after his arrival in Torah Vodaath, Reb Reuven was delivering a *shiur klali* when one of the *talmidim* raised a problem. Reb Reuven pondered and then, without hesitation, admitted that the *talmid* was right and that a section of the *shiur* must be discarded.

From the time that Reb Shraga Feivel founded Bais Medrash Elyon in Monsey in early 1944, Reb Reuven divided his time between Monsey and Williamsburg.[8] The first half of the week was spent with the *talmidim* in Williamsburg, and the latter half, including Shabbos, with the advanced students in Beis Medrash Elyon. In late 1951, Reb Reuven suffered a stroke, which greatly limited his

power of speech and freedom of movement, and made it impossible for him to deliver *shiurim* or remain active. His mind, however, remained clear, and in the six years remaining to him, he kept informed of events in Torah Vodaath, and the Jewish world as a whole, despite his intense suffering and forced inactivity.

Rabbi Yaakov Kamenetsky

Reb Yaakov Kamenetsky, who was to guide Torah Vodaath for nearly a quarter of a century, had much in common with Reb Shraga Feivel, and the two quickly forged a bond of great intimacy. Breadth of interests and scrupulous honesty were two traits for which both were justly famed.

---

8. In addition to his duties in Torah Vodaath, Reb Reuven also served as the first head of the Moetzes Gedolei HaTorah of Agudath Israel of America.

In the course of a *shiur* on *Pirkei Avos*, Reb Shraga Feivel revealed something of the esteem in which he held Reb Yaakov. A true *talmid chacham*, he said, is a walking *mussar sefer* from whom it is possible to learn how to speak, how to act, and how to think like a Jew. One of the students asked, "Is there anyone in the Mesivta from whom we can learn in this fashion?" Reb Shraga Feivel did not answer immediately, and an air of tension hung over the room.

After several moments, he said that it was impertinent (*chutzpah*) to ask such a question in public, but since it had been asked, he would respond. To answer the question, Reb Shraga Feivel said, would require knowledge of every aspect of someone's life, and since he lacked such knowledge about most of the staff of the Mesivta, he could not comment with respect to them. Nevertheless, he continued, "There is one person among us, whom I know both in the yeshivah and in his private life, and I have already come to the conclusion that every movement, every word, every act of his is exactly in accord with the *Shulchan Aruch*. He can indeed serve as the kind of model we were discussing. I am talking about HaGaon Rabbi Yaakov Kamenetsky."[9]

Reb Shraga Feivel was ever on the alert to attract gifted personalities to the Mesivta. Such a person was Rabbi Yitzchak Schneider, a Talmudic genius, who was erudite and expert in the entire Talmud, and also knowledgeable in Kabbalah. In addition to a brilliant mind, he had a deep understanding of people, sensitivity, genuine humility, refined character — and a sense of humor that eased many a difficult situation. He had the gift of being able to bring people around to his opinion, even if they did not at first agree with him. Reb Shraga Feivel considered Rabbi Schneider to be more gifted than himself.

In about 1941, Reb Shraga Feivel invited Rabbi Schneider to become associate *menahel* of the Mesivta. He remained in Torah Vodaath only until the end of the decade, but during his tenure made significant contributions to the Mesivta's progress.

---

9. This incident took place in the first or second year that Reb Yaakov was in the Mesivta.

Rabbi Gedaliah Schorr

At the same time that Reb Reuven and Reb Yaakov were coming into Torah Vodaath, a young American product, twenty years their junior, was continuing his meteoric rise to the top echelons of the yeshivah. His name was Rabbi Gedaliah Schorr, and, according to no less an authority than Rabbi Aharon Kotler, he was the first *talmid chacham* of world-class stature produced in America. Though born in Galicia, Reb Gedaliah came to America when he was only 10 years old, and all of his training — except for a year after marriage when he learned in Kletsk under Rabbi Aharon Kotler — was in Torah Vodaath. Rabbi Meir Shapiro, the initiator of the *Daf Yomi,* pronounced him, while he was still in his teens, the finest mind he had met in America and one of the finest anywhere in the world.[10]

Reb Gedaliah was the outstanding product of Torah Vodaath in Reb Shraga Feivel's lifetime. The latter introduced Reb Gedaliah to the writings of the Sfas Emes when he was still young, and Reb Gedaliah committed large sections to memory. He would later do the same to the vast body of Midrashim, *Ramban* on the Torah, the *Maharal,* and many of the giants of Chassidus, including Reb Tzadok HaKohen and the Izhbitzer Rebbe. Each of these interests was carefully nurtured by Reb Shraga Feivel, who could often be heard telling Reb Gedaliah to *"gib a kook* (give a look)" at a certain *Ramban, Maharal,* or Reb Tzadok.[11]

10. Rabbi Moshe Sherer.
11. Rabbi Avraham Abba Freedman.

Reb Gedaliah represented the ideal around which Reb Shraga Feivel had shaped Torah Vodaath — a combination of Lithuanian *lamdus*, the *bren* (spiritual arousal) of Polish Chassidus, Hungarian *tzidkus*, and the sincerity and optimism of America. Reb Shraga Feivel appointed his protege to give the fourth *shiur* in the Mesivta when he was still in his early 20's and not yet married.[12] Even at that young age, and for the next forty years, he dazzled his students with his unique combination of Talmudic genius and command of all areas of Torah thought. With equal facility, he discussed the difficulties posed by Rabbi Akiva Eiger on the Gemara and offered startling new insights into the *Maharal* or *Sfas Emes* or his own original interpretations of Midrashim. For two generations of American-born boys, Reb Gedaliah was the hero who proved that America, too, could produce great *talmidei chachamim*.

---

12. Reb Shraga Feivel suggested to Reb Gedaliah, when the latter was still in his teens, that he give a *daf yomi shiur* in the fledgling Zeirei Agudath Israel of Williamsburg. From then on, Reb Gedaliah served as the unofficial *rav* of the Williamsburg Zeirei, in which role he exercised a major influence on the development of the Agudah movement in America.

Chapter 12

The Boss

R EB SHRAGA FEIVEL'S POSITION IN THE MESIVTA WAS perhaps unique in the annals of yeshivos. He was not the *rosh yeshivah* in any conventional sense — indeed he never gave a regular Gemara *shiur*. Nor was he the *mashgiach* or *menahel ruchani*, as those terms are generally understood in yeshivos. Perhaps the best description is the title by which he was known to generations of Torah Vodaath students: "The Boss." He set policy for the Mesivta and stimulated and guided the faculty and students, collectively and individually, and because his demands were wise and practical, they were regularly accepted. His guidance included training in the crucial value of time and punctuality, training in the manner and decorum of *davening*, and teaching *neginah* (singing with feeling and spiritual elevation) and explaining its importance. Nor did he stop with such "educational" duties. He undertook responsibility to provide for needy students, including refugees, and he made sure that the Mesivta dining room served sufficient, nutritious food. For young men who were forced to leave the Mesivta to go to work to help support their families, which was not uncommon, especially during the Depression, he acted as a surrogate father and continued to be their "*rebbi*." Clearly, the title Boss was very apt.

As such he chose the *maggidei shiur* in the yeshivah, decided what classes would be given, raised much of the Mesivta's budget, and, in general, assumed responsibility for the development of every student. Yet despite the fact that the Mesivta was his creation, he never viewed himself as anything other than an employee — and never took a front seat. When there was a shortage of money to pay salaries, he absolutely refused to take his own until all of the *maggidei shiur* had received theirs.[1] Once he asked that his $70-a-week salary be decreased by $15 in order to reduce the financial burden on the Board of Directors.

Nor did he appropriate any of the external trappings of rule. His personal conduct was unassuming, and he dressed, even on Shabbos, like an ordinary person. His students had their own explanations for his refusal to wear rabbinic garb. He once told Rabbi Elchonon Wasserman that he dressed as he did because "that is how I dressed when I learned Torah in Pressburg."[2] Others were sure that in his modesty, he did not consider himself a true *rav* and therefore was unworthy to dress as such. It could well be that he felt he would have more influence on American boys if dressed neatly and in modern, though restrained, style. Others felt that he did not want to appear as a "professional rabbi," whose "job" it was to advocate religion. Whatever the reason, he was addressed as Mister and even dressed as a "mister."[3]

REB SHRAGA FEIVEL ARRIVED IN THE *BEIS MEDRASH* EVERY morning before the *davening* began. After Shacharis, he returned

Reb Shraga Feivel's Daily Schedule

home for a meager breakfast, usually consisting of hot cereal and a glass of milk. On his way back to the yeshivah,

---

1. Rabbi David Talansky, one of the veteran administrators in Mesivta Torah Vodaath.
2. Rabbi Moshe Yechezkel Samuels.
3. Rabbi Yitzchak Karpf.

he was always filled with enthusiasm, as he planned his day and thought about new approaches he wanted to try. "I never walked to the Mesivta without a feeling of renewal," he said.

The first lesson he taught every day did not take place in the classroom, and it was always the same: the value of every moment. At the start of every school day, the first sight that greeted Mesivta students was invariably Reb Shraga Feivel standing at the entrance of the Mesivta, pocket watch in hand, waiting for the learning to begin. As a latecomer passed by, he would glance alternately at his watch and at the offender, with a look of absolute astonishment on his face. His curt *"Gut Morgen"* was usually all that was needed to be said, though repeated offenders occasionally received more of a reprimand. One such student arrived five minutes late and completely out of breath one day. "What's your excuse today?" asked Reb Shraga Feivel. The hapless boy had to admit, *"Rebbi*, I was running so fast, I didn't have time to think of an excuse."[4]

He simply could not understand how anyone, whether *rebbi* or student, could possibly come a moment late to study Torah. "Aren't we striving to build *Yiddishkeit* in America?" he demanded of the *rebbeim* and boys alike. "And if so, how can we afford to waste a minute?"[5] In later years, when he taught a 9 a.m. class in the auditorium, he was always in his seat waiting to begin five minutes early. ("I'm not a punctual person," he would say. "A punctual person is on time; I'm always five minutes early.")

The sanctity of time was a lesson he hammered home in countless ways. *"Bachurim, zeht austzunitzen di zeit* — Boys, be sure to make good use of your time," was a constant refrain. "Learn, and if you don't want to learn, play ball. But don't just sit around," he would tell them. The idea of doing nothing was anathema to him.[6] He em-

---

4. Rabbi Ephraim Wolf.

5. Rabbi Avraham Pam.

6. Rabbi Yaakov Greenwald.

A classroom in the yeshivah

phasized how much could be achieved in even a few minutes.[7] Thus he explained the verse, "The days of our years contain within them (בָּהֶם) seventy years" (*Tehillim* 90:10): "Within a few days — בָּהֶם — you can compress the achievements of seventy years."[8]

Reb Shraga Feivel visited every classroom daily. Though these classroom visits were of necessity brief, with a few well-chosen words directed to the *rebbi* or the *talmidim*, he had the ability to inject new life into the learning.

Part of each day was set aside for private discussions with individual boys. At minimum, Reb Shraga Feivel tried to speak to each boy privately twice a year. These talks

An early graduating class of Yeshivah Torah Vodaath

---

7. He was filled with admiration for Rabbi Aharon Kotler's ability to use every single minute. He and Reb Aharon once emerged from a meeting at which Reb Aharon had actively participated in the discussion of some pressing communal matter. Before they had even reached the elevator, Reb Aharon was already muttering under his breath, "Now, I understand Rabbi Akiva Eiger's *kushya*." He had returned instantaneously to his Torah learning.

8. Chinn, "Ohr Shraga," p. 7.

The psalm continues, לִמְנוֹת יָמֵינוּ כֵּן הוֹדַע, *Make known to us how to count our days properly*, i.e., teach us the proper use of our time. *Sidney Greenwald*.

An advanced class in Gemara

Discussing a shiur in the Mesivta library with Rabbi Yitzchak Meyer Traube

allowed Reb Shraga Feivel to gain an intimate picture of each boy — who his friends were, what he did after school, what he liked to read in his free time, his opinions on various subjects. At the same time, the discussions with "the Boss" gave the students a feeling of importance and made them want to show themselves worthy of his attention.

Reb Shraga Feivel chose the best *maggidei shiur* he could find, and while he gave them independence in their teaching, he stimulated them to ever-greater accomplishment. His only direct connection to the Gemara learning was to give periodic examinations to see how students were progressing. Nevertheless he maintained a close connection with the *rebbeim*. When the *rebbeim* gathered together for lunch, Reb Shraga Feivel used the informality of the hour to good advantage. Not infrequently a chance remark would provide him with important information about a particular stu-

The Mesivta beis medrash

dent or class.[9] Sometimes he would drop a comment without any obvious intent that would in the flash of an eye develop into a lively discussion of how to teach Torah.[10] Through such informal contacts, he would often convey a message subtly, without teachers' meetings.

If a young *rebbi* wanted to discuss teaching or particular students, Reb Shraga Feivel was available. In 1939, Rabbi Avraham Pam, today the *rosh yeshivah* of Torah Vodaath, was appointed a *rebbi* in the Mesivta. He reports that Reb Shraga Feivel spent hours together with him discussing the boys in his *shiur* and what each one needed. Rabbi Pam never ceased to be amazed by Reb Shraga Feivel's attention to every little detail concerning the *shiur*. From time to time, he would suggest, for instance, that the *shiur* move on to the next *sugya* (topic), because the boys had absorbed as much as they could without becoming confused or bored.

Late afternoon was the time for Reb Shraga Feivel's various *shiurim*. Most nights, he also returned to the Mesivta during the evening *seder* (session). If by chance, the *rebbi* in charge of night *seder* could not attend, Reb Shraga Feivel himself would supervise and be available to answer any questions the boys might have. When the hour grew late, he would urge the boys to put an end to their learning for the night so that they would not be tired the next day. He used to tell the dorm supervisor, "If the boys learn too late into the night, you will lose your reward in *Olam Haba*."[11] Only on Thursday night did he permit them to stay late.

---

9. Rabbi Avraham Pam.

10. The lunch hour also provided the *rebbeim* with an opportunity to discuss Torah with one another. One *rebbi* would raise a problem that was bothering him, and the rest would offer their solutions. Rabbi Shmuel Kushelevitz once described these discussions as reaching into different parts of the entire Talmud. Yet no matter where the talk of this group of *talmidei chachamim* ebbed and flowed, Reb Shraga Feivel showed himself to be as at home in the Gemara as any of them. After a while, it no longer surprised these stalwarts of the best Lithuanian yeshivos to find that "Mister" Mendlowitz was their equal in Gemara learning. *Rabbi Avraham Pam.*

11. Rabbi Hershel Mashinsky.

FOR A LONG TIME, REB SHRAGA FEIVEL CONSIDERED HIMSELF
subject to the authority of the Board of Directors of Torah

Relations With the Board

Vodaath. Inevitably, the perspectives of Torah educator and successful businessmen conflicted at times, but in general, the relationship between Reb Shraga Feivel and the board was one of mutual respect. He came from a tradition that did not devalue working for a living and had himself struggled in business at various times. Business experience gave him an appreciation of what life in the business world was like and the challenges faced by the board members.

There was one drawn-out conflict between him and the board. Convinced that there had to be entertainment at the annual fund-raising dinner, the directors refused to follow his advice not to invite a theatrical personality or group to perform; otherwise, they insisted, the event would be a failure. That did not stop until Reb Shraga Feivel founded Torah Umesorah. Its first dinner had two innovations: First, there was no theatrical entertainment, and all the speeches were intended to inspire the guests with the feeling that the work of the organization was sacred and was the only guarantee of the survival of the Jewish people. Second, Reb Shraga Feivel seated the distinguished Torah personalities at the dais while the supporters were in the audience. (As for Reb Shraga Feivel himself, he sat on the side, of course.)

From the very beginning, Reb Shraga Feivel viewed part of his task as giving the members of the board more of a Torah perspective. He started a periodic *shiur* for the board members almost from the moment he was appointed principal of Torah Vodaath elementary school.

Reb Shraga Feivel raised large sums of money for Torah Vodaath, Holocaust rescue work, Torah Umesorah, other institutions, and for countless individuals. Those sums are a reflection of his success in educating an older generation of *baalebatim* in the importance of supporting Torah education and causes. It was his forceful personality that attracted many of the first substantial supporters of Torah

Joseph Rosenzweig   *Harry Herskowitz*

causes in America. He solicited not just their money but their commitment to the cause.

In time, Reb Shraga Feivel assembled a group of backers willing to support him in whatever direction he led. Among these was Joseph Rosenzweig, one of the first religious millionaires in America. Reb Shraga Feivel referred to him as a *"tzaddik in tzedakah."*[12] Reb Shraga Feivel always addressed him as Reb Yosef, not the more familiar "Joe," by which he was universally known. And Rosenzweig, in turn, invariably greeted Reb Shraga Feivel, "Mister Mendlowitz, what can I do for you and how much is it going to cost this time?"

Another crucial supporter was Harry Herskowitz, head of the New York office of the Internal Revenue Service, who had widespread connections and always treated Reb Shraga Feivel with great deference. *Gedolei Yisrael* considered him America's model *baalebos*. At the wedding of his daughter, Herskowitz called his fellow directors into a private room before the *chuppah* and told them, "How can I bring my daughter to the *chuppah* when the *rebbis* in the yeshivah

---

12. It was his donation of $100,000 with which the Vaad Hatzalah began. *Rabbi Alexander Linchner.*

Joseph Shapiro

Moses Feuerstein

still haven't been paid?" His fellow directors answered the appeal, and the necessary money was collected immediately.[13]

Though he worked hard to raise the sights of Torah Vodaath supporters, Reb Shraga Feivel did not attribute his success as a fund-raiser to these efforts. He told his students that the generosity with which *baalebatim* support yeshivos is one of the proofs that Torah is from Heaven. It is natural, he said, that Jews, who are distinguished by their merciful hearts, give generously to hospitals, orphanages, and other institutions for the needy. But what is truly miraculous is their support for Torah study, even when they personally have little connection to that study.

Henry Hirsch

13. Other prominent contributors included Samuel Herskowitz, Henry Hirsch, Joseph Shapiro, Samuel and Moses Feuerstein, and Joseph Rosenzwieg.

Reb Shraga Feivel (on the right) with Henry Hirsch

Fund-raising was never easy for Reb Shraga Feivel. He once asked Yaakov Leshinsky to accompany him on a visit to a certain well-to-do man. Reb Shraga Feivel asked the man for $500, but the man replied that he could afford to give no more than $300 at that time. Leshinsky was amazed to see Reb Shraga Feivel blush brightly, as he told the man that he would wait until he could afford $500. Later Leshinsky asked him, "Why did you blush like that? It's not the first time you ever collected money." Reb Shraga Feivel told Leshinsky he was by nature a giver, not a taker, and that he sometimes blushed when he solicited funds.

Only his overwhelming sense of mission allowed him to undertake a task so contrary to his nature. To make the task easier, he tried to internalize the feeling that he was not seeking a favor from the giver, but offering him an opportunity of incomparable value. He used the metaphor of an insurance policy to persuade prospective donors. Contributions to support Torah, he explained, are the best insurance policy one can have when he completes his "one hundred and twenty" years in this world.

That attitude also served to protect him from disappointment. Once he and his student Sender Gross were collecting funds for Torah Umesorah. The secretary of a certain businessman whom they went to visit told them that he was not in his office, which was a patent lie. Gross was incensed, but Reb Shraga Feivel was unfazed. "I wanted to do him a favor, but you cannot force a favor on someone if he is not ready to accept it," he explained.

Certainly Reb Shraga Feivel's success as a fund-raiser was not due to a gift for flattery. He once visited a well-to-do man on behalf of Torah Vodaath. Before he could even begin his appeal, the man launched into a series of complaints about how Torah Vodaath was being run. Reb Shraga Feivel cut him short. "My dear friend, I came here in search of financial assistance, not to hear your criticisms." Taken aback, the man nevertheless wrote out a large check to the Mesivta. Once the check was firmly in hand, Reb Shraga Feivel told him, "Now I'm prepared to hear your criticism."[14] His original curt response was because it seemed that the critic was looking for an excuse not to contribute; once it was clear that he wanted to support the Mesivta, his constructive criticism was welcome.

From time to time, Reb Shraga Feivel returned to Scranton to raise funds. On one of those trips, he visited a former student from his Scranton days, who had prospered in business, but had not remained religious. As soon as he entered the house, Reb Shraga Feivel burst out, "*Oy, oy,* I am going to be scorched in the fires of *Gehinnom* on your account — that I taught such a student." That he was in the man's house to ask for money did nothing to temper his rebuke. Still, the man gave a large sum to Torah Vodaath.

Students saw that Reb Shraga Feivel was always respectful of the board members, whether or not they were present, but they learned an even more important lesson from observing his relations with the board: He showed not the slightest bit of deference to its members simply because they were wealthy. During a Friday morning class in the early 40's, one of the office workers entered the *shiur* room and announced that Mr. Samuel Feuerstein was calling from Boston. In those days, long-distance phone calls were rare. Moreover, Feuerstein was one of Torah Vodaath's biggest supporters, as well as president of Torah Umesorah, a project very close to Reb Shraga Feivel's heart. Nevertheless Reb Shraga Feivel told his assistant, "Tell Mr. Feuerstein that I'm teaching a *shiur* and cannot come to the phone." Ten minutes later the assistant was back at the door to say that Mr. Feuerstein had called back. Reb Shraga Feivel repeated his

---

14. Alter Pearl.

Samuel Feuerstein

earlier response and went back to teaching. Another ten minutes passed, and the hapless assistant returned looking very uncomfortable at having been placed in the cross-fire between Feuerstein and Reb Shraga Feivel. This time Reb Shraga Feivel told him, "Tell Mr. Feuerstein that if he never wants to talk to me again, that's his prerogative. But I will not interrrupt a *shiur.*"[15]

Every boy in that class knew how important Samuel Feuerstein was to Torah Vodaath and that he was one of the biggest contributors in the country to Orthodox causes. Thus Reb Shraga Feivel's refusal to interrupt the Torah learning was a concrete lesson in the importance of every minute of Torah learning, even at the risk of monetary loss.

The board members knew that Reb Shraga Feivel was prepared to resign at any minute rather than compromise his principles. He once told the Board of Directors, "I'm richer than you are because I'm prepared to feed my family just tea and bread without butter, and you are not capable of doing that."[16]

The first time he met Reb Yaakov Kamenetsky, at the dedication of the new campus of Yeshivas Ner Israel in 1943, Reb Shraga Feivel discussed with Reb Yaakov a problem that he was then having with the board. The board wanted *rebbeim* to punch a time clock, and Reb Shraga Feivel felt that this was an affront to their dignity. Yet as an employee, Reb Shraga Feivel asked Reb Yaakov, was he obliged to obey the board's order? Reb Yaakov told him that as far as matters of educational policy went, he was not beholden to the board. Rather Reb Shraga Feivel should view himself as free to follow his

---

15. Heard by Rabbi Zev Cohen from his father, the late Feivel Cohen, who was in the class that morning.

16. Rabbi Shimshon Appelgrad, a fund-raiser for Torah Vodaath.

own judgment. Reb Shraga Feivel was impressed with Reb Yaakov's solution to the problem, especially since it comported so closely with his own approach to the board on other occasions.

In 1945, Reb Shraga Feivel was eager to appoint Rabbi Reuven Grozovsky as *rosh yeshivah* to fill the void left by Rabbi Shlomo Heiman's protracted illness and passing. After describing to the board Reb Reuven's greatness as a teacher of Torah, Reb Shraga Feivel told them that he would leave the room to let them deliberate. When he returned, he was informed that the board had been unable to reach a consensus. Hearing this, Reb Shraga Feivel said, "Gentlemen, I wanted to give you the merit of hiring Reb Reuven. That you have lost. I must appoint Reb Reuven and I will."[17]

---

17. Heard by Rabbi Zev Cohen from his father, the late Feivel Cohen.

Chapter 13

Guide for Life

I T WAS NATURAL THAT, WHEN THEY FIRST CAME TO KNOW
him, young students, and even adults, felt intimidated by Reb
Shraga Feivel's greatness, impressive personality, and aura of
authority; only later could they learn and appreciate his
warmth, concern, and dedication to the welfare of everyone who
needed his help or guidance. Nor can it be denied that, as head of
Torah Vodaath, he had to project authority in order to carry out his
chinuch program and mold *talmidim*.

AWE, TINGED WITH FEAR, WAS THE FIRST EMOTION THAT MOST
students experienced upon meeting Reb Shraga Feivel.[1] His piercing
First eyes seemed to take in everything at a glance:
Impressions Many students were convinced that he could look
at them and know everything they were thinking.
Often their strategy was to avoid him. As one former student put it,

---

1. Rabbi Moshe Aharon Stern.

Mike Tress

"What 14-year-old boy doesn't have something to hide? We tried to steer clear as much as possible because we were sure that as soon as he laid his eyes on us he would know what we were up to."[2] When boys playing stickball during recess or before school glanced up and saw Reb Shraga Feivel with his pocket watch in his hand, "the ball seemed to stop in mid-flight."[3] Word that "the Boss is coming" was enough to send tremors through the lunchroom.[4]

Even adults were awed in his presence. Mike Tress, the dynamic leader of the Agudath Israel Youth Council, told Rabbi Hershel Mashinsky that there was no one who "cast such an aura of *yiras hakavod* (veneration)" as Reb Shraga Feivel. "He speaks authoritatively and he knows what he is talking about. You can't disagree with him," Tress said. And if that is how a successful businessman and community leader felt, how much more so did teenage boys tremble in front of him.

Even the power of Reb Shraga Feivel's emotions could bewilder younger boys. When he broke down sobbing in class over the Exile of the *Shechinah* and tragedies that befell the Jewish nation, they could only sit uneasily, unable to comprehend the origin of such strong feelings. They realized that something was demanded of them, but did not know how to respond.

He had neither the desire nor the ability to be a "pal" to his students. All forms of frivolity and wasting time were anathema to

---

2. Jack Klausner.
3. Abe Dicker.
4. Rabbi Yaakov Greenwald.

him. Even with his own children, he was not given to outward displays of affection. The halachah forbids kissing one's children in shul so that a person will never forget that his love of his children is secondary to the love of his Creator.[5] To Reb Shraga Feivel the whole world was a place for the worship of *HaKadosh Baruch Hu*, and thus there were always limits on his physical expressions of affection, whether to his own children or his students. In this respect, his students were treated no better and no worse than his children.

He avoided every form of personal *kavod* (honor), but he demanded respect. It never occurred to his students, for instance, to make him the subject of their *grammen* (humorous doggerel) on Purim.

THE AWE ALWAYS REMAINED, BUT IN TIME IT CEASED TO DOMInate the students' feelings about Reb Shraga Feivel. Over the course

Educate the Youth in His Way of years, many students came to love him intensely, as the person most responsible for shaping them into whatever they eventually became.

For many — perhaps most — the key to the development of that love was that Reb Shraga Feivel showed each student the respect of knowing him as an individual. His first piece of advice to those embarking on a career in *chinuch* was: Never stint on the time for talking to your students. Much of his day was devoted to regular conferences with students, and he was always available for any student who wanted to speak to him. As a consequence, the common phenomenon of a student falling between the cracks and feeling that no one in the institution was aware of his existence or his problems did not occur in the Mesivta. Reb Shraga Feivel not only knew each student by name, he knew his family situation, personality, plans for the future, and spiritual level at any given time.

There was nothing perfunctory about the private conferences. The way that Reb Shraga Feivel listened with complete attention encouraged boys to pour out their hearts. Boys who were having

---

5. *Rama* to *Orach Chaim* 98:1.

trouble in school or outside opened up to him in ways that they did with no one else. They knew that he never gave pat, platitudinous answers to problems that concerned them deeply, but rather encouraged them to speak freely without constraints of time or subject matter. Then, because his advice did not flow quickly or profusely — each piece of advice was carefully weighed — it was that much more powerful when it did come. One message, however, was consistent: Only within the framework of the Torah can a Jew experience real happiness in life and as part of *Klal Yisrael*.

Because he knew each student so well, Reb Shraga Feivel was able to guide each according to his individual needs and talents. He had no set approach; the approach varied according to the character of the student. No two were approached in the same way. He spoke to them differently, selected different works of *mussar* and *hashkafah* to learn with them according to their backgrounds and personalities, and directed them toward the life goals best suited to them.

Sometimes, for instance, a particularly bright but restless boy was given more leeway than would have been given to another student. A certain Yankele used to employ his considerable intelligence to finding ever more ingenious ways to upset the smooth functioning of the Mesivta. One time he picked the lock on the bulletin board in the Mesivta lobby, on which the names of the staff were listed, and rearranged the movable letters to spell out previously unheard-of positions for the various members of the administration. It did not take long to discover the culprit. Reb Shraga Feivel invited Yankele into his office, and spoke to him at length, without once mentioning his most recent offense. During that conversation, Reb Shraga Feivel learned everything about Yankele's background, his thoughts, and his aspirations. It was clear to Reb Shraga Feivel that a boy as full of life as Yankele required some special treatment.[6]

---

6. Chinn, "Ohr Shraga," p. 7.

Moshe was another exceptionally talented student, a rare genius, who had a difficult time submitting himself to the normal yeshivah discipline. Schedules were completely foreign to him, and he would come and go as he pleased. Though he was several years younger than the *talmidim* in Bais Medrash Elyon, Reb Shraga Feivel finally sent him there in the hope that, if given the independence he craved, he would settle down and apply himself. But when he heard that Moshe had traded a set of *Chiddushei HaRashba* for a phonograph, Reb Shraga Feivel let him be expelled for good. All the patience that he had previously shown Moshe came to an abrupt end. "If he has no appreciation of the value of Torah," Reb Shraga Feivel said, "there is no hope for him."[7]

Rabbi Zelik Epstein noted that there was a common characteristic among Torah Vodaath students — namely a feeling of responsibility for the *klal* — but it was less a matter of indoctrination than osmosis; *bachurim* simply absorbed Reb Shraga Feivel's dedication to others. His respect for the individuality of the *bachurim* was reflected in the fact that there was never an identifiable Torah Vodaath student. In most yeshivos, there is a certain style, and the yeshivah attracts students whose personalities are suited to that particular approach. Over time, students in the yeshivah come to resemble one another not only in their approach to a Gemara but in such externals as the way they dress and speak. In many cases there is an unconscious effort to imitate the *rosh yeshivah*. "Every yeshivah," Rabbi Yaakov Kamenetsky said, "is a *Sedom* bed: Boys are cut or stretched to fit the yeshivah." But that was never true, said Reb Yaakov, of the Mesivta under Reb Shraga Feivel.[8]

Rabbi Moshe Wolfson describes this phenomenon: "We are used to the fact that each yeshivah has its own particular approach, and

---

7. Ibid.

8. Reb Yaakov said that this encouragement of individuality was a quality that the Mesivta shared with Slabodka Yeshivah under the Alter. In Slabodka, the primary influence on a young *bachur* was usually one of the advanced students, not the *rosh yeshivah*. In developing their own *derech halimud*, younger *bachurim* gravitated toward the older *bachur* who, they found, was the best role model for them. *Sidney Greenwald.*

it is understood that those who are not suited to that approach will not find their place in that particular yeshivah. Reb Shraga Feivel's approach was different. One could say that he had no approach to education, or, more accurately, that he had a different approach for every *talmid*. The number of his students equaled the number of educational approaches he employed. He fulfilled Rashi's definition of 'a man in whom the spirit dwells,' one capable of responding to the differing spirit of every individual in *Klal Yisrael* (see *Rashi* to *Bamidbar* 27:18)."

Respect for the individuality of students meant guiding them in a path designed to employ all their natural *middos* (character traits) — both the desirable and the undesirable ones. Reb Shraga Feivel found support for this approach in *Chazal's* description of the *yetzer hara* as "iron that is placed over the fire" (*Avos d'Rav Nosson* 16). As long as the iron is in the fire, he pointed out, it can be shaped into a wide variety of useful vessels.[9] A father once asked Reb Shraga Feivel what he could do to curb his son's wildness. Reb Shraga Feivel told him that it would be a mistake to try and remove every trace of the boy's boisterousness — a false imposition on his nature. "What you have to do," said Reb Shraga Feivel, "is channel his natural *lebedikeit* (liveliness) into a greater devotion to Hashem's mitzvos."[10]

Reb Shraga Feivel's knowledge of the students allowed him to find just the proper form of rebuke when necessary. Very often, that rebuke was blunt in the extreme. He was once asked why he did not emulate the method normally followed by *mashgichim* of beginning their *mussar* with words of *Chazal*, which then serve as a springboard for a more personal message. He replied, "They want me to put their mistakes into a *pasuk* (verse)?"[11] The sharper his criticism,

---

9. He also saw in this *Chazal* support for the chassidic approach, which stresses the redirection of negative character traits, over what he saw as the *mussar* approach of trying to completely uproot negative traits.

10. Rabbi Elias Schwartz, *V'shee-non-tom*, vol. I, p. 263.

11. Rabbi Moshe Aharon Stern.

however, the more concise it was likely to be; Reb Shraga Feivel was ever mindful of *Chazal's* advice: "Do not reprove over and over."

Sometimes even a few perfectly aimed words could leave a mark for a lifetime. One student complained that he was torn between his learning and his emotional drives. Reb Shraga Feivel reminded him of one short phrase in *Tehillim* (38:4): אֵין שָׁלוֹם בַּעֲצָמַי מִפְּנֵי חַטָּאתִי, *There is no peace in my bones because of my sins,* meaning that there is always a tug of war between the *yetzer tov* and the *yetzer hara.* A person's drives are reinforced by his actions; vigilance over one's conduct will end the inner conflict. Those words had a profound effect. That student went on to become a well-known Torah educator.

As a teenager, Hertzl Shechter was invariably a few minutes late for Reb Shraga Feivel's 9 a.m. *Tanach* shiur, and one day he received a notice that "the Boss" wanted to speak to him. Shechter entered Reb Shraga Feivel's office trembling. "*Nu,* Hertzl, when are you going to start coming on time?" Reb Shraga Feivel asked. Shifting uncomfortably in his seat, Shechter could manage nothing more than: "*Im yirtzeh Hashem.*" But Reb Shraga Feivel was not to be put off so easily. "*Nein,*" he began shaking his head, "not *im yirtzeh Hashem. Im yirtzeh Hertzl* — no, not if Hashem wants; rather if *Hertzl* wants." That terse comment rendered Shechter a hyperpunctual person to this day.

Sometimes tears became the chosen instrument of rebuke. Overhearing two boys talking in the *beis medrash* about matters far removed from the Gemara in front of them, he exclaimed, "It is I who is going to be called to judgment. I, the student of the *geonim* of Chust and Unsdorf." The tears that followed such a declaration were worth a dozen *mussar shmuessen.*

As sharp as the reproof could be, it was always tempered by the students' recognition of Reb Shraga Feivel's love. That love was expressed in many ways, large and small. One Lag B'Omer, in the early years of the Mesivta, he took a group of students with him to a sun-drenched park, as had been the custom in his native Hungary. As they boarded a trolley car, the conductor remarked jocularly, "Not all your sons, I assume." Without hesitation, but with a twinkle in his eyes, Reb Shraga Feivel answered, "Yes, they are all my

Reb Shraga Feivel

sons."[12] His love was the condition that enabled him to be so biting in his rebuke at times without losing his students. They felt that whatever he said was for their benefit, not a means of venting his spleen.

In his eyes, every boy was an unpolished diamond, and his guiding light was the dictum of the Baal Shem Tov: "In order to influence someone else, one must always focus on his good points." While recognizing that all education requires both "the right hand that draws close" and "the left hand that pushes away," Reb Shraga Feivel always emphasized that the right hand must be dominant. He had seemingly unlimited patience for even the most troublesome *talmidim*. "Will I get any reward because I did not ruin the sons of *Admorim* (chassidic *Rebbes*) who came to learn in the Mesivta?" he asked. "Isn't our principal task to worry about those who have never tasted the sweetness of Torah and Judaism?"[13] With these boys, he went step by step.

One such boy came from Brazil with a very limited knowledge of halachah. Rabbi Moshe Rivlin, the dorm supervisor, was aghast to see him walking along the street one Shabbos and pull a handkerchief from his pocket. When Rabbi Rivlin tried to explain the prohibition against carrying in a public domain on Shabbos, the boy looked at him as if he were crazy and called him a "fanatic" for thinking that there could be any problem with carrying a handkerchief. Rabbi Rivlin was afraid that it might be impossible to keep the

---

12. Rabbi Hershel Leiman.
13. Elimelech Terebelo.

boy in the Mesivta. But Reb Shraga Feivel felt otherwise. He called the *talmid* into his office and had a long conversation with him concerning the basic principles of Shabbos. Today that "transgressor" is numbered among the outstanding Torah educators in Brooklyn.[14]

Attending to Material Needs as Well as Spiritual

REB SHRAGA FEIVEL DEVOTED HIMSELF COMPLETELY TO EVERY student, and his fertile mind never stopped developing stratagems for each one according to his individual needs. A typical problem was dealing with parents who wanted to take their sons out of the yeshivah. One such student had a great desire to learn despite a very average intellect, but his parents wanted him to go to work and relieve some of the financial pressures on the family. Reb Shraga Feivel sent the boy's parents a letter announcing that in recognition of their son's outstanding abilities in learning, the Mesivta had decided to offer him a full scholarship, covering room and board, and to provide him with a monthly stipend, as well. From then on, the parents raised no further objections to their son, the *"talmid chacham,"* pursuing his studies.

A widowed mother who lived far from New York sent her three orphaned sons to the Mesivta to learn. The youngsters had a difficult time adjusting to the Mesivta and particularly to living in a dormitory, and after a few days, they fled the Mesivta and returned home. When he learned what had happened, Reb Shraga Feivel telephoned their mother and begged her to send her sons back. "If the dormitory is not for them," he told her, "they can live with me just like my own children." And that is what happened. The boys lived in the Mendlowitz household, and Reb Shraga Feivel personally looked after them. It was not too long before the boys were ready to live in the dormitory, and they grew to be *bnei Torah* of note.[15]

One of Reb Shraga Feivel's closest *talmidim* was Elimelech Terebelo, who first came to the Mesivta from Detroit at the age of 19.

---

14. Rabbi Shaul Rowner.
15. Rabbi Yaakov Leshinsky.

Though he came from a religious family, Terebelo had little background in Torah learning. He insisted that he was prepared to sit in a class with boys much younger than himself, but Reb Shraga Feivel feared that he would ultimately be broken by the experience of being five years older than his classmates. Instead Reb Shraga Feivel found a special *chavrusa* (study partner) for Terebelo, who prepared him for Rabbi Shlomo Heiman's *daf shiur*, where the students were his age and older, and then reviewed it with him afterwards, until Terebelo was able to understand the *shiur* on his own.

The *chavrusa* Reb Shraga Feivel chose for Terebelo was a young refugee from a very distinguished family. He had arrived in America in 1940 with only the clothes on his back. Reb Shraga Feivel was moved by his plight, and instructed one of his assistants to pay a stipend to the young man every week. But when Reb Shraga Feivel saw that receiving charity was repugnant to the young man, he looked for another way to supply some of his monetary needs. Learning with Melech Terebelo was the answer.

Reb Shraga Feivel was also eager that the young refugee eat at least one meal a day in a restaurant, but knew that he would refuse any money proffered for that purpose. One day he told the young man that a famous *talmid chacham* from Russia had arrived in Williamsburg. It was not befitting the honor of the older Torah scholar to eat in the Mesivta dining hall, said Reb Shraga Feivel, and he wanted to provide the man with his meals in a nearby restaurant. He asked the young refugee as a favor to accompany the older scholar so that he would not be forced to eat all his meals alone. Only years later did the young man learn that the story was largely a ploy to make sure he had adequate meals.

Another young European refugee arrived together with his family just before the war. The boy's parents had no ready means of support and their financial situation was desperate. The *bachur* told Reb Shraga Feivel that he had received a generous monthly stipend in the Mirrer Yeshivah in Europe and asked him for a similar stipend. Reb Shraga Feivel immediately began learning with the *bachur* the Rambam's description of the spiritual devastation that follows from deriving one's sustenance from learning Torah (*Hilchos*

Talmud Torah 3:10). He felt that some of the Lithuanian yeshivos went too far in emphasizing that Torah scholars are the aristocracy of the Jewish people and that, as a consequence, even young students developed an attitude of entitlement. But after giving the 16-year-old *bachur* three days to absorb this lesson, Reb Shraga Feivel began providing him with a large monthly stipend to help his family.[16]

A prominent rabbi recalls that he lost his father while he was still a teenager in the Mesivta. Reb Shraga Feivel called him in after the *shivah* and inquired about his mother and brothers. Did the family need help? Knowing that the family had always struggled financially, Reb Shraga Feivel handed the *talmid* a few dollars and said, "You need spending money." The boy said that his mother would not permit him to accept it. When the interview ended, Reb Shraga Feivel said, "You should know that my door is always open to you, whatever you need."

Later that year, the *talmid* decided that he would like to go to Camp Mesivta for the summer. He applied to Rabbi Rivlin, who served as camp registrar, only to be told that there was no room; registration was closed. The *talmid* said, "I have only one request. Please speak to Mister Mendlowitz." Later that day, Rabbi Rivlin found the *talmid* and told him, "Mister Mendlowitz said that for you we must always find room."

Rabbi Ephraim Oshry, spiritual leader of the Bais Medrash Hagadol on the Lower East Side, relates that when he and another rabbi came to the United States from concentration camps after the war, they were housed, by HIAS, the Hebrew Immigrant Aid Society, in an inexpensive hotel. Only one person visited them and showed an interest in their welfare — Reb Shraga Feivel, who offered them positions in the Mesivta.

As unconcerned as he was with his own physical needs, Reb Shraga Feivel was extremely attentive to those of his students. If

---

16. Rabbi Hershel Mashinsky.

he saw that a certain boy at Camp Mesivta was particularly frail or pale, he would insist that he remain for an extra session of the camp, whether or not he could afford to pay. He did not let weaker boys fast on minor fast days, and was known to occasionally send a *masmid* (exceptionally diligent student) to the graduate division in rural Monsey, New York, for ten days of more relaxed learning in the country.[17] Catching one *masmid* learning under a tree at Camp Mesivta, rather than playing baseball with the rest of his bunk, Reb Shraga Feivel scolded, "Did you come here for that?"[18]

> He made it a point to know the financial situation of every student. Someone who is now one of the leading philanthropists in the Orthodox Jewish world was a young student in Torah Vodaath during the Depression, and he suffered real want. Reb Shraga Feivel knew that the boy's father had passed away and that the family had no money. "Before he would talk to me about an afternoon *chavrusa*," he remembers today, "he always made sure that I had eaten a filling lunch. The memory of how he always asked me about my mother and the situation at home left an impression that time has not erased." Prior to Yom Tov one year, Reb Shraga Feivel gave needy *talmidim* money to buy new suits. When one of them protested that he had never given him money before, Reb Shraga Feivel replied, "Until now your father was working."

Reb Shraga Feivel taught his students that a Jew has to look for better ways to do acts of *chesed* (kindness) just as he has to look for new accomplishments in his Gemara learning, and he himself exemplified this effort. Before Pesach, he would arrange with clothing manufacturers, such as Berman and Feinerman, and in later years Lester Udell, to supply Yom Tov suits for poor boys. Realizing that

---

17. Rabbi Shmuel Mendlowitz.
18. Dr. Jerry Fink.

the boys would feel uncomfortable if they were sent to pick up the suits themselves, he went with them.[19]

Students' problems were his own. Meilach Silber came to America as a refugee in 1939, and made the long daily commute from the Bronx to the Mesivta. Shortly after the family's arrival, Meilach's father was hospitalized, and the boy would stop every morning at Mount Sinai Hospital, on his way to the Mesivta, to bring his father kosher food. The commute and the stop resulted in his being late to the Mesivta a number of days in a row. The first two times that Reb Shraga Feivel chastised him, Silber said nothing. But the third day, he broke down and told Reb Shraga Feivel about his father's illness and the family's other problems. Reb Shraga Feivel dissolved in tears when he realized the pressures under which the young boy was laboring. He immediately wanted to know: What do you need? What can I get you? Rabbi Silber, who went on to become the respected principal of the Yeshivah of Eastern Parkway, always attributed the inspiration for his decision to enter *chinuch* to Reb Shraga Feivel's concern with every aspect of his situation.[20]

During Reb Shraga Feivel's reign at Torah Vodaath, tuition was not a bar to anyone who wanted to learn. One day as he was walking through the hall, he heard the sobbing of a woman in the financial office. Going in to investigate, Reb Shraga Feivel found a woman who had three sons in the yeshivah begging for a tuition reduction. Reb Shraga Feivel signaled to one of those working in the office to follow him out of the room. Once they were outside, he told his assistant, "Let's go see for ourselves how she is living." It was only a few blocks from the Mesivta to the woman's apartment. Knocking on the door, Reb Shraga Feivel and his assistant were admitted to a tiny apartment whose very walls cried out the poverty within. Reb Shraga Feivel stopped only long enough to leave a few dollars on the table.

Back in the Mesivta office, he berated those who refused to grant the tuition reduction. "You are dealing here with *dinei nefashos* (mat-

---

19. Rabbi Alexander Linchner.
20. Yerucham Silber.

ters of life and death). In the time you stood here arguing with her about whether to reduce her tuition from $5 to $3 dollars a month, you could have gone out and collected much larger sums." He instructed the office staff that from then on they were to look favorably upon all requests for tuition reductions.

Reb Shraga Feivel's heart melted at the sight of the survivors who arrived in America after the war. He set up a special class in the yeshivah for a group of boys in their middle-to-late teens who had been cruelly denied any chance to learn during the war. In charge of the class was Rabbi Pinchas Briskman, a *talmid* of the prewar Mirrer Yeshivah. Rabbi Briskman's task was to bring his charges up to the level where they would be able to enter the regular *shiurim* in the yeshivah. One day one of his students asked him a particularly sharp question, and Rabbi Briskman went to share his excitement with Reb Shraga Feivel. Reb Shraga Feivel's face lit up with joy at the news, and he told Reb Briskman, "*Baruch Hashem*, you could not have given me better news than that."

DURING THE DIFFICULT YEAR AND A HALF SPENT RECUPERATING in Liberty, New York, one of Reb Shraga Feivel's resolutions was to

Developing the Individual

spend more time thinking about the life goals of every student and not just concern himself with how they were faring in the Mesivta. The underlying assumption of all his guidance was that each Jew has a particular destiny in life and a specific contribution to make to *Klal Yisrael.* The key was to help each student identify the special qualities with which Hashem imbued him and find the task for which those abilities made him uniquely suited.

In the *Zichronos* section of Mussaf of Rosh Hashanah we say, "The remembrance of every created thing passes before You, the deeds of a man (מַעֲשֵׂה אִישׁ) and his appointed task (וּפְקוּדָתוֹ)." From this we see, Reb Shraga Feivel taught, that we are judged on two scales: one according to our performance of mitzvos — מַעֲשֵׂה אִישׁ — and one according to whether we have fulfilled the task for which we were uniquely created — וּפְקוּדָתוֹ. And it is by no means certain, he would add, that the first judgment is more severe than the second. Even if our slate of *aveiros* (transgressions) is relatively clean, we can still expect a strict judgment if we have not fulfilled the purpose for which we were created.

A classic example, he said, is Navos HaCarmeli, a righteous man who met a terrible end at the hands of the wicked King Achav and Queen Ezevel. *Yalkut Shimoni* attributes his fate to the fact that he neglected his mission. He had a beautiful voice and would lead the prayers in Jerusalem on every festival. One festival, without good cause, he did not go to Jerusalem, thereby interrupting his practice of glorifying God's Name and disappointing the throngs who longed to be inspired by his prayers. Reb Shraga Feivel summarized, "When you are not fulfilling the task for which you were created, you have missed your *raison d'etre*."

He forced each student to think hard about what he should be doing with his life and to focus on himself as an individual. He once asked one of the older students in the Mesivta what he intended to do after leaving the Mesivta. The student had heard Reb Shraga Feivel say so many times that the battleground for the future of American Jewry was the field of Jewish education, that without much thought, he answered, "*Chinuch.*"

Reb Shraga Feivel was unimpressed with the response, which he correctly saw as an attempt to please him, not based on any serious reflection. He pointed out to the young man that teaching is a career for which one must prepare himself. In the course of the conversation, Reb Shraga Feivel asked the *talmid* whether he was good with his hands. Assured that he was, he advised him to become a *shochet* or a *mohel*. "You are a *y'rei Shamayim*," Reb Shraga Feivel told him, "and there is a shortage of such *shochtim*."

He was constantly on the lookout for talent that needed nurturing. One year during the Purim festivities, he discovered that one of the students was gifted at expressing deep ideas in rhymes. Reb Shraga Feivel was eager to find out the precise extent of the student's writing talent and asked him to compose a Hebrew essay for him. Many months later, after a class on *Akdamos*, Reb Shraga Feivel launched into a discussion with that student of the brilliant poets who had once graced *Klal Yisrael* and how our talent for poetry, along with other aesthetic sensibilities, had been drained by the prolonged *galus*. He then told him, "I read your essay with great joy. You have a real talent for writing. But alas, who in our day can write a poem like *Akdamos*?" The very comparison to the author of *Akdamos* — even one weighted so heavily in favor of its author, Rabbi Meir ben Yitzchak of Worms — indicated to the student that he should continue developing his thought and means of expression.[21]

Discovering someone's talent was not enough; the means had to be found to place it in the service of *Klal Yisrael*. A large part of the original conception of Torah Umesorah[22] was to harness the widest possible array of talents on behalf of Torah education: the artistry of Berl Merling; the writing talent of Charles Wengrovsky; the organizational skills and dedication of Sender Gross and Bernard Goldenberg. Yiddel Turner came to the Mesivta after having already been a violinist with the Philadelphia Philharmonic. Reb Shraga Feivel did not permit him to give up his violin just because he had come to learn Torah, and he frequently asked Turner to play for him. In time, Turner used his musical genius to form one of the first successful Orthodox wedding bands.

Not only did Reb Shraga Feivel develop in his *talmidim* talent that was already apparent, he uncovered latent, undiscovered abilities. Given how critical he could be, both with respect to himself and others, some saw it as a paradox that so many of his students had the strength to go out into the unsown wilderness that was America in the 1940's to found day schools and other Torah institutions.[23] Yet the paradox was more apparent than real. True, he was quick to show his annoyance to any expression of conceit; he was wont to respond, "*Die vas blozzen fun zich* (those who blow their own horn) ...*"

---

21. Rabbi Avraham Abba Freedman.

The student in question was Rabbi Moshe Wolfson, today *mashgiach* of Torah Vodaath, who has a poetic feel for language and is the author of many works of *hashkafah*.

22. See Chapter 25 below.

23. Rabbi Shubert Spero.

But at the same time, he built up his students with the sense that each one of them had a unique task in life that Hashem had assigned to him alone. Moreover, he so fired them with enthusiasm to do something for *Klal Yisrael* that questions of whether they had the necessary talents for a particular job faded into the background.

Their humility served his *talmidim* well in many difficult situations. Because the goal of building Torah was always paramount, they were content in positions where the potential for accomplishment outweighed their paltry salaries. "Our students always think that they deserve less than they are offered," Reb Shraga Feivel once commented, "and as a consequence they are always happy with what they are given. The main thing for them is that Torah grow and be glorified."[24]

Concern for the future of his *talmidim* also meant attending to practical issues of how they would earn a living. He tried to find careers that would provide a sufficient livelihood for a family, leave time for learning, and not require compromises in their *Yiddishkeit*. For a short period of time, he even had some diamond-cutting machines brought into the Mesivta so that students could learn the trade. And when teaching diamond-cutting on the premises proved impractical, he personally raised for some students the $1,000 needed for an apprenticeship as a diamond cutter.[25] Another time, early in the history of the Mesivta, his son-in-law Rabbi Sender Linchner recalls with amusement, he became enamored of bricklaying as a trade. He pointed out that bricklaying was honest labor that would not drain all a person's mental energies and leave him too tired to learn at the end of the day. And the strong bricklayers union insured a decent livelihood.[26]

When older students confronted important life decisions, it was usually Reb Shraga Feivel whom they consulted. Not only did he

---

24. Elimelech Terebelo.

25. Yonah Zev Herskowitz.

26. Bricklaying was in those days seasonal labor from which one could earn enough in a few months to live for the rest of year, which could then be spent in learning. *Rabbi Nesanel Quinn.*

know them better than anyone else, it was he who was primarily responsible for shaping their worldview. One of the outstanding students of the Mesivta lost his father at a young age, and, in order to support his family, he took a job as the principal of an afternoon Talmud Torah. After his first year in that position his mother and older sister urged him to return to full-time Torah learning, even though the family was still poor. The young man was loath to let his mother and siblings depend on the sister's earnings for their support. Reb Shraga Feivel agreed with the mother and sister; if his Torah was so important to them he should accede to their entreaties.

On the other hand, he was disturbed to see the wife of one of his students loaded down with packages and leading two small tots behind her because she did not want to ask her husband for help and thereby take him away from his Torah studies. "One has to know when yes and when no," he would say on such occasions. He advised all newlywed students to learn at home at night rather than leave their wives alone.

Even on those rare occasions when a student did not seek his advice, he did not wait to be asked for his opinion. He once learned that a certain *shidduch* had been suggested to one of his students. Though the student had not asked his opinion, as most did in similar circumstances, Reb Shraga Feivel did not wait to be asked before voicing his disapproval; his feeling of responsibility for his *talmidim* did not permit him to stand on etiquette where he saw a danger to a *talmid*.

THE LOVE THAT DEVELOPED BETWEEN REB SHRAGA FEIVEL AND his students over a period of years thus had nothing of the superficial about it, but it was that much deeper for not being given easy expression. It took some students years to discover his deep, even passionate love for them. As a student in the Mesivta, Rabbi Moshe Aharon Stern once overheard a telephone conversation in which Reb Shraga Feivel was describing a *talmid*. The effusion of warmth and love in his description took Rabbi Stern completely by surprise since the students were not used to hearing those kind of words directly from him.

Bonds of Love

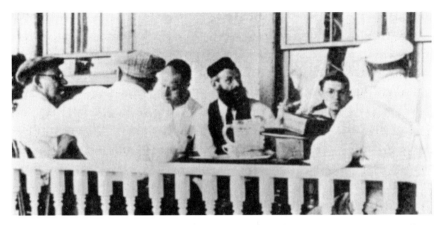

Reb Shraga Feivel convalescing in Liberty

A letter written during his time of confinement in Liberty to a student on the eve of his marriage captures the bonds of love joining him to his students:

> My beloved dear one, who is bound to me very deeply in the recesses of my heart. I am permitting myself to describe to you how powerful is my desire to rejoice with you and to cause you to rejoice at your *simchah*. I do not exaggerate when I tell you how many years I have waited and longed for this moment and how many times I have pictured in my mind's eye how I would dance in front of you at your wedding.
>
> But "many are the thoughts of men" . . . This too [i.e., my inability to come] is no doubt also for the good. But know, my dear friend, that it is only my three-dimensional body, bound by the constraints of time and space, that will not be with you. My soul, unconstrained by distance and above all time and space, the true "I," which is joined to you with all its might, will have a large share in your *simchah*.[27]

27. Reb Shraga Feivel concluded the letter with an invitation to the *chasan* and *kallah* to visit him, together with some *bachurim* from the Mesivta, during the week of *sheva berachos* so that he could prepare for them a "meal like that of Shlomo HaMelech in his time."

Reb Shraga Feivel once came to the *chasunah* (wedding) of a close *talmid* directly from a meeting of Vaad Hatzalah devoted to descriptions of the ghastly conditions in the concentration camps and ghettos of Eastern Europe. Profound grief was etched on his face. As he stood there immersed in his thoughts, the *chasan* came over and said, "*Rebbi*, you told me so many times, 'My rejoicing will reach up to the Heavens at your *chasunah*.' " Reb Shraga Feivel's face underwent an immediate transformation, and he began dancing until he had no more strength to stand.[28]

His *talmidim* fully reciprocated his love for them. Those closest to him credited him with everything they were or would ever be. In their eyes, he had done nothing less than fashion their spiritual beings. Even those who seemed to hold themselves aloof from his embrace nevertheless felt themselves to be his products. Rabbi Moshe Aharon Stern recalls being astonished one Simchas Torah when one of the *talmidim* who had appeared resistant to Reb Shraga Feivel's approach suddenly started showering him with kisses after a few drinks.

---

28. Rabbi Mannes Mandel.

Chapter 14

Know What to Answer

O NE OF THE MOST IMPORTANT GIFTS REB SHRAGA
Feivel gave his students was the intellectual where-
withal to deal with the challenges posed to tradition
by *Haskalah*, the so-called Enlightenment, and modern
science. Though he had no secular education other than what he
gleaned from his reading, he was acutely sensitive to the questions
that might trouble intellectually curious modern youth.[1] He did not
give *shiurim* dealing specifically with such issues as evolution, Bible
criticism, and the age of the universe, but the *shiurim* he gave in classical texts often included material relevant to these and similar
topics.

While still in Hungary, Reb Shraga Feivel began preparing himself to address such issues, which played a large role in the
development of German Reform. Reb Shraga Feivel did not un-

---

1. Rabbi Shubert Spero.

derestimate the powerful pull of the Enlightenment, especially for those who had grown up in a society based on its assumptions — e.g., individual autonomy, the inevitability of human progress, and human reason as the arbiter of faith and morality. And he girded himself for battle with a careful study of the Orthodox thinkers who had preceded him into the fray.

In crafting his response, he turned first to the works of Rabbi Samson Raphael Hirsch, which constitute the most comprehensive presentation of Judaism in a modern idiom and are addressed to Jews for whom the Enlightenment is an integral part of their intellectual baggage. The entire Hirschian *oeuvre* cannot be appreciated without an understanding of how deeply and in what ways the Age of Reason had undermined the old bastions of faith.[2]

Dr. Nathan Birnbaum

Among the modern Jewish authors he read and recommended to others were Dr. Nathan Birnbaum, Dr. Isaac Breuer, Rabbi David Zvi Hoffman, and Aharon Marcus. Significantly, each of these thinkers was either born or spent most of his life in Germany, where the Enlightenment made its earliest inroads among the Jewish population; each of them lived on the cusp between modernity and tradition; each of them addressed, in one way or another, issues

Dr. Isaac Breuer

---

2. See Dr. I. Grunfeld's excellent introduction to Rabbi Hirsch's *Horeb* for a full treatment of this subject.

raised by the confrontation between the two; and some of them had pursued a tortuous road in their personal search for a path as Jews in the modern world.

Dr. Nathan Birnbaum, for instance, was a modern-day Yisro, who played a major leadership role in many of the late 19th- and early 20th-century secular Jewish movements, prior to returning to the faith of his fathers.[3] His *Confession* (originally named *Gottesvolk*) was a clarion call to Jews to awaken to the revolutionary nature of Judaism and to join together in the battle against paganism in its modern guise. *Gottesvolk* urged a reawakened consciousness of the Jewish people's Messianic task of sanctifying themselves and the world.[4] Isaac Breuer was Rabbi Hirsch's grandson, as well as one of the leading ideologues of Agudath Israel. At the same time, he was a neo-Kantian thinker whose *Neue Kuzari* appropriated many of Kant's insights in the service of Judaism. Reb Shraga Feivel admired Breuer's term "meta-history," which describes God's control of historical events in the service of His ultimate goal. Rabbi David Zvi Hoffman, head of the Hildesheimer Seminary in Berlin, took the leading role in responding to the so-called "Bible critics." His commentaries to *Bereishis, Vayikra,* and *Devarim* constitute perhaps the most systematic refutation of their theories. Aharon Marcus was born in Germany and studied philosophy at university. While still a young man, he traveled to Eastern Europe where he became a Radomsker chassid. His *Chassidismus* sought to convey something of the spirit of Chassidism to German Jews raised in a very different tradition,

---

3. In 1883, a decade before the Jewish world had heard of Herzl, Birnbaum founded the journal *Self-Emancipation* devoted to spreading the idea of a resurgent Jewish nationalism. Twenty years later, having become convinced that Eastern European Jewry was the repository of all that was most vital in Jewish culture, he founded *Der Weg* (The Way) to promote outstanding Yiddish writers. Shortly after the founding of Agudath Israel, he was appointed general secretary of the movement.

4. See Editor's Introduction to Dr. Birnbaum's *Confession*, the first volume published in the Jewish Pocket Book Series of the Agudath Israel Youth Council of America in 1946.

and, as such, was equally relevant to American-born students of the Mesivta.[5]

Reb Shraga Feivel considered Rabbi Hoffman's works important in preparing students for דַע מַה שֶׁתָּשִׁיב לְאֶפִּיקוֹרוֹס, *Know what to respond to a heretic* (*Pirkei Avos* 2:19). The other three produced important classics in Jewish thought. He quoted Rabbi Meir Don Plotzki, the great Polish *rav*, who said that Nosson Birnbaum's *daas Torah* was comparable to that of anyone he knew.

Confronting Challenges Head On

REB SHRAGA FEIVEL WAS EXCEPTIONALLY OPEN TO QUESTIONS; he encouraged his students to bring him the problems raised by their secular reading rather than let them fester. When he was living in Monsey, a group of Mesivta students drove up every Sunday for a *shiur* in *Kuzari*. In one of those *shiurim*, Reb Shraga Feivel mentioned the metaphor of "the ocean of life" used by Rabbi Yehudah HaLevi. Jack Klausner, one of those present, recalled having seen the same expression in the writing of the British biologist J.B.S. Haldane, and he wondered whether Haldane was using it in the same fashion. After class he mentioned Haldane to Reb Shraga Feivel, and the latter told him to bring the book with him the next week. Reb Shraga Feivel kept the book for several weeks before returning it to Klausner with the comment that Haldane's usage paralleled that of the *Kuzari*.[6]

Klausner would ask Reb Shraga Feivel many questions based on his scientific reading. For instance, both carbon dating and the fact

---

5. Reb Shraga Feivel not only recommended these authors to others, he continued to study them himself. His student Yonah Zev Herskowitz occasionally visited him in his home. One time, Reb Shraga Feivel was reading *Chassidismus* and another time studying Rabbi David Zvi Hoffman's Biblical commentary.

6. Reb Shraga Feivel was not always so responsive to students' queries. If he felt the student was not genuinely interested in understanding the Torah viewpoint on the issue under discussion, but rather in flaunting his independence of mind, he could be very curt.

One time a small group of students who prided themselves on their knowledge of philosophy presented him with a number of questions that had arisen in the course of their studies. He responded sharply and refused to engage in any discussion of the issues with them.

Given his vast knowledge of all aspects of Jewish thought, he could easily have answered their challenge, but he felt that an angry response would do more to make that we can observe light from stars millions of light years away suggest that the universe is far older than according to our *Mesorah* (Torah tradition). Many solutions are given to this apparent discrepancy, but Reb Shraga Feivel sensed that Klausner did not find any of them completely satisfactory. Finally he told him, "There is no verse that does not apply in every generation, and in the section dealing with the false prophet it says that the false prophet will, in fact, produce a sign or wonder (*Devarim* 13:2). For you, carbon dating is such a sign or wonder. But then the Torah tells us that, on the basis of those signs and wonders, the false prophet will say, 'Let us follow other gods that you did not know and we shall worship them.' About this attempt to lure us into the worship of false gods we are warned, 'Do not hearken to the words of that prophet … for Hashem, your G-d, is testing you' (ibid. v. 3)." Having been shown on many other occasions how the Torah addressed problems raised by scientific theories, Klausner found that his faith was not affected by them at all.[7]

The reason why the A-mighty created such problems of faith, Reb Shraga Feivel explained, was to allow room for freedom of choice. If questions of faith were not to exist, then belief in a Creator would be so obvious and logical that it would be imperative.

---

them realize the danger of the path upon which they were embarking. (He subsequently confided to others who were present that their queries were easily answered.) In *Pirkei Avos* (2:19), he said, we are taught: "Know what to answer an *apikorus.*" The *Tanna,* however, refrains from revealing the content of that answer because he did not consider it fit to print. With an *apikorus,* the *Tanna* is teaching us that we have to know not only *what* to answer but *how* to answer — i.e., in as sharp a fashion as possible. *Rabbi Eliyahu Yehoshua Geldzhaler.*

7. That particular insight of Reb Shraga Feivel was one of those that has remained with Klausner for over fifty years. On another occasion, Reb Shraga Feivel showed him what he considered the Torah's most nearly explicit mention of the eternity of the soul. After prescribing death by stoning for one who offers up his child to Molech, Hashem adds, "I shall concentrate My attention upon that man, and I shall cut him off from among his people" (*Vayikra* 20:2-3). This cutting off refers to the destruction of the soul, not to a punishment in this world, for two verses later, Hashem once again states that He will concentrate His attention upon the perpetrator if *beis din* fails to act. Since the second verse refers to Hashem acting in lieu of *beis din,* which metes out corporal punishment, the first verse can refer only to a spiritual punishment, i.e., excision of the perpetrator's eternal soul.

Rabbi Shlomo Rotenberg in the 1950's

Reb Shraga Feivel not only grappled with the questions that his *talmidim* brought to him, he made sure that they would be able to answer those of others. Around the same time that Bais Medrash Elyon opened in Monsey, Reb Shraga Feivel brought to Monsey another group of twelve students.[8] The program he designed for them was in some sense a continuation of the earlier *Aish Dos.*[9] A number of those chosen for this program had spent some time in college — usually in night school while learning during the day in the Mesivta — and virtually all had shown talents that suggested they were well suited to careers as educators or as *klal* activists.

During their little more than a year in Monsey, Reb Shraga Feivel exposed them to a wide range of classes. He devoted much of his own time to this group. Rabbi Zelik Epstein was their *rebbi* for Gemara. In addition, he brought in Rabbi Shlomo Rotenberg to teach them Jewish history, Rabbi Mordechai Schwab to teach the works of Rabbi Samson Raphael Hirsch, Rabbi Samson Raphael Weiss to teach *hashkafah*, Rabbi Zelig Fortman and Rabbi Pinchas Teitz to teach homiletics, and Rabbi Hershel Leiman to lecture on pedagogy.

Rabbi Hershel Leiman

One Sunday, toward the end of the students' time in Monsey, Reb Shraga Feivel brought out a Conservative spokesman to speak to the students. He wanted to see if they were capable of refuting his arguments. When the man's presentation was finished, Reb

8. Among the members of this group were Sidney Greenwald, Jack Klausner, Chaim Meir Listoken, Hershel Mashinsky, Berel Schwartz, Shubert Spero, Moshe Weitman, and Moshe Wolfson.

9. See Chapter 24 below.

Shraga Feivel told his *talmidim* to respond to his arguments. He just sat there with his arms folded across his chest as the debate ensued, and he was not disappointed by the way his students defended their position.[10]

Reb Shraga Feivel never denied that wisdom was to be found among the nations. His efforts to limit the reading of his students did not stem from narrow-mindedness. On the contrary, there were students to whom he recommended scientific books and even works of psychology. He felt that with sufficient guidance, knowledge of the wonders of creation and of the depths of the human psyche could be of great value to certain students.[11]

Rather than stifle his students' intellectual curiosity, he redirected it. He once noticed that one of the younger boys in the Mesivta spent his Fridays haunting the Jewish bookstores of the Lower East Side. In those days, these bookstores were largely frequented by *maskilim*. Reb Shraga Feivel was concerned that the boy's interest in Jewish history would lead him to the modern Jewish historians whose findings he would be ill equipped to refute. His fears were confirmed one day when he asked him what he read in the bookstores. The boy replied that he read mostly the history works of Jewish historians who wrote from a secular point of view, and with much misinterpretation and distortion. Reb Shraga Feivel took $25 out of his pocket and told him to purchase a set of the works of Zev Yavetz instead.[12]

---

10. Jack Klausner.

The Jewish Theological Seminary was a lure for some of the career-minded yeshivah students in those days. Many, if not most, of the students at JTS came from Orthodox homes, and the lines of demarcation between JTS and Orthodoxy were far less clearly delineated than they are today. To many seeking a career in the rabbinate, the Conservative movement seemed the wave of the future. In many Orthodox shuls, the only people in attendance were women and older men, but few if any young people, while the Conservative movement was attracting first- and second-generation Americans. *Sidney Greenwald* and *Jack Klausner*.

11. Sidney Greenwald.

12. Rabbi Bernard Goldenberg.

FOLLOWING MANY YEARS WHEN TORAH VODAATH STUDENTS did not attend college, some students broke ranks after 1940. The vast

Dealing With College

array of *shiurim* that he taught in the late afternoon were, in part, an effort to show the students that whatever intellectual stimulation they might find in a college philosophy course could be found in the classic Jewish texts, and that the riches of the Torah far surpassed whatever they could gain in secular institutions.[13] He countered college classes in philosophy and psychology with *Kuzari, Moreh Nevuchim,* and *Nefesh HaChaim.*[14]

In this approach, he was following the path laid out by Rabbi Yisrael Salanter, the founder of the *Mussar* movement almost a century earlier. He realized that *Haskalah* (Enlightenment) could not be fought with bans and prohibitions; it had to be opposed with an even more powerful spiritual force from within Judaism. The words of Rabbi Yechiel Yaakov Weinberg describing Rabbi Yisrael Salanter's approach apply with equal force to Reb Shraga Feivel:

> Rejection of the secular *Haskalah* is not enough . . . It is the nature of a new cultural trend to seep in through small crevices. Fighting it with prohibitions and excommunications alone will not stem the tide, for the spirit of man is not to be stemmed by mere force.
>
> The suppression of the spirit in itself is of no value. It cuts short spiritual development and results in but a spiritual sterility. *The sole defense against a cultural movement breaking in from the outside is the establishment of an opposing cultural force, and the opening of doors to a fresh trend of thought, stemming from the very depth of our Jewish soul* (emphasis added).[15]

Reb Shraga Feivel did not sever his ties with students who went to college, most of whom continued to learn in the Mesivta and attended school at night. Rather he attempted to counteract the effects of the ideas to which they were exposed. He encouraged college stu-

---

13. Yonah Zev Herskowitz.

14. Sidney Greenwald.

15. Rabbi Yechiel Yaakov Weinberg, "The Mussar Movement and Lithuanian Jewry," in *Men of the Spirit,* Rabbi Leo Jung, ed., p. 243.

dents to share with him what they had learned so that he could show them the Torah perspective on the same issues. Reb Shraga Feivel felt that every ideology must contain a germ of truth or it could not exist. What he sought to show his students was how that germ of truth had been distorted.[16]

In the case of individual boys who he was convinced could not handle college, he made every effort to prevent them from attending. He told the boys that when he had learned in Pressburg, one of the best students in the *beis medrash* went to university without in any way changing his dress from what it had been in the yeshivah. When he returned to visit the yeshivah, the *rosh yeshivah* told him that he was the most dangerous of all, because by remaining externally the same he gave the impression that one could go to university and remain a *y'rei Shamayim*. "If you're going to college to earn a living — to be a doctor, lawyer, or accountant — the *frum* world needs these things. But if you are going for an education, you are wasting your time," he told one group of students.[17]

The major reason for his objection to college attendance was that professors sought to propound a way of life contrary to the Torah, and listening to such theories in a classroom atmosphere, where the professor is an authoritative figure, will be harmful to *emunah*. A *talmid* attending college reported that in his professor's first lecture, he asked the class, "How many of you are of the persuasion that this universe has a G–dly Creator?" Out of a class of fifty-five, only two raised their hands. Without comment, the professor continued his lecture. Later in the semester he posed the same question, and only one student had the temerity to raise his hand.

He chose not to place an absolute ban on college,[18] while, at the

---

16. Elias Karp.

17. Rabbi Elias Schwartz.

18. From Rabbi Shlomo Heiman's arrival in 1935 through 1940, students in the Mesivta were not allowed to attend college nor — thanks to the love of learning inculcated by Reb Shlomo — did they wish to go. When Rabbi David Leibowitz left the Mesivta with the *beis medrash* students, Reb Shraga Feivel and Reb Shlomo had to begin from scratch with a small nucleus. That being the case, Reb Shraga Feivel chose to strive for an ideal situation where there would be no outside influences on the Mesivta.

same time, clearly conveying to the students that their decision to go was highly problematic and not one to be undertaken lightly.[19] To have forbidden boys attending college from continuing in the *beis medrash* would, in many cases, have resulted in their leaving the Mesivta and the ultimate loss of Reb Shraga Feivel's influence over them.[20] And there was another danger. He feared that if he told a *talmid* that college was forbidden and he nevertheless went, either due to his own desires or parental pressure, that student would come to view himself as a rebel against Orthodoxy and no longer bound by its rules. Dire predictions that college was the end of one's life as a religious Jew could thereby become self-fulfilling prophecies.[21]

When the pressures to attend college became very strong, he placed certain constraints on those who wished to attend. He would insist that certain boys learn full-time in the *beis medrash* for a period of time before going to college. He told one mother who was pressuring her son to go to college full-time, "You are *shechting* (slaughtering) your son."[22] With some students, he directed their selection of courses: He urged many of his students, for instance, to study German so that they would be able to read Rabbi Samson Raphael Hirsch's works, which were then available only in German.

Reb Shraga Feivel's approach to college was typical of his lifelong method of balancing the optimal against the possible. He always kept before himself a vision of where he was headed, but he did not move faster than the traffic would bear. Another example of this balancing of the ideal and the possible — perhaps trivial in itself — can be seen in his approach to the growing of beards. In his native Hungary, it was common for *yeshivah bachurim* to wear beards, and

---

19. His approach to college was carefully calibrated to the individual student. He told one boy that under no circumstances should he attend. The boy went anyway and did not remain religious. *Jack Klausner.*

20. Rabbi Zelik Epstein.

21. It must also be remembered that the primary threat from college fifty years ago was in the realm of ideas, and these Reb Shraga Feivel felt himself capable of countering and tempering to some extent. Today the liberation from virtually all moral restraints is the primary threat from college, and there is no reason to think that Reb Shraga Feivel's position would remain the same.

22. Rabbi Shubert Spero.

he was once asked why he did not encourage Mesivta students to do the same. He replied that America was not yet ripe, and that *bachurim* with beards would find it difficult to get married.[23]

Nevertheless he personally placed great value on a beard as a distinctive mark of a Jew. As a young man on a train from Hungary to Hamburg, he found himself seated together with a gentile intellectual. The two began to talk, and the gentile was surprised and impressed by Reb Shraga Feivel's breadth of knowledge. Toward the end of the journey, the gentile asked him how as a modern man he could still wear a beard. Reb Shraga Feivel replied that Jews had once been forced to wear a yellow badge as a sign of shame. Only as it dawned on the gentile public that Jews are also human beings entitled to equal rights was this practice gradually abandoned. But, in fact, said Reb Shraga Feivel, Jews *are* different: They are distinguished by their traits of mercy, kindheartedness, and sense of shame — and this inhibits them from sinning. A beard, he concluded, is a sign of a Jew's distinctiveness. The gentile shook his hand and said, "I respect you."[24]

Yet he never made a fetish of a beard or any other external sign. He once pointed at two former students, one of whom had a beard and the other of whom was clean shaven. Of the first he commented, "He absorbed the *chitzonius* (the external) from me"; and of the second, "He absorbed the *penimius* (internal)."[25]

Reb Shraga Feivel had a unique ability to tailor his approach according to the spiritual level of the American students of that generation while making them aware, at the same time, of the ideal. Jack Klausner was one of the group of twelve students for whom Reb Shraga Feivel created a parallel program to Bais Medrash Elyon in Monsey. At home, he had always studied with classical music in the background, and he decided to bring a radio to Monsey. His friends warned him, "Wait and see what the Boss says when he finds out," but being an intrepid young man Klausner decided to

---

23. Rabbi Nesanel Quinn.

24. On another occasion, he went to visit a *talmid chacham* who was very ill. He took the man's hands in his, and told him that if he would promise to stop shaving, his condition would improve.

25. The Admor of Reitzfert.

tell Reb Shraga Feivel before he found out for himself. Reb Shraga Feivel replied, "Yes, a radio. You know in Unsdorf they once found a boy reading a newspaper, and they threw him out."

But the conversation did not end there. Reb Shraga Feivel went on to ask whether Klausner had always listened to a radio at home. Told that he had, Reb Shraga Feivel allowed him to keep the radio, but only on condition that his room did not become a *moshav leitzim* (a gathering place of idlers).

Chapter 15

A Kotzker

"IF I WERE TO CHARACTERIZE MY FATHER-IN-LAW IN one word," said Rabbi Sender Linchner, "I would say he was a Kotzker."[1]

Cheshbon HaNefesh

But this description is incomplete — because Reb Shraga Feivel created a synthesis of Kotzk, Frankfurt, Chasam Sofer, and Bobov.

Kotzk rejected indulgence in material pursuits, such as amassing money, seeking comfort, eating gluttonously, taking pride, and pursuing fame.

The Kotzker Rebbe demanded from his followers complete immersion in Torah study and *avodas Hashem*, and that they take from the world only the barest necessities. Whoever did not fit this pat-

---

1. A reference to Rabbi Menachem Mendel Morgenstern, the Kotzker Rebbe, famed for his pithy profundity. He was the *Rebbe* and peer of Rabbi Yitzchak Meir Alter, the Chiddushei HaRim, founder of the Gerrer dynasty, and the Rebbe and father-in-law of the Avnei Nezer, founder of the Sochatchov dynasty. He attracted brilliant people and his disciples included many descendants of the greatest Torah scholars of the preceding generation, including Rabbi Leibel Eiger, grandson of Rabbi Akiva Eiger; the grandson of Rabbi Aryeh Heller, the Ketzos HaChoshen; and the son-in-law of Rabbi Yaakov Lorberbaum of Lisa, the Nesivos HaMishpat.

tern was not admitted to his circle of chassidim.

From Frankfurt, Reb Shraga Feivel adopted self-discipline and consistency. Like the Chasam Sofer, Reb Shraga Feivel would not compromise on matters of principle and religion, and he advocated complete renunciation of relations with the Conservative and Reform movements.

From Bobov and others he adopted cordial and pleasant interpersonal relations.

These constitute the creed of Reb Shraga Feivel. He wanted no money — how could he accumulate money when others were in need?

He wanted no honors — honors tend to make a person self-centered rather than being oriented *l'shem Shamayim* (for the sake of Heaven). He avoided indulgence in physical comforts — these might prompt one to escape from strenuous effort *l'shem Shamayim*.

His doctrine was to allow absolutely no compromise of halachah in public and private life, to value Torah learning above money and renown, to maintain genuine humility, and to be actively involved in helping people in need.

Reb Shraga Feivel lived with the times. His normal disposition was one of joy and good humor. But when faced by a suffering person he was all grief and even moved to tears. In the time of lament over the *churban Beis HaMikdash, churban* Yerushalayim, and tragedies of *Klal Yisrael*, he melted away in tears and sobs, like a bereaved person.

Reb Shraga Feivel defined the basis of Kotzker Chassidus (chassidic thought) as the recognition that all that a person possesses, all his talents, all his achievements, are solely by the grace of Providence. In this description of the Kotzker, one hears a description of Reb Shraga Feivel himself. He explained the commandment to love Hashem with all one's soul to mean that a person should subdue his natural inclination to feel self-sufficient. Rather, he should realize that his very being, as well as the entire universe, is the creation of Hashem, Who continuously gives us life, might, and understanding. All our successes are because of His Providential help.

The Kotzker Rebbe was justly famed for his uncompromising honesty with himself, and the same could be said of Reb Shraga

Feivel. "What is the most important thing in life?" he asked his *talmidim*. "It's *cheshbon* — to judge honestly if one is living up to one's own potential."[2] That remark reveals the quality of *emes* (truth) that underlay every aspect of his personality. For him, honesty did not mean merely being truthful and avoiding fraud. It meant subjecting himself to an unrelenting and uncompromising scrutiny.

A student once asked him what works of *mussar* he should study. Reb Shraga Feivel's reply was a surprise. A *mussar sefer*, he said, can help, but "true *mussar* is that which one gives to oneself." *Mussar* works can point out the evasions and self-deceptions to which we are all prey, but the real work lies in an honest evaluation of oneself and one's actions.[3] He would say that a *mussar sefer* should be studied with two eyes, one in the *sefer* and the other on the learner himself.[4]

The Torah, said Rabbi Samson Raphael Hirsch, is Divine anthropology: It teaches us how man and his world look through the eyes of his Creator. And that is how Reb Shraga Feivel judged himself — not according to the standards of the world or by comparison to others — but through Hashem's eyes. From the Torah's point of view, the material world is the most fleeting of way-stations on the road to eternity. Reb Shraga Feivel's loathing of luxury and his incredulity at the energy spent on its pursuit is but one reflection of the extent to which he had adopted that perspective. His unfathomable humility was another. He acknowledged and honored any good quality he observed in another, but his own considerable talents he regarded as an unearned gift from Heaven, for which he deserved no credit. After one of his children was happily married, he exclaimed, "The A-mighty has now paid me for all I have done. Now I must start from scratch!"

---

2. Chinn, "Ohr Shraga," p. 7.
3. Yaakov Michoel Jacobs.
4. Rabbi Nesanel Quinn.

OF ALL THE *AVEIROS* (TRANSGRESSIONS) IN THE TORAH, TAUGHT
Rebbe Simchah Bunim of P'shis'cha, falsehood is the only one from

Far From Falsehood which we are specifically enjoined to *distance* ourselves (see *Shemos* 23:7). And of all the forms of falsehood none is so hard to avoid as self-deception,
for every man "is close to [i.e., loves] himself," and is apt to justify
even his errors. Reb Shraga Feivel fought to maintain his objectivity
and to remove any personal interest from his decisions.

As *menahel* of the Mesivta, he strictly avoided any trace of nepotism and never gave a position of any kind to one of his sons or
sons-in-law. When his son-in-law Rabbi Yitzchak Karpf was appointed a *maggid shiur* in the Mesivta, Reb Shraga Feivel felt
compelled to assure his students that he had not been involved in
the appointment.[5] Toward the end of his life, he asked that his son
Shmuel not receive any preferential treatment regarding admission
to the *kollel* of Bais Medrosh Elyon.[6]

In the spring of 1933, shortly after the birth of his first child, Reb
Shraga Feivel's oldest son, Moshe Yitzchak, lost his job and was left

At the wedding of Rabbi Yitzchak Karpf to Reb Shraga Feivel's daughter

---

5. Rabbi Yaakov Michoel Jacobs.
6. Rabbi Yaakov Leshinsky.

without any means of support. With no money for rent, he and his family had no choice but to accept the offer of a room from the Globinger family, which owned a farm in Connecticut. While living there, Moshe Yitzchak learned that one of the *rebbis* in the elementary school of Torah Vodaath was about to resign. He hitchhiked to New York and asked his father to speak on his behalf to Rabbi David Stern, the principal of the elementary school. But Reb Shraga Feivel refused on the grounds that Rabbi Stern might feel obligated to favor his son over other candidates. Moshe Yitzchak was forced to go to Rabbi Stern himself, and, as it turned out, he did not obtain the position.

At the wedding of Rabbi Yitzchak Karpf to Reb Shraga Feivel's Daughter

A *talmid* once asked Reb Shraga Feivel for a letter of recommendation for a rabbinic position, and even provided him with an already composed letter for his signature. After reading the letter, which contained exaggerated praise of the student, Reb Shraga

Rabbi David Stern

Feivel said he could not sign it. The student protested that he needed the letter only to show to the directors of the synagogue and promised to tear it up immediately afterwards. "No one will know," he told Reb Shraga Feivel. "But I will know," was Reb Shraga Feivel's curt reply.

His refusal to have an expense account is another good example of how scrupulous he was on any issue concerning himself personally. After an evening of raising funds for Torah Vodaath, he usually went home by subway, and on the rare occasions when he took a taxi, he paid for it out of his own money, without ever asking to be reimbursed by Torah Vodaath.[7]

Reb Shraga Feivel pointed out to his students that in the Ne'ilah service on Yom Kippur we pray that no "foreign money" should come into our hands, and he was scrupulous in this regard.[8] He once went to a certain wealthy donor in an attempt to raise money for a poor chasan and kallah (bride and groom). The donor seemed surprised by the request, and pointed out to Reb Shraga Feivel that he had just given him $1,500 a few months earlier. Reb Shraga Feivel was shocked by the response: He quickly deduced that someone whom he had asked to secure a personal loan on his behalf had instead solicited an outright gift from this donor. He was devastated by the realization that personal gifts had been sought on his behalf, and insisted on paying the man back immediately. He refused to even consider the man's offer to apply the $1,500 to a gift for the poor couple.[9]

Gezel (theft), Reb Shraga Feivel taught, is not limited to stealing money from someone or defrauding him. In the Yom Kippur vidui (confession), he explained, we have to know that included in the category of not accepting help under false pretenses is receiving any form of support from the yeshivah and not learning properly. Money is donated to the yeshivah to support Torah learning, and if the condition of its gift is not fulfilled, then accepting the support is not honest.

---

7. Rabbi Nesanel Quinn.

8. The care they both showed with regard to monetary matters was one of the reasons that Reb Shraga Feivel and Rabbi Yaakov Kamenetsky felt such a strong natural affinity for one another. On Reb Yaakov's scrupulousness in this regard, see Reb Yaakov, pp. 342-349.

9. Rabbi Yaakov Leshinsky.

He could be caustic about the exaggerated praises that have become so much a part of common parlance. Hearing someone referred to as a "*gaon amiti* (true genius)," he was likely to ask, "As opposed to what — a false *gaon*?"

Rejection of Luxury

IN HIS AVERSION TO ALL FORMS OF LUXURY, REB SHRAGA FEIVEL self-consciously patterned himself after Rebbe Chaim of Sanz, the Divrei Chaim, who once said, "If I were to hear that one of my children was pursuing luxuries, I could not live with it."[10] The cupboard in the Mendlowitz house was never filled, and Mrs. Mendlowitz never saw a full weekly salary — much of it had already been given away by the time Reb Shraga Feivel reached home. The Mendlowitz family lived according to the Chida's comment on the Mishnah in *Pirkei Avos* (1:5), "Let the poor be members of your household": The Chida would interpret homiletically: Let the members of your family be poor — teach them to live frugally, so you will have money to spend on holy things and to help those less fortunate.

The mixture of scorn and pity on his face whenever he saw Jews involved in the pursuit of the pleasures of this world said more than any words. He viewed the pursuit of luxury as the most obvious sign of an excessive attachment to the physical world. One Erev Rosh Hashanah, he published in *Dos Yiddishe Licht* an analysis of the pernicious effects of being too bound to the material world:

> What yesterday was a luxury has today become a necessity. This attitude places a financial strain on a person that might adversely affect his capacity to perform mitzvos and *chesed*. The average person is not able to live without an excess of material possessions. Such a person must earn all his knowledge of the world by painstakingly climbing the ladder of knowledge rung by rung. And there is a limit to how high he

---

10. Gross and Kaminetsky, p. 569.

will ever reach. But those who succeed in disentangling themselves from the material world are capable of reaching extraordinary insights in a flash, beyond their normal capacity.

To overindulge in sensual pleasures, says the *Sefer HaChinuch*, is to set up an obstruction between oneself and what is spiritual and sacred.

Reb Shraga Feivel found no time for irrelevant pastimes; life is momentous, and to waste time is to waste life. He advised his married students not to follow the prevailing American custom of making the largest room in the house the living room. Instead, prominence should go to the dining room. The living room, he noted, is a place for leaning back in an easy chair and relaxing with the newspaper, and if it is the central room in the house, reading the newspaper will become the central activity. The dining room, by contrast, is a place where one learns at the table with his children or *chavrusa*, and where the family gathers together for Shabbos and Yom Tov meals.[11]

He harbored the deepest suspicions about the corrupting influence of money, suspicions that he transmitted to his closest *talmidim*. Rabbi Yosef Levitan once tutored a boy privately for an extended period, and out of gratitude the boy's parents sent him a large gift of money. He promptly sent the money back together with a letter explaining his response. In that letter, we can clearly discern Reb Shraga Feivel himself speaking:

> I must beg of you a thousand pardons for my return of the money ... But I could not forget the words of my master and teacher, Reb Shraga Feivel Mendlowitz: "Anyone who hopes to be successful in transmitting our heritage to his students must be completely pure of any desire other than that his students absorb the Torah into the very fiber of their beings ..." To accept money from you for learning [with your son] would introduce precisely such an interest into my

11. Chinn, "Ohr Shraga," p. 9.

teaching … Reb Shraga Feivel also used to say that a *rebbi* needs special *siyata d'Shamaya* (Heavenly assistance) in order to teach boys in need of special help, and for that he must make himself worthy …

I have often felt guilty about taking money from the yeshivah for teaching Torah, but what can I do since I must feed my family? I have not yet reached the level described by *Chazal:* "If he is worthy, the sustenance will be provided by others."

You know that my only ambition in life has been to learn and teach Torah and to be satisfied with a bare minimum of the pleasures of this world. Material things are not my desire, and I would therefore feel exceedingly guilty about taking money from you . . . I am convinced that *HaKadosh Baruch Hu* is testing me with your generous offer to see if after all these years of learning Torah I am still completely bound to this material world or whether I have the strength to withstand its temptations.[12]

The only real enjoyment Reb Shraga Feivel ever had from money was giving it away. Here, too, the model was the Divrei Chaim, who never retired for the night without having disbursed every penny in the house to the poor.[13] He frequently borrowed money on behalf of

_____

12. Reb Shraga Feivel once said of Rabbi Levitan that all his efforts in establishing the Mesivta were worth it to have produced one Yosef Levitan. Rabbi Levitan first came to the yeshivah from public school just before his bar mitzvah. At that time, he knew nothing more than how to *daven,* and the principal Dr. Stern told him that all the classrooms were crowded and there was no physical place for him in the yeshivah. Yosef countered that he was prepared to sit in the first or second grade, but that he wanted to learn in a yeshivah. Dr. Stern showed him that even in the lower grades there was absolutely no room for an extra desk, but the boy would not be denied. He asked Dr. Stern for a note that he had wanted to come to yeshivah but had been refused. "When I get to *Shamayim* (Heaven), it might turn out that I was supposed to be a big *talmid chacham,*" he told Dr. Stern, "and I want a note that it was your fault that I wasn't." At that point, Dr. Stern relented. For two years, Levitan sat in the aisle of a classroom with boys five or six years younger than he, until he was able to join his own age group. *Rabbi Moshe Linchner.*

13. Rabbi Mannes Mandel.

some worthwhile project. At times his personal debts reached $60,000 or $70,000, despite the frugality with which he lived.[14] One day in 1938 one of the creditors of the long-defunct *Dos Yiddishe Licht* came to the Mesivta seeking payment on a bill of $100. Even though Reb Shraga Feivel was not personally liable for the debts incurred by the paper, he immediately went to his office and found the money to pay the man. When he had departed, Reb Shraga Feivel announced to those present, "You cannot imagine my happiness. For the first time in my life, I don't owe money to anyone." With a smile he added that he ought to celebrate by giving a *kiddush*, "but I can't because I will have to borrow money to do it, and then I will be in debt again."[15]

As stinting as he was with himself, he was extremely concerned with the material well-being of others. The Board of Directors of Torah Vodaath finally had to instruct him not to be involved in salary negotiations with the staff of the Mesivta, since he so readily acquiesced to every request for a raise. A bookbinder once came to his office and complained that he had delivered bound books to the Mesivta, but was told to return in a few days because no money was available. Reb Shraga Feivel immediately went to the comptroller and told him that the Mesivta was no less bound than others by the injunction, "That same day you shall pay [the worker] his wages" (*Vayikra* 19:13). The man was paid on the spot.

When Rabbi Yaakov Kamenetsky first came to Torah Vodaath from Toronto, the apartment he had rented for his family near the Mesivta was not yet vacant, and he and his family had no place to live. Reb Shraga Feivel immediately vacated his apartment near the Mesivta and moved with his family to Monsey until Reb Yaakov's apartment was ready. "Everything about him impressed me," Reb

---

14. Rabbi Alexander Linchner.
   Only after his death did it become known that he was supporting a number of poor families in Williamsburg.

15. Rabbi Nesanel Quinn.
   He had freed himself from indebtedness at that time because he was preparing to settle in *Eretz Yisrael*, his lifelong ambition.

Yaakov said later, "but nothing so amazed me as his concern with the well-being of others."

One of Reb Shraga Feivel's greatest triumphs as an educator was that he was able to pass on his own attitude toward money to his *talmidim*. A *baalebos* whose daughter had recently married one of those students came to Reb Shraga one day to complain about his son-in-law. "I have given him support and he has a salary of his own from his job as a *maggid shiur*, and yet he doesn't save a penny for the future. Everything, to the last penny, goes to *tzedakah*," the man complained. The father-in-law did not receive the hoped-for sympathy. "Those who surround me," Reb Shraga Feivel told him, "don't know what it means to save. We have too much to do with our money."[16]

FEW HAVE EVER WORKED SO HARD AT CONCEALING THEIR essence as did Reb Shraga Feivel. He dressed in the manner of any

Humility Williamsburg *baalebos* of his day. The *tallis katan* worn over his shirt was concealed by a vest that was seldom taken off, and his *peyos* were tightly rolled and barely visible.

He steadfastly refused to answer to the title rabbi. Just being called for an *aliyah* was enough to make him blush.[17] A *gabbai* in the Mesivta once made the mistake of calling him for an *aliyah* as "*Moreinu V'Rabbeinu HaRav* Shraga Feivel ben Moshe." Eyes blazing, Reb Shraga Feivel rebuked him, "*You* are giving *me semichah?*"[18] No *gabbai* ever made that mistake again.

An officer of the Agudath HaRabbanim once had to introduce Reb Shraga Feivel to some strangers. Since Reb Shraga Feivel insisted that he be called "Mister," the officer assumed that he was not worthy of the title of *menahel* (principal) or *rosh yeshivah*, and fumbled for what to say. Sensing his discomfiture, Reb Shraga Feivel came to the rescue. "Tell them I'm the janitor of the Mesivta," he suggested.

---

16. Rabbi Alexander Linchner.
17. Yonah Zev Herskowitz.
18. Rabbi Hertzl Shechter.

Rabbi Yitzchak Ruderman

Reb Shraga Feivel traveled from New York to Baltimore for the dedication of the Garrison Boulevard campus of Ner Yisrael in 1943.[19] When the master of ceremonies announced, "Now we will hear words of blessing from HaRav Shraga Feivel Mendlowitz of Torah Vodaath," no one stirred. Even as hundreds of heads turned expectantly towards the next speaker, Reb Shraga Feivel remained firmly planted in his place, muttering to those closest to him, "There must have been some mistake . . . I'm not Rav Mendlowitz; I'm Mister Mendlowitz."

Yet it would have made no difference if the unfortunate master of ceremonies had called upon "Mister" Mendlowitz, Reb Shraga Feivel would never have spoken in public. He did, however, contribute $400. The *rosh yeshivah*, Rabbi Yitzchak Ruderman, commented later that of all the dignitaries invited to the dedication, only Reb Shraga Feivel made such a contribution.[20]

Public attention of any sort caused him real pain; any honor was

---

19. The dedication ceremony turned out to be of great significance for the future of the Mesivta. Rabbi Yaakov Kamenetsky was present, as the father of two sons learning in Ner Yisrael and as a cousin of Rabbi Ruderman, and the dedication was the occasion of Reb Yaakov's first meeting with Reb Shraga Feivel. The two men established an immediate rapport.

Both Reb Shraga Feivel's modesty and his generosity made a favorable impression on Reb Yaakov. And for his part, Reb Shraga Feivel had a glimpse of the wisdom with which Reb Yaakov was one day to guide the Torah world in America.

20. Years later, Rabbi Ruderman still remembered that Reb Shraga Feivel was the most joyous participant at the *rikud* (dancing) after the dedication ceremony. Rabbi Ruderman found it incredible that someone who had his own institution to worry about could take such satisfaction in the success of another institution. *Sidney Greenwald.*

anathema. He did not permit people to take his photograph, and when they ignored his wishes, he would demand that they give him the film.[21] When his *talmidim* placed a congratulatory message in the *Jewish Morning Journal* upon the engagement of his son Avraham Mordechai, Reb Shraga Feivel's responded, "Why do they have to make a show out of everything? Whose business is it that I made a *shidduch* for my son?"

Reb Shraga Feivel and Mr. Berish Lampert escorting R' Avraham Mordechai Mendlowitz to his chuppah, Lag B'Omer 5707 (May 7, 1947)

During the week-long festivities surrounding the *Chanukas HaBayis* (dedication) of the new Mesivta building on South Third Street in 1941, for which he had raised the bulk of the money, Reb Shraga

R' Avraham Mordechai Mendlowitz at his chuppah; behind the chasan are Reb Shraga Feivel and Reb Reuven Grozovsky

Feivel steadfastly refused to sit on the dais.[22] (Yet when someone asked him why he was sitting in the back with the other onlookers, he replied, "I can run things just as well from here as from the dais."[23])

---

21. Chinn, "Ohr Shraga," p. 11.
22. Rabbi Joshua Silbermintz.
23. Heard from Avrohom Gross by his nephew Rabbi Yehoshua Leiman.

Despite founding and guiding Torah Umesorah, he had no official position in the organization and was not mentioned in any organizational material produced in his lifetime. A journalist once asked him for an interview concerning Torah Umesorah. Reb Shraga Feivel readily consented on one condition: that his name not appear anywhere in the article. At the end of an interview lasting several hours, in which Reb Shraga Feivel discussed all aspects of the new organization's efforts, the interviewer protested that it was impossible to properly describe an organization without mentioning who ran it. "No, no," Reb Shraga Feivel insisted, "that is precisely what I had in mind when I said that my name could not appear." When the journalist persisted that he could not write an article without mentioning him at all, Reb Shraga Feivel told him, "In that case, don't write."

There was no cause so important that he would consent to be seated on the dais or to be honored in any way. The Board of Directors of Torah Vodaath once tried to persuade him to be the honoree at the yeshivah's annual dinner. "I'm building Torah here," he told the board, "and the Torah was not given in order that Feivel should be honored." Protest as they might that their sole intention was to raise as much money as possible, he could not be budged. "That Feivel will taste *kavod* at the banquet is certain, but that the yeshivah will raise more money in this fashion is uncertain, and the rule is 'אֵין סָפֵק מוֹצִיא מִידֵי וַדַּאי, *an uncertainty can never displace a certainty.*'"

Only once did he consent to speak outside the context of an ongoing *shiur* to his students in the Mesivta or to *baalebatim* in Williamsburg.[24] Reb Shraga Feivel's shunning of the limelight is sufficient by itself to explain his refusal ever to address the general public. But in addition, he was first and foremost a *mechanech* (educator), who sought to teach in a way that would move his students to action. As such, he felt that the effect of his words depended to a

---

24. He spoke in 1947 to a group of Pirchei Agudath Israel youth leaders, after months of badgering by his student Sidney Greenwald, who was then national director of Pirchei. Even then he spoke only on condition that he not be introduced. Afterwards he expressed regrets even about this speech. *Rabbi Shmuel Mendlowitz.*

large extent on his personal relationship with every listener. Speeches, in his opinion, generally had nothing more than a superficial and short-lived impact — something that held no allure for him.

He could be acerbic in poking fun at those who busy themselves with the pursuit of honor. During a *shiur* on *Shaarei Teshuvah* of Rabbeinu Yonah, he commented, "At my age, people start thinking about the fantastic *levayah* (funeral) they'll have and who will be there." He went on to mock all the ways in which people routinely engage in the pursuit of honor.[25] "Woe to those who sell their *Olam Haba* for a little *kavod* (honor)," was a constant theme of his.[26]

Flattery, like public recognition, posed the danger of bringing one to pride, and was something from which Reb Shraga Feivel fled. In the early days of Torah Umesorah, he exerted himself until he developed perforated ulcers. His doctor told him that his life was in danger, and that he must lie on his back perfectly still for days. A *talmid* came to visit and told him that when he *davened* for health in *Shemoneh Esrei*, his *kavannah* (intention) was for one whose illness affects all of *Klal Yisrael*, as opposed to those whose illness adversely affects only their family and a limited number of people. Reb Shraga Feivel reprimanded him saying, "To a person in critical condition, you don't give compliments."

EVEN AMONG *ROSHEI YESHIVAH* WHO ARE EXCEEDINGLY MODEST in everything concerning their behavior, there is often one prerogative

Sharing His Talmidim

that they reserve for themselves: that of shaping the learning and character development of their *talmidim*. Reb Shraga Feivel was the primary influence on almost every boy who passed through the doors of Torah Vodaath during his lifetime and he had very definite ideas about how they should be educated. Yet he deliberately sought to expose them to the widest possible array of Torah influences, because every *talmid chacham* has an outstanding quality different from those of others.

---

25. Rabbi Eliyahu Yehoshua Geldzhaler.
26. Gross and Kaminetsky, p. 554.

He was too keen an observer not to know that he was charismatic, but he consciously sought to negate that charisma. One day, after a particularly inspiring *Tanya shiur*, his students insisted on accompanying him home. As they reached his building, he turned to them and said, "*Az ihr volt gekent meine rebbeim, volt ihr mir ungeshpign a fillen ponim* — If you had known my teachers, you would spit in my face."[27] On one Simchas Torah, while dancing with his *talmidim*, he slipped and fell. As the boys helped him to his feet, they heard him saying to himself, "*Oy, die bizyonos zeinen gut* — Oh, the humiliations are good." Prior to his fall, the boys had been completely entranced, and he viewed his fall, unintended though it was, as valuable for having broken the trance and for having prevented him from experiencing any pride in his hold over his students.[28]

Despite the strong sense of mission that had guided him from early adulthood, he was even prepared to withdraw from Torah Vodaath if he felt that by doing so the students would benefit. In

1929, three years after the founding of the Mesivta, when the student body had increased greatly in numbers as well as in the standard of learning, he decided that he had given his *talmidim* all that he was capable of, and that a greater *talmid chacham* than he was needed to bring them to a higher plateau. To that end, he brought Rabbi Moshe Dov Ber Rivkin from Jerusalem to become *menahel* of the Mesivta. Rabbi Rivkin was a renowned *talmid chacham*, a

Rabbi Moshe Dov Ber Rivkin

27. Rabbi Alexander Linchner.
    To convey how unseemly is the pursuit of fame, he once related how the Maggid of Mezeritch fasted to know why he had been punished by becoming famous.
28. Ibid.

prudent person who understood people, and a dedicated *chassid* with many years of succesful experience as a *menahel* in Jerusalem — in short, he was Reb Shraga Feivel's ideal candidate.

In his great modesty, Reb Shraga Feivel saw no reason not to think that this step was for the greater good of the Mesivta. To his situation he applied the well-known rabbinic saying, "Just as I have been rewarded for my expounding (דְּרִישָׁה), so will I be rewarded for my withdrawal (פְּרִישָׁה)." For the next two years, he learned Torah almost the entire day, selling insurance part-time to support his family. His only ongoing connection with the Mesivta was to *daven* with the *talmidim*.[29] Reb Shraga Feivel returned to the Mesivta only in 1931 after the Board of Directors forced him to do so in a *din Torah*. To mitigate Rabbi Rivkin's pain at having been removed from his position, the *beis din* ruled that he be the *rebbi* of the class just before the *beis medrash*.

As attached as they were to him, his students were able, after his death, to draw close to other powerful personalities. That, too, was part of his legacy. Some of his closest *talmidim* became Klausenburger or Satmar chassidim, while in the Mesivta they gravitated to Rabbi Gedaliah Schorr, and to the Lithuanian *gedolim*, such as Rabbi Reuven Grozovsky and Rabbi Yaakov Kamenetsky. Not only did he teach his students to draw from a broad range of the classics of Jewish thought in formulating their own *hashkafos*, he opened them up to as many contemporary greats as possible. He provided a ready forum in the Mesivta for any Torah giant who arrived in America. Both the Klausenberger Rav and the Satmar Rav gave their first public *shiurim* in America in Torah Vodaath. When the Klausenberger asked Reb Shraga Feivel what kind of *shiur* he should give, the latter was embarrassed by the question and replied that it

---

29. For some of the older *talmidim,* who complained that his departure had left them rudderless, he continued to give private *shiurim* in his home. Over a period of six months, he also gave an early morning *shiur* in Tractate *Shabbos* for a group of his closest *talmidim*. Reb Shraga Feivel would explain each new Mishnah according to the halachic conclusions derived from it, before proceeding to the Gemara. To push the boys, he used to tell them that if they themselves did not ask *Tosafos'* questions on the Gemara or the Maharsha's questions on *Tosafos,* their learning lacked sufficient application. *Rabbi Nesanel Quinn.*

to tell the *Rav* how to give his *shiur*. The Satmar Rav not only gave a Gemara *shiur* but, at Reb Shraga Feivel's request, also spoke against going to college and growing long pompadours. Among the other *geonim* to give *shiurim* in Torah Vodaath over the years were Rabbi Meir Shapiro, Rabbi Meir Don Plotzki, Rabbi Baruch Ber Leibowitz, Rabbi Elchonon Wasserman, Rabbi Aharon Kotler, Rabbi Avraham Kalmanowitz, the Ponevezher Rav, and the Bobover Rav.

Reb Shraga Feivel sent his *talmidim* to the *tischen* of the many *Rebbes* in Williamsburg or the Lower East Side — the Kopitchinitzer Rebbe, the Boyaner Rebbe, the Novominsker Rebbe, the Amshinover Rebbe, the Modzhitzer Rebbe — and to the newly arrived Lubavitcher Rebbe in Crown Heights.

Rabbi Avraham Kalmanowitz   *The Bobover Rebbe*   *The Modzhitzer Rebbe*

The Kopitchinitzer Rebbe   *The Novominsker Rebbe*   *The Boyaner Rebbe*

Not only did Reb Shraga Feivel expose his students to a wide array of charismatic Torah leaders, he went out of his way to let them see the extent to which he felt himself subservient to them. He shadowed Reb Elchonon Wasserman during the latter's prolonged stay in the United States in the late 30's, never missing an opportunity to seek Reb Elchonon's *daas Torah* concerning the Mesivta or the dangers confronting *Klal Yisrael*.

Before the Satmar Rav's arrival, Reb Shraga Feivel talked frequently to his students about how the Rebbe did not sleep in a bed from one Shabbos to the next, but punctuated his learning with short naps while still seated. When the Satmar Rav's ship anchored in New York harbor on *Shabbos Shuvah* of 1946, Reb Shraga Feivel sent a delegation of Torah Vodaath students to greet him, a three-hour walk from Williamsburg.[30] He himself ate the salty fish the Rav passed out at his *tisch*, though he ordinarily never touched fish because of his ulcers. "Yankele, *dos iz a rebbe* — Yaakov, *this* is a *rebbe*," he told Yaakov Leshinsky, a *talmid* from a strong Lithuanian background.

He was always on the alert to meet any great Torah authority who arrived in America. When Rabbi Meir Don Plotzki, the Ostrover Rav, came in 1926 to raise funds for the Mesivta of Warsaw, he and Reb Shraga Feivel spent a number of hours in private conversation. After Rabbi Plotzki's return to Europe, they exchanged letters concerning various aspects of Jewish history, a subject in which they both had great expertise. Rabbi Meir Shapiro, the Rav of Lublin, was a guest in Reb Shraga Feivel's *succah*, where the two danced and sang together until late at night.

Rabbi Meir Don Plotzki

---

30. Rabbi Hershel Mashinsky.

A large contingent of Torah Vodaath students was also present to greet Rabbi Aharon Kotler at Penn Station on his arrival in 1942.

The Chofetz Chaim

At a gathering in his honor, Rabbi Shapiro insisted that Reb Shraga Feivel sit next to him. "Why do you honor *me*?" Rabbi Shapiro demanded of those present. "You should be honoring *him*! He is building a yeshivah in a spiritual desert. Do you think it is greater to build a yeshivah in Poland? I wish I could sit next to him in *Gan Eden*."[31]

Reb Shraga Feivel venerated the Chofetz Chaim. When his future son-in-law Rabbi Sender Linchner went to study under the Chofetz Chaim in Radin in 1931, Reb Shraga Feivel wrote him that if he were in Rabbi Linchner's place in Radin, "I would be the happiest person on the face of the earth." In the last days of his life, he expressed regret over two things: never having breathed the air of *Eretz Yisrael* and never having met the Chofetz Chaim.

In the middle of a halachic dispute with a Lithuanian *rosh yeshivah* one day, Reb Shraga Feivel adduced a proof to his view from one of the Chofetz Chaim's halachic works. The *rosh yeshivah's* only response was: "If that's what Reb Yisrael Meir says, then I disagree with him." Reb Shraga Feivel retorted, "It's a pity the Chofetz Chaim was not a chassidic Rebbe. He would have had at least 100,000 followers who knew how to value him properly."

REB SHRAGA FEIVEL'S HUMILITY WAS BUT THE EXTERNAL MANI-festation of an even more essential trait: his success in concealing his

Nistar Mendlowitz

greatness. Those who knew him well always felt that no matter how much he revealed, much more was concealed. Even his occasional sobbing in public was seen by his close students as nothing more than an un-

---

31. Rabbi Shmuel Mendlowitz.

sobbing in public was seen by his close students as nothing more than an uncontrollable eruption of the powerful currents that were constantly flowing beneath the surface.

It was left to the Ponevezher Rav to most succinctly catch this aspect of his personality. During his eulogy when Reb Shraga Feivel's remains were taken to his beloved *Eretz Yisrael*, the Rav said, "He wanted to be called not Rav Mendlowitz, but *Mister* Mendlowitz. I say he was not *Mister*, but *Nistar* (Hidden One) Mendlowitz."

The Ponevezher Rav

Few of those who knew him for many years had an inkling of his wide knowledge of Gemara and *poskim*. They assumed that his learning was confined to *Tanach* and works of Jewish thought. Yet Rabbi Chaim Heller stated as he walked after Reb Shraga Feivel's *aron* (bier), "He knew *Shas*." And students who stole a glance into his *Tur* and *Shulchan Aruch* found them covered with his annotations.

In not publicizing his erudition, he resembled the Alter of Slabodka who was seldom seen with an open Gemara. Reb Shraga Feivel himself often expressed his admiration of Polish chassidim for three things: learning much Torah, being clever, and concealing their virtues from others. And he himself excelled in each of these areas.

Chapter 16

Man Against the Flood

R EB SHRAGA FEIVEL'S SENSE OF HIMSELF AS NOTHING
other than Hashem's agent allowed him to withstand the
pressures of public opinion with equanim-
ity. On any issue, he could be counted on to
stake out an independent position without
fear of ridicule or ostracism. And when convinced of his own opinion, he did not hesitate to share it even with great Torah authorities
whom he held in awe.

No Compromise

During Reb Elchonon Wasserman's prolonged stay in America
in 1938 and 1939, the great *rosh yeshivah* of Baranovitch had a profound influence on many different groups in the Orthodox world.
On one occasion, however, the *Jewish Morning Journal* carried an
announcement that Reb Elchonon would be giving a *mussar
shmuess* in an institution that Reb Shraga Feivel considered inconsistent with genuine Torah spirit. Reb Elchonon had been invited
there by a group of the institution's wealthy supporters, who

Rabbi Elchonon Wasserman (center)
in Camp Mesivta, 1938

were also prepared to contribute desperately needed funds for Reb Elchonon's yeshivah. By speaking there, Reb Shraga Feivel felt, Reb Elchonon would inadvertently be lending his prestige to the institution and its views.

Reb Shraga Feivel sent two of his *talmidim* to the Broadway Central Hotel on the Lower East Side, where Reb Elchonon was staying, with the following message:

American Jewry has been waiting for an upright and honest Jew, one who cannot be swayed by personal flattery or money for his yeshivah. Until now, many *gedolim* have come to America, and even though they did not look with favor on this institution, they gave *shiurim* there, because of the money they hoped to obtain for their yeshivos. If Rabbi Wasserman follows their example, it will be clear to all that there is no more truth in the world.

The two young rabbis visited Reb Elchonon in his hotel on *Motza'ei Shabbos* and delivered Reb Shraga Feivel's message word for word. Reb Elchonon replied that he had initially refused to present a halachic discourse to the group in question. But when asked to deliver a *mussar shmuess* instead, he felt constrained to accept on the basis of a tradition he had received from the Chofetz Chaim. The Chofetz Chaim had said, "Even if the Bolsheviks would invite me to give a *mussar shmuess*, I would go."

Nevertheless, in the end, Reb Elchonon did not speak there. No sooner had the two messengers left than someone else brought Reb Elchonon the Sunday issue of the *Morning Journal*, which was known to be printed on Shabbos. Reb Elchonon was extremely upset that his hosts had seen fit to advertise his speech in a paper printed on Shabbos, and he immediately canceled his appearance.[1]

Reb Shraga Feivel deplored the tendency toward ever-greater halachic leniencies undertaken in the hope that such leniencies would make it easier to hold wavering Jews within the Orthodox camp. He felt that just the opposite was the case: In a generation of flight from Orthodoxy, even otherwise valid leniencies had to be avoided. The decline had been set in motion, he once said, when rabbis ruled that it was not necessary to have a *minyan* present for a *bris.* All the awe that had always surrounded the induction of an infant Jewish boy into the covenant of Avraham Avinu was thereby diminished, and eventually circumcision was performed by physicians, and not as prescribed by halachah.

"If the rabbis of America were capable of the same long view as the Chasam Sofer in his time," he said, "they would never have started with such *kulos* (leniencies), and we would never have reached our present situation." His uncompromising stance on halachic issues was a direct outgrowth of his awareness that the halachah is not ours to cede.

ONE OF THE FREQUENT OBJECTS OF HIS RIDICULE WAS THE Yiddish press of his day. Though he did not object to his students **The Yiddish** reading the Yiddish papers so that they would be **Press** informed about what was happening to Jews around the world, he was appalled by the papers' frequent careless way with the truth. It is said that whoever heard the Kotzker Rebbe's *"feh"* when he handled money never thought about money the same way again. And the same could be said of anyone who ever heard Reb Shraga Feivel's *"feh"* as he threw down the *Morning Journal* in disgust.[2]

At a time when many Orthodox Jews carried the *Morning Journal* to shul in the morning in their *tallis* bags, Reb Shraga Feivel was openly dismissive. Rabbi Shlomo Heiman once asked a student what the secular date was, and when the student did not know, Reb

1. Rabbi Nesanel Quinn.
2. Rabbi Alexander Linchner.

Shlomo suggested that he look in the *Morning Journal.* Reb Shlomo added that this information probably constituted the only true words in the paper. When the student told this story to Reb Shraga Feivel, he replied caustically, "Even the date is incorrect since the Sunday edition is printed on Shabbos." On Friday, the *Morning Journal* published an expanded edition, concerning which Reb Shraga Feivel used to say, "Every day it's a lie, and on Friday it's a double lie."[3]

IN REB SHRAGA FEIVEL'S DAY, THE ORTHODOX WORLD, INCLUDing most of Torah Vodaath's leading supporters, was almost entirely in the Religious Zionist (Mizrachi) camp. Yet despite his passionate love of *Eretz Yisrael* and his intense concern with settlement activity in the Land, Reb Shraga Feivel did not hesitate to openly criticize Mizrachi, even when doing so posed a threat to the financial well-being of Torah Vodaath. He objected to the Mizrachi because of its "centrist" position, which means being halfway between the authentic Torah position and secular Zionism.

On Mizrachi

He was once asked what possible objection could be raised to the slogan of Mizrachi: "The Land of Israel for the People of Israel according to the Torah of Israel." He responded that the Mizrachi slogan could be likened to wearing a right-handed glove on one's left hand. The Mizrachi slogan placed the Land of Israel above the people of Israel and both above the Torah. The traditional view, however, has always been that the Jewish people were created for the Torah — i.e., in order that the Torah could be realized in the world — and not the Torah for the Jewish people. In truth the slogan of the Jewish people throughout the ages has been: "The Torah of Israel for the People of Israel in the Land of Israel." The Mizrachi's change in the order of priorities, argued Reb Shraga Feivel, contained an entire worldview, and determined how different interests would be balanced against one another. By placing the Torah third on its list of priorities, he said, Mizrachi had already been party to many compromises of the Torah for the benefit of the Land or People.[4]

---

3. Rabbi Bernard Goldenberg.
4. Rabbi Nesanel Quinn.

These views were neither kept private nor confined to the Mesivta. In the 30's and 40's, there was virtually not an event or *simchah* in the religious world that did not begin with the playing of the Zionist national anthem, *Hatikvah*. During the playing of *Hatikvah*, all those present would stand. Not Reb Shraga Feivel. He did not even bother to leave the room, but rather sat fixed in his place. "Their hope (*tikvah*) is not ours," he explained, "for it does not include the *Beis HaMikdash* or the coming of Mashiach."

At the wedding of a Torah Vodaath student with a graduate of Herzliah, a Zionist school which stressed Hebrew studies, Reb Shraga Feivel and his students sat as usual during the singing of *Hatikvah*. The bride's principal indignantly demanded an explanation. Reb Shraga Feivel told him, "You would have to be a drunkard like the one who composed these lyrics to stand while his words are being sung."[5]

Reb Shraga Feivel was determined to keep Mizrachi out of Torah Vodaath. He refused to hear of an effort to enlist Torah Vodaath students to collect funds for Keren HaYesod, despite the fact that the chairman of Keren HaYesod in America happened to be one of Torah Vodaath's major contributors. When the latter found out about Reb Shraga Feivel's opposition, he demanded to know his reason.

Reb Shraga Feivel explained that, as important as his contributions to the Mesivta were, the educational principles upon which Torah Vodaath was founded were even more precious. How could *yeshivah bachurim* collect for a fund that supported schools in *Eretz Yisrael* dedicated to uprooting Torah values from their students, and *moshavim* and *kibbutzim* that had declared war against religious observance?[6]

On one occasion, a delegation of the Mizrachi Council for Jewish Education, which included Rabbi Zev Gold, one of the founders of Torah Vodaath, sought permission to observe classes.

---

5. Ibid.

    Naftali Herz Imber, author of the lyrics of *Hatikvah*, was a drunkard whose personal life was shameful. He was even reputed to have converted to Christianity at one point in his life.

6. Yonah Zev Herskowitz.

"If you wish to visit the Mesivta as private citizens," Reb Shraga Feivel told the delegation, "you are more than welcome, but I cannot let you visit the yeshivah as the official representatives of Mizrachi."

The festivities surrounding the dedication of the new Mesivta building on South Third Street in 1941 required Reb Shraga Feivel to walk a delicate line between all the various Orthodox groups. The dedication was the occasion for introducing the concept of a yeshivah *al taharas hakodesh* (for pure Torah learning) to the broader Orthodox public, and Reb Shraga Feivel was determined that there should be the widest possible spectrum of Orthodox groups in attendance. For that reason, the dedication ceremonies lasted seven days, with representatives from all the various Orthodox groups offering congratulatory speeches.

Among the dignitaries who attended was Rabbi Yitzchak Isaac Herzog, then Ashkenazi Chief Rabbi of Palestine. In honor of his visit, there was considerable pressure on Reb Shraga Feivel to display the Zionist flag together with the American flag and to play *Hatikvah*. Instead Reb Shraga Feivel redesigned the Zionist flag for the occasion. Between the blue bars, he had stitched in the prophet Malachi's exhortation to the Jewish people on their way into exile: "זִכְרוּ תּוֹרַת מֹשֶׁה עַבְדִּי, *Remember the Torah of my servant Moshe.*"

That solution pleased no one. The Zionists objected to the "desecration" of the Zionist flag and those affiliated with Agudath Israel criticized him for having used the Zionist flag in any form. But Reb Shraga Feivel remained staunch in his position. To the first group, he explained that there could be no Jewish national identity not founded on the Torah of Moshe Rabbeinu; to the second, he argued that Torah and *Eretz Yisrael* are the natural possessions of the Jewish people and that these concepts were well expressed by the newly designed flag.

In honor of Rabbi Herzog's visit, he requested that Seymour Silbermintz, a musically gifted Mesivta student, compose a new *niggun* (melody) put to the words of Rabbi Avraham Yitzchak Kook's *Shir Emunah*. When there were complaints from Mizrachi guests about the failure to play *Hatikvah*, Reb Shraga Feivel referred to the reputation of its lyricist as a drunkard. He asked in wonder how they could prefer the words of one who was often found drunk in the gutter to those of Rabbi Kook.

Neither the redesigned flag nor the newly composed *niggun* should be viewed as mere ploys. Reb Shraga Feivel believed in national symbols as long as they reflected the Jewish people's identity as *Am HaTorah*, the nation of the Torah. His effort to find such symbols captures at a deeper level Reb Shraga Feivel's refusal to concede anything to Mizrachi or secular Zionists in terms of the love of *Eretz Yisrael*. "They say we are not Zionists," he once said at the conclusion of a class filled with his love of *Eretz Yisrael*, "but it is we who are the true lovers of Zion."

Reb Shraga Feivel did not permit anything to cloud his *ahavas Yisrael*. Two directors of the yeshivah once approached Mr. Abraham Lewin, the yeshivah's president, with the request that he enroll two Jewish boys who had been in a Catholic orphanage for a long time. Mr. Lewin refused, on the grounds that boys who had been kissing a crucifix for such a long time would not be willing to accept Torah and mitzvos. Both sides agreed to let Reb Shraga Feivel make the final decision. Reb Shraga Feivel ruled that the boys should be accepted. He contended, "Better that they should be *posh'ei Yisrael* (sinful Jews) than *son'ei Yisrael* (haters of Jews)." The boys were admitted and at least one of them became an observant Jew.[7]

Hearing his criticisms of Zionism, someone once told him, "I too hate the Zionists. They should be cursed."

"*Chas v'chalilah* (Heaven forbid)!" Reb Shraga Feivel interjected. "To the contrary: They should be blessed, along with all those who are building up our Holy Land. I only pray that they observe mitzvos. But *chalilah* to curse or hate them. They are *tinokos shen-ish'bu* (people who never received a Jewish education and so were led astray)."[8]

In this attitude, Reb Shraga Feivel echoed Rabbi Yosef Chaim Sonnenfeld, the *rav* of Jerusalem. Chaim Weizmann once asked him, "How could a *tzaddik* hate the Zionists who are his fellow Jews?" Reb

---

7. Rabbi Nesanel Quinn.

8. Rabbi Hershel Mashinsky.

Rabbi Yosef Chaim Sonnenfeld

Yosef Chaim replied, "I will prove to you that I love the Zionists. For a loved one, a person wishes only the best. To me the most precious things in the world are the Torah and mitzvos, and I wish these for every Zionist. I object only to their anti-Torah actions."

After hearing a well-known rabbi give a fiery *derashah* against the secular Jews in *Eretz Yisrael*, Reb Shraga Feivel expressed his displeasure with the tone of the speech. "True, it is hard for us to reach the *ahavas Yisrael* of Reb Levi Yitzchak of Berditchev," he said, "but we are all commanded to keep far away from hatred of our fellow Jews."

Pirkei Avos, Reb Shraga Feivel once noted, teaches us to receive everyone with a cheerful face (בְּסֵבֶר פָּנִים יָפוֹת; 1:15) and with joy (בְּשִׂמְחָה; 3:16). *Simchah*, he explained, refers to the inner joy we should feel at meeting a fellow Jew. But even if we cannot reach that level, we are required at the very least to show our fellow Jews a pleasant face. He himself worked hard to reach the level of inner joy in the presence of another Jew.

Chapter 17

Seething Spirit

THE JUXTAPOSITION OF THE COLD INTELLECTUAL WITH the person of powerful emotions is by now a literary commonplace. Reb Shraga Feivel, however, proved that the dichotomy is a false one, for he was at once a thinker of depth and a man of the most powerful feelings. If anything, he demonstrated that thought at its deepest level must stir the emotions and that, conversely, only an aroused soul will be spurred to push the boundaries of intellectual inquiry. Rabbi Reuven Grozovsky captured well these intertwined aspects of his personality:

> Reb Shraga Feivel was a genius of the soul, *possessed of a powerful mind and a fiery heart.* To a degree seldom found, he burned with love of Hashem, love of Torah, love of the Jewish people. But at the same time, his great intellect taught him *how* one must love Hashem and *how* one must love the Jewish people.
>
> He understood better than others that the command "Love Hashem, Your G-d" includes the command "Make

Him beloved to mankind," and from his great love of *Klal Yisrael* he devoted his days to bringing the Jewish people close to their Father in Heaven.

THE ENTIRE CREATED WORLD CRIED OUT TO REB SHRAGA FEIVEL the presence of the Creator, and he tried to bring his students to the

Reading From the Siddur of David HaMelech

same level of sensitivity. One Erev Shabbos,[1] Rabbi Moshe Aharon Stern hid near Reb Shraga Feivel's home next to Bais Medrash Elyon to catch a glimpse of Reb Shraga Feivel in an unguarded moment. From his hiding place, he watched Reb Shraga Feivel stand on the porch for a long period of time, with his eyes cast upwards, repeating the words of the *Zohar*: "His glory fills the entire world; He encompasses the entire world, and there is no place without Him. All the wonders of the universe are but a representation of His glory that proclaims to humanity that there is a Creator.

Reb Shraga Feivel viewed the world as an open prayer book. He *davened* near a window and frequently looked out during *davening.* When a layman asked why he did so, Reb Shraga Feivel explained to his students, "He thinks I'm looking out, but actually I'm looking in."[2] Nature was for him "the *siddur* of David HaMelech," who sang, "the Heavens proclaim the glory of Hashem," and when he looked out the window, he was simply exchanging the printed *siddur* for that of David HaMelech.[3]

The natural world was alive for him. The sight of a slender branch of a tree broken under the weight of a heavy snow was enough to disturb him. When he watched the leaves rustling in the wind, he actually saw them singing praises to Hashem. During his year of confinement in Liberty, one of his doctors begged him not to become so excited by the sight of leaves waving in the breeze. Reb

---

1. During the summer, when the days are long, Reb Shraga Feivel went to the *mikveh* and completed his Shabbos preparations six or seven hours before Shabbos. Those hours were spent in anticipation of the Shabbos Queen. By the time he reached *Lecha Dodi*, in *Kabbalas Shabbos,* he was already transported to a higher world. *Rabbi Moshe Aharon Stern.*

2. Chinn, "Ohr Shraga," p. 10.

3. That is how he explained his habit of looking out the window to his student Elias Karp.

Shraga Feivel only laughed and asked, "Is it really possible to view them like an unthinking animal?" He would say, "Let's look at Yeshayah's prophecy, 'The Heavens shall be rolled open like a scroll' (*Yeshayahu* 34:4). If the Heavens are a scroll, we should learn from them that there is a Creator." He would quote the Kotzker that the world is a book and the Torah is its commentary.

He was once walking with a group of *talmidim* when one of them absentmindedly picked a leaf off a tree. Reb Shraga Feivel stopped in midsentence. "Don't you know," he asked the hapless offender, "that the whole creation sings a song to the Creator — every plant, every blade of grass? When you pulled that leaf off the tree, you cut off its song in the middle." One still day, he pointed out the window to a tree on which a single leaf on the very top was rustling in the wind. "That leaf is the *chazzan*," he said, "and all the other leaves are listening to his prayerful song." That is how he viewed nature — as an ongoing song of praise.

And if he could see every leaf as part of the Divine plan, how much more so a human being. He was shaken by the news that atom bombs had been dropped on Hiroshima and Nagasaki. "Even if we had heard that so many cats, and not people, had been killed, it would cause us great pain," he said. He feared that America would be subject to Divine Judgment for not having first revealed the power at its disposal by dropping an atom bomb on an uninhabited island.[4]

Reb Shraga Feivel taught his students to see Hashem's hand in nature. Viewing a majestic mountain range, he pointed out to a group of *talmidim* the harmony in the panorama before them. And yet, he added, if we were to view this scene from close-up, many of the elements that seem to us harmonious at a distance might well appear discordant. From that perspective, we might see only a disorderly mass of details, in no apparent relation to one another. It is the long view, which allows us to take in the whole scene at once,

---

4. Rabbi Avraham Abba Freedman.
   Reb Shraga Feivel was acutely sensitive to any human suffering. He found it hard to be a *sandek* at a *bris* because the pain of the infant troubled him. His grandson, Rabbi Moshe Linchner, recalls that on rare occasions when Reb Shraga Feivel was a *sandek* he would look straight ahead, and avoid watching the circumcision.

that provides the harmony. So is it with the Torah. A particular halachah may strike us as difficult to understand. Yet when viewed from the perspective of the entire Torah, the *din* is just one more perfectly fitted element.

He showed his followers how David HaMelech had viewed the natural world. One *shalosh seudos* at Camp Mesivta, he went to the window and stared out at the red sky turning to night. "Come, *kinder* (children), let us see how to view everything in the natural world," he said. "Doesn't David HaMelech sing, 'The young lions roar after their prey and seek their food from Hashem' (*Tehillim* 104:21)? If we were asked why they roar, we would answer simply that they roar out of hunger. But David HaMelech saw it differently; he saw in their roaring a thirst for the Divine — 'they seek their food from Hashem.' "

Reb Shraga Feivel in Camp Mesivta

And with that, he sang, "הַכְּפִירִים שֹׁאֲגִים לַטָּרֶף, *The young lions roar for their prey*," in the *niggun* attributed to the Shpoler Zeide. He led the boys in lively dancing until the final verse — יִתַּמּוּ חַטָּאִים מִן הָאָרֶץ (may sins disappear from the earth). Then he abruptly brought the dancing to a halt. "See how David HaMelech made a fine distinction: Let the *sins* (חַטָּאִים) disappear, not the *sinners* (חוֹטְאִים)."

An Aesthetic Sensitivity

JUST AS THE BEAUTY OF THE NATURAL WORLD ATTESTS TO Hashem's presence, so too does man's Divinely endowed power to create works of beauty. Reb Shraga Feivel encouraged his students to develop their aesthetic sensibility as a means of drawing close to Hashem. He was fond of quoting Rabbi Samson Raphael Hirsch on the verse (*Tehillim* 29:4): קוֹל ה' בֶּהָדָר, *The voice of Hashem is in everything beautiful*: "The same Divine voice that one hears in the Law, and that commands man to develop all his talents in harmony with that Law, is the same voice that speaks to you whenever you perceive harmonious beauty in nature. The very same law through which Hashem carries out His will in every creature is the law through which Hashem commands you to develop your human personality."

Insisting that his students keep their possessions in order and garments neat and clean was one of the means by which he developed that aesthetic sensibility.[5] When the first group of *Aish Dos* students arrived in Monsey in the summer of 1943, Reb Shraga Feivel asked them to clean up the grounds before they began learning.[6] Reb Shraga Feivel hired professional gardeners to plant flowers and shrubs. If there was litter on the grounds, he expected his students to pick it up. Those who just passed it by were likely to feel his lash. How could they not perceive the litter as an offense against the beauty of G-d's world?

The janitor in the Mesivta once rebuked the boys for not keeping the premises cleaner. "A religious person who learns the Bible has a greater responsibility to be clean," he told them. When the incident was reported to Reb Shraga Feivel, he exclaimed, "What a *chillul Hashem* that the gentile understood that and the *bachurim* didn't."[7]

Arousing students' sensitivity to anything unsightly was, in his view, a necessary prelude to a proper appreciation of the wonders of the creation. The long exile, he felt, had weakened the aesthetic sensibility of Jews. He used to say, "Every Jew is by nature a poet, but *galus* has dulled our sensitivity."

---

5. Rabbi Moshe Wolfson.

6. Rabbi Shmuel Mendlowitz.

7. Rabbi Yisrael Spinner.
   Reb Shraga Feivel lived in fear of any trace of *chillul Hashem*, often saying that it would be better to close the Mesivta than for there to be a trace of *chillul Hashem* associated with it. During World War II, he forbade the *talmidim* from walking in large groups to *Tashlich* for fear that the sight of a large number of Orthodox boys not serving in the army, when so many families had sons serving overseas or who had been killed, would create animosity toward Orthodox Jews. For the same reason, he flew the American flag in Monsey. *Rabbi Shmuel Mendlowitz.*

No beauty so stirred Reb Shraga Feivel as that of music. He liked to quote the Baal HaTanya to the effect that "anyone who lacks an appreciation of music also lacks an understanding of Chassidus."[8] And he regularly demonstrated a deep understanding of music. One *Seder* night, a group of *talmidim* came to his home after midnight, as was their custom. They found Reb Shraga Feivel in a state of high exaltation. He asked Yitzchak Rosengarten, one of the boys in the Mesivta who was particularly musical, to sing a famous *Chabad niggun*. Rosengarten complied with the request, but for some reason left out the concluding stanza. As he was singing, Reb Shraga Feivel sat quietly, with his eyes closed in intense concentration, but as soon as he finished, Reb Shraga Feivel instantly snapped to attention and called out, "You must have left something out. This *niggun* is arranged in ascending order of worlds from the lower to the upper, and I still do not feel that we have reached the world of *Atzilus*."

He used to explain that each of the instruments mentioned in the final psalm — shofar, psalter, harp, timbrel, stringed instruments, flute, loud-sounding cymbals, and stirring cymbals — arouses a different emotional response: This one arouses tears, another happiness, and yet another encourages deep reflection. Taken as a whole, the message is that one must serve Hashem with every emotion.[9]

Reb Shraga Feivel was extraordinarily responsive to music. Someone once shared with him one *Rebbe's* explanation of the Yiddish expression: "*A chazzan iz a nar* — A chazzan is a fool." The *Rebbe* had explained that in the upper worlds the courtyard of melody and that of *teshuvah* are located close to one another, and thus the *chazzan* was a fool for not having jumped from one to the other. Reb Shraga Feivel's dry comment on this *vort*: "Whoever said that has no appreciation of music; otherwise he would have realized that anyone who is privileged to enter into the courtyard of melody has no desire ever to leave it."

---

8. In the same vein, he would quote the Chasam Sofer's observation that *niggun* is an aspect of *ahavas Hashem*. Yonah Zev Herskowitz.

9. See Hirsch, *Tehillim* 150.

When Yiddel Turner played the heartrending *"Keili, Keili, lamah azavtani*, My G-d, My G-d, why have You abandoned me?"* on his violin, Reb Shraga Feivel would sit there, his eyes tightly shut and a look of intense concentration on his face. So emotionally wrenching was Turner's playing for him that it not infrequently provoked one of his ulcer attacks.[10] Yet when he was in excruciating pain, it was often the sweet sounds of Turner's violin that provided him with his only relief. At those moments, he would say, "Yiddel, please make sure to be there as well at the moment when my soul leaves this world . . . In those few moments of your playing, I was able to think as deeply as I normally can in six hours."[11] *Motza'ei Shabbos* he often asked Turner to play the Modzhitzer Rebbe's *niggun* to *"Mimkomcha Malkeinu Sofi'a* — From Your dwelling place, our King, appear." He once told Turner, "Yiddel, I marvel at your playing, but even more do I marvel at the violin itself. How can strings of catgut speak so deeply to the soul?"[12]

REB SHRAGA FEIVEL WAS BY NATURE UNUSUALLY EMOTIONAL and sensitive. Yet it would be a mistake to understand the constant

Alive to Hashem's Presence outpouring of feeling as merely the result of a sensitive nature. The powerful feelings that constantly surged to the surface came from something much deeper. Every Jew, writes Rabbi Yehudah HaLevi in *The Kuzari*, is endowed with a special capacity for awareness of Hashem. Prophecy is the highest expression of this capacity, but every Jew has the potential to feel a closeness to Him.

That sensitivity to Hashem's presence was found in Reb Shraga Feivel to a particularly acute degree. He frequently quoted the

---

10. Chinn, "Ohr Shraga," p. 10.

11. Rabbi Yisrael Spinner.

One Shabbos, the boys began singing a *niggun* to *Mizmor L'David* (*Psalms* 23) that Benzion Shenker had brought back to Torah Vodaath from the Modzhitzer Rebbe's *tisch*. Reb Shraga Feivel called for the boys to sing it over and over. He was especially moved by the melody to the words, "Though I walk in the valley overshaded by death, I will fear no evil for You are with me." Finally, he told them that he hoped that this *niggun* would be sung at the moment his soul departed from the world.

12. Rabbi Avraham Abba Freedman.

words of the Baal HaTanya on his deathbed, as he pointed to the beams of the ceiling above his head: "I don't see here just wooden beams, but the Divine Presence that brought them into existence."

Even Reb Shraga Feivel's everyday speech reflected the degree to which his thoughts were constantly on Hashem. No joke was without a double meaning. Passing out the drinks on his last Simchas Torah, he jokingly referred to the liquor as firewater. The next day he confided to one of his students that he had been thinking about what Rabbi Shneur Zalman of Liadi writes in his *Likkutei Torah* on the statement of *Chazal:* Even though the fire [on the altar] was from Heaven there was a mitzvah to add earthly fire as well.

He lived with a sense of obligation to give of himself entirely to Hashem. "You shall love the L-rd Your G-d with . . . all your resources (בְּכָל מְאֹדֶךָ)" meant for him that one must use whatever plenitude he has been blessed with — i.e., all his talents — to serve Hashem.[13] The anthem of Torah Vodaath under Reb Shraga Feivel was drawn from *Sefer Chareidim*: "In my heart I will build a tabernacle to His glory . . . And there I will bring an offering — my unique, indivisible soul." There were few boys in the Mesivta who did not know the words by heart and sing them with great fervor.

Years of the deepest reflection had given the most abstract ideas an overwhelming immediacy for him. His voice trembled as he read the *kvittel* (personal petition) that the Ohr HaChaim had sent to be placed in the cracks of the *Kosel* (the Western Wall), in which he addresses the *Shechinah* with the words of Shlomo HaMelech: יוֹנָתִי, תַמָּתִי אֲחֹתִי, רַעְיָתִי, *My sister, my beloved, my dove, my perfect one* (*Shir HaShirim* 5:2).

Tanya (ch. 24) describes a person who sins as having disgraced the King Himself; adding that there is no greater manifestation of the Exile of the *Shechinah*. He likens a sinner to someone who inflicts unspeakable humiliation on the king. These words were no mere metaphor for Reb Shraga Feivel. They pierced deep into his heart, and every time he taught this section of *Tanya*, he was visibly shaken by the metaphor.

---

13. Rabbi Hershel Mashinsky.

On the last Simchas Torah of his life, Reb Shraga Feivel sat in the waning light with his *talmidim* in Bais Medrash Elyon singing the haunting melody of R' Aisik of Kahliv, *"Galus, galus, vie lang bist du, Shechinah, Shechinah, vie veit bist du* — Exile, exile, how long you are; *Shechinah, Shechinah,* how distant You are." He told his students how the Divrei Chaim used to send his *chassidim* to R' Aisik, as the Divrei Chaim put it, "to study in the yeshivah of *galus HaShechinah*." For his students Reb Shraga Feivel was a *rosh yeshivah* in the same yeshivah.

Reb Shraga Feivel sought to give his students the same awareness of Hashem's presence. He once gave a parable to illustrate how the awareness of Hashem's presence depends on sensitizing oneself to it. Twin brothers were separated at birth: One was raised in the house of a well-to-do banker and the other on a farm. Many years passed and the two brothers were reunited one day in the bustling city. As they stood talking on a busy street, the brother raised on a farm suddenly stopped to listen to the sweet song of a lark. His banker brother heard nothing. On the other hand, when someone nearby dropped a coin, the brother raised in a bank heard its jingling on the pavement immediately while the other brother heard nothing. Each heard what he had trained himself to hear.[14] Reb Shraga Feivel trained his students to sense Hashem everywhere.

Accepting Suffering With Love

R' SHALOM BER OF LUBAVITCH ONCE SAID OF HIMSELF THAT IF HIS veins were cut they would be found flowing with Chassidus. On this comment, Reb Shraga Feivel added, "And if they cut my veins, they would find them flowing with *bitachon* (trust) in Hashem." Nowhere was that *bitachon* more manifest than in the way he dealt with his lifelong ulcer attacks,[15] which sometimes left him totally immobilized. Somehow he was able to use his ability to concentrate on the most profound Torah concepts not only to overcome the pain but to lead a life of almost unparalleled productivity.

---

14. Rabbi Elias Schwartz, *Delving Within*, pp. 189-90.

15. Milk and crackers were his daily fare for a period of sixteen years.

From time to time, when the pains were the most intense, he would call the Mesivta office and ask that a student be sent over to be with him. Invariably the student would arrive and find him with a *sefer* in hand. He would apologize for having summoned the student and explain that the only relief he could find was in works that required his full concentration. His son Shmuel remembers being awakened early one morning by the sound of his father pacing back and forth in his room. When he knocked on the door, he found his father with the Ramchal's *138 Gates of Wisdom*[16] in his hand. Only by immersing himself with all his concentration in this work, he told his son, could he find relief from the terrible pains he was then suffering.

Of course no amount of immersion in Torah could help him forget the pain all the time. Other mental stratagems were needed as well. The trick of overcoming debilitating pain, Reb Shraga Feivel told one *talmid*, is to remember that life is a long series of individual moments. With that in mind, "there is no pain that cannot be borne for the moment. And as for what's ahead: There's no sense in worrying about what one does not yet feel."[17]

Finally, when nothing else helps, the recognition must come that even the pain comes from a benevolent G-d. Reb Shraga Feivel's *matzeivah* (gravestone) describes him not just as having accepted suffering but as having rejoiced in it: שָׂמֵחַ בְּיִסּוּרִין. He used to explain the verse (*Tehillim* 62:6): אַךְ לֵאלֹקִים דּוֹמִי נַפְשִׁי כִּי מִמֶּנּוּ תִּקְוָתִי, *Only for G-d my soul waits quietly, for my only hope comes from Him*, in the following manner: "אֱלֹקִים refers to the Divine quality of strict judgment as reflected in the bitter afflictions that cleanse and purify the soul, and without which Man would be utterly without any chance to stand before Hashem. Therefore דּוֹמִי נַפְשִׁי, *my soul remains silent*, in the face of these afflictions, for my hope comes only from Hashem Who has thus afflicted me in order to purify me."

---

16. This work was particularly dear to Reb Shraga Feivel. One day his student Yisrael Spinner noticed that he was especially happy. Reb Shraga Feivel told him that he had just finished *138 Gates of Wisdom* for the fifteenth time.

17. Chinn, "Ohr Shraga," p. 14.

Chapter 18

Chassid

REB SHRAGA FEIVEL WAS A CHASSID; HE WAS DEEPLY rooted, both emotionally and intellectually, in the chassidic milieu in which he grew up. Most of his central ideas — Hashem's immanence in every aspect of creation; the centrality of prayer; the importance of joy, song, and dance; the study of the classic chassidic literature; the importance of having a *rebbe* or other spiritual leader; the need to subordinate one's sense of self in favor of a *Klal Yisrael* identity — have their source in the works of the leading thinkers of Chassidism. His stress on joy, his appreciation of the *amcha Yid* (the simple Jew), his favorable view of working for a living[1] — all these are typical of chassidic communities.

It has been said that there is no such thing as a generic chassid — that every chassid is of necessity a chassid of a particular *Rebbe*.[2] If

---

1. Everywhere in the Torah where the seventh day is described as a day of rest, he noted, it is preceded by a description of the preceding six days as days of work.

2. Rabbi Nechemia Polen, review of *Leaping Souls: Rabbi Menachem Mendel and the Spirit of Kotzk* by Chaim Feinberg, *Jewish Action*, Summer 1995, p. 51.

so, Reb Shraga Feivel was an exception to the general rule. In Chassidus, as in the larger world of Jewish thought, he was too open to differing approaches ever to bind himself exclusively to one approach. And he was too independent minded to hew exactly to a previously trodden path. Thus the more he learned, thought, met others, and saw how various approaches succeeded with various types of people and in various surroundings, the more he developed as a person and as a chassid. To say that he was not the same as the chassidim among whom he grew up is not to say that he in any way disapproved of or considered his way better than theirs; it means only that he grew constantly throughout his life.

REB SHRAGA FEIVEL HAD THE WARMEST ASSOCIATIONS WITH the chassidic world of his youth. He once described for his students

Emotional Roots

a Rosh Chodesh meal in which the tablecloth was a torn *tallis katan* and the only food was borscht. The chassidim gathered around the wobbly table sang *Barchi Nafshi*[3] with such feeling that the borscht spilled and the makeshift tablecloth was dyed a deep red. "Never in my life was I again privileged to experience such an elevated moment," he said, when describing the scene to his students.[4]

He was a walking storehouse of chassidic lore, both what he had picked up in his youth and what he had gathered from his voracious study of chassidic works. Chassidic stories, related with great animation, spiced his *shiurim*, and he showed students that a chassidic story also has to be "learned" to be properly understood.[5]

He rejoiced in the creation of a vibrant chassidic world in America by the survivors who arrived in the aftermath of the war. He told Yosef Binyamin Wulliger that he felt like reciting the *Shehecheyanu* blessing when he saw him come to his *chuppah* wearing a *shtreimel.* He was pleased when a group of chassidic students, led by the current Bostoner Rebbe, Rabbi Levi Yitzchak Horowitz, formed a group

---

3. *Tehillim* 104, the song of the day for Rosh Chodesh.
4. Rabbi Eliyahu Yehoshua Geldzhaler.
5. Ibid.

The Klausenburger Rebbe

called *Re'im Ne'emanim* (Loyal Friends) that gathered for *melaveh malkah* and Rosh Chodesh meals.

His excitement at hearing from *talmidim* about the *tischen* of the recently arrived Klausenburger Rebbe, Rabbi Yekusiel Yehudah Halberstam, made the experience of those *tischen* even dearer to the *talmidim*.[6] When *talmidim* returned from the celebrations following the Klausenberger Rebbe's remarriage, Reb Shraga Feivel eagerly debriefed them about every detail of the festivities.[7]

The Mesivta was the first yeshivah in America to install its own *mikveh*,[8] and the installation of a *mikveh* preceded the arrival of the first students in Bais Medrash Elyon in Monsey, as well.[9] The importance of a *mikveh* in Reb Shraga Feivel's eyes was only one example of his lifelong emphasis on *kedushah* (holiness). That quest for *kedushah* in all its aspects could be seen as well in the relish with which he repeated Rabbi Hirsch's question: Why did the Kohen Gadol immerse himself in the *mikveh* after completing the entire service of Yom Kippur? The final immersion in the *mikveh*, Rabbi Hirsch answered, is to ensure that the *kedushah* (holiness) of the day continues to accompany the Kohen Gadol even as he returns to his mundane tasks. Just so, Reb Shraga Feivel always emphasized, a Jew should always carry with him the spiritual exaltation that he experiences on special occasions in his life.

---

6. Rabbi Hershel Mashinsky.

7. Rabbi Eliyahu Yehoshua Geldzhaler.

8. When Reb Shraga Feivel sent a *bachur* to find a wealthy donor for the *mikveh*, he told him ironically that he would have a better chance of success if he said he was collecting for a swimming pool.

9. Rabbi Eliyahu Yehoshua Geldzhaler.

R' Shraga Feivel at the wedding of one of his childeren; Rabbi Avraham Pam is seated in the background (right) and Rabbi David Bender is seated on the left (facing forward)

At the same wedding: Seated (left to right) at table in foreground: Mr. Abraham Lewin, Rabbi Shmuel Kushelewitz, Rabbi Yisrael Chaim Kaplan. Seated (left to right) at table in background: R' Binyamin Wilhelm and Rabbi Shimon Goder

As the students in Bais Medrash Elyon returned from *Tashlich* one Rosh Hashanah, near the end of his life, Reb Shraga Feivel summoned them to his side. "After all the day's effort, I still don't feel I've reached the level of *Malchiyos*, of declaring and accepting the total sovereignty of G-d. I want you to help me. Let's see if together we can arouse ourselves to some taste of *Malchiyos*. He then began to sing slowly from the Rosh Hashanah *davening*, "וְיֵדַע כָּל פָּעוּל כִּי אַתָּה פְעַלְתּוֹ, *Let everything that has been made know that You are its Maker*," drawing the *talmidim* into the *niggun* with him. They sang *niggun* after *niggun*, and then Reb Shraga Feivel drew them into a circle to dance to וְעַל כֵּן נְקַוֶּה לְּךָ, *Therefore we put our trust in You*. Rabbi Yisrael Chaim Kaplan, the *mashgiach*, a Lithuanian *gadol* who had never been exposed to chassidim, entered and looked at those singing and dancing on the Day of Judgment as if they had taken leave of their senses. When they were done, Reb Shraga Feivel thanked his students for having helped him reach his goal. For their part, the American *bachurim* had tears of *hisorerus* (spiritual arousal) streaming down their faces.[10]

Rabbi Shraga Moshe Kalmanowitz

Reb Shraga Feivel worked hard to create within the Mesivta the feelings of brotherhood that are the hallmark of chassidic groups. In this he succeeded to a remarkable degree. "The *talmidim* in Bais Medrash Elyon," said Rabbi Moshe Aharon Stern, "were like brothers. We sat together at the same tables with the stars of the *beis medrash* — such future *roshei yeshivah* as Simchah Schustal, Don Ungarisher, Shraga Moshe Kalmanowitz — and addressed one another by our first names."

To create that sense of brotherhood, he used the brotherly spirit of Chassidism. In the singing and dancing in a circle of chassidic gatherings, all are equal, all parts of the same circle — the greatest scholar

10. Rabbi Moshe Aharon Stern.

and the simplest Jew — and so it was in the Mesivta as well. Reb Shraga Feivel struggled hard against elitism based purely on Torah scholarship and strived to eradicate feelings of disregard for unlearned Jews. He once overheard a student, recently arrived from Europe, ridiculing the way in which a simple Jew recited *parashas hakorbanos* (the list of the Temple sacrifices) during Shacharis. When this Jew reached the phrase כֶּבֶשׂ אֶחָד (one lamb) of the *korban tamid* (the daily offering), he had drawn out the word אֶחָד as if he were reciting the first verse of *Krias Shema*, and with the same facial expression.

Reb Shraga Feivel told the *bachur* that his amusement at this sight was evidence of his deficient spiritual sensitivities, not of his superior understanding. What should have struck him was how this simple Jew had been able to accept the yoke of Heaven on himself even in the אֶחָד of the *korban tamid*.[11]

Ultimately, however, Reb Shraga Feivel was not primarily interested in making chassidim of his students. If that happened, he was pleased, but he was also pleased if a student held fast to his own time-honored Lithuanian or German customs. All Jewish *minhagim* were dear to him in this respect. Rabbi Sheah Geldzhaler was once invited to Reb Shraga Feivel's home for the Shemini Atzeres meal. In keeping with his custom, Reb Shraga Feivel ate his Shemini Atzeres meals in the *succah*, while Rabbi Geldzhaler, whose family followed the Galician *minhag*, did not. At the beginning of the meal, Reb Shraga Feivel immediately set his confused *talmid* at ease. "Don't worry, you'll eat in the part of the *succah* under the roof," Reb Shraga Feivel told him.

He then took the occasion to stress the special importance of preserving one's *minhagim*, especially in the wake of the Holocaust. "Today when almost nothing survives of the holy communities of Europe, each of us is obligated to hold fast to the precious customs of his ancestors, who sacrificed their lives for those customs. Neither their Torah nor their *minhagim* must be forgotten. Should those customs be lost because those who kept them have been sacrificed on the altar?"[12]

---

11. Rabbi Yisrael Spinner.

12. Reb Shraga Feivel taught students to be proud of their differing *minhagim* (customs) and not to try to conform to the standard of others. Shortly after his arrival in

FAR MORE IMPORTANT THAN MAKING CHASSIDIM OF HIS STU-
dents was giving them a taste of the depths of chassidic thought.

The Goal of Chassidus The great chassidic thinkers exerted an extremely strong pull on him. Reb Tzadok HaKohen of Lublin, was, in his opinion, the deepest of Jewish philosophers. On Erev Shabbos, as he awaited the onset of Shabbos, he was most often found studying the *Likkutei Torah* of Rabbi Shneur Zalman of Liadi[13] or *Sfas Emes*. In his final illness, when he was confined to bed, he frequently asked his son Shmuel to read to him the stories of Rabbi Nachman of Breslov.

Chassidus, Reb Shraga Feivel taught, remains completely focused on G–d. The words of Rabbi Shneur Zalman of Liadi, the Baal HaTanya, speaking to G–d, as it were, captured this focus for him — "I want not Your Gan Eden; I want not Your *Olam Haba*; I seek only to be attached to You."[14] On the practical plane, Chassidus provides the tools to continue to reach toward G–d, even when obstacles arise. If there is an impediment blocking one's path to G–d, one has to go around it or find a way of ignoring it — with an emphasis on constructive activities, learning or a *niggun*, for instance — but above all, do not stop your ascent by becoming preoccupied with removing the obstacle.[15]

In this he followed the counsel of the Chiddushei HaRim, founder of the Gerrer dynasty, who spoke to his disciples on Erev

---

America from Belgium, Sheah Geldzhaler approached Reb Shraga Feivel and told him that his father had insisted that he inquire about the kashrus in the Mesivta. Some might have been insulted by the inquiry, but Reb Shraga Feivel went out of his way to praise the new student for fulfilling his father's request. He told him to tell the cooks that he was to be served *milchigs* only. "If your father told you to inquire, you have to be more careful about what you eat than other students," Reb Shraga Feivel explained.

The kitchen staff, however, received the request for *milchig* meals less warmly, and made fun of the young boy for his "*meshugasen* (crazy ideas)." Only when Reb Shraga Feivel himself walked the three flights down from his office to the kitchen was the matter taken care of.

13. Reb Shraga Feivel once saw his son Shmuel turning the pages of *Likkutei Torah* one after another. He told him that if he was not capable of thinking deeply about what he was learning it was pointless to study *Likkutei Torah* at all.

14. Rabbi Shmuel Mendlowitz.

15. Rabbi Elias Schwartz, *Delving Within*, p. 49.

Yom Kippur and urged them not to be preoccupied on Yom Kippur with analyzing their sins; that would lead to depression and prevent them from focusing on how to improve themselves. In earlier, greater generations, the order of priorities followed the verse, "סוּר מֵרָע וַעֲשֵׂה טוֹב, *Turn from evil and do good*" (*Psalms* 34:16), but in inferior generations the verse must be interpreted: "Turn from evil *by* doing good." Rather than being absorbed in one's shortcomings, Chassidus taught that one should focus on elevating himself, and the shortcoming would fall away as a result.

Once when he was confined to bed for a prolonged period, someone obtained for him a hospital bed that allowed his head to be elevated. Reb Shraga Feivel found in that bed a useful application to everyday life. This bed, he said, can be compared to Chassidus: Just as the bed lifts you up, so Chassidus lifts you up, it elevates you, and makes you feel like a prince, so you do not wish to sin.

DESPITE THE CHASSIDIC CORE OF HIS BEING, REB SHRAGA FEIVEL shaped boys who did not come from chassidic families and were not

A Yeshivah for Everyone headed in that direction, no less than boys who ended up as devoted followers of the Klausenburger Rebbe or the Satmar Rebbe. A chassidic student of the Mesivta might reminisce, "*Even* Yankel, the Litvak, was a *talmid*." But Yankel, the Litvak, would reply with fervor, "And I say, *even* Sheah, the chassid, was a *talmid*."[16]

Reb Shraga Feivel's respect for every Torah approach, and his ability to synthesize and find the common ground between apparently divergent approaches, was something his *talmidim* picked up from him. Those *talmidim* came from every group in the Orthodox world. Some *talmidim* from chassidic homes ultimately went much further in their Chassidus than anything their parents could have imagined, and some from nonchassidic backgrounds were certainly drawn to Chassidus under Reb Shraga Feivel's influence. On the other hand, nonchassidic students never felt that they were out of place, nor did Reb Shraga Feivel try to draw them away from their background. Old divisions between chassidim and *misnagdim* were

---

16. Rabbi Yaakov Leshinsky.

checked at the door of Torah Vodaath, which was built on Reb Shraga Feivel's unique melding of the two approaches. Each student could grow in the way he chose for himself, without slighting other approaches. The golden era of Bais Medrash Elyon was a perfect example of this. It had chassidim and *misnagdim* and everything in between, but these divergent streams added flavor, not conflict, to the yeshivah.

When he spoke about the bitter divisions that had plagued *Klal Yisrael* in the past, and particularly about those between chassidim and *misnagdim*, Reb Shraga Feivel would mention the famous parable, attributed to Rabbi Yisrael Salanter and others. There was a rich man with two sons-in-law, one who ate no *fleishigs* (meat) and one who ate no *milchigs* (dairy dishes). For many years, the rich man fed them both in his house according to their tastes. One sat at one table with his family eating meat and the other sat at a second table with his family eating dairy. Eventually, however, the father-in-law lost his fortune and served the whole family bread and potatoes. "Now that we can afford neither meat nor dairy delicacies," he said to his sons-in-law, "why sit at separate tables?"

"Similarly today," said Reb Shraga Feivel, "we lack the greatness, the scholarship, the zeal, the intensity of early chassidim and *misnagdim* — we have neither meat nor dairy — and there is no point eating at separate tables."

Chapter 19

An Education in Responsibility

IF THE TALMIDIM OF REB SHRAGA FEIVEL SHARED ONE THING in common, it was a sense of responsibility for their fellow Jews.

For the Klal No subject so dominated his teaching or private conversation as the obligation upon every Jew to be concerned with the fate of his fellow Jews. Among the most important words in his vocabulary were "*Klal Yisrael*," and his constant question was: What are you doing for *Klal Yisrael*?[1]

He repeated two verses very often: כֹּל הַנִּקְרָא בִשְׁמִי וְלִכְבוֹדִי בְּרָאתִיו יְצַרְתִּיו אַף עֲשִׂיתִיו, *Everyone who is called in My Name, for My honor have I created him; I fashioned him; yea, I have made him* (*Yeshayahu* 43:7); and כֹּל פָּעַל ה' לַמַּעֲנֵהוּ וְגַם רָשָׁע לְיוֹם רָעָה — *Hashem has made everything for His own purpose, even the wicked for the day of evil* (*Mishlei* 16:4). To the latter verse he would add the homiletical interpretation that even the spiritual darkness of a wicked person

---

1. Rabbi Elias Schwartz.

must be transformed through repentance to the spiritual light symbolized by *day*. Every person and everything in the world was created for Hashem's honor. Even the wicked person brings honor to Hashem on the day when he receives his punishment. If even the *rasha* (wicked person) brings glory to Hashem, Reb Shraga Feivel used to say, how much more so must *we* act for His glory, though we be no more than insignificant human beings. And since *Klal Yisrael* is the principal bearer of Hashem's honor in this world, the improvement of its situation is the greatest possible glorification of Hashem.[2] He interpreted the verse, דּוֹר לְדוֹר יְשַׁבַּח מַעֲשֶׂיךָ, *One generation will praise Your creations to another* (*Tehillim* 145:4), to mean that each generation has an obligation to improve and make Hashem's world more praiseworthy, and thereby give praise to the Creator.

When Adam and Chavah sinned and were banished from the Garden of Eden, G-d reduced the productive power of the earth. Henceforth, people would till and plant and be rewarded with thorns and limited crops — and the Torah describes this decrease as a curse for the earth.[3] How was it a curse for the inanimate *earth*, rather than just for Adam? Reb Shraga Feivel explained that every part of Creation was designed to be productive. For the earth to be condemned to relative futility, to be denied its capacity to produce crops, was a curse. Similarly, he said, any person who does not live up to his creative potential has been denied a blessing.[4]

The principal distinction between man and other living creatures, said Reb Shraga Feivel, is that the latter receive life and sustenance from Hashem without feeling an obligation to share with others. Man's primary purpose, after striving to perfect himself, is to concern himself with improving his fellow man. Thus the Midrash (*Vayikra Rabbah* 14) comments that if a man is not worthy, he is told that even the lowly *yitush* (flea) was created before him. The message of the Midrash, Reb Shraga Feivel explained, is that a person

2. Sidney Greenwald.

3. *Bereishis* 3:17.

4. Rabbi Nesanel Quinn.

who partakes of G-d's bounty — who breathes His air, who eats His food, who benefits from His knowledge — yet feels no responsibility to share his money, food, or knowledge with others, serves no purpose in the Creation. To such a person we say, "If you, like the flea, are not contributing to others, there was no need for you to be created. The flea already preceded you."[5]

Reb Shraga Feivel stressed that a Jew cannot concern himself with his individual spiritual state apart from that of the Jewish community around him. The Sages' teaching, אַל תְּהִי רָשָׁע בִּפְנֵי עַצְמֶךָ, *Do not judge yourself to be a wicked person* (*Pirkei Avos* 2:18), may also indicate, he said, that anyone who limits his efforts to himself alone — who is בִּפְנֵי עַצְמֶךָ, *for himself* — is derelict in his obligation. Even Torah learning, without a concern for others, said Reb Shraga Feivel, is not enough: *Toras chesed*, the Torah of kindness, is Torah taught to others; do not keep your Torah for yourself.

All Jews are linked in a common fate, Reb Shraga Feivel insisted, and it is sinful to remain aloof in times of Jewish tragedy; personal righteousness without a concern for the rest of humanity is inadequate. Throughout the Holocaust, he challenged his students to do more for the Jews of Europe. He cited the verse, כִּי הַשָּׁתוֹת יֵהָרֵסוּן צַדִּיק מַה פָּעָל, *When the firm foundations are destroyed, what has the righteous man wrought?* (*Tehillim* 11:3), as explained by Rabbi Samson Raphael Hirsch: "When the very foundations of society are destroyed, of what avail has a righteous man been to himself or to the world with all his righteousness?"[6]

This concept is one of the fundamental ideas of Chassidus. As the Sfas Emes taught, a Jew must be willing to sacrifice everything, even his portion in the World to Come, on behalf of *Klal Yisrael*, and the exemplar of this principle is Moshe Rabbeinu. Rather than allow Hashem to destroy the Jewish people and create a new nation from him, Moshe insisted that his fate be linked to that of the Jewish people: If they were to be blotted out, Moshe told Hashem, his name too should be erased from the Torah.

---

5. Sidney Greenwald.
6. Rabbi Ephraim Wolf.

REB SHRAGA FEIVEL KNEW THAT LOVE FOR *KLAL YISRAEL* IN THE abstract was worthless if not based on the love of individual Jews

Sensitizing to Others

making up *Klal Yisrael.* Thus he first made *chesed* concrete in countless everyday actions. Younger boys in the Mesivta learned to be sensitive to the needs of the students sitting next to them in class or the *beis medrash.* Better students, for instance, were actively pushed to help weaker ones.[7]

Once he noticed two *talmidim* carrying chairs to a classroom. Reb Shraga Feivel asked one of them, "For whom are you bringing this chair?" He answered, "For myself." He asked the same question of the other boy, and the answer was the same. Reb Shraga Feivel chided, "*You* brought a chair for yourself, and *you* brought a chair for yourself. So you're both just *schleppers.* If each of you had brought a chair for the other, each of you would have done a *chesed.*"[8]

Reb Shraga Feivel sensitized his students about their responsibility to their fellow Jews. "Understand, my sons, to love, to *truly* love, means to know what brings pain to your friend, without being told."[9] *Pirkei Avos* teaches that retribution for a person's misdeeds is meted out with a person's knowledge and without his knowledge.[10] The Baal Shem Tov explains that when a person comes before the Heavenly Court and defends himself, he is shown that he condemned others who did the same thing he did. If so, how can he defend himself when he failed to defend others who committed the same sin? His defense is then rejected. In other words, when someone criticizes others, he may well be passing judgment on himself.[11]

The goal, of course, was to create a sensitivity to the needs of others that would eventually embrace all *Klal Yisrael.* And indeed the trademark of Torah Vodaath students was the feeling that they had

---

7. Rabbi Joshua Silbermintz.

8. Chinn, "Ohr Shraga," p. 9.

9. Rabbi Elias Schwartz, *V'shee-non-tom*, Vol. I, p. 129.

10. *Pirkei Avos* 3:20.

11. Rabbi Elias Schwartz, *Delving Within*, p. 206; *V'shee-non-tom*, Vol. 1, pp. 220-221.

been personally given the task of changing the face of American Jewry. "You have been drafted in a time of crisis. *Klal Yisrael* is waiting for you," was Reb Shraga Feivel's frequent refrain. In times when assimilation and low birthrates prompt predictions that the Jewish population of the world will decline precipitously, *mesiras nefesh* (self-sacrifice) is demanded from every Jew. The frogs sent to plague Egypt entered the stoves of the Egyptians knowing that they would be burned, and from their example Chananiah, Mishael, and Azariah deduced that they too should enter Nebuchadnetzar's fiery furnace in order to sanctify G-d's Name. "From this we learn," Reb Shraga Feivel would declare, "that when Hashem gives us a mission to fulfill, we have no right to consider our personal interests."

"It is remarkable to what an extent he planted in us a feeling that we who had been fortunate to learn Torah held the whole spiritual fate of American Jewry in our hands," recalls Elimelech Terebelo. "Even when I had been in the yeshivah only a short time, and had barely begun to realize my ambitions in learning, Reb Shraga Feivel had already instilled in me a sense of obligation to worry about all those Jewish boys who had not had the opportunity to attend a yeshivah or who lived in towns far from any yeshivah." Mesivta students were never allowed to forget that no matter how happy they were in the *beis medrash*, they represented a pitifully small fraction of the Jewish world and that most of their contemporaries had never even seen a Gemara.

WHEN IT WAS TIME FOR STUDENTS TO LEAVE THE *BEIS MEDRASH*, Reb Shraga Feivel pushed them toward *klal* work and fired them

Directing Into Klal Work
with a sense of mission that allowed them to overcome the myriad obstacles that they were certain to confront. Whenever he talked to a student about his plans for the future, he reminded him that those plans must acknowledge a duty to give something back to *Klal Yisrael*. "Your first concern should be not what you can get out of the position," he told them, "but what you can give."[12]

---

12. Gross and Kaminetsky, p. 562.

Equally important, he gave his students the confidence that they would succeed. To a student who complained that Reb Shraga Feivel's expectations of him were beyond his capabilities, he said, "America is an אֶרֶץ לֹא זְרוּעָה" (literally: an unsown land), a place where the לֹא (no or *not*) is planted everywhere. All one hears is, 'I'm not capable; I can't.' " One of his favorite verses was what Hashem told the prophet Yirmiyahu when he said he was too young to admonish his people: "Don't say I am but a youth; everywhere that I send you, there shall you go" (*Yirmiyahu* 1:7).[13]

His mark was on his students. Aryeh Leib Kramer, a product of the Mesivta, founded the Inter-Yeshivah Student Council to convince boys in elementary yeshivos to continue on to yeshivah high schools. In many respects, the council proved to be the forerunner of all American *kiruv* work. When New York State allowed public-school children an hour a week of so-called "Release Time" for religious study, Torah Vodaath students volunteered to teach the classes. Camp Agudah, which throughout the 40's taught the basics of *Yiddishkeit* to boys from outside the yeshivah community, was staffed primarily by Mesivta students, and the head counselors were almost all Reb Shraga Feivel's *talmidim*.[14]

When Torah Umesorah began its activities, it was students of the Mesivta who went from city to city trying to register boys and girls for the local day schools. Abish Mendlowitz and Shubert Spero, for instance, spent a summer recruiting for new day schools in Detroit and Cincinnati." Freddy Wolf and Elimelech Terebelo traveled from town to town, sleeping at night in railway stations to save money, as they scouted out possible communities for day schools.[15]

The adventures of Moshe Weitman and Sidney Greenwald in Montreal show the extent to which Reb Shraga Feivel's students were willing to walk into fire for him. Greenwald was born in Hungary and was not yet an American citizen. Though Weitman was a native American, he lacked both a passport and a birth cer-

---

13. Rabbi Avraham Pam.

14. See *They Called Him Mike*, pp. 217-230.

15. Rabbi Ephraim Wolf.

tificate.[16] Understandably the parents of both boys strongly opposed their going to Montreal for fear that they would have difficulty reentering the United States.

Nevertheless they were determined to go. When they explained their problem to Reb Shraga Feivel, he turned to the Mesivta's registrar and said, "Schevelowitz, *klap op a brief* (type up a letter)." The result was a letter that read: "To Whom it May Concern. Sidney Greenwald and Moshe Weitman are traveling to Montreal on business of Mesivta Torah Vodaath. Please extend them every courtesy." Greenwald and Weitman explained to Reb Shraga Feivel that such a letter was worthless. So he told the registrar to affix to the letter the Mesivta's corporate seal, consisting of a mass of red wax with the Torah Vodaath imprint stamped on it.

Despite the unpromising nature of this document, the two young men did not want to disappoint their *rebbi*. At the border crossing, on the way out of the United States, the customs agent told them, "I'll let you out of the United States, but you are going to have problems getting back into the country." Nevertheless they proceeded. In three weeks in Montreal, they succeeded in recruiting enough students to open a day school and boarded the train to return. At the Rouse's Point border crossing, however, the customs official took one look at their letter and sent it to his superior. The train was held up for an hour while Customs considered the fate of the two young idealists. Finally, at 11 p.m. came the unexpected order to let the train go on with all its passengers.[17]

Like the frogs in Egypt, Weitman and Greenwald had ignored their fate and considered only Reb Shraga Feivel's orders.

---

16. The hospital in which he was born had burned down, with its records.
17. Sidney Greenwald.

Chapter 20

Father of the Yeshivos

WERE REB SHRAGA FEIVEL TO HAVE GUIDED ONLY Torah Vodaath for a quarter of a century, his place as the preeminent Torah educator in America in the first half of this century would be secure. Yet, in addition, he played a major role in establishing Mesivta Chaim Berlin, Telshe Yeshivah, and Bais Medrash Govoha of Lakewood. And he provided crucial assistance to three of the great chassidic leaders who arrived after the Holocaust — the Satmar Rav, the Klausunberger Rav, and Rabbi Michoel Ber Weissmandl — that helped them gain their first footholds in America.

He never recognized any distinction between his yeshivah and others. In his mind there existed only one large yeshivah — the yeshivah of the *Ribbono Shel Olam* — of which all yeshivos were branches. Rabbi Yaakov Kamenetsky once captured Reb Shraga Feivel's uniqueness in this regard:

> Every *rosh yeshivah* thinks his yeshivah is the best or that it soon will be. For Reb Shraga Feivel it was different. To

soon will be. For Reb Shraga Feivel it was different. To him, as long as there was Torah it did not matter where it was — whether it be Telshe or Lakewood. That is why we find something unusual about graduates of Torah Vodaath. Other yeshivos breed loyalty. But Torah Vodaath is different. Reb Shraga Feivel implanted the attitude that it does not matter what yeshivah one is attached to — it is all Torah.[1]

There are two things that no head of a yeshivah will ever give up

Rabbi Michoel Ber Weissmandl

willingly: a good student and a major financial supporter. Yet Reb Shraga Feivel did both — and not just once but many times over the course of twenty years. At a time when there were barely fifty advanced *talmidim* in all of America, Reb Shraga Feivel provided many of his best *bachurim* to help start Telshe and Lakewood, and helped the yeshivos raise money as if they were his own. In the annals of the yeshivos from Volozhin to the present, there is almost no comparable example.[2]

1. *Reb Yaakov*, pp. 153-54.

2. Rabbi Zelik Epstein has noted an interesting parallelism in the transmission of the Torah: New eras often begin with a dramatic act of self-renunciation. Thus the era of the *Tannaim* started when the Bnei Beseira recognized that Hillel's learning far surpassed their own and voluntarily stepped down as the heads of the Sanhedrin in favor of him. Similarly, the transmission of Torah from Babylonia to Spain began when the *rav* of the community in Cordoba realized that a captive who had been brought in chains into the *beis medrash* was far greater than he in learning. He instructed the community to redeem the captive and appoint him *rav* of the community. That captive, Rabbi Moshe ben Chanoch, was the first great teacher of Torah in Spain. Yet none of this would have occurred except for the humility of the previous *rav* of Cordoba, who is virtually unknown today. And so it was that Torah learning in America today began with one who gave no consideration to himself but thought only of the need to spread Torah among American Jews.

THE LARGEST CONCENTRATION OF JEWS IN NEW YORK CITY IN the 30's and 40's, after the Lower East Side, was in the Brownsville

Founding of Mesivta Chaim Berlin
section of Brooklyn. Yet Brownsville's 300,000 Jews lacked a single high school-level yeshivah, until 1936. That year Reb Shraga Feivel decided that Yeshivas Chaim Berlin, which then continued only until eighth grade, should develop its own mesivta, although a large percentage of its graduates enrolled in Torah Vodaath.

Reb Shraga Feivel's son-in-law, Rabbi Sender Linchner, was then a rabbi in the largest shul in East New York, the neighborhood adjacent to Brownsville, and among his congregants was the president of Yeshivas Chaim Berlin, Mr. Moshe Meltzer. Reb Shraga Feivel told his son-in-law that he should prevail upon Meltzer to expand the yeshivah. Meltzer's initial response was that the money could never be raised for such an expansion, especially in the depths of the Depression. From the first day that he mentioned the idea to Mr. Meltzer, however, Rabbi Linchner gave him no peace until he finally agreed to undertake the project.

By the time Mesivta Chaim Berlin opened its doors, the school year had already begun, and any of its elementary-school graduates interested in attending a Mesivta were already enrolled in Torah Vodaath. Reb Shraga Feivel solved the problem by sending every Brownsville boy in Torah Vodaath to Chaim Berlin. Later he established a rule that any boy who lived closer to Chaim Berlin than to Torah Vodaath would not be accepted in the Mesivta. That he was thereby diminishing his own enrollment made no difference to him.

It was also Reb Shraga Feivel — again working behind the scenes through Rabbi Linchner — who

Rabbi Yitzchak Hutner

brought Rabbi Yitzchak Hutner to Chaim Berlin, and thus ensured its development into one of the premier yeshivos in America. From the time that Rabbi Hutner first came to the United States, Reb Shraga Feivel had been encouraging him to start his own yeshivah. He assured Rabbi Hutner that if he rented a shul and opened a yeshivah, it would soon be filled to capacity.[3] And when the Mesivta of Chaim Berlin opened, Reb Shraga Feivel saw it as the perfect opportunity for Rabbi Hutner.[4]

Rabbi Eliyahu Meir Bloch

Telshe Yeshivah opened in 1941 with three students from England, six *bachurim* who had previously learned in Telshe in Lithuania, and several Americans, among them Bernard Goldenberg, Hillel Bodek, and Yitzchak Sheiner, all from Torah Vodaath.[5] At a shul in Williamsburg, Goldenberg had first heard Rabbi Eliyahu Meir Bloch announce his intention of opening a new yeshivah. Goldenberg was mesmerized by Rabbi Bloch and eager to be a pioneer of the new Telshe Yeshivah, despite the fact that he was then close to finishing

---

3. Sidney Greenwald.

4. This was the second time that Reb Shraga Feivel had secured a position for Rabbi Hutner. When the eminent Orthodox layman Irving Bunim was appointed by the Board of Directors of Rabbeinu Jacob Joseph School (RJJ) to recommend a new *menahel,* he naturally turned to Reb Shraga Feivel for advice. Reb Shraga Feivel recommended Rabbi Hutner, who was new in America and almost completely unknown. Despite never having heard of Rabbi Hutner, Bunim took Reb Shraga Feivel's advice. Shortly thereafter, Rabbi Hutner approached Reb Shraga Feivel and asked him for two *rebbeim* to teach in RJJ. Reb Shraga Feivel sent two of his closest *talmidim,* Rabbi Anshel Fink and Rabbi Nesanel Quinn, who brought to RJJ much of the spirit of Mesivta Torah Vodaath.

5. Rabbi Goldenberg was one of the founders of Torah Umesorah and Rabbi Sheiner is Rosh Yeshivas Kamenitz in Jerusalem.

his studies for *semichah* in Torah Vodaath. Both Rabbi Shlomo Heiman and Goldenberg's father, however, were strongly opposed to his leaving Torah Vodaath, but Reb Shraga Feivel encouraged him, saying, "Go help start a yeshivah."

Reb Shraga Feivel gave the same advice to Rabbi Nochum Velvel Dessler when the latter arrived in America via Siberia on a visa procured by Torah Vodaath. After learning for a time in the Mesivta, Dessler, who been a *talmid* of pre-war Telshe, was invited to join the new Telshe in Cleveland. One of his *rebbeim* advised him strongly against going to Cleveland, which he described, very accurately, as a

Rabbi Nochum Velvel Dessler

spiritual wasteland. Reb Shraga Feivel, however, told him, "I say go and have a part in the building of a yeshivah. And Hashem will help you turn the wasteland into a famous place of Torah."[6] Reb Shraga Feivel added that he would personally do everything possible to ensure Telshe's success — a promise he more than fulfilled.

It was Reb Shraga Feivel who first suggested to Rabbi Eliyahu Meir Bloch and Rabbi Mottel Katz that they open their yeshivah in Cleveland. They had already received a less-than-warm welcome for their proposed yeshivah from the Orthodox rabbinate in a number of cities. Reb Shraga Feivel told them that they should go instead to Cleveland, a city then dominated by the Reform rabbinate.[7] Reb

---

6. That prophecy came true. Rabbi Dessler eventually founded Hebrew Academy of Cleveland, a model institution, which he still leads.

7. The leading rabbinic figure in Cleveland was Abba Hillel Silver, the Reform and Zionist leader.

Earl H. Spero

Shraga Feivel also urged the Spero brothers of Cleveland, who were among his supporters, to assist Rabbis Bloch and Katz in building Telshe. At Reb Shraga Feivel's *levayah*, Rabbi Bloch told one of his students, "We are walking after the *mitah* (bier) of one to whom Telshe Yeshivah owes its founding and its continued existence."

Soon after Rabbi Aharon Kotler's arrival in America in 1941, he expressed to Reb Shraga Feivel the desire to open in America a yeshivah like the one he had left behind in Kletsk. Without hesitating, Reb Shraga Feivel chose some of the Mesivta's best — including Rabbi Elya Svei, Rabbi Moshe Eisemann, Rabbi Tzvi Genauer, Rabbi Yisrael Kanarek, and Rabbi Yaakov Weisberg — and sent them to Reb Aharon. He knew that only the very best *talmidim* could understand Reb Aharon's *shiurim*, and those were the *talmidim* he sent. The *roshei yeshivah* in the Mesivta were understandably upset to lose such prize pupils and complained to Reb Shraga Feivel. He told them unapologetically, "Our task is to cause Torah to flourish, and Reb Aharon cannot be *rebbi* for students of a lower caliber." It was to such deeds that Reb Aharon referred when he said of Reb Shraga Feivel, "Who can compare to him? His every action is *l'shem Shamayim* (for the sake of Heaven)!"

Rabbi Avraham Yaffen

What Reb Shraga Feivel did for Telshe and Lakewood was repeated in time for Yeshivas Chachmei Lublin in Detroit, and Yeshivas Bais Yosef (Novardhok), under Rabbi Avraham Yaffen, in Boro Park. Reb Shraga Feivel also helped establish a number of yeshivos for survivors from Europe after the war. Rabbi Michoel Ber Weissmandl, whose unrelenting efforts to rouse the West to save the Jews of Europe had fallen on deaf ears, described the *seiver panim yafos* (a warm demeanor) with which Reb Shraga Feivel greeted him, as sharply contrasting with the reception he received elsewhere. Reb Shraga Feivel offered Rabbi Weissmandl whatever help he could in reestablishing the Nitra Yeshivah in Mt. Kisco, New York.

After the war, Rabbi Moshe Neuschloss, the Sederheller Rav, established a yeshivah in Czechoslovakia for nearly a hundred survivors. The gates of *Eretz Yisrael* were closed by the British Mandatory authorities, and entry to America was limited by immigration restrictions. To obtain a student visa, foreigners needed a sponsoring institution willing to take responsibility for the student and capable of showing that it was a suitable facility. Through mutual friends, Rabbi Neuschloss was given Reb Shraga Feivel's name and contacted him to see whether Torah Vodaath could supply the necessary papers. Torah Vodaath had long since filled up its quota of such visas, but Reb Shraga Feivel asked Rabbi Hutner, as a personal favor, to have the necessary papers sent by Chaim Berlin.

Even after receipt of the necessary affidavits from Chaim Berlin, "the way was not paved with roses," as Rabbi Neuschloss wrote to Reb Shraga Feivel. Most of the boys had no citizenship papers of any kind, and such papers could only be obtained with the payment of substantial bribes to the Czech authorities. Once again, Reb Shraga Feivel responded quickly and sent Rabbi Neuschloss several thousand dollars. Embarrassed as he was to have to write to Reb Shraga Feivel yet a third time, Rabbi Neuschloss had no choice but to inform him that the boys were dressed in rags totally unsuitable for the journey to America. Again Reb Shraga Feivel sent money, to cover the cost of providing the boys with suitable clothing.

Upon reaching the United States, Rabbi Neuschloss decided that his yeshivah would be better located outside of New York City. Reb Shraga Feivel obtained a large building on Long Island for the yeshivah, and he used to travel personally from Williamsburg to Long Island by train to make sure the yeshivah had what it needed. He also persuaded Mr. Harry Hershkowitz, at that time the most active member of the Board of Torah Vodaath, to take a special interest in Rabbi Neuschloss' yeshivah.

THOUGH DIRECTING TORAH VODAATH *BACHURIM* TO OTHER
yeshivos was the most dramatic of Reb Shraga Feivel's sacrifices on
Sharing the behalf of yeshivos other than his own, he was no
Wealth less generous with his financial resources, even
when that generosity was at the expense of Torah
Vodaath. To help Mesivta Chaim Berlin establish itself, he told some
of his largest donors — including Benzion Eliyahu Fruchthandler —
who lived in closer proximity to Chaim Berlin than to Torah Vodaath,
that they should henceforth direct their support to Chaim Berlin.

Benzion Eliyahu Fruchthandler

Near the end of his life, when he
was already very weak, Reb Shraga
Feivel heard that the Klausenburger
Rav was holding a meeting to raise
funds for the network of yeshivos
and girls schools that he had established in the Displaced Persons
camps in Europe. Reb Shraga Feivel
immediately announced that he
would attend, to the shock and dismay of his students and family.
They could not understand why he
felt he had to go in such a weakened
condition. Seeing their concern, Reb
Shraga Feivel explained, "He's a
Yid, a *talmid chacham*, a *tzaddik*.
Besides, he was spared from the fire,
and he speaks in the name of all the *Yidden* over there who need
our help. Now is no time to think about ourselves or anything
gashmiyus'dik (material)." He went to the meeting and pledged to
raise $10,000.

Reb Aharon Kotler was so surprised when he heard of Reb Shraga
Feivel's contribution that he called him to find out whether the story
was true. Reb Shraga Feivel told Reb Aharon that he felt obligated to
do whatever the Klausenberger Rav asked, out of respect for him
and what he had been through.

Reb Shraga Feivel gave the Satmar Rav, Rabbi Yoel Teitelbaum, a similar gift of $10,000 shortly after the *Rebbe's* arrival in America.[8] At the very time Reb Shraga Feivel was giving $10,000 to the Klausenburger Rebbe and the Satmar Rebbe, Torah Vodaath was laboring under its own severe financial burdens.

Where he obtained all the money he gave away remains a mystery. Much of it appears to have come in the form of personal loans. On his deathbed, he carefully instructed his family of the necessity of repaying his personal debts.

The Satmar Rav with his attendants

Every director of an institution that relies on charitable gifts zealously guards his lists of contributors for fear that any gifts given to other institutions will be at his expense. Not so Reb Shraga Feivel. When Rabbi Avraham Kalmanowitz opened the Mirrer Yeshivah in Brooklyn, Reb Shraga Feivel offered him the names and addresses of all the supporters of Torah Vodaath. In addition, he intervened actively with Rabbi Leo Jung of the Manhattan Jewish Center to obtain large sums for the Klausenburger Rav, the Satmar Rav, and for Rabbi Weissmandl from a fund under Rabbi Jung's control. These gifts exceeded in most cases the amounts that Torah Vodaath itself had been receiving from the fund.[9]

EREV YOM KIPPUR 5703 (1942), HE AND RABBI LINCHNER WENT TO visit the great Sephardi *baal tzedakah* (philanthropist), Isaac Shalom,

A Worldwide Operation on behalf of Torah Vodaath. In the course of their conversation, Shalom shared with Reb Shraga Feivel a concern that was very much on his mind: the lack of any organized Torah education in North Africa, Iraq, and Iran, and the consequent inroads being made in these coun-

---

8. Reb Shraga Feivel also offered his hand to the Bobover Rebbe in the latter's postwar efforts to establish a network of *chadarim*, girls schools, and yeshivos.

9. Rabbi Avraham Abba Freedman.

tries by the Alliance and other nonreligious groups. At the end of the conversation, Shalom held out a check of $5,000 to Reb Shraga Feivel. But Reb Shraga Feivel refused to accept it. Even though Torah Vodaath was badly in need of funds, Reb Shraga Feivel told Shalom, "The Holocaust ended European Jewry. A new epoch is starting in which Sephardim will be at the center. You are the only one who understands this, so you must devote yourself to the Sephardim." On the basis of that meeting, Shalom established Otzar HaTorah, which over the next two decades established Jewish schools and yeshivos for tens of thousands of Jewish children in Arab lands. Many of the current generation of Sephardi *roshei yeshivah* in *Eretz Yisrael* and elsewhere were trained in yeshivos established by Otzar HaTorah.[10]

In the early 40's, Reb Shraga Feivel also became interested in the situation of South American Jewry. While the Mirrer Yeshivah was still in Shanghai awaiting American visas for its students, Reb Shraga Feivel proposed to Rabbi Avraham Kalmanowitz that the yeshivah should relocate to South America. Most of South American Jewry, he pointed out, was Yiddish-speaking, relatively prosperous, and as yet unassimilated. At the same time, there was virtually no spiritual sustenance for them in South America. The Mirrer *talmidim* could provide that sustenance, Reb Shraga Feivel argued, and at the same time be assured of a solid base of support. The proposal was given serious consideration by the Mirrer contingent in Shanghai, but in the end, they decided that prospects for them were brighter in the United States, and that they deserved some security after their six years of suffering.

REB SHRAGA FEIVEL VIEWED A YESHIVAH AS A PUBLIC INSTITUtion, not as a "business" run for the benefit of the proprietor. His goal was never that Torah Vodaath be acknowledged as the "best"

Yeshivah for the Klal yeshivah in America, but that it do everything possible to advance the cause of Torah.

His task, as he saw it, was to do that which others were not doing, not to compete with others. Thus he was perfectly

---

10. After his *petirah,* found among Reb Shraga Feivel's papers were documents attesting to his support for the pioneering educational efforts of Rabbi Yitzchak Meir Levi in Iran as well. Rabbi Levi was originally sent to Iran by Chief Rabbi Yitzchak Isaac Herzog, and succeeded in setting up schools and yeshivos in numerous Jewish communities.

willing to merge his Bais Medrash Elyon with Rabbi Aharon Kotler's Bais Medrash Govoha in Lakewood, even though Bais Medrash Elyon was the better established of the two.[11] He saw no need, as he put it, to become a "chain store" if Reb Aharon was committed to building his own *kollel*.[12]

Rabbi Aharon Kotler

Similarly, Torah Vodaath's admission policy was governed by the question: How can the yeshivah have the greatest impact on American Jewry? The idea of a yeshivah taking only the brightest boys was completely foreign to him. Torah Vodaath in his day would no more have turned down any boy from Williamsburg than a Satmar yeshivah today would turn down a boy from a Satmar family.[13] He saw Torah Vodaath as serving a community and *Klal Yisrael*, not as some sort of private enterprise.

Boys from weaker Jewish backgrounds were not only admitted, they were eagerly sought out. The recruiting trips, in which boys from Eastern Pennsylvania, Baltimore, and Rochester were bused into Williamsburg for a Simchas Torah in Torah Vodaath, were aimed precisely at boys with little background in Torah learning and scant halachic knowledge.[14] Even where the boys came from nominally *shomer Shabbos* homes, their knowledge of halachah was often woefully weak.[15]

Reb Shraga Feivel emphasized that the success of the recruiting trips would be determined by how many boys remained in the yeshivah after Simchas Torah. To that end, the entire emphasis was on making sure they thoroughly enjoyed the Yom Tov. If that meant enticing them with a Brooklyn Dodgers game and bowling, so be it.

---

11. Rabbi Shmuel Mendlowitz.

12. Jack Klausner.

13. Rabbi Yisrael Belsky.

14. For a fuller account of the recruiting trips see *They Called Him Mike*, pp. 118-121.

15. In the Orthodox communities throughout Pennsylvania, which were the main targets of the recruiting trips, it was not uncommon, for instance, for Orthodox Jews to carry on Shabbos in the public domain. *Yonah Zev Herskowitz*.

One time some of the visiting boys shined their shoes on Yom Tov. Reb Shraga Feivel gave instructions that nothing should be said to them. "First let us bring them to Torah Vodaath, then we'll have plenty of time to take care of them religiously," he said.[16] It was precisely such boys whom Reb Shraga Feivel was most eager to bring into Torah Vodaath. Only by greatly expanding the range of those exposed to Torah learning, he felt, would a foothold for Orthodoxy be created in America.[17]

He was also prepared to use Torah Vodaath as a partial remedy for the almost total absence of Torah education in South America.

A group of talmidim from South America, with their rebbi, Rabbi Moshe Yechezkel Samuels, who was a chavrusa of Rabbi Shlomo Heiman
(L-R standing) Shaul Rovner, Yaakov Hutner, Yerachmiel Blumenfeld, Yoel Genauer, Mordechai Lichtenstein, Asher Lightman.
(L-r seated) Shlomo Kuznitzki, Moshe Yechezkel Samuels, Shimon Miller

---

16. Rabbi Joshua Silbermintz.

17. Even he might have been surprised by the number of boys from weak Jewish backgrounds who went on to be numbered among the next generation's leading *talmidei chachamim* and *roshei yeshivah*. He took particular pride in the boys who came from homes that were only nominally *shomer Shabbos* or less, who went on to excel in their Torah studies, and would frequently remark when looking at such students that all his efforts in building the Mesivta were worth it just for them. Many of those students would have difficulty being accepted at any mainstream yeshivah today, when Reb Shraga Feivel's conception of a yeshivah as a public institution seems a quaint anachronism.

Rabbi Moshe Yechezkel Samuels   *Rabbi Gedaliah Schorr (left) with Rabbi Yerachmiel Blumenfeld, who was Chief Rabbi of Brazil*

When Rabbi Mordechai Tzikanovky, the *rav* of Rio de Janeiro, wrote in 1948 asking whether Torah Vodaath would be willing to accept eight youngsters from Rio, Reb Shraga Feivel replied with alacrity that he would. When the boys arrived, Reb Shraga Feivel hired a special *rebbi* for them, to facilitate their integration into the yeshivah. That was just the beginning of a process that would bring hundreds of South and Central American boys to Torah Vodaath over the next twenty years. Many of these boys subsequently returned to South America where they played leading roles in establishing Torah schools and institutions on the continent. Others became major supporters of these institutions.

A story is told of a *rosh yeshivah* who had studied under the Alter of Kelm in his youth and one day had the pleasure of showing the Alter around his yeshivah. He pointed to the two hundred *talmidim* learning diligently and exclaimed, "What *k'vod Shamayim* — What honor for Heaven!" The Alter, however, was less impressed. "Tell me," he asked his former student, "would you say the same thing if it were someone else's yeshivah?"

No such suspicion ever attached to Reb Shraga Feivel. He never confused *k'vod Shamayim* with his own honor or sought anything but the former.

Chapter 21

Visionary

I T IS CUSTOMARY TO THINK OF DREAMERS AND MEN OF AC-
tion as if they were two inherently separate categories of
people. Yet we find that Yosef HaTzaddik is described in the
Torah as both "a man of dreams" and as an אִישׁ מַצְלִיחַ, *a successful man.*[1] The prominence of dreams in his life in no way
prevented him from being successful in every practical matter to
which he put his hand. Reb Shraga Feivel, Rabbi Avraham Pam
notes, also combined the qualities of vision and practical success;
they went hand in hand. He constantly dreamed of measures that
were needed to put *Yiddishkeit* on a firm footing in America and,
again like Yosef, Hashem granted him success in bringing them
into being.

Many of his dreams were realized; some were not. But because
he never attributed success or failure to his personal merit, failure

---

1. *Bereishis* 39:2.

did not faze him. Nothing of value, Reb Shraga Feivel knew, would be achieved by those unwilling to risk failure and disappointment. The more worthy the undertaking the more obstacles likely to be thrown in his path by the Satan. Thus when he succeeded in raising the money to purchase a building for the Mesivta on South Third Street in a relatively short span of time, the very ease with which the money was gathered was a cause of concern; good things rarely come easily.[2]

His fertile mind was constantly hatching new plans. All his life, he suffered from being surrounded by those who lacked his breadth of vision. Those who objected to this or that idea on philosophical grounds rarely bothered him, but he had no patience for people who viewed every plan as an unattainable dream for which the time had not yet come.

The wealth of his ideas is astounding both in its multitude and its diversity.[3] In the late 20's, he joined a project to create an exclusively religious neighborhood in Pelham Bay in the Bronx, and as early as the 40's he was one of the first to see the potential of then-rural Monsey as a Jewish center. On the property he purchased there in 1943, he envisioned establishing an ideal, self-supporting Torah community, with homes for dozens of families. A diamond factory would offer a livelihood to yeshivah graduates and a wine-making operation would raise money for the yeshivos. The husbands would work part of the day and learn the rest of the time.[4] Such ambitious ideas did not come to fruition, but he was the father of the present-day Torah metropolis of Monsey.

---

2. Rabbi Yisrael Spinner.

3. His lively imagination was well attuned to the possibilities offered by new technologies. He was fascinated by the changes in communications technology forecast over the next twenty years, which he foresaw would provide access to Torah for tens of thousands of Jews located far from major Torah centers or unable to attend *shiurim* in person. To introduce his *talmidim* to the possibilities while imbuing them with a Torah perspective on how to regard technological advances, he took Rabbi and Mrs. Berl Belsky to a major science exposition in 1939. *Berl Belsky.*

4. Elimelech Terebelo.

Reading Material

REB SHRAGA FEIVEL WAS ONE OF THE FIRST TO APPRECIATE THE importance of providing appropriate reading material for the expanding religious population. The stories of Rabbi Marcus Lehmann, he told his students, had done as much to save German Jewry as the philosophical writings of Rabbi Samson Raphael Hirsch.[5] In 1948, Reb Shraga Feivel invited Rabbi Yechezkel Rottenberg, the founder of Netzach Press in *Eretz Yisrael*, to the United States, with the promise that he would organize investors to allow Rabbi Rottenberg to dramatically increase the scope of his publications. Reb Shraga Feivel succeeded in enlisting the support of the Spero brothers, Yechezkel (Earl) and Chaim Yitzchak.[6] In addition, he encouraged Rabbi Rottenberg to use his time in America to recruit people capable of writing material for the religious public. Reb Shraga Feivel himself was responsible for the printing of classic works of both Halachah and Aggadah, which were then unobtainable in America.[7]

Girls Education

REB SHRAGA FEIVEL WAS ONE OF THE FIRST TO RECOGNIZE THAT the Torah education available for girls would ultimately have no less an effect on the nature of Jewish life in America than Torah education for boys.[8] In the summer of 1923, he wrote an editorial in *Dos Yiddishe Licht* decrying the total lack of Torah education for girls:

---

5. Berl Belsky.

6. Among the works produced with money provided by the Speros were: biographies of Rabbi Moshe Mordechai Epstein of Slabodka, Rabbi Menachem Ziemba of Warsaw, Sarah Schenirer, Rabbi Yehudah Leib Zirelson of Kishinev; the writings of the famous *baal teshuvah* and Agudah activist Dr. Nathan Birnbaum; *Judaism* by Rabbi Yitzchak Zailer, and *Torah and Science* by Rabbi Avraham Wolf.

7. In 1943, with the support of the Feuerstein Foundation, he published the following works under the name of Daas Press: Rabbi Akiva Eiger's *Drush V'Chiddush* and *She'eilos U'Teshuvos, Mesillas Yesharim,* and a volume containing four classic *mussar* works: *Shaarei Teshuvah* of Rabbeinu Yonah, *Orchos Chaim* of the Rosh, *Tomer Devorah* of Rabbi Moshe Cordovero, and *Kitzur Sefer Chareidim* of Rabbi Elazar Azkari, as abridged by the *Chayei Adam.*

8. He immediately grasped the crucial insight of Sarah Schenirer in this regard, despite the fact that many of the leading Torah scholars of his native Hungary were opposed to the Bais Yaakov concept.

We have as yet done nothing in America for Jewish girls . . .
It is as if they have been sentenced at birth to remain blind
to any knowledge of Torah.

In our lack of concern for girls education we are committing a great sin. We our pushing our daughters away from
Judaism with our own hands — can we then be surprised
when our grandchildren [are far indeed from anything
Jewish]?

Why do we show less concern for our daughters than
other people for theirs? Why do the Catholics go to such efforts with respect to the education of their daughters . . .
while we abandon ours without a trace of Jewish education?

In 1924, Reb Shraga Feivel and his close friend Binyamin Wilhelm
opened an afternoon Talmud Torah for girls in Williamsburg called
Beth Jacob Hebrew School. One of the few places where an
Orthodox girl could gain some familiarity with Torah was in one of
the handful of informal Shabbos groups that Mrs. Fruma Leah
Mandel, a widow living in Brownsville, began organizing in her
neighborhood in the late 20's. After moving to Williamsburg in the

Sarah Schenirer

early 30's, Mrs. Mandel organized
groups there as well. The Mendlowitz
girls were among her first
Williamsburg recruits.

Not until 1935 did the first elementary schools for girls on the Bais
Yaakov model open in Williamsburg.
Not just one but two schools opened
that year, and they joined together two
years later under the name Bais
Yaakov. In 1937, the legendary
Rebbetzin Vichna Kaplan, known as
the Sarah Schenirer of America, arrived in America from the Bais Yaakov
Seminary in Cracow. Soon after, she
expressed a desire to open a Bais

Yaakov Seminary. Reb Shraga Feivel brought her two of his daughters — Channah and Rivkah — and told her, "Take my daughters and build a seminary around them." Rebbetzin Kaplan began the first Bais Yaakov Seminary in America at her dining-room table, with seven high-school girls.

At the very outset of her teaching in America, Rebbetzin Kaplan asked Reb Shraga Feivel what should be the focus of her message to her students. He replied, "They should avoid luxuries." Besides his support and advice, Reb Shraga Feivel made one other crucial contribution to the success of the pioneer Bais Yaakov Seminary. At that time, Rabbi Baruch Kaplan, Rebbetzin Kaplan's husband, was giving a Gemara *shiur* in the Mesivta. Reb Shraga Feivel told him that the seminary needed him and suggested that he give up his *shiur* in order to place the seminary on a firm footing. "A teacher can have only one task," Reb Shraga Feivel told him, "and now the young women in the seminary take precedence." Leaving the Mesivta was a bitter pill for Rabbi Kaplan, and before agreeing he consulted Rabbi Aharon Kotler, who was then on a visit in the United States. Reb Aharon confirmed what Reb Shraga Feivel had already told him: "The seminary needs you more, and that, too, is *harbatzas Torah*."

REB SHRAGA FEIVEL WAS THE FATHER OF ORTHODOX CAMPING in America. He recognized early on that the ten week-long summer

Orthodox Camping

vacation could destroy a whole year's spiritual growth. The immense amount of free time offered too many temptations — from movies to mixed swimming at the beach. In addition, all the momentum in Gemara learning built up over the course of the year was quickly dissipated over such a long break without any structured framework of learning.

But Reb Shraga Feivel also viewed the summer-camp experience in a very positive way. He saw that a properly constructed summer experience could be the foundation of the entire school year and, in some areas, more might be achieved during the summer months than during the school year itself. During the year, the boys still spent many hours each day outside the yeshivah, but during the summer the entire day could be structured as a learning experience — from *Modeh Ani* in the morning to *Hamapil* at night.

Camp was not to be a mere continuation of the school year in a different setting. Reb Shraga Feivel appreciated the importance of relaxation and rejuvenation after the rigors of the school year, but he did not want that relaxation to come in the form of "killing time," a concept that was anathema to him. The beautiful natural environment of the Catskills would, he felt, draw forth emotions from the boys that were normally stifled in the hustle and bustle of the city. Reb Shraga Feivel's soul was alive to the wonders of nature, and the picturesque Catskills allowed him to share with the boys his own sense of the perfection of Hashem's creation. He felt freer in camp than in the Mesivta to give full vent to his poetic soul, as well as to show his love for his *talmidim* in a demonstrative fashion.

In 1928, the Mesivta's third year, Reb Shraga Feivel borrowed money to rent a farmhouse in Mountaindale, New York, where the Mesivta students spent the summer with him and Rabbi David Leibowitz. He put all his energy into the camp that first year. Two boys who were sleeping outside on a hot night once woke up at 4 a.m. to see him plucking the chickens for the Shabbos meals.[9] Running the camp, and raising the money to keep it going, completely drained his energies, and, over the course of the summer, he lost twelve pounds from his already gaunt frame.

The next year was the beginning of the Great Depression, and with it went any chance of raising sufficient money for the camp. For the next eight years, he could not open the camp again. Though he was able to create a learning environment for the older boys in the Mesivta during the summer, it still pained Reb Shraga Feivel to see his beloved *talmidim* learning in a sweltering *beis medrash* in the summer months, rather than in the invigorating rural setting of the mountains.

---

9. Rabbi Alexander Linchner.

By 1936, Reb Shraga Feivel had convinced a group of supporters of the importance of a camp, and Camp Mesivta came into being. Again the entire fund-raising burden was on him, and funds ran out during the summer. Before *Kinnos* on Tishah B'Av morning, Reb Shraga Feivel called over Rabbi Linchner and told him that they had to leave immediately for Ellenville to raise money. Eight years earlier, when Rabbi Linchner had himself been one of the campers, he had been unnerved by the power of Reb Shraga Feivel's emotions during *Kinnos*. And he was surprised that anybody who experienced the words of *Kinnos* so intensely was willing to forgo them, even to save the camp. In a fund-raising effort that lasted all day, the largest contribution that Reb Shraga Feivel and Rabbi Linchner received was $5.00 and the next largest was $1.50. "Mainly we succeeded in collecting *bizyonos* (humiliations)," remembers Rabbi Linchner.

In 1937, a campsite was purchased in Ferndale, near Liberty. Reb Shraga Feivel himself selected it, high on a hill, with a breathtaking view of the surrounding forests. He trusted that the magnificence of the view would inspire the boys with reverence for Hashem.

Camp Mesivta drew boys from other yeshivos as well as the Mesivta, and became the model for many of the camps that dot the Catskills today. Reb Shraga Feivel instituted the practice that was to become standard in all the learning camps of having *gedolim* visit the camp for anywhere from a few days to weeks. The experience of being able to see Reb Elchonon Wasserman on a daily basis for a couple of weeks during his stay in America in 1938 had a profound effect on the *bachurim*. Rabbi Shlomo Heiman and later Rabbi Yaakov Kamenetsky used to spend most of the summer in Camp Mesivta. For

R' Shraga Feivel (seated, right) and Rabbi Shlomo Heiman (seated, center) in Camp Mesivta. Seated at left, in the white suit, is Mr. Jacob I. Samuel, a philanthropist. Standing on the right is Moshe Yitzchok Menlowitz.

R' Shraga Feivel in Camp Mesivta

several years, Rabbi Moshe Feinstein and Rabbi Avraham Kalmanowitz were among the visitors, and the Bobover Rav would come for a *melaveh malkah*.

Typically, Reb Shraga Feivel was not interested solely in the success of *his* camp, but that as many boys as possible benefit from the experience of an Orthodox summer camp. His student Sidney Greenwald was the head counselor of Camp Agudah in the late 40's, and he complained to Reb Shraga Feivel that he was having difficulty finding suitable counselors for the coming summer. Part of the problem was that the postwar draft was still in effect, and boys with deferments as divinity students were afraid that a summer spent as camp counselors might jeopardize their deferments. But Reb Shraga Feivel viewed the summer-camping experience as so important for the campers that it was worth the risk. He told Greenwald to select anyone he wanted as a counselor from the Mesivta *beis medrash*, and he would prevail upon them to go to Camp Agudah.

In 1966, several years after Camp Mesivta closed down, Rabbi Zelik Epstein and Rabbi Nesanel Quinn opened a successor, learning camp in Greenfield Park. At Reb Zelik's initiative, it was named Camp Ohr Shraga — Bais Medrash L'Torah, in recognition of Reb Shraga Feivel's pioneering role in Orthodox camping.

Chapter 22

Do Not Stand By Your Brother's Blood

A T NO TIME WAS REB SHRAGA FEIVEL'S INTENSE EMPA-
thy for his fellow Jews more evident than during the
years of the Holocaust. From the time the first revela-
tions of the Nazi atrocities reached America, he was a
man possessed. He never again ate meat.[1] "There is already enough
killing in the world," he explained.[2]

Even on Shabbos, the constant awareness of the suffering of Jews
in Europe overwhelmed him. The joy that had always radiated from
him was replaced by involuntary sighs and tears. When he sang
Tzur Mishelo at the end of the Shabbos meal, and came to the stanza,
רַחֵם בְּחַסְדֶּךָ, *Be merciful in Your kindness upon Your nation*, he would
cry. His wife implored him not to turn the Shabbos meal into Tishah

---

1. Rabbi Yaakov Leshinsky.
2. Rabbi Shmuel Mendlowitz.

B'Av and to recall the halachic prohibition against mourning on Shabbos.

Reb Shraga Feivel did not content himself, however, with tears. He was deeply involved in rescue work in addition to his responsibilities in the Mesivta. He felt that his work for Torah was too important to be curtailed, but eventually he asked Rabbi Aharon Kotler whether he should put aside all his other responsibilities and concentrate exclusively on rescue work. Reb Aharon agreed with him that saving Torah was no less important than saving a life, and he therefore had no choice but to continue directing the Mesivta, along with the *hatzalah* (rescue) work.[3]

Affidavits and Fund-raising

AS DESPERATE JEWS SOUGHT AMERICAN IMMIGRATION VISAS after Hitler's rise to power, and especially after the German takeover of Austria (March 13, 1938) and *Kristallnacht* (November 9, 1938), Reb Shraga Feivel became known as one of those who would act immediately and energetically on all requests from abroad for papers. He personally signed as many affidavits guaranteeing financial support for would-be immigrants as his meager resources would allow. Despite the financial risk to which each affidavit exposed the sponsor, Reb Shraga Feivel would have signed many more had it not been futile. (In general, only affidavits signed by those who could show significant assets had any chance of being relied upon by the American consuls with authority to issue visas.[4]) In addition, he personally went from shul to shul beseeching Jews to sign affidavits.

Reb Shraga Feivel's efforts bore fruit. Among those for whom he obtained affidavits was Rabbi Yechiel Michel Schlesinger, a *dayan* in Frankfurt-am-Main, who later founded Yeshivas Kol Torah in Jerusalem. (Rabbi Schlesinger did not use the affidavit, however, since he was able to obtain a visa to enter Palestine.) Before the war,

---

3. Rabbi Avraham Abba Freedman.

4. For an explanation of the visa process and the role of affidavits of financial support in that process, see *They Called Him Mike*, pp. 250-51.

Reb Shraga Feivel issued the papers that brought to America Rabbi Joseph Breuer[5] and all his students of the Yeshivah in Frankfurt, and those of Yeshivas Arugas HaBosem, named after his *rebbe*, in Zielsheim. In addition, he was active in the committee to save the Gerrer Rebbe, the Imrei Emes.[6]

Julius Steinfeld

Reb Shraga Feivel was also one of the major fund-raisers for the rescue activities of Agudath Israel of America and Zeirei Agudath Israel of America. In late 1943, Moreinu Jacob Rosenheim, president of the World Agudath Israel, and Julius Steinfeld, who had stayed in Vienna for three years after the Nazi takeover — at great personal risk — heading the activities of the Viennese Agudah,[7] came to Torah Vodaath to speak to Reb Shraga Feivel. The immediate cause of their visit was a series of letters Rosenheim had received from the Nitra Rav and his son-in-law Rabbi Michoel Ber Weismandl describing the possibility of ransoming Jews hiding on the Polish side of the Polish-Hungarian border and bringing them to Hungary, which had not yet been subjected to the Nazi extermination machine.

Rosenheim explained to Reb Shraga Feivel the necessity of a major fund-raising campaign in response to the Nitra Rav's letters.

---

5. Rabbi Breuer was the son of Rabbi Shlomo Zalman Breuer and the grandson of Rabbi Samson Raphael Hirsch. He became the spiritual leader of the German community in Washington Heights for more than forty years. Reb Shraga Feivel offered him a position in the Mesivta but Rabbi Breuer declined, in order to create the Washington Heights community.

6. The Imrei Emes eventually escaped to Palestine together with his son and successor, the Bais Yisrael; another son, the Lev Simchah, who suceeded the Bais Yisrael; his son-in-law, Rabbi Itche Meir Levine, who became the leader of Agudath Israel in *Eretz Yisrael*; and his youngest son, Pinchas Menachem Alter, the recently deceased Gerrer Rebbe, known as the Pnei Menachem.

7. See *They Called Him Mike*, pp. 285-87, for a description of the activities of the Viennese Agudah after the Nazi takeover and Steinfeld's role.

When Reb Shraga Feivel asked Rosenheim and Steinfeld how much they hoped to raise, they replied that their goal was $100,000. Reb Shraga Feivel could not contain himself. "Such a small amount when we are talking about saving lives! I will personally raise that much, and together we cannot aim for anything less than a million dollars!"[8]

Reb Shraga Feivel immediately gathered the entire staff of Torah Vodaath and spoke with passion of the great sin of standing by while the blood of one's fellow Jew is shed. Every member of the staff pledged a full month's salary, despite the fact that most could barely make ends meet. Later Reb Shraga Feivel addressed the entire student body and ordered that the Mesivta be closed for three days to allow the students to canvass the entire city and beyond in search of every nickel and dime to be had. Teams of boys covered the streets of New York. Subways, apartment houses, and housing projects resounded to their appeals.[9] Meanwhile Reb Shraga Feivel took out personal loans to make up any shortfall in the money collected. After the three days, Reb Shraga Feivel presented $50,000 to the Vaad Hatzalah rescue organization, and before long he completed his pledge of $100,000.[10]

Besides fund-raising, Reb Shraga Feivel was involved in efforts to publicize the Nazi atrocities in Europe. When Rabbi Michoel Ber Weismandl succeeded in smuggling out of Europe a detailed report of the number of Jews killed by country to date, Reb Shraga Feivel had Elimelech Terebelo translate it, and he tried to give it the widest possible circulation. Toward the end of the war, he sent a warning to the Hungarian Jews, urging them to flee and not rely on the fact that the Nazis had not yet occupied their Hungarian ally. The very ground was burning beneath their feet, Reb Shraga Feivel wrote, and the great fire that had gone out from Germany was now headed

8. Rabbi Alexander Linchner.

9. Gershon Kranzler, "Setting the Record Straight," *The Jewish Observer*, November 1971, p. 12.

10. Rabbi Nesanel Quinn.

in their direction. In case there were any who had refused to flee Hungary for fear that it was impossible to lead a fully Jewish life in the West, Reb Shraga Feivel added that such was no longer the case in America.

Though filled with anger at the apathy of Stephen Wise and Abba Hillel Silver, the recognized leaders of America Jewry, Reb Shraga Feivel went personally to Wise to beg him to use his influence with President Roosevelt.[11] Later he commented bitterly that American Jewry had been like a patient anesthetized prior to a painful operation. It was as if they had been lulled to sleep during one of the greatest tragedies in Jewish history.[12]

With the unconditional surrender of Germany and Hitler's suicide, Reb Shraga Feivel expressed his feelings with the last lines of *Al Naharos Bavel* (*Tehillim* 136), "Praiseworthy is He Who repays you in accordance with the manner that you treated us. Praiseworthy is He Who will clutch and dash your infants against the rock." Rabbi Sheah Geldzhaler still remembers him entering the *beis medrash* of Bais Medrash Elyon with the news of Germany's defeat, and telling the *talmidim* to recite *Hallel* without a blessing. During the entire *Hallel*, he stood with his faced pressed in a handkerchief to wipe away the flowing tears. A few months later, even the consolation at the Nazis' defeat was forgotten with the news of pogroms in Kielce and elsewhere, in which scores of Jewish survivors were murdered by Poles as they tried to return home.

EVEN AS HE MOURNED FOR WHAT HAD BEEN DESTROYED, REB Shraga Feivel busied himself with whatever could be done for the

Helping the Survivors
surviving remnant. The United States showed little guilt over its negligible efforts to save Jewish lives, and the strict American immigrant quotas were not relaxed. One of the few ways around those quotas

---

11. Rabbi Shmuel Mendlowitz.
12. Rabbi Eliyahu Yehoshua Geldzahler.

was through student visas, which did not count against quota numbers. Though theoretically only those intending to return to their native lands and with the ability to do so were eligible for student visas — something that was true of none of the impoverished, homeless survivors — Torah Vodaath brought hundreds to America on student visas. Once in the United States, their chances of being able to remain increased substantially.

The issuance of a student visa required the applicant to show that he had been accepted for a course of study in a recognized institution, and the institution had to demonstrate that it was capable of providing the applicant with the necessary instruction and room and board. Showing that they were indeed providing the students with an education was not always easy for the sponsoring institution. Many of those coming to the United States on those visas had been out of any formal educational structure for more than six years and were not capable of fitting into a regular yeshivah schedule. Nevertheless, Reb Shraga Feivel did not hesitate to bring as many refugees as possible to America, and went to great ends to provide special programs for them. In financial papers filed with the government, the Mesivta submitted that it had the capacity to accept another three hundred students, which would have doubled the size of the high school and *beis medrash* departments.

Rabbi Moshe Lonner

Torah Vodaath never asked a penny from any of these students. When it was suggested to Reb Shraga Feivel that he should at least charge a fee to cover the expense of the paperwork, he curtly brushed the suggestion aside. "When you do a *chesed*," he said, "you do it completely."[13] Although Torah Vodaath may have been the most generous in this regard, its Williamsburg neighbors,

---

13. Rabbi Moshe Lonner, longtime General Studies principal of Torah Vodaath, supervised the student-visa program.

Yeshivas Chofetz Chaim and the Bais Yaakov Seminary, as well as other yeshivos, also brought over large numbers of survivors.

ONLY HIS LONG VIEW OF JEWISH HISTORY AND ABSOLUTE TRUST in Hashem allowed Reb Shraga Feivel to retain his optimism in the

Putting the Holocaust in Perspective

wake of the Holocaust. In a prescient essay on Jewish history in *Dos Yiddishe Licht*, written in 1923, he noted:

> Anyone who views Jewish history from its beginning until the present sees one long miracle. After each national nadir — which for another nation would have meant permanent destruction — the Jewish people bloomed again; after each deathblow there was a new revival ...
>
> How can this be explained? With the ordinary principles of history? Certainly not! Every historian who views Jewish history with the same eyeglasses he uses to view world history remains perplexed with head bowed, and must admit, "I don't understand."[14]

In Channah's lyrical, prophetic song of thanks to Hashem for answering her prayer by giving her a child, Shmuel, she described Hashem with the word צוּר, *Rock*, saying "There is no rock (צוּר) like

---

14. In the same article, Reb Shraga Feivel set forth much of his philosophy of Jewish history. That history, he wrote, is distinguished from the history of the nations of the world by the questions to which it addresses itself. Not "What?" and "When?" but "Why?" is the question that the student of Jewish history is called upon to ask. At all times, the search is for the guiding hand of Providence in the events of history. Just as there is no place in which G–d's presence is not felt, so too there is no epoch in which His presence is not found. Nowhere more than in Jewish history is G–d's providential control over the affairs of man more evident, and that history stands as the clearest refutation to the existence of a "natural" order guided by its own rules and independent of G–d's control.

Reb Shraga Feivel noted another unique feature of Jewish history. The history of other nations is limited to the past; that of the Jewish people also encompasses the future. The same prophets who explain the reasons for the events of our past are the prophets who have predicted our ultimate destiny. And while other nations derive their sustenance from the history of past greatness, the Jewish people derive theirs from the knowledge of their ultimate role in bringing the knowledge of G–d to all the nations of the world.

our G-d" (*I Shmuel* 2:2). The Sages give a deeper meaning to the word צוּר, which they read as צָיָיר, *artist*: "There is no artist (צָיָיר) like our G–d" (*Berachos* 10a). Reb Shraga Feivel interpreted this Gemara with a parable that encapsulates his efforts to put the Holocaust into perspective.

> When a small child draws a person, it is obvious from the start that the circle on top is the face, the line going down is the body, and the lines projecting outward are the arms and legs. But when a master artist paints a person, he may start with a stroke of bright red, which, to the uninitiated viewer appears to ruin the canvas. Only when the painting is completed will it be obvious why the stroke of red was needed for contrast. So, too, Hashem is painting a masterful panorama of history. As the painting develops, there are strokes that we see as unnecessary or detrimental. But when the painting is done, it will be obvious that every stroke was necessary for the perfection of the picture.[15]

Meeting Rabbi Avraham Pam in the hall one day during the war, Reb Shraga Feivel began the verse from *Michah* (7:8), "Let my enemies not rejoice," and waited for Rabbi Pam to complete the verse, "though I have fallen, I will rise . . . and though I dwell in darkness, Hashem is my light." During the Holocaust, this verse and another from *Tehillim* (90:15): "Gladden us according to the days You afflicted us," were frequently on his lips, and he sang them both to the *niggun* of "*Samcheinu* — Gladden us."[16]

The Midrash links the tears that Hashem "has made us drink in great measure" (*Tehillim* 80:6) to the three tears that Esav shed when

---

15. Rabbi Zev Leff, *Outlooks and Insights,* pp. 65-6.

16. Rabbi Shmuel Mendlowitz.

Reb Shraga Feivel's linking of the two verses with one *niggun* is interesting. In his *Essay on Redemption,* the Ramchal writes that the verse in *Tehillim* parallels the prophecy of *Michah*. In *Shaarei Teshuvah* (2:5), Rabbeinu Yonah quotes the verse from *Michah* and adds: "One who trusts in Hashem must hope, in the gloom of his anguish, that the darkness will be the cause of light."

he learned that Yaakov had "stolen" his blessings. "Just imagine," Reb Shraga Feivel said, "if the wicked Esav has been so compensated for three tears, how much more so will Hashem compensate us for all our suffering."[17] The terrible tragedy that had befallen European Jewry only deepened his faith in that eventual compensation.

17. Rabbi Hertzl Shechter.

Chapter 23

Spreading Torah

THE CURE FOR AMERICAN JEWRY, REB SHRAGA FEIVEL felt, could be summarized in one term: Jewish education. **Jewish Education — the Key** Accordingly, a career in *chinuch* was the goal he set for most of his close students. When Rabbi Nesanel Quinn expressed the desire soon after his marriage to spread *Yiddishkeit* outside of the New York area, Reb Shraga Feivel was overjoyed. He wrote to Rabbi Quinn, "As I have already told you many times in person, my opinion is the same as yours: Each of us is obligated to spread Torah to every corner [of the country] where we are able. And I am sure that you will merit to build a home filled with Torah, as a result of your determination to do so."[1]

---

1. Rabbi Nesanel Quinn. Reb Shraga Feivel insisted, however, that Rabbi Quinn make sure that his new bride was in full agreement with his determination to leave the main center of Jewish life. "I am hopeful that she will give her agreement to this holy undertaking," he concluded, "because it is indeed the task for which we all have to be ready to sacrifice ourselves."

Even though the weekly salaries of educators were less than half of what one could hope to earn as a rabbi, only in a few special cases did he direct students toward careers in the rabbinate. "As a rabbi," he told his older students, "you'll be dealing with the *baalebatim*. How much can you do with *baalebatim*? But if you work with children, you'll have spiritual satisfaction — and you'll be building *Klal Yisrael*."[2] If American rabbis had used the time spent preparing *derashos* to educate the children in their shuls, he noted bitterly, they might have accomplished much more.

The quality for which most American rabbis were then judged — their speaking ability — was in his eyes of little value, in comparison with the importance of educating children.[3] When his son-in-law Rabbi Sender Linchner was rabbi of a large shul in East New York, Reb Shraga Feivel would invariably greet him when he returned from his Shabbos-morning *derashah*: "*Nu, mein Rabbi, vos host du heint geplapelt* — So, my Rabbi, what did you prattle about today?"[4] And it was not unheard of for him to ask a rabbi whose sermon was based on a news item in the daily press, "Is there really nothing appropriate for a sermon in our Torah literature?"

For many years, Rabbi Zelig Fortman taught a homiletics class in the Mesivta. One day Reb Shraga Feivel happened to sit in on the class when one of the best students in the Mesivta was due to speak. When he was finished, the student, who went on to be a well-known pulpit rabbi, asked Reb Shraga Feivel what he thought. "A fine speech, interesting ideas on a wide range of topics, but what was Jewish about it?" Although the student had quoted many

---

2. Rabbi Elias Schwartz.

3. At best, he considered public speaking ineffectual, and therefore did not view the rabbinate as part of the revolutionary spiritual vanguard he was fashioning. *Rabbi Avraham Pam.*

At worst, he saw many in the American rabbinate as having betrayed their trust. His characterization of much of the American rabbinate — "*Deineh firrers zenen farfirrers* — Your leaders are misleaders" — consciously echoed that of the prophet Yeshayahu: "The guides of this people mislead, and the guided ones are devoured" (*Yeshayahu* 9:15).

4. Chinn, "Ohr Shraga," p. 9.

verses from *Tanach*, Reb Shraga Feivel explained, "There was no *maamar Chazal* (a saying of our Sages)."[5]

THE TRANSFORMATION OF AMERICAN JEWRY THAT REB SHRAGA Feivel envisioned depended on the creation of a cadre of teachers

Instilling a Sense of Mission

who burned with a sense of mission. He once sent Sender Gross, later one of the founders of Torah Umesorah, to a distant community for the *Yamim Noraim*. When he returned, Reb Shraga Feivel asked him how many Sabbath observers he found there. Gross expressed doubt that there was even one fully *shomer Shabbos* Jew. "And when you realized that," Reb Shraga Feivel asked him in amazement, "didn't you cry bitterly?" Only those capable of crying over the state of American Jewry, he said, would be able to change it.

And only those who were aflame with the desire to bring Torah to an American Jewry that had lost its heritage would find the necessary means of communication. How are we to teach the words of Torah? he asked. The answer can be found in the first paragraph of *Shema*: "And these words that I command you this day shall be *al levavecha* (on your hearts), and you shall teach them to your children." From an overflowing heart, from your heart to their souls — there is no other way.[6]

Rabbis Avraham Abba Freedman and Shalom Goldstein, two *talmidim* who entered careers in *chinuch* outside the New York area, returned to visit their *rebbi* with a sense of failure that they had not been able to change the language of instruction in Detroit from English to Yiddish. Reb Shraga Feivel, however, did not share their disappointment. "English is the students' native language, their 'soul language,' " he explained, "and if you want to find the path to their hearts you have to reach them in the language of their soul."

When they challenged him that he had always taught in Yiddish, Reb Shraga Feivel replied that if he had ten more years left he would

---

5. Rabbi Shubert Spero.
6. Chinn, "Ohr Shraga," p. 10.

learn an idiomatic English. He had not done so earlier only because he never dreamed that he would remain for so many years in America before moving to *Eretz Yisrael*.[7]

And how would an educator know when he was successful? Reb Shraga Feivel also found the answer to that question in the first paragraph of *Shema*: "And *you shall teach them* to your children to speak in them, when you are sitting in your house and *when you are going on the way.*" Can we really expect, he asked, that the children will continue to learn when their father or teacher is far away, not looking over their shoulder? Only if we teach in a way that pierces deeply into their souls and makes them love Torah can we hope that even when we are not at home, they will still be sitting with a *sefer*, when we *are going on the way.*

BY THE LATE 30'S, THE FIRST STAGE IN REB SHRAGA FEIVEL'S PLAN for a Torah revolution was well under way. At least in the New York

Aish Dos

area, there were hundreds of Torah Vodaath graduates with an appreciation of Torah study and a commitment to uncompromising Orthodoxy. The time had come for the second stage: the creation of a group of dedicated educators who would spread knowledge of Torah to far-flung Jewish communities. Reb Shraga Feivel realized that it was difficult for European-trained *melamdim* to transmit *Yiddishkeit* to increasingly Americanized Jewish youth, and that the Torah educators of the future would be drawn from among the ranks of the *talmidim* produced in Torah Vodaath and the handful of other yeshivos then in existence. The advent of the Holocaust made this need a matter of spiritual life and death.

Chinuch (education) was then too closely associated with the image of the *"melamed."* Tragically, assimilated American Jews lacked respect for such teachers and even, very unfairly, made them an object of ridicule. It is true, however, that many *melamdim* were unskilled in their craft and even unlearned. The stock image of the *melamed*, unfortunately, was of someone who became a teacher

---

7. Ibid., pp. 9-10.

A group of students in the Aish Dos program, Spring Valley, 1941. (Right - left): Front row: R' Meyer Lubin, R' Moshe Wolfson,
R' Berel Schwartz, R' Simcha Wasserman, Zissel Walkenfeld, R' Shmuel Mendlowitz, R' Sholom Goldstein, zt"l.
Second row: Meyer Strassfeld, R' Yisrael Spinner, R' Moshe Weitman, R' Shlomo Weinberger, R' Heshie Mashinsky, Yitzchak
Schwinder, R' Avrahom Abba Friedman. Top row: R' Avish Mendlowitz, R' Eliyahu Moshe Shisgal, zt"l, Lennie Kestenbaum,
R' Milton Terebelo, R' Mendel Eller.

because he could do nothing else.[8] The first requirement, then, was to raise the prestige of *mechanchim* (educators). To do that Reb Shraga Feivel conceived of an advanced institute for training *mechanchim*, which would attract committed students from all the yeshivos in America. Reb Shraga Feivel firmly believed that *mechanchim* needed training, just like any other professional. At the same time, he never believed that courses in pedagogy could compensate for a lack of commitment on the part of the teacher. "A love of children and a spirit of *mesiras nefesh* for Torah is worth more than all the courses in pedagogy," he said.[9]

Aish Dos (literally: Fire of Faith), the name Reb Shraga Feivel gave his proposed institute, captured his philosophy of education. Ideas, he felt, are best transmitted when packaged in a person. The pre-eminent requirement for an educator, in his view, was that he burn with a fire for *Yiddishkeit*. Only those whose souls were aflame would succeed in igniting a spark in American children largely ignorant of what it meant to be a Jew.

In 1943, Reb Shraga Feivel began to put his plan into action. He took the unprecedented step of purchasing a large property in rural Monsey, then nearly two hours' drive from Torah Vodaath. Today Monsey is famous as an intensely Orthodox town and a center of Torah and chassidic life, but in those days it had only a handful of Jews and not even a shul. He envisioned the sixteen-acre plot with its two buildings as the home of *Aish Dos*. The property cost $13,000, and Reb Shraga Feivel took out a personal loan for the $3,000 down payment. He was confident that many students with outstanding potential as *mechanchim* would flourish there, away from the distractions of the city. "Skyscrapers," he once said, "block out the *Ribbono Shel Olam*."[10]

That summer, Reb Shraga Feivel brought with him to Monsey thirty students, who constituted what was to be the founding class of the

---

8. Sidney Greenwald.
9. Rabbi Elias Schwartz.
10. Rabbi Moshe Aharon Stern.

Rabbi Simchah Wasserman

Rabbi Yerucham Levovitz

new *Aish Dos.* This group of young men would be the Reb Chiyas of their generation.[11] Reb Shraga Feivel made it clear that they were not being trained to be rabbis or *poskim,* but to be the educators of the next generation of American Jews.

Directing the Gemara learning of the *Aish Dos* program was Rabbi Simchah Wasserman, the son of Rabbi Elchonon Wasserman, who had already gained a reputation in his native Lithuania and later in Strasbourg for his ability to explain difficult concepts in the Gemara and for his knack of relating to people of varying backgrounds.[12] More than forty years later, Reb Simchah recalled the way that Reb Shraga Feivel had inspired him, as well as the students, with a sense of obligation to teach Torah wherever there are Jews. As a young man in the Mirrer Yeshivah, Reb Simchah was once discussing with the great Mirrer *Mashgiach,* Rabbi Yerucham Levovitz, the Sages' parable for the desire to teach Torah:

---

11. Rabbi Chiya said to himself, "I will prevent Torah from being forgotten from Yisrael." He would go from town to town, where there were no teachers of Torah. In each town he would gather about him five boys, each of whom would be taught one *sefer* of *Chumash,* and another group of six boys, each of whom would be taught one *seder* of Mishnah. Each one would be instructed to teach what he knew to the others (*Kesubos* 103b).

12. Reb Shraga Feivel's first choice to head *Aish Dos* was Rabbi Yaakov Kamenetsky, who was at that time still serving as a *rav* in Toronto. He felt that Reb Yaakov, by virtue of his wide-ranging knowledge — including Hebrew grammar, *Tanach,* and Jewish history — in addition to his greatness in Talmud and Halachah, was ideally suited for a program designed to be broader than the normal yeshivah curriculum. Reb Yaakov, however, did not accept the offer. See *Reb Yaakov,* p. 150.

Students in the Aish Dos program, summer 1943

1. Heshy Mendlewitz (from Scranton) 2. Heshy Mashinsky 3. Avraham Abba Freedman 4. Meyer Lubin 5. Kestenbaum 6. Meyer Strassfeld 7. Rabbi Simchah Wasserman 8. Weinberger 9. Shalom Goldstein 10. Moshe Wolfson 11. Moshe Weitman 12. Eli Halberg

More than the calf wants to nurse, the cow wants to give (*Pesachim* 112a). "Don't think," said Reb Yerucham, "that the cow wants to nurse only because it must rid itself of an excess of milk. The cow wants to nurse because the calf needs her milk. But," Reb Yerucham had concluded, "you are a young man, and you won't understand this yet."

It was Reb Shraga Feivel, said Reb Simchah, who showed him the full meaning of that *mashal* for the first time. In the appreciation of a Jew's responsibility for the *klal* and the recognition that with every talent with which Hashem favors a person only comes a greater obligation to help others, said Reb Simchah, "Reb Shraga Feivel was my *rebbi*."[13]

Most of the day in *Aish Dos* was spent learning Gemara, just as in any advanced yeshivah. Reb Shraga Feivel himself tested the

Rabbi Shlomo Rotenberg

bachurim on their progress in Tractate *Shabbos*.[14] History, *Chumash* with Midrash, and lecture technique were taught by Rabbi Shlomo Rotenberg, who had only recently escaped from Europe and who, over the next five decades, would revolutionize the teaching of Jewish history in the Orthodox world; *hashkafah* by Rabbi Samson Raphael Weiss, formerly of the Wurzburg Teacher's Seminary and for many years the executive director of Young Israel; and homiletics by Rabbi Zelig Fortman, who had been Rabbi Moshe Feinstein's *chavrusa* in Europe. Others with expertise in their fields, such as Rabbi Philip Biberfeld and Rabbi Pinchas Mordechai Teitz, supplemented the traditional yeshivah curriculum.

---

13. Rabbi Wasserman's remarks were made at a *yahrzeit* gathering of Reb Shraga Feivel's students in 1987.

14. Rabbi Wasserman testified that Reb Shraga Feivel had total command of the tractate with all the *Rishonim* (early commentators).

Rabbi Rotenberg became one of the most powerful influences on the *Aish Dos* contingent. Reb Shraga Feivel recognized his depth and inspirational qualities, and enlisted him to give voluntary — and very well-attended — classes in the Mesivta, on Jewish history and the weekly *Sidra* with Midrash.

But most important of all to the development of the students in *Aish Dos* were the various *shiurim* of Reb Shraga Feivel. In Torah Vodaath, he had been wont to divide the *talmidim* into different groups and to give each what he felt they needed most. With the small group of pioneers in Monsey, he was able to tailor his *shiurim* even more precisely than he had in the Mesivta.

A number of the participants in *Aish Dos* had already begun college studies while learning in the Mesivta, and Reb Shraga Feivel spent a great deal of time with these students individually. He wanted to impress upon them that any intellectual stimulation they had found in their college studies could be found to a higher degree within Torah. The energy he invested in these students was all aimed at one goal: that they should feel that all their joy in life consisted of being a better, more elevated Jew.[15] Rabbi Shalom Rudensky recalls that one student protested that his professors were brilliant and learned. Reb Shraga Feivel replied that the caliber of a person is not determined by the extent of his knowledge. He concluded tartly, "A donkey that knows seventy languages is still a donkey."

Even fifty years later, the short existence of *Aish Dos* remained a vital memory to all who participated. Above all, they remember the impact on their development of close, intensive contact with Reb Shraga Feivel. That contact, says Rabbi Moshe Aharon Stern, "left a more lasting impression than anything we heard in his *shiurim* or

---

15. Sometimes the other students would be envious of all the time that Reb Shraga Feivel invested in deep intellectual discussions with the young men who had been to college. He would tell the complainers that they not only did not need these discussions, but that the *emunah peshutah* (innocent faith) that they had as a heritage from their ancestors could be threatened by exposure to college. He used to give them a *mashal* to explain why what was good for one could be damaging to another: "Someone with a weak constitution like myself, who suffers from ulcers, would be thrown into excruciating agony by a rich gourmet meal that would do justice to a royal table." *Rabbi Moshe Wolfson.*

that we learned from the *sefarim* we studied. We *davened* together, we ate together, we experienced nature together, we spent many nights on the grass under the stars as he addressed our souls."

> We were typical American boys who loved sports and wanted to have a good time. Striving for spiritual elevation and an appreciation of the depth of *Yiddishkeit* were far from us. Yet he impressed upon us that the sole task in life is to do the will of our Father in Heaven.
>
> We knew the Mishnah in *Pirkei Avos* that this world is like an entrance hall. But he provided us a real-life example of someone who lived his life that way. He showed us what it means to "set Hashem before [oneself] always."

One night the boys were gathered on the grass listening to Reb Shraga Feivel, who was sitting on the stairs leading up to the main building. As he was speaking, mosquitos descended on the boys, and soon everyone was scratching himself furiously. In the dark, Reb Shraga Feivel could not see what had happened, but he sensed the disturbance. When one of the students explained what had happened, he was perplexed: "If there was a swarm of biting insects here, I, too, would have felt it." For their part the boys were equally amazed that he had not been bitten at all. The next day, however, as they were learning *Yalkut Shimoni* on *Mishlei* with Reb Shraga Feivel, they had their explanation. On the verse, *"When a man's ways are pleasing to Hashem, even his enemies make peace with him"* (Mishlei 16:7), *Yalkut Shimoni* interprets the word "enemies" as referring to mosquitos.[16]

REB SHRAGA FEIVEL HOPED TO ATTRACT GIFTED STUDENTS FROM the Mesivta and other yeshivos to *Aish Dos*, because in his mind,

An Unfulfilled Dream
there was no more important task at hand than establishing new Torah schools throughout the country, and he saw that this could only be

---

16. Reb Shraga Feivel himself once offered another explanation for the fact that insects never bothered him: He could not recall ever having killed a fly.

The Bais Medrash Elyon dormitory and dining-room building

Bais Medrash Elyon, with dormitory on second floor

achieved by people of talent and commitment. It soon became clear to him, however, that his vision was not universally shared, and the *roshei yeshivah* would not send their best *talmidim* to *Aish Dos*.

Because of such opposition, Reb Shraga Feivel did not renew *Aish Dos* for a second year. Though *Aish Dos* itself never fulfilled his high hopes, time would show that Reb Shraga Feivel had picked his students well. Most of them eventually did go on to distinguished careers in *chinuch*, in fulfillment of his vision.

Reb Shraga Feivel renamed his Monsey property Bais Medrash Elyon, and it became the advanced institute for noncollege students, primarily from the Mesivta, but it attracted top *bachurim* from other yeshivos as well. Reb Shraga Feivel did not abandon his plans for a teaching institute, however, just the dream of drawing students from other yeshivos. Almost simultaneously with the opening of Bais Medrash Elyon in the fall of 1944, he brought another group of twelve students with him to Monsey for a program called *Bais Medrash L'Mechanchim*. That program was basically a continuation of *Aish Dos* and lasted for almost a year and a half under Reb Shraga Feivel's close tutelage.[17] As with the original contingent from *Aish Dos*, virtually all went on to become active in *klal* work and *chinuch*.[18]

Although *Aish Dos* and *Bais Medrash L'Mechanchim* were his most ambitious programs to train Torah educators, he had undertaken this mission in Torah Vodaath several years before. Almost every one of the first generation of American-born yeshivah principals was a student of Reb Shraga Feivel and the product of one of his programs for *mechanchim*. Among them were Rabbi Mannes Mandel, of Yeshivah of Brooklyn; Rabbi Elias Schwartz, of Toras Emes in Boro Park; Rabbi Eliyahu (Leon) Machlis, of Ohel Moshe in Bensonhurst; Rabbi Sender Gross, of the Hebrew Academy of Greater Miami; Rabbi Bernard Goldenberg, of Torah Umesorah; and Reb Shraga Feivel's son-in-law, Rabbi Berel Greenbaum, of the Yeshivah of Spring Valley.[19]

Neither *Aish Dos* nor *Bais Medrash L'Mechanchim* were designed merely to produce one-dimensional educators. Reb Shraga Feivel

---

17. The program subsequently continued in Torah Vodaath itself under the direction of Rabbi Joseph Elias.

18. Among the students were Rabbi Moshe Wolfson, Rabbi Hershel Mashinsky, Rabbi Shubert Spero, Rabbi Moshe Weitman, Rabbi Berel Schwartz, Chaim Meir Listoken, Sidney Greenwald, and Jack Klausner. Rabbi Zelik Epstein headed the Gemara studies, and besides Reb Shraga Feivel the staff included Rabbi Shlomo Rotenberg, Rabbi Mordechai Schwab, who taught the writings of Rabbi Samson Raphael Hirsch, and Rabbi Heshy Leiman.

19. All the aforementioned were participants in an earlier summer program that Reb Shraga Feivel ran in Torah Vodaath for future *mechanchim*. At the end of the course Reb Shraga Feivel arranged for the students to receive official certification from the Jewish Education Committee. But when a required part of their oral examination in Hebrew included questions on the poetry of Bialik and Chernochovsky, Reb Shraga Feivel halted the proceedings. "*Chevra, kumt, mir geiyen* — Boys, come, we're leaving," he told his students as he ushered them out of the room. In parting, he assured the head of the JEC that they would all be fine teachers without the JEC's certification.

Students learning in Bais Medrash Elyon   Students on the lawn of Bais Medrash Elyon

was also trying to create ambassadors for Torah, suited to the unique and sometimes hostile atmosphere of America. He knew that when a *yeshivah bachur* was in shul with a *minyan* of *baalebatim*, he would not, unfortunately, be judged by how well he understood *Tosafos* or Reb Chaim Brisker, but by whether he could *lain* (read from the *Sefer Torah*), make a knot on *tefillin*, decide a question concerning a *Sefer Torah*, and the like. If he could do all these things, then Torah learning would assume more prestige in the eyes of *baalebatim* — hence Reb Shraga Feivel emphasized this kind of practical knowledge in such programs as *Aish Dos*.[20]

THE HOLOCAUST CHANGED REB SHRAGA FEIVEL'S PERSPECTIVE

Bais Medrash Elyon on the importance of establishing *kollelim* in America. Most of the great scholars of Europe, including most of the upcoming generation, had been murdered. No longer would it be possible to rely on a steady stream of *talmidei chachamim* from Europe. Already in 1937, Reb Shraga Feivel had corresponded with Reb Aharon Kotler about establishing a *kollel*, but now he realized that producing Torah scholars of depth was an urgent priority. Thus, in the fall of 1944, Reb Shraga Feivel opened Bais Medrash Elyon, bringing to Monsey the

---

20. Sidney Greenwald.

first group of eighteen young scholars willing to commit themselves to a program of exclusive Torah learning.

Bais Medrash Elyon was explicitly designed to be an elite institution, and he carefully chose each of those budding scholars for his potential to one day be a *rosh yeshivah*.[21] Yet the production of *roshei yeshivah* did not become Reb Shraga Feivel's exclusive preoccupation even after the Holocaust. He spent at least as much time with the group of twelve students he brought up to Monsey at the same time, whom he groomed for a future in *chinuch* and *klal* work. He once told Yaakov Leshinsky, one of the first students in Bais Medrash Elyon, that his goal was to produce soldiers, whereas others were primarily concerned with producing generals. "If I produce a thousand soldiers," he said, "I know that out of that group will come a certain number of generals. But if one sets out to produce only generals, who knows if there will be any soldiers?"[22]

The Monsey of 1944 was nothing like the thriving Jewish center of today. The area was still almost completely rural farmland. In fact, the yeshivah was always referred to as "Spring Valley," after the nearby village; Monsey's population was so sparse that its existence was virtually unknown. Looking at one of the steeples on the old mansion housing Bais Medrash Elyon one day, Reb Shraga Feivel exclaimed, "I wonder what merit the gentile who built this mansion a hundred years ago possessed that one day it would house such a holy yeshivah."[23]

Rabbi Reuven Grozovsky, the *rosh yeshivah*, divided his week between the Mesivta in Williamsburg and Bais Medrash Elyon,

---

21. Rabbi Shmuel Mendlowitz.

22. He went on to highlight the difference in approach with one of his typically sharp *meshalim*. After the Red Army defeated the White Army in the Russian civil war, many of the former White Army generals fled Russia for Paris. There many of them became taxi drivers; in fact, a large percentage of the Parisian taxi drivers at a certain point were Russian emigres. The dramatic decline in status was naturally very hard for many of these ex-officers to take, and so they opened up an emigre nightclub, to which they would repair at night wearing their White Army uniforms, replete with a chestful of medals. There they would address one another as General So-and-so. That, said Reb Shraga Feivel, is a general without soldiers.

23. Rabbi Eliyahu Yehoshua Geldzhaler.

coming to Monsey the second half of the week and remaining there through Shabbos. Rabbi Yisrael Chaim Kaplan was the *mashgiach*. He had been a *maggid shiur* in the Brisker Rav's yeshivah prior to the war and was the son-in-law of the great Mirrer *Mashgiach*, Rabbi Yerucham Levovitz. He lived in the yeshivah all week, returning to his family in Williamsburg for Shabbos.

The level of the learning was very high. Rabbi Reuven Grozovsky pronounced the quality of learning equal to that in preWar Kamenitz,[24] the only difference being that in Kamenitz the *talmidim* had learned in poverty, which the American *bachurim* had never experienced. Among the early *talmidim* were many who went on to become *roshei yeshivah*: Rabbi Simchah Schustal, Rabbi Don Ungarisher, Rabbi Hillel Zaks, Rabbi Gershon Zaks, Rabbi Hershel Zaks, Rabbi Yitzchak Scheiner, Rabbi Moshe Feigelstock, Rabbi Shraga Moshe Kalmanowitz, Rabbi Chaim Grozovsky, Rabbi Sheah Schiff, Rabbi Shmuel Mendlowitz, Rabbi Sheah Geldzahler, and Rabbi Yaakov Moshe Kulefsky.

Reb Shraga Feivel lived with his family in a house adjacent to the grounds of Bais Medrash Elyon, which allowed him to have the sort of individual contact with each *bachur* that he longed for. As the Mesivta had grown, Reb Shraga Feivel constantly fretted that he was losing his personal feel for each boy committed to his care. He felt that it was impossible to have an accurate sense of more than two hundred boys, and the Mesivta had long since grown past that number. Though he recognized that there were advantages to a larger institution, Reb Shraga Feivel nevertheless tended to think that they were outweighed by the lack of personal intimacy.

In Monsey, however, he could work personally with each student. Every day after the official learning *seder* was over, he would take a different student for a long walk. He used the time to build up the student and to deepen his perspectives on life. Living in such close proximity to the *bachurim*, he was in a position to show them how to interact with one another as part of an extended family.

---

24. A reference to the yeshivah of Reb Reuven's father-in-law, Rabbi Baruch Ber Leibowitz, in which Reb Reuven had been a *rosh yeshivah* before escaping to America.

Above all, his goal was to ensure that Bais Medrash Elyon would produce not just *talmidei chachamim* but *anshei ruach*, people of spirit, with deep Torah perspectives.[25] In part, that goal was achieved in the classroom. He was now teaching advanced students, who had committed themselves to years of Torah study, undiluted by any other pursuits. As a consequence, he was able to give classes in *Tanya* and *Reb Tzaddok* at a much deeper level than in the Mesivta. But Reb Shraga Feivel also took advantage of his close proximity to the *talmidim* and the various contexts in which he met them to convey much of his spirit informally. The *bachurim* never knew when they would be privy to another startling insight that would open up new vistas for them. One *Motza'ei Shabbos*, which was the first night of *Selichos* prior to Rosh Hashanah, the *bachurim* made a *melaveh malkah* in the dining room. Unexpectedly, Reb Shraga Feivel appeared. "A *melaveh malkah* before *Selichos*? I knew chassidim in the previous generation who made the *melaveh malkah* only after reciting *Selichos*." The students were silent, and then Reb Shraga Feivel resumed speaking:

> In truth, there is a place for both *minhagim*. We find in *Tanna d'Vei Eliyahu* that David HaMelech said, "My fear is produced by my rejoicing. My rejoicing is produced by my trembling." When you recite *Selichos* tonight after the *melaveh malkah*, it will be fear produced by rejoicing, but you should know that there is also a path of rejoicing that emanates from trembling.

Reb Shraga Feivel did not live to see the full flowering of Bais Medrash Elyon, passing away in only its fourth year. It grew into the premier postgraduate yeshivah *kollel* in America, a status it held throughout the 50's. But at least he had the pleasure of setting Bais Medrash Elyon on course toward its ultimate greatness. In 1951, Rabbi Reuven Grozovsky suffered a debilitating stroke. After that the yeshivah was led by Rabbi Yisrael Chaim Kaplan with Reb Shraga Feivel's greatest *talmid*, Rabbi Gedaliah Schorr, assuming an ever-greater role, finally becoming *rosh yeshivah*.

---

25. Rabbi Eliyahu Yehoshua Geldzhaler.

Chapter 24

Torah Umesorah: Spreading Torah Throughout America

MUCH OF THE LAST FOUR YEARS OF REB SHRAGA
Feivel's life was dedicated to Torah Umesorah, the
National Society for Hebrew Day Schools, which he
founded in 1944. At a time when there were less
than forty yeshivos and day schools in all of the United States, and
only five or six outside the New York metropolitan area, he set himself the goal of putting a Jewish day school in every community
with a thousand Jewish families. Paraphrasing President Herbert
Hoover's promise, "A car in every garage, a chicken in every pot,"
he chose as Torah Umesorah's motto, "A day school in every community."[1]

Torah Umesorah was the final outgrowth of the central insight
that had guided him since his arrival in America: Without Torah education there would, within one generation, be nothing left of

---

1. Sidney Greenwald.

genuine Torah observance in America. His own sense of urgency was further heightened by the Holocaust, which left American Jewry as the largest Jewish community in the world. For every Torah school in Europe that had been destroyed, he was determined to build a new one in America.

He was a man possessed with the imperative necessity of spreading Torah to the hinterlands of America. As remnants of the Torah leadership of Europe made their way to America, Reb Shraga Feivel was quick to enlist their support for the idea. On his lips was the Midrash (*Yalkut Shimoni, Shoftim* 68) that discusses why 72,000 Jews died in internecine fighting at Givat Binyamin (see *Judges* Ch. 20). The Midrash lays the blame on the members of the Great Sanhedrin. They should have gone from city to city to teach the people, until Hashem's Name would become great in the eyes of all, says the Midrash. Instead, as soon as they came into the Land, each ran to his vineyard and his olive trees, and said to himself, "I am at peace with myself."[2]

In an anonymous proclamation published in the *Jewish Morning Journal* on Rosh Chodesh Elul[3] of 5705 (1945), Reb Shraga Feivel gave expression to the sense of desperation that was driving him. He mentioned no organization, made no appeal, listed no phone numbers. The proclamation consisted only of Reb Shraga Feivel sharing his understanding of the situation with his fellow Jews. In large type at the top of the page was a verse from *Yeshayahu* (59:21): *My* וּדְבָרַי אֲשֶׁר שַׂמְתִּי בְּפִיךָ לֹא יָמוּשׁוּ מִפִּיךָ וּמִפִּי זַרְעֲךָ וּמִפִּי זֶרַע זַרְעֲךָ אָמַר ד׳ *words that I have placed in your mouth will not be withdrawn from your mouth, nor from the mouth of your offspring, nor from the mouth of your offspring's offspring, said Hashem.*

Reb Shraga Feivel explicitly linked the overwhelming tragedy suffered by European Jewry with the demands of the hour. "We

---

2. This same Midrash was used by the Alter of Novardhok to encourage his students to found yeshivos all over Eastern Europe.

3. The publication of the proclamation was deliberately timed to coincide with the first shofar blasts of *Elul*, which call all those who are asleep to awaken and consider their duties to man and G-d.

have to ask ourselves whether we fulfilled our obligations to our brothers in Europe and to *Klal Yisrael* with our tears and sighs and clasped hands." While it was too late to bring the millions of Jews slaughtered in Europe back to life, he acknowledged, it was still possible to create a vibrant *Yiddishkeit* in America. Few American Jews could say with a clear conscience with respect to what had happened in Europe, "Our hands did not shed this blood" (*Devarim* 21:7). The question of the hour, however, was whether they would show the same indifference — for which they stood condemned at the bar of history — to the spiritual devastation taking place in America.

"Will we let the golden chain of Torah going all the way back to Sinai come to an end in this land of freedom!?" was his challenge to American Jewry. The future of Torah Jewry, he insisted, was in the hands of the Jews of America, and it was incumbent upon them to commit themselves to building a new institution for every one that was destroyed. Only at the bottom of the page, in very small print, did the words Torah Umesorah appear at all: "Talking to you is a Jew whose heart bleeds for the physical and spiritual devastation of our generation, and who hopes that Torah will be built in America in the spirit of Torah Umesorah."

THE FUND-RAISING RESPONSIBILITY FOR THE NEW ORGANIZA-tion fell entirely upon Reb Shraga Feivel.[4] The initial $150,000 raised

Lining Up Support

came entirely from major supporters of Torah Vodaath. Reb Shraga Feivel knew that the money given to him for Torah Umesorah would likely come at the expense of the Mesivta, but he offered his contributors no respite from his solicitations. "Yes, I will be back before long collecting for the Mesivta, and I will ask you for large sums, but why should it matter to you who is collecting the money? We are talking about a completely new organization unconnected to the Mesivta. If someone else were doing the collecting, you would not refuse him. So why should you close your hands just because I also raise money for the Mesivta?"

---

4. Rabbi Bernard Goldenberg.

(Left to right): Rabbi Aharon Kotler, Rabbi Reuven Grozovsky, and Rabbi Yitzchak Hutner at a Torah Umesorah dinner

With his deep sincerity and earnest persuasiveness, he prevailed upon Mr. Samuel Feuerstein of Boston to become the first president of Torah Umesorah.[5] With his dignified appearance and refined character, Feuerstein was an aristocrat of the American Torah world. Twenty-five years later, Feuerstein, who served as president of Torah Umesorah until his death in 1983, recalled his first discussions with Reb Shraga Feivel:

> I was on a short vacation in Atlantic City when I received a telephone message that Reb Shraga Feivel was on his way to see me on an urgent matter. That alone was enough to shock me since I knew that he was in poor health and that the trip would drain him greatly. When he arrived, only after repeated entreaties on my part did he agree to rest briefly before revealing the purpose of his visit . . .
>
> The strenuous efforts he had made to visit me made a deep impression on me. The subject of his concern gave him no rest. "In this bitter hour, we must establish yeshivos in America," he said. "We can no longer be content with one

---

5. Other major early supporters were Irving Bunim, Anshel Fink, Moses Feuerstein, Harry and Sam Hershkowitz, Frank Newman, Joseph and Ira Rosenzweig, and Joseph Shapiro.

Torah Vodaath. All the Jews in Europe are trapped or already dead and the fortresses of Torah destroyed. We have to start everything over again from scratch."

He asked me to undertake the formation of an organization called Torah Umesorah for the purpose of establishing day schools throughout America. "Money I could have obtained with a telephone call," he told me, "just as I have always done with you. But this time I need something more. I need encouragement. I need someone whose heart is aflame to share with me the burden."

Mr. Feuerstein did not refuse.

By June 1944, Reb Shraga Feivel had held Torah Umesorah's first annual dinner, at the Hotel Astor. Though he was content to live in a drab apartment, Reb Shraga Feivel was a shrewd-enough student of character to recognize the importance of an impressive opening in one of New York's most elegant hotels. With great effort, he brought 115 guests, and he instituted two important changes in the program, changes that spoke volumes about the direction of the new organization and its seriousness of purpose. There was no entertainer on the program, as was then *de rigueur*, and the dais was made up of rabbis and *roshei yeshivah*, with the major contributors seated below, a complete reversal of the-then universal practice. The dire predictions that wealthy contributors would resent not being on the dais did not materialize. Meanwhile, the man who had almost single-handedly brought Torah Umesorah into existence seated himself inconspicuously among the guests.

Enlisting the Gedolim

NOR WERE THE *GEDOLIM* PRESENT JUST FOR SHOW. FROM THE beginning, Reb Shraga Feivel established the principle that the organization would be run by the Rabbinic Administrative Board, which would have absolute policy-making and veto power over every aspect of the organization's operations. His success in enlisting the support of virtually every major American *rosh yeshivah* and leaders of the Orthodox rabbinate is evident in the composition of the first Rabbinic Administrative Board. Rabbi Aharon Kotler was its chairman, and he continued in that capacity until the end of his life. Other members were Rabbi Eliyahu Meir Bloch, Rabbi Chaim Yitzchak Block, Rabbi Moshe Feinstein, Rabbi Reuven Grozovsky, Rabbi Yitzchak Hutner, Rabbi Avraham Yaffen, Rabbi Yaakov Kamenetsky, Rabbi Mordechai Katz, Rabbi Yaakov Meir Lessin, Rabbi David Lifshitz, Rabbi Yaakov Yitzchak Ruderman, Rabbi Yehudah Leib Seltzer, Rabbi Eliezer Silver, and Rabbi Mendel Zaks.

Securing the intimate involvement of the *roshei yeshivah* in the operations of Torah Umesorah from the very beginning was a masterstroke that contributed greatly to the organization's ultimate success. Above all it ensured that *daas Torah* (Torah wisdom and judgment) would guide Torah Umesorah as it navigated some very tricky and uncharted seas. There were, for instance, few, if any, communities outside of the New York area with a large enough Orthodox population to support a school without attracting both students and financial support from the broader Jewish community. The vast majority of students in the early years came from homes where neither Shabbos nor kashrus was observed strictly. Torah Umesorah thus had to find a way to relax standards from the ideal, without, at the same time, relaxing them so much as to vitiate the whole purpose of establishing Orthodox day schools in the first place. Without the wisdom of the *roshei yeshivah* to guide it and their prestige to back it up, Torah Umesorah could never have negotiated this tightrope.

One of the recurring issues in almost every new community was separate classes for boys and girls. Ideally, in the view of the Rabbinical Administration Board, boys and girls should have been segregated from an early age. Yet insistence on this principle would have doomed any chance of establishing schools anywhere outside of New York City, where there were neither the financial resources nor the will to support early gender segregation. The determination as to how to proceed required an individual *psak*, based on such factors as local resources, availability of teachers, school enrollment, and local resistance, with respect to every new school.[6]

Another common problem was that in many cities the only available facility for a school was owned by a Reform or Conservative congregation, and a difficult decision had to be made whether to rent those facilities or make a major investment, for which there was usually no local support, in a new building. Many of the day schools started in makeshift, one-room "schoolhouses."[7]

R' Shraga Feivel and other Torah personalities traveling by special train to the National Conference on Torah Education in Cleveland

The involvement of the *roshei yeshivah* was crucial for another reason: It ensured that many of the

R' Shraga Feivel and Rabbi Aharon Kotler at the Cleveland conference

rebbeim entering the Torah Umesorah system would be drawn from the ranks of their students.[8] In addition, the contact with a large cross-section of the world's leading Torah giants at the annual Torah

---

6. Dr. Joseph Kaminetsky, *Memorable Encounters*, p. 95.

7. Ibid., pp. 95ff.

8. At the same time, most of the *roshei yeshivah* opposed the creation of any type of teacher-training program in their yeshivos that would help prepare their graduates to enter a classroom. Teacher seminaries had traditionally been associated with the *maskilim* in Europe, and this was one reason for the resistance of the *roshei yeshivah*. A more important consideration was the reluctance to dilute in any way the atmosphere of pure learning in the yeshivos. Only Reb Shraga Feivel continually tried to create such an institute within his yeshivah. Eventually his quest reached fruition with funds provided by Mr. Joseph Shapiro, with which Torah Umesorah instituted the Joseph Shapiro Teachers Training Program, with sessions held in Torah Vodaath.

Umesorah convention was a source of inspiration for the teachers in the field, whose jobs were inevitably difficult ones and rarely provided more than bare subsistence, not to mention environments that were hardly sympathetic to their lofty spiritual aspirations.

The most impressive of these annual conferences in Reb Shraga Feivel's lifetime was the National Conference on Torah Education held at Telshe Yeshivah in 1947. All the expenses of the conference, including a specially chartered overnight train from New York City that brought the leading *roshei yeshivah,* were covered by Herbert and Ben Spero of Cleveland. Despite his ill health and the urging of his family and doctors that he not make the strenuous trip, Reb Shraga Feivel was there too, though he did not speak publicly. The conference allowed principals and teachers far removed from the center of Jewish life to share with one another the problems they confronted and to seek the advice of the leaders of Torah Jewry in America.

FOR THE POSITION OF NATIONAL DIRECTOR OF TORAH Umesorah, Reb Shraga Feivel tapped Rabbi Dr. Samson Raphael

Living on Idealism

Weiss, a relatively recent refugee from Germany, who had been one of the main teachers in the *Aish Dos* program. In three years as principal of the Talmud Torah in

Rabbi Dr. Samson Raphael Weiss

Detroit, Rabbi Weiss had quadrupled enrollment and added a girls program as well. With the exception of Rabbi Weiss, the early staff of Torah Umesorah was made up entirely of Reb Shraga Feivel's *talmidim.* In charge of day-to-day activities were Sender Gross and Bernard Goldenberg. When Reb Shraga Feivel had approached them to help him create Torah Umesorah, they had both given him the same answer: Gross agreed on condition that Goldenberg would be involved, and Goldenberg agreed on condition that Gross would be involved.

(Left to right): Dr. Joseph Kaminetsky,
Rabbi Sender Gross, Rabbi Bernard Goldenberg

Rabbis Weiss, Gross, and Goldenberg were the only paid staffers. This skeleton staff was somehow supposed to found schools in communities where none existed, provide those schools with the staff and educational material they needed, serve as an ongoing resource for school principals to consult as problems arose, and to publicize the virtues of day school education across North America. Much of the actual fieldwork of recruiting students and establishing schools was done by a dedicated band of volunteers led by Freddy Wolf and Elimelech Terebelo, and included Mendel Eller, Charles Batt, and Leon Machlis, all of whom were also students of Reb Shraga Feivel. Two more *talmidim*, Berl Merling, a talented artist and writer, and Charles Wengrov, a gifted writer, had a major hand in the creation of *Olomeinu*, Torah Umesorah's children's magazine, which is now in its sixth decade.

The early Torah Umesorah survived on idealism and little else. For example, Bernard Goldenberg worked to put out an edition of *Olomeinu* during the week of his *sheva berachos*. The story of the founding of a day school in Minneapolis gives some taste of Reb Shraga Feivel's inspirational role in the organization. The proclamation placed in the *Morning Journal* had caught the attention of a few Yiddish-speaking Jews in the St. Paul-Minneapolis area. Somehow they had heard of Torah Umesorah, and they wrote seeking assistance in creating a day school in St. Paul.

One cold wintry day in 1946, as Bernard Goldenberg accompanied Reb Shraga Feivel from the Torah Umesorah offices at 132 Nassau Street in downtown Manhattan to the Williamsburg bus stop, Reb Shraga Feivel took the letter from Minnesota out of his pocket and showed it to Goldenberg. When Goldenberg had finished reading it, Reb Shraga Feivel suggested that he travel to Minnesota in a day or two.

To Goldenberg's protest that he had no idea of how to get to Minnesota, Reb Shraga Feivel quipped, "Are you too lazy to find out?" And to his next plea that he had no clue as to how to begin a day school once he arrived, Reb Shraga Feivel simply suggested that he look up the Jew who had written Torah Umesorah.

Two buses to Williamsburg passed and Goldenberg had still not given Reb Shraga Feivel his answer. As yet another bus approached, Reb Shraga smiled wearily at his *talmid* and expressed his hope that there would yet come a day when they would say about him what Yirmiyahu had said of *Klal Yisrael*. His curiosity piqued, Goldenberg asked Reb Shraga Feivel to tell him what Yirmiyahu had said.

A big smile on his face, Reb Shraga Feivel replied, "Yirmiyahu said: *I recall for you the kindness of your youth, the love of your nuptials, your following Me into the Wilderness, into an unsown land*" (*Yirmiyahu* 2:2). He repeated the last phrase, "בְּאֶרֶץ לֹא זְרוּעָה, *into an unsown land.*" Placing his hand on Goldenberg's shoulder, he said, in a play on words, "Go to Minnesota, to a land where the לא, the negativism, the disbelief — the *lo* (not) — is sown. Go to that wilderness and start a school." Reb Shraga Feivel knew full well that it was deeply and firmly implanted in the consciousness of American Jews that Torah Judaism cannot be sown in America, but he would not accept such defeatism — and Bernie Goldenberg would not accept it either. The young man accepted his marching orders and the result was a day school in Minnesota that same year, the first of many schools to be founded by Rabbi Goldenberg.[9]

Nearly fifty new schools were established in Reb Shraga Feivel's life-

---

9. This vignette is adapted from Rabbi Goldenberg's short chapter, "A Land Not Sown," in *Memorable Encounters*, Dr. Joseph Kaminetsky's memoirs.

time alone. Every success — and every failure — had its own dramatic story. Gross and Goldenberg traveled to Buffalo to try to rouse some interest in a day school, and while there, they attended the tenth-anniversary dinner of the Buffalo Board of Jewish Education. The chairman of the board began his speech with a direct attack on the idea of a day school, which he labeled "undemocratic and un-American." Unfortunately for him, a reporter from the local newspaper was there, and the next day's headline read, "Parochial Schools Called Undemocratic." The article brought an outraged response from the Catholic diocese, which listed all the Catholic school alumni who had fallen in World War II or earned medals. The chairman of the Board of Jewish Education was forced to beat a hasty retreat in public. He clarified that only *Jewish* parochial schools are undemocratic.

On another occasion Goldenberg was about to speak in a smaller town in upstate New York. As he sat on the podium, he noticed a distinguished-looking older woman, wearing a mink coat, enter and sit in the front row. As soon as Goldenberg rose to speak, she leaped to her feet, yelling, "You Jew you, you East Sider you, you Communist you, get out of my town." Pandemonium broke out, and he never had a chance to speak. Later he found out that the woman was the widow of the town's richest Jew, who had built the community center and the Reform Temple.

IN 1946, RABBI WEISS LEFT TORAH UMESORAH TO BECOME THE Executive Director of Young Israel. His departure created a major

Dr. Joseph Kaminetsky

gap in the organization. He not only possessed the worldly experience that his younger colleagues still lacked, but was a peerless orator and a distinguished *talmid chacham*. The fact that he was a product of the Mirrer Yeshivah and the holder of a German doctorate lent luster to the organization he headed.

To replace him, Reb Shraga Feivel chose Dr. Joseph Kaminetsky, a graduate of Yeshiva College and then the national vice president of Hapoel Mizrachi. There were many at the time who viewed that choice as an uncharacteristic lapse of judgment on Reb Shraga Feivel's part, and, as Dr. Kaminetsky notes with bemusement in his

Dr. Joseph Kaminetsky

Rabbi Yitzchak Isaac Sher

memoirs, many of the doubters never made peace with his appointment for the nearly thirty years that he served as national director of Torah Umesorah.

But Reb Shraga Feivel knew exactly what he was doing. He understood that the crucial work of convincing Jews in distant communities of the importance of a full-day Torah education would require someone with whom local *baalebatim* could identify. At the same time, the scouting reports of Bernard Goldenberg and Sender Gross attested to Dr. Kaminetsky's deep commitment to spreading Torah values. As a young college student he had been drawn to the Slabodka *Rosh Yeshivah*, Rabbi Yitzchak Isaac Sher, and would have followed him back to Slabodka but for the responsibility of helping support eight younger brothers and sisters.

The fledgling Torah Umesorah was threatening to the Jewish federations and other establishment organizations around the country, and had managed to stir a great deal of overt animosity in its short existence.[10] The easiest charge for those who feared an Orthodox educational system was

---

10. Mizrachi, which in those days viewed itself as the spiritual leader of American Orthodoxy, immediately established a competing educational organization, which closed after a few years with little to show for its efforts.

that Torah Umesorah was a group of yeshivah products totally un-qualified to run a modern school. Dr. Kaminetsky's doctorate in education from Columbia, something virtually unknown in Jewish education at the time, went a long way towards silencing those crit-ics. In addition, as principal of Manhattan Day School, he had developed the only complete day-school curriculum in America.

For his part, Dr. Kaminetsky was reluctant to leave his positions as principal of the Manhattan Day School and principal of the Talmud Torah in Rabbi Leo Jung's Jewish Center. The turning point came when he was asked to address a group of Torah Vodaath students who were preparing for careers in *chinuch.* That night one of the stu-dents was getting married, and Dr. Kaminetsky was invited to attend. What he saw at the *chasunah* amazed him. The emotion with which Reb Shraga Feivel sang *Od Yishama* and the depth of the love between the *talmidim* and Reb Shraga Feivel was something for which nothing in his background had prepared him. He returned home from the *cha-sunah* that night and told his incredulous wife, "I'm a chassid of Reb Shraga Feivel, and I'm going to work for Torah Umesorah."

For the last two years of Reb Shraga Feivel's life, Dr. Kaminetsky indeed joined Rabbis Goldenberg and Gross as chassidim of Reb Shraga Feivel, as well as co-workers.[11]

Every morning Sender Gross would *daven* in the same *minyan* as Reb Shraga Feivel in Torah Vodaath, and afterwards they would dis-cuss Torah Umesorah. He would then bring the day's marching orders from "the Boss" to the office. As Dr. Kaminetsky recalls:

> Every day there was a new vision, a new project proposed. We lived in an atmosphere charged with challenge and en-thusiasm. Even in absentia, Reb Feivel moved us no end. He not only had the power to inspire and lift our sights, but also the capacity to encourage us whenever our spirits were low.[12]

---

11. Nevertheless, he could not crack the circle of Reb Shraga Feivel's *talmidim.* One time he expressed to Reb Shraga Feivel a desire to attend some of his *shiurim.* Reb Shraga Feivel told him, "You are my co-worker, not my *talmid.*"

12. *Memorable Encounters,* op. cit., p. 77.

In those two years, says Dr. Kaminetsky, the staff of Torah Umesorah saw miracles on a regular basis that they could never have anticipated in their most optimistic moments. They also absorbed inspiration for a lifetime. Dr. Kaminetsky's own *mesiras nefesh* for the organization was legendary. Over a period of thirty years, he was home for no more than every other Shabbos.

THE TRANSFORMATION OF DETROIT FROM A SMALL BACKWATER on the American Jewish map into a vibrant Orthodox community

Detroit — A Model of Inspiration
was largely fueled by Yeshivah Beth Yehudah, which became a full-day school in 1944. Thus Detroit demonstrates the impact that Torah Umesorah-sponsored day schools could have on communities throughout America. More, Beth Yehudah was built almost entirely by *talmidim* of Reb Shraga Feivel or those who had come under his sway. Nowhere was his inspiration more intensely felt than in the sense of mission his followers brought to Detroit.[13]

The first principal of Yeshiva Beth Yehudah full-day school was Rabbi Simchah Wasserman, who had headed the learning program of *Aish Dos* and there imbibed Reb Shraga Feivel's message that the first order of business for American Orthodoxy was the creation of day schools around the country. In 1951 he was succeeded by Rabbi Joseph Elias, who had headed *Beis Medrash L'Mechanchim*, a successor program to *Aish Dos*. Rabbi Avraham Abba Freedman, a graduate of *Aish Dos* and a devoted *talmid* of Reb Shraga Feivel, became Yeshivah Beth Yehudah's first full-time teacher in 1944. He had originally been recruited by Rabbi S. R. Weiss to teach in the Talmud Torah. Two years later, he was joined in Detroit by his Mesivta *chavrusa* and fellow *Aish Dos* alumnus, Rabbi Shalom Goldstein. Until his passing in 1984, the dynamic Rabbi Goldstein

---

13. The information on Yeshivah Beth Yehudah is derived from C. Danhi's article "Rebbis in Shirtsleeves: The Golden Days of Detroit's Yeshivah Beth Yehudah," in *Visions*, and was confirmed by a number of interviews with products of Yeshivah Beth Yehudah and the Detroit Bais Yaakov.

was at the forefront of every new Torah initiative in Detroit, including the founding of a Bais Yaakov, of which he was principal from its inception in 1965 until his death. Rabbi Chaim Schloss, a Bais Medrash Elyon alumnus, was another one of Reb Shraga Feivel's emissaries in Yeshivah Beth Yehudah's early years. Another Torah Vodaath *talmid*, Rabbi Shmuel Elya Cohen, was Rabbi Goldstein's general studies principal and succeeded Rabbi Goldstein after his premature death.

Reb Shraga Feivel's *talmidim* did not come to Detroit to find jobs but to build a community. They were not attracted by the lure of relatively higher salaries in an "out-of-town" community, for such material inducements did not exist in those days. Salaries and the other terms of employment meant nothing to them. Their "jobs" may have been teaching in the classroom, but the classroom was only one venue among many in which they waged their campaign to transform Detroit Jewry. Their watchword was *Chazal's* interpretation of the opening words of Shema: "וְאָהַבְתָּ אֵת ד' אֱלֹקֶיךָ, *You shall love Hashem, your G-d*, שֶׁיְּהֵא שֵׁם שָׁמַיִם מִתְאַהֵב עַל יָדְךָ, [*to love G-d means to act in such a way*] *that the Name of Heaven should become beloved through you*" (*Yoma* 86a).

Before the term *kiruv*, or outreach, had even been coined, the Yeshivah Beth Yehudah *rebbis* were a full-time *kiruv* organization. Every Friday night, the population of the two-block area near Yeshivah Beth Yehudah, in which most of the *rebbeim* lived, would swell by twenty to forty boys — most of whom were from non-observant homes — spending Shabbos in the homes of their teachers. Friday night typically ended in singing and storytelling around the overflowing Goldstein table. Every weekday, one of the Beth Yehudah *rebbis* — Rabbi Freedman, Rabbi Goldstein, or Rabbi Yaakov Levy, another Torah Vodaath product — would drive the yeshivah's schoolbus to pick up boys for the morning *minyan*. School remained in session during Chol HaMoed Succos so that students from nonreligious families would be able to eat their meals in a *succah* and perform the mitzvah of the Four Species. On Purim, too, there were regular sessions, so that all the students could participate in the rituals of the day. For many years, Rabbi Levy spent the week prior to Succos building *succos* for families that would otherwise not have had one. The building materials were procured by Beth Yehudah students, led by Rabbi Freedman, on foraging trips to lumberyards, where they asked for contributions of used doors and the like and loaded them into a U-haul.[14]

The *rebbeim* were constantly on the lookout for new opportunities to expand their contacts with students. Ice-skating, tobogganing, and auto shows were just a few of the activities for which groups of boys piled into their *rebbeim's* dilapidated cars. There were cross-country bus trips to Williamsburg for visits to matzah bakeries and *tzitzis* factories and to give the students a taste of a large Jewish community.[15] Telshe Yeshivah, Torah Vodaath, and Lakewood were other frequent destinations, and over the years many Beth Yehudah graduates continued their studies in those institutions.

Every boy attracted to the yeshivah was a story in himself. Rabbi Freedman used to go to local hospitals to visit Jewish patients. Inevitably every discussion included questions about the patient's children, their schooling, and a pitch for a day-school education. Rabbi Nachman Kahn and Rabbi Freedman once spent every night for a week pleading with recent immigrants, who felt their son's English had improved enough for him to be enrolled in public school, not to take him out of the yeshivah. A few years later, the same parents decided to send their son to a Federation-sponsored summer camp. But the *rebbis* forestalled this plan as well. The night before the boy was to leave for camp, Rabbi David Reiss and Rabbi Shmuel Kaufman told the startled parents that a full scholarship had been arranged for their son to spend the summer in an Orthodox camp, including three weeks at Camp Agudah. Today that boy is the educational director of a day school with seven hundred students.

---

14. The number of *succos* in the community is one good measure of the changes in Detroit over the last half-century. In 1944, there were no more than fifty in the entire community; today there are more than a thousand.

15. Rabbi Freedman continues to lead these bus trips to New York. Today, however, the participants are more likely to be new immigrants from the former Soviet Union, who have had little previous exposure to Judaism.

The cadre of *rebbis* was not only enthusiastic, but endlessly creative. Rather than relax with their families or concentrate on their own learning during the summer, the *rebbis* of Yeshivah Beth Yehuda founded and staffed a day camp. They did not forget Reb Shraga Feivel's message that the summer provides an opportunity for further growth in a completely different setting. The morning in camp was spent in learning and the afternoons in sports and other recreational activities. Rabbi Levy was the tour guide for a variety of overnight expeditions. Before such activities were widespread, Detroit pioneered a Thursday-night *mishmar* in the yeshivah game room, Shabbos-night Mishnayos groups, and Shabbos-day learning groups for the boys. The weekly *melaveh malkahs* were a throwback to Reb Shraga Feivel's *shalosh seudos* table, at which many of the Yeshivah Beth Yehudah *rebbis* had been nurtured. The singing and dancing and *varmkeit* (warmth) of Torah Vodaath were transplanted to Detroit. Beth Yehudah *rebbis* canvassed homes to recruit students for the yeshivah, as Reb Binyamin Wilhelm had done when Torah Vodaath was a derided dream.

One of the problems confronting youngsters in Detroit, Rabbi Goldstein realized, was that growing up in a small Orthodox community, they might feel like misfits, far removed from normal social life. To counteract that sense of social isolation, he undertook to organize national Bais Yaakov conventions in the early 60's, so that Detroit girls could meet their counterparts from other cities. He was also one of the first to encourage girls to attend a seminary in Israel after graduating high school, and girls from Detroit quickly gained a reputation for providing the *ruach* (spirit) in their respective seminaries, which continues to this day. That *ruach* was largely a function of what Rabbi Goldstein had imparted to them, both in school and on their many outings together.

Torah Umesorah is one of Reb Shraga Feivel's most enduring legacies. His impossible dream of a day school in every Jewish community has become a reality. The handful of day schools in existence when Torah Umesorah was founded has blossomed into six hundred schools today, with a total enrollment of over 135,000 children.

And in many of the two hundred communities in which Torah Umesorah affiliated schools are found today, the local day school has been largely responsible for whatever exists of Torah Judaism.

Reb Shraga Feivel used to say that if just one Jewish child in Kansas City learned to say *Krias Shema,* all his efforts on behalf of Torah Umesorah would be worthwhile. As a consequence of his vision, hundreds of thousands have learned *Krias Shema* and much more.

Chapter 25

In Love With Zion

"I AM IN THE WEST BUT MY HEART IS IN THE EAST," Rabbi Yehudah HaLevi's immortal description of his own position in Spain, applied no less to Reb Shraga Feivel. The earth and stones of *Eretz Yisrael* were as real to him as those upon which he trod every day. Of all his sacrifices on behalf of *Klal Yisrael*, says Rabbi Moshe Wolfson, none was as great as his remaining in America despite his intense yearning for *Eretz Yisrael*.

Opposite the entrance to his apartment, where he could see it as he sat at his table, in big black letters were the words: אִם אֶשְׁכָּחֵךְ יְרוּשָׁלַיִם תִּשְׁכַּח יְמִינִי, *If I forget you, O Jerusalem, let my right hand forget its skill* (Psalms 137:5), and, indeed, *Eretz Yisrael* was never far from his consciousness. The merest mention of *Eretz Yisrael* was enough to release Reb Shraga Feivel's strongest emotions. Just hearing the name Yerushalayim or Zion caused him to lose all balance, like the lovesick maiden in *Shir HaShirim* (2:5): כִּי חוֹלַת אַהֲבָה אָנִי, *for I am sick with love.*[1] Whether it was teaching the lament of Yirmiyahu over the fallen Jerusalem; or "By the waters of Babylon," recited by the exiles after the destruction of the First Temple; or the blessing in *Shemoneh Esrei,* "to Jerusalem, Your city, return in mercy," he could never fully restrain himself.

He never tired of telling his students that *Eretz Yisrael* is the natural place for every Jew. Only there can a Jew flourish to his maximum potential. A Jew's life outside of *Eretz Yisrael* inevitably has a truncated, unnatural quality. He is like a polar bear removed from his Arctic habitat and placed in the Bronx Zoo.[2]

Any Jew who does not at least dream of going up to *Eretz Yisrael,* he said, is surely lacking something in his *Yiddishkeit.*[3] And he expressed amazement that anyone who considered himself a good Jew could possibly go seven days without thinking of some way in which he could improve the lot of settlers in *Eretz Yisrael* or otherwise improve the Land.[4] On a Yom Tov, he would repeat the Midrash: "The Congregation of Israel says before the Holy One, Blessed is He, 'Because I did not keep one day of Yom Tov as was fitting in *Eretz Yisrael,* I am forced to keep two days of Yom Tov in exile.' "[5]

Reb Shraga Feivel did not content himself with theoretical statements about how precious *Eretz Yisrael* is. His entire life he was busy with plans to make *aliyah.* With every stage in Torah Vodaath's development, he again asked himself whether he had succeeded in placing it on a sufficiently firm basis that he could leave for the Holy Land.

---

1. Elias Karp.

    In his emotional attachment to *Eretz Yisrael,* he was like his *rebbi* the Unsdorfer Rav. Seeing his students looking at him with a puzzled look one day, after the mention of *Eretz Yisrael* had provoked an emotional outburst, Reb Shraga Feivel told them, "Just reading the Mishnah 'One who brings a *get* from across the sea to *Eretz Yisrael* ...' was enough to bring my *rebbi* to tears."

2. Rabbi Nesanel Quinn.

3. Rabbi Yaakov Leshinsky.

4. Rabbi Elimelech Terebelo.

5. Rabbi Shmuel Mendlowitz.

His partner in all these plans was his dearest friend from Scranton and Williamsburg, Rabbi David Eisenberger. From Reb Shraga Feivel's first days in Scranton, they planned how they would go to *Eretz Yisrael* with their families. Finally, in 1938, Reb David decided that the time was ripe to realize their lifelong dream. He resigned his position as a *rebbi* in the yeshivah and left for *Eretz Yisrael*. Reb Shraga Feivel delayed his own departure in order to conclude his work in the Mesivta, but, to his enormous disappointment, Heaven had other plans. Reb David waited expectantly in Bnei Brak for his friend, but the rendezvous never took place. In this, Reb Shraga Feivel could be compared to the Baal Shem Tov, the Vilna Gaon, and the Chofetz Chaim, all of whom set out for *Eretz Yisrael*, but for reasons unknown to us, were forced to turn back.

ALMOST FROM THE EARLIEST DAYS OF THE MESIVTA, REB SHRAGA Feivel involved his *talmidim* in concrete plans for making *aliyah*. He

Plans for Building the Land

formed an organization named *Yesod Hamaaleh* whose members committed themselves to the ideal of settling *Eretz Yisrael*. Later the name of the organization was changed to *Torah V'Avodah*. At the initial meeting of *Torah V'Avodah*, Reb Shraga Feivel asked Reb Itche Gershtenkorn, the founder of Bnei Brak, to address the members. Gershtenkorn pictured Torah communities flourishing across the Land, while at the same time mentioning the numerous obstacles to realization of that vision.

Members of *Torah V'Avodah* set up a fund specifically designated for their planned settlement in *Eretz Yisrael*. The group went so far as to choose candidates who would be given training in agricultural science. Reb Shraga Feivel's oldest son, Moshe Yitzchak, was one of the first slated for *aliyah* and even spent time on a farm, learning agriculture.

All this planning, however, never came to fruition. In the midst of the Great Depression, when Torah Vodaath was unable to pay its *rebbis*, the yeshivah's president asked *Torah V'Avodah* to lend all its funds to Torah Vodaath. That loan effectively brought *Torah V'Avodah* to an end.

Though nothing concrete came of plans for a Torah Vodaath settlement in *Eretz Yisrael*, Reb Shraga Feivel succeeded in instilling many of his students with a burning love for the Land. When Rabbi Avraham Makitowsky (later famous as Eliyahu Kitov) came to America before the creation of the State to sell shares in a corporation to create *chareidi* industries, his most enthusiastic supporters were students of Reb Shraga Feivel, who had been raised on his vision of religious Jews building and farming the Land with their hands.[6] Jack Klausner spent three months at that time learning about the manufacture of neon lighting in order to run a factory that the Spero brothers of Cleveland had agreed to establish in *Eretz Yisrael*.[7]

One student who did emigrate to *Eretz Yisrael* under the British Mandate was the late Rabbi Moshe Aharon Stern, who became famous as *mashgiach* of Yeshivas Kamenitz in Jerusalem. After World War II, the British yielded to great public pressure and "magnanimously" allocated thirty-two immigration certificates to the Jewish Agency, of which only two were granted to Agudath Israel. Stern approached Mike Tress, the leader of Agudah, whom he knew well, and asked if he could have one of the certificates. Tress told him, "You'll have to ask the Boss." As close as he was to Stern, Reb Shraga Feivel refused to hear of him taking one of the certificates since he was still unmarried; an entire family could go on the certificate — why should it be wasted on an individual?

Instead, the certificate was granted to Daniel Goldstein and his family, but two days before the boat was due to sail, Mrs. Goldstein

---

6. Rabbi Makitowsky's organization was called PAGI (Poalei Agudath Israel, but was not related to the political party of the same name), and succeeded in establishing a construction firm, bakery, and printing press. PAGI built the first houses in the Bayit Vegan neighborhood of Jerusalem, which was then a summer resort, and also the PAGI neighborhood, which was right on the Jordanian border and absorbed heavy bombardment in the War of Independence. Makitowsky came within a few hundred votes of being elected to the first Knesset on the list of PAGI, which was then considered somewhat to the right of Agudath Israel. *Rabbi Nachman Bulman* and *Jack Klausner.*

7. Nothing ever came of that plan because the Histadrut put too many restrictions on it for the Speros' taste. Elimelech Terebelo, another member of the original PAGI group in Torah Vodaath — which included Moshe Weitman, Alter Perl, Sidney Greenwald, and Jack Klausner — did succeed in coming to *Eretz Yisrael* in the early 50's, where he was active in the projects of Zeirei Agudath Israel and the Karlin Stolin institutions.

became ill and they could not go. Again, Stern approached Reb Shraga Feivel, and this time the Boss told him he could have the certificate on one condition: "You cannot travel to *Eretz Yisrael* like an *Amerikaner*. An *Amerikaner* takes one whiff and comes running back. That's not what I want. If you go there, you have to go with the intention of remaining. If you marry there, then I can consider it as if I sent a family to *Eretz Yisrael*."[8]

The Chazon Ish

When the War of Independence broke out and the country was invaded by five Arab armies, Stern's parents begged him to return to America until after the war, and even sent tickets for him and his family. Moshe Aharon consulted the Brisker Rav and the Chazon Ish. The Brisker Rav told him to stay and assured him that he would not be in danger. The Chazon Ish told him to stay, and gave him a sealed letter to send to his parents. Years later, Stern learned that the Chazon Ish had written that there were only a handful of such young men in the country and that he was needed in *Eretz Yisrael*. He stayed, with his parents' blessing.

OF ALL REB SHRAGA FEIVEL'S EFFORTS ON BEHALF OF THE reestablishment of religious life in *Eretz Yisrael*, none would have

Support for Bnei Brak

such long-range effect as the timely assistance he provided to Reb Yitzchak (Itche) Gershtenkorn, the founder of Bnei Brak.

---

8. Reb Shraga Feivel commented that Rabbi Moshe Aharon Stern merited to live in Israel for the same reason that Yehoshua merited to lead the Jewish people into the Land. The Midrash says that Yehoshua arranged the benches in Moshe Rabbeinu's *beis medrash*, and so too Rabbi Stern always put away the *sefarim* in the Mesivta *beis medrash*. Jack Klausner.

Rabbi Yitzchak Gershtenkorn

A year after the founding of Bnei Brak in 1924, Gershtenkorn desperately needed funds to meet the payments for the land and to start commercial enterprises that would provide a living for the Jews he wished to attract from Poland and other European countries. He had high expectations that the Fourteenth Zionist Congress, to be convened in Vienna in the summer of 1925, would make a substantial allocation toward the expansion of Bnei Brak. But despite the large budget for settlement activities, not a single penny was allocated for Bnei Brak. The idea of a city of religious Jews, or of attracting such Jews from Europe, apparently held little appeal for any of the Zionist groups represented in Vienna.

Gershtenkorn saw his life's dream vanishing in front of his eyes. His last hope was to raise funds for the project in America. Arriving in New York in 1928, he first tried his luck in the *kloizen* and *shtieblach* of Polish-born chassidim. There he had little success. Next he tried the official Orthodox organizations — Agudas HaRabbanim and Mizrachi — with a similar lack of response. After two weeks, he had almost nothing to show for his efforts.

The new year of 5689, however, brought him better fortune. As he exited the *mikveh* on Erev Rosh Hashanah, he was greeted by Reb Shraga Feivel and Binyamin Wilhelm, who recognized his picture from one of the Yiddish papers and who urged him to *daven* in Torah Vodaath that night. From the minute he entered the *beis medrash*, Rabbi Gershtenkorn wrote later in his diary, he was enveloped in the familiar confines of a *"beis medrash* filled with chassidim from Poland and Galicia. They stood crowded together, but *davened* with the same *nusach*, the same chassidic fire [that I was used to from Poland], and a feeling of being uplifted came over me that did not depart the entire holiday."

Reb Itche ate his meals with Reb Shraga Feivel. Later he would describe him as "one of the rare souls of the generation, a person of exemplary *middos*, who loves Zion from the depths of his soul. When he spoke about *Eretz Yisrael*, he became transported by his great yearning for it."

On the second day of Rosh Hashanah, Reb Shraga Feivel honored his guest by asking him to speak before the shofar blowing. In the course of speaking about *Akeidas Yitzchak*, Rabbi Gershtenkorn reminded his listeners of the Midrash that Yitzchak Avinu never left *Eretz Yisrael*, never getting further than Bnei Brak. His emotion-laden words had a powerful impact, and immediately after the holiday was over, a group of chassidim, with Reb Shraga Feivel at their head, came to offer him whatever help they could.

Reb Itche asked them to purchase shares of the Bank of Agriculture and Industry, which he had established in order to finance various small factories in or near Bnei Brak. Reb Shraga Feivel was the first to purchase shares, and many others followed his lead. The next day, the Fast of Gedaliah, Reb Itche was able to send a check for $6,000 back to *Eretz Yisrael*, the first monies he had collected since leaving home months before.

The support of those who *davened* in Torah Vodaath revived Reb Itche's spirits, and he remained another five months in America, seeking support for Bnei Brak. His fund-raising in America ended as it had begun — in Williamsburg. Reb Shraga Feivel prevailed upon Yaakov Feiner, one of those who *davened* regularly in Torah Vodaath, to host a parlor meeting for Reb Itche. This gathering, too, was very successful, and provided funding for a substantial expansion of Bnei Brak.

Reb Itche never forgot Reb Shraga Feivel's kindness. At the *hakamas hamatzeivah* (placing of the gravestone) for Reb Shraga Feivel in the Shomrei Shabbos cemetery in Bnei Brak, Reb Itche expressed the wish to be buried next to Reb Shraga Feivel: "מִי יִתְּנֵנִי שָׁכֵן שֶׁל מַר, *If only I could be this man's neighbor!*" And so it was that twenty-three years later the founder of Bnei Brak was brought to his final resting place near Reb Shraga Feivel.

The halachah prohibits leaving a sharp knife on the table during *Bircas HaMazon* because someone had once become so distraught over the destruction of Jerusalem and the Jewish suffering of the time that he plunged a knife into his heart while reciting the blessing "Build Yerushalayim." That halachah could have been said with Reb Shraga Feivel in mind, so intense was his feeling for *Eretz Yisrael*.

Chapter 26

Final Months

R EB SHRAGA FEIVEL ALWAYS DEFINED HIMSELF IN TERMS of his duties as an enlisted recruit of *Klal Yisrael*. That identification with the collective fate of *Klal Yisrael* only intensified in the final months of his life. During that period, he was fully absorbed with the epochal events surrounding the creation of the State of Israel. He followed closely the months of political maneuvering and debates leading up to the United Nations vote for the partition of Palestine and the subsequent struggle of the infant Jewish state for survival in the face of the onslaught by the combined Arab armies. The state of his health fluctuated, often in tandem with the news from *Eretz Yisrael*.

IN THE LAST YEARS OF HIS LIFE, REB SHRAGA FEIVEL TRIED TO divide his time between the Mesivta and Bais Medrash Elyon in

Bidding Farewell to the Mesivta
Monsey. He moved his residence to a small house adjacent to Bais Medrash Elyon, but spent several days a week in the Mesivta,

Rabbi Yaakov Kamenetsky

*(Left to Right): R' Anshel Fink,
Reb Shraga Feivel,
Rabbi Gedaliah Schorr*

where he slept on a couch in his office. As his health deteriorated, however, he realized that he could no longer bear the strain of commuting between Bais Medrash Elyon and the Mesivta and sleeping in his office.

Less than a year before his passing, Reb Shraga Feivel spoke to the Mesivta student body after Minchah. In a voice brimming with emotion, he described to the students something of the history of the Mesivta, including his own role, which he said ranged from *menahel* to building manager. He was leaving the Mesivta, he said, to devote himself entirely to Bais Medrash Elyon and Torah Umesorah, and in his place, he appointed Rabbi Yaakov Kamenetsky and Rabbi Gedaliah Schorr.[1] In a few words, he described the *maalos* of each: Reb Yaakov, he said, was a *mushlam*, a complete *gaon*, and Reb Gedaliah the rising star in the entire yeshivah world.[2]

Though there were few students who had not seen Reb Shraga Feivel cry before, then it had always been over some abstract concept still far from their grasp — the Exile of the

---

1. Earlier Reb Shraga Feivel had appointed a *Vaad* to run the Mesivta, with Rabbi Yitzchak Schneider as its head and Rabbi Yaakov Kamenetsky and Rabbi Gedaliah Schorr as *menahalim*. Rabbi Alexander Linchner and Rabbi Nesanel Quinn were also members of the *Vaad*. Rabbi Schneider left the Mesivta for personal reasons around the time that Reb Shraga Feivel appointed Rabbi Kamenetsky and Rabbi Schorr as his successors. At one point he had spoken with Rabbi Shlomo Rotenberg about his possible involvement in the *hanhalah*.

2. Sidney Greenwald.

Shechinah, the beauty of *Eretz Yisrael,* the pain of *Klal Yisrael.* But this time, as he choked back the tears while saying good-bye to his beloved Mesivta, the boys could not restrain their own tears.

ON FRIDAY, NOVEMBER 29, 1947, THE UNITED NATIONS DEBATED the issue of partitioning the British Mandate for Palestine into two

The U.N. Declaration
countries, one Arab and one Jewish. Reb Shraga Feivel prayed fervently for partition. He had no radio in his house, but that Friday he borrowed one and set it to the news, leaving it on for Shabbos. He waited with such tense anticipation to hear the outcome of the U.N. vote that he did not come to *shalosh seudos.* When he heard the U.N.'s decision to establish a Jewish state, he stood up and recited the blessing הַטּוֹב וְהַמֵּטִיב, *Who is good and Who does good.*[3] Without losing sight of the antireligious nature of the leaders of the *yishuv* in *Eretz Yisrael,* he nevertheless saw the creation of a Jewish state as an act of Providence and as a cause for rejoicing. At the very least, there would now be one country in the world whose gates would be open to the thousands of Holocaust survivors still languishing in Displaced Persons Camps in Germany and Austria.[4]

Reb Shraga Feivel gave voice to the ambivalence with which religious Jews around the world greeted the creation of an independent Jewish state in *Eretz Yisrael* nearly two millennia after the destruction of the *Beis HaMikdash* by Titus' army. On the one hand, there was the recognition that the new state led by those raised in ideologies hostile to Torah was not the return of the Davidic kingdom for which they had prayed so long. Yet coming a scant three years after the greatest tragedy in modern Jewish history, it was hard not to

---

3. In 1948, after the Arabs attacked the newly declared Jewish state and soldiers were falling on the battlefield, several *roshei yeshivah* taunted Reb Shraga Feivel for having recited the blessing. Reb Shraga Feivel turned to Rabbi Aharon Kotler, who agreed with him that the favorable U.N. resolution was indeed worthy of the blessing. *Rabbi Nesanel Quinn.*

4. He once said that even though *Eretz Yisrael* is controlled by nonreligious and antireligious Jews, one must still admit the good that *HaKadosh Baruch Hu* had done in causing the gates to the Land to be open once again to Jewish immigration. *Rabbi Yehoshua Schiff.*

hope that the new state was a harbinger of a new life for the survivors.

In a famous parable, Reb Shraga Feivel compared the new state to a breech birth. When a baby is born normally, head first, Reb Shraga Feivel said, the delivery is easiest and safest for the mother, and augurs best for the future development of the infant. In the context of the establishment of Jewish political sovereignty in *Eretz Yisrael*, a "head-first birth" would have been one in which the great Torah leaders — the true heads of the nation — led the way. But even in a breech birth, despite the danger to the infant, one can still hope that it will live and be healthy. Perhaps *Chazal* were referring to the legs-first manner in which the new state was born, Reb Shraga concluded, when they said (*Yalkut Shimoni* to *Amos*, 549), "In a generation that rejects Hashem — expect the footsteps of Mashiach."[5]

Four days after the United Nations vote, on 19 Kislev,[6] Reb Shraga Feivel spoke in Bais Medrash Elyon, to present his *talmidim* with a Torah perspective on the event. He began by emphasizing that in the absence of prophecy no one could interpret the U.N. declaration with any certitude.[7] Nevertheless the whole tenor of his remarks reflected his hope that the moment was a positive one for the Jewish people.[8] He described three aspects of the final redemption: the redemption of the Land, the ingathering of the exiles, and the return of the Divine Presence to her proper place. The redemption of the Land is the first of the three. The Sages (*Megillah* 17b) explain why the blessing over fruitfulness of the Land [בִּרְכַּת הַשָּׁנִים] comes before

---

5. Chinn, "Ohr Shraga," p. 13.

6. The day is the *yahrzeit* of the Maggid of Mezritch, when Reb Shraga Feivel annually held a *seudah* with his *talmidim*. *Rabbi Yehoshua Geldzhaler.*

7. The account of this speech is based on the notes of Rabbi Yaakov Homnick, which were subsequently published in his pamphlet, "*Nitzanei Torah B'America: R' Shraga Feivel Mendlowitz.*"

8. Even the Brisker Rav, one of the strongest opponents of Zionism, said of the U.N. vote that it was "a smile from Heaven, but the rulers of the State ruined it." Quoted in Rabbi Shlomo Wolbe's *Bein Sheshet LeAsor*, p. 146.

the blessing for the ingathering of the exiles [מְקַבֵּץ נִדְחֵי עַמּוֹ יִשְׂרָאֵל].
The prophet Yechezkel says: "And you, mountains of Israel, shall
shoot forth your branches and lift up your fruits to My people Israel,
for they are soon to come" (Yechezkel 36:8). In other words, the physical rebirth of the Land and its release from foreign domination is
the prelude to the return of the exiles.

Reb Shraga Feivel suggested that the present moment paralleled
the return of the exiles from Babylonia under Ezra and Nechemiah,
which had come about only through the permission of a gentile
ruler, King Cyrus. Just as Cyrus in his time had his own reasons for
allowing the Jewish exiles to return to Jerusalem, so the nations of
the U.N. no doubt had interests of their own that they sought to advance by allowing a Jewish state. But, in the final analysis, "The
heart of a king is in Hashem's hands; He directs it where He wants"
(Mishlei 21:1).

Reb Shraga Feivel followed his comparison of the U.N. and Cyrus
to its logical conclusion. While agreeing that the Torah leaders of the
past two generations had been absolutely correct in directing their
followers to have nothing to do with the Zionist movement,[9] the
question of the hour was: What should the Torah world do now after having witnessed Heavenly intervention? To that question, there
could be only one answer: It was incumbent upon all bnei Torah to
do everything in their power to ensure that the voice of Torah increase and be heard in the new state:

> It is our duty to participate in the building of the State, phys-
> ically and spiritually . . . The choice is in our hands. Will we

---

9. In the 1,870 years from the destruction of the Second Temple to the present moment,
he pointed out, Zionism had no role to play for the first 1,820. Only because of generation after generation of believing Jews, ever ready to cast themselves into the flames
or extend their necks to the executioner's sword rather than betray their G-d, were
there still Jews today. Had we followed the path of Mendelssohn, whose children and
followers almost without exception became apostates or assimilated totally, there
would have been no Jews left to become Zionists. Yet, Theodore Herzl, an assimilated
Jewish journalist who covered the Dreyfus trial, came to the conclusion that Jews
would find safety only in their own land.

make ourselves a high wall and go up, as they failed to do in the days of Ezra . . . ? If causeless hatred prevails among us, the arousal of Divine favor from above could all be lost. We must be the pioneers of Torah. We must form a nation worthy of the Land, a nation of Torah.

The thrust of his remarks was that the future of *Eretz Yisrael* would be determined by the response of religious Jews to the new opportunity. If they rose to the challenge, he suggested, it would be possible to create a land filled with Torah. Reb Shraga Feivel noted that those who failed to take advantage of Cyrus' permission to return to the Land are severely criticized in both the Gemara and Midrash (*Shir HaShirim Rabbah* 8:9). The Sages give the following interpretion to the verse in *Shir HaShirim* (8:9): אִם חוֹמָה הִיא נִבְנֶה עָלֶיהָ טִירַת כָּסֶף וְאִם דֶּלֶת הִיא נָצוּר עָלֶיהָ לוּחַ אָרֶז, *If her faith and belief are strong as a wall [notwithstanding incursions from without] we shall become her fortress and beauty, building her city and Holy Temple, but if she wavers like a door [succumbing to every alien knock], with fragile cedar panels shall we then enclose her.* The Talmud (*Yoma* 9b) comments that if Israel's faith had been strong like a wall and the people had unanimously followed Ezra back to *Eretz Yisrael*, they would have been privileged to have the full glory of the *Shechinah* in the Second *Beis HaMikdash*, just as it had been in the First. But since only a small minority followed Ezra, the *Shechinah* was lacking in the Second Temple. Instead of being like silver, which never rusts, the people were likened to cedar, which warps and rots. Those who remained in Babylonia, writes Rashi (to *Yoma* 9b), prevented the *Shechinah* from returning to dwell in the Second *Beis HaMikdash*. Reb Shraga Feivel strongly implied that the Jewish people should not miss such an opportunity a second time by remaining aloof from the fate of the Land or being reticent about going there.

In response to those who claimed that Providence would not have made the United Nations the instrument to make such a gift to the Jewish people, Reb Shraga Feivel compared the current phenomenon to the events of Purim. In that miracle, the Sages saw

Hashem working His will through Achashveirosh, clearly an unworthy person. Do *Chazal* not tell us, he asked, that the first steps of the final redemption will go very slowly, to be followed by a sudden burst of light, just as the sun suddenly appears in the morning?[10]

Many wondered how the nations of the world, who had inflicted untold suffering on the Jewish people in both the recent and distant past, could be the instrument of their salvation. The same question had been asked at the time of Cyrus, Reb Shraga Feivel pointed out. The Jewish people had queried *HaKadosh Baruch Hu* as to why Daniel, Chaggai, Zechariah, and Malachi had not been the ones to bring about the miracle (*Midrash Shir HaShirim* 5:4). In answer to that question, the *Ohr HaChaim* writes that the nations of the world are also the creations of Hashem and have a purpose: "For then I will change the nations [to speak] a pure language, so that all will proclaim the Name of Hashem, to worship Him with a united resolve" (*Tzephaniah* 3:9). After what they inflicted upon the Jewish people and what they allowed the Nazis to do, Reb Shraga Feivel speculated, the nations of the world had lost all right to exist. But since they, too, are part of the Divine plan, Hashem had allowed them to continue to exist by making them the instruments of good to the Jewish people.

In a similar vein, he also explained why the secular Zionists might have been chosen to play such a fateful role in the history of the Jewish people. In every Jew, he explained, there is a spark of *kedushah* (holiness) — *dos pintele Yid* — which is his inheritance from the *Avos*. Every Jew is both an individual and a part of the collective body of Israel. As long as he does not sever his bonds to the nation, that little spark is not extinguished, no matter how numerous his sins. Divine Providence might have arranged that the secular Zionists play a major role in the redemption of *Eretz Yisrael* precisely in order to maintain their connection to *Klal Yisrael*.

In a conversation with the Satmar Rav, shortly after his talk on the U.N. declaration, Reb Shraga Feivel was subjected to the

---

10. *Midrash Shir HaShirim* 6:10; *Yerushalmi Berachos* 1:1; *Yerushalmi Yoma* 3:2.

sharpest criticism for his "Zionist leanings." Later he told his family, "I could have answered him *Chazal* for *Chazal*, Midrash for Midrash, but I did not want to incur his wrath, for he is a great man and a *tzaddik*." He added with a twinkle, "And besides, he has a fiery temper."

The Satmar Rav told a group of Torah Vodaath students who wanted to hear his views, that the U.N. declaration was no cause for rejoicing and nothing of permanence could be created by Jews who have left the path of the Torah. He asked, "Do we not say twice a day in the second paragraph of *Shema* that if the Jewish people turn astray and serve alien gods 'they will be swiftly banished from the goodly land which Hashem gives you'? "

When these words were repeated to Reb Shraga Feivel, he stood his ground. Certainly the Satmar Rav is right, he told his students, that nothing of lasting significance can be created by those removed from Torah, but building the Land they can do, and for that they will also receive a reward in Heaven. The prediction of swift banishment in *Shema*, he insisted, refers to those in whom sin is so ingrained that there is no hope of *teshuvah*. For now, we can still hope that slowly they will return to their Father in Heaven.[11, 12]

He did not deny that there was merit in opposing views, nor did he think that his reading of events was beyond question. To those close to him he admitted that others might be right from a logical point of view, but nevertheless maintained "my heart tells me that our approach is the right approach."

Of course, he did not let his feelings alone guide him. In Rabbi Moshe Chaim Luzzatto's *Daas Tevunos*, he found support for his view. There the Ramchal specifically describes the period of *Ikvesa d'Meshicha* (the time before the coming of Mashiach) as one in which Hashem does not guide the world according to the normal calcula-

---

11. Rabbi Eliyahu Yehoshua Geldzhaler.

12. Someone once scorned the gentile nations who built projects in Jerusalem, with their names attached to them. To this, Reb Yosef Chaim Sonnenfeld responded, "Let them build. They destroyed much; now let them build."

tions of reward and punishment. At that time, events will take place regardless of the merit of the generation.

And in the writings of his beloved Reb Tzadok HaKohen of Lublin he found a hint that there would be a time in which the aggressive stance of the Zionists would succeed. After the sin of the spies, Moshe Rabbeinu warned those who regretted their original lack of faith that they should not attempt to go into *Eretz Yisrael* by force: וְהִיא לֹא תִצְלָח, *it will not be successful*. Reb Tzadok HaKohen adds, however, "*Now* it will not succeed, but there will be another time when it will succeed. That will be in the time of the footsteps of Mashiach."

AFTER THE U.N. VOTE FOR PARTITION, JEWISH SETTLERS IN ISRAEL were subjected to increased attacks from Arab bands supported by

Reconsidering His Stance

the Arab League. Meanwhile, the British, who were still the Mandatory power, systematically prevented the Jewish population from defending itself and intensified their efforts to disarm the Jewish populace, searching Jewish homes with Geiger counters and confiscating every weapon they found. In the face of renewed fighting in Palestine, the United States wavered in its support for the partition plan, and it appeared that the U.N. declaration might come to naught.

On Rosh Chodesh Adar II, March 11, 1948, Reb Shraga Feivel spoke again in Bais Medrash Elyon. That day the Jewish Agency office in Jerusalem had been blown up, and Reb Shraga Feivel's tone was more subdued than in the wake of the U.N. declaration. Reb Shraga Feivel's ostensible subject was the well-known Gemara in *Nedarim* (81a) that attributes our present exile to the failure of the Jews at the time of the Second Temple to make a blessing on Torah study. Only at the very end did he mention *Eretz Yisrael* at all, and his remarks reflected his intense grief at the bloodshed in Palestine. It seemed from his talk that he wished to prepare the *talmidim* for possible disappointment.

He found in the words of *Yeshayahu* (26:17-18) a description of the current situation of the Jewish people. After prophesying about the future redemption, the prophet spoke about Israel's suffering in exile, likening the expectant nation to a woman in the throes of child-birth. "Like a pregnant woman close to giving birth . . . so were we before You, Hashem. We have conceived and gone into travail . . . salvations were not performed in the land, and the [wicked] who dwell on the earth did not fall."

Despite the intensity of labor pains, a mother is able to bear it, he explained, because each new pain brings her closer to the birth of her child, and the more intense the pain, the closer the birth. Exile is pregnancy, and Redemption is birth, he said. The horrors of the Holocaust, then, should have been the intense pangs that precede birth. And yet we must recognize that we might have been wrong, that the time for the Redemption was not yet at hand, that the Land will not yet be redeemed nor the evil be destroyed from the world.

In such a situation, Reb Shraga Feivel continued, the Jewish people have no choice but to return to their traditional role of waiting: "Jews know how to wait . . . We can wait another 'hour' in the great sea of time." And if the nations now do not stand by their promise to allow a Jewish state, we shall be no more despondent than we were before their declaration. In the meantime, the only thing for us as Jews to do, he said, was to heed the prophet's further advice: לֵךְ עַמִּי בֹּא בַחֲדָרֶיךָ וּסְגֹר דְּלָתְךָ בַּעֲדֶךָ חֲבִי כִמְעַט רֶגַע עַד יַעֲבָר זָעַם, *Go, my people, enter your rooms and close your door behind you; hide for a brief moment until the wrath has passed* (26:20).

We must always ask ourselves: "Am I any closer to my Creator than in the year past? Than I was ten years ago?" Even while learning Torah, we must never forget that the purpose of that learning is to bring one ever closer to Hashem.

ONCE FULL-SCALE WAR BROKE OUT AFTER THE STATE OF ISRAEL declared its existence on May 14, 1948, Reb Shraga Feivel's

Heart in Zion
thoughts were never far from *Eretz Yisrael*. A group of students saw him outside the Mesivta building one day talking excitedly with Rabbi Gedaliah Schorr and gesticulating rapidly with the newspaper held in his hand. "If I were your age," he told the students, "I would take a gun and go

to *Eretz Yisrael.*"[13] At the same time, he worried about the destructive effect of a prolonged war on Jewish souls.[14]

Just two weeks after the Declaration of Independence, the Jewish quarter of Jerusalem, including the Western Wall, fell to the Arabs. Every Jew living there was either killed, taken prisoner, or exiled from the ancient walls of Jerusalem. After the Shabbos-eve meal, as he reached the words, "Have mercy, Hashem, on Israel, Your nation, and on Yerushalayim, Your city," in *Bircas HaMazon*, Reb Shraga Feivel burst out in violent sobbing, which brought on a massive heart attack. The doctors were immediately summoned and had him carried to his bed with orders that he must remain absolutely still. He was confined to bed for weeks before he was able to move. Even when he was under the oxygen tent, those attending him saw his fists beating on the side of the bed and heard him repeat over and over again, *"Vos vet zein mit Eretz Yisrael?* — What will be with *Eretz Yisrael?*"[15]

REB SHRAGA FEIVEL DID NOT DECEIVE HIMSELF ABOUT HIS chances for recovery. He told his *talmid* Mannes Mandel, who was

Preparing for the End

sitting by his bed, "My wife thinks that when I get better we'll go back home to Williamsburg. But I know that from here, we will go straight to *Eretz Yisrael.*"

"I'm not afraid of death," he told another student, "but I am terrified when I think to Whom I will be accountable."[16]

For the first time, he complained about pain. Pain was his constant companion, he told his son Shmuel, and all his life he had combated it with dreams of projects yet to be completed. But now he could no longer dream of the future.[17]

---

13. Rabbi Shubert Spero.

14. After the bombing of the King David Hotel by the Irgun, he expressed his fears about the long-range consequences of Jewish boys learning how to shoot and kill.

15. Chinn, "Ohr Shraga," p. 13.

16. Rabbi Yaakov Leshinsky.

17. When the pain abated, his natural optimism returned as well. He told one *talmid* who visited on a day when he was well enough to learn Mishnayos, "Moshe Rabbeinu

Too weak to concentrate in the way he was accustomed, he complained that he was unable to prepare himself properly for the World to Come. "All one's life is a preparation for this day . . . All life teaches a person how to die . . . And in the end he is too weak to uplift himself." He used his situation to teach others. A sick person cannot properly do *teshuvah* (repentance), he said. Thus this verse should be read not as a statement, but as a question: "You reduce man to pulp, and You say, 'Repent'?" (*Tehillim* 90:3). Yet, despite the pain, he sought to fully experience the passage from this world to the next. Frequently on his lips was Rebbe Yitzchak of Vorki's play on the words of the nighttime *HaMapil* prayer, הָאֵר עֵינַי פֶּן אִישַׁן הַמָּוֶת, *Illuminate my eyes, lest I die in my sleep:* Illuminate my eyes, lest I sleep through my death.

A few days before his *petirah*, Reb Shraga Feivel told Rabbi Linchner that, as the son-in-law of a person who had endured suffering, Rabbi Linchner would succeed in his creative efforts. Reb Shraga Feivel cited a letter of the Chofetz Chaim, in which he strongly advised a student of his not to break off an engagement, because the prospective bride's father had suffered greatly in his life and the merit of his suffering would benefit his future sons-in-law.[18]

His youngest son, Shmuel, often read him the tales of Rabbi Nachman of Breslov, and when he had the strength, Reb Shraga Feivel would explain the deeper meaning hidden in the simple stories.[19] Another work he requested frequently was the recently published edition of the Baal Shem Tov on the Torah, from which Shmuel would read only a few lines at a time. Even those few lines often caused him to become so excited that the doctors threatened him with the loss of this privilege if he did not learn to listen calmly. "How can I hear words from a work like this without being transformed?" Reb Shraga Feivel demanded.

---

pleaded to be allowed to enter *Eretz Yisrael*, if only as a bird to sing to *HaKadosh Baruch Hu*. How much more fortunate am I to be able to learn Mishnayos." *Rabbi Nesanel Quinn.*

18. Rabbi Alexander Sender Linchner.

19. Rabbi Eliyahu Yehoshua Geldzhaler.

LITTLE MORE THAN TWO WEEKS BEFORE REB SHRAGA FEIVEL'S
petirah, the Satmar Rav came to Monsey for the wedding of one of

Final Days Reb Shraga Feivel's students. The *chasunah* took
place on Erev Shabbos, and the Satmar
Rav remained in Monsey over Shabbos.
On Shabbos afternoon, he came to visit
Reb Shraga Feivel, who was confined to
his bed, which had been placed on the
porch of his home. Before the Rav's arrival, Reb Shraga Feivel asked for a pill to
steady his weak heart.

Satmar Rav

Those two giants sat facing one another
for a long time without either one uttering
a single word. Tears formed in the corners of Reb Shraga Feivel's
eyes and remained there throughout the meeting.

The last days of his life were by no means given over exclusively
to preparing himself for death. The future of *Klal Yisrael* remained the
focus of his thoughts. Two days before the end, he called Rabbi
Linchner to his bedside. "You know how dear Torah Umesorah is to
me. It's my *liebling* (my favorite). See to it that it continues to grow."
But uppermost on his mind remained the fate of *Eretz Yisrael*. "*Tu
eppes far Eretz Yisrael* — Do something for *Eretz Yisrael*, for the Torah
education of Israeli youth," was his last wish to Rabbi Linchner. "I
feel that I will be charged in Heaven with not having done enough
for *Eretz Yisrael*."[20]

Torah Vodaath, of course, was not forgotten. In his last conversation
with Rabbi Nesanel Quinn, Reb Shraga Feivel begged him to guard

---

20. Rabbi Linchner heeded Reb Shraga Feivel's final wishes. Just after Pesach the following year, he visited *Eretz Yisrael* for the first time as the guest of the Ponevezher
Rav. In the course of that trip, Boys Town Jerusalem and its companion institution
Mesivta Merom Zion were born. Today, nearly fifty years later, Boys Town, on the outskirts of Jerusalem's Bayit Vegan neighborhood, occupies a campus of nearly ten
square blocks, and has provided a Torah education and professional training to thousands of Israeli youth, most of them products of the large immigration of Oriental Jews
in the early years of the State.

two things in the Mesivta "like the pupil of your eye": דער האָר וואָהר דער — און די ביסעל חסידות — the thread of truth and the bit of Chassidus.[21] His final testament to his students was "to do everything possible to spread Torah."

On 3 Elul, at 7 o'clock in the morning, Reb Shraga Feivel's heart beat its last, just as he finished *Bircas HaTorah* (the blessings on the Torah). The news reached Bais Medrash Elyon, where the *talmidim* had already gathered to say *Tehillim*, prior to Shacharis. The stunned *talmidim* rushed to the *mikveh* to immerse themselves, so that they could participate in the *taharah* (preparation of the body for burial).

From Monsey, the funeral procession proceeded to Williamsburg, where thousands had gathered at the Mesivta on South Third Street to pay their final respects. The streets surrounding the Mesivta were filled, as the *aron*, covered by a *tallis*, was brought up to the *beis medrash* and circled the *bimah* seven times.

In accord with Reb Shraga Feivel's repeated instructions, no eulogies were said. The verse-by-verse recitation of *Tehillim* was the only means for the large crowd to express its pain. It was arranged for Rabbi Yaakov Kamenetsky to eulogize Reb Shraga Feivel at graveside, but the bus bringing Reb Yaakov lost its way and he arrived only after the completion of the burial. Many of those closest to Reb Shraga Feivel were sure that the total absence of eulogies was Providentially arranged in keeping with his deepest wishes.

If he had not merited to see *Eretz Yisrael* in his lifetime, Reb Shraga Feivel hoped to do so in death. Thus he was buried in America on the express proviso that when peace came to the Land and conditions permitted, he would be reburied in Bnei Brak. Two years later, Rabbi Alexander Linchner had Reb Shraga Feivel's body transported to *Eretz Yisrael* for reburial in Bnei Brak, the city he had helped so much in its infancy.[22]

21. The *hor vor* (thread of truth) to which Reb Shraga Feivel referred meant, in Rabbi Quinn's opinion, to be genuine in the service of the A-mighty. The *bissel Chassidus* referred to the joy in the service of the A-mighty and the accent on personal humility.

22. Buried close by are the Chazon Ish; Rabbi Eliyahu Eliezer Dessler; Rabbi Yitzchak Isaac Sher, the Slabodka *Rosh Yeshivah*; Rabbi Mordechai Pogramansky, the greatest student of the prewar Telshe Yeshivah; and Rabbi Yitzchak Gershtenkorn, the founder of Bnei Brak.

Ponevezher Rav   *Rabbi Yechezkel Levenstein*

Reb Pinchas Mandel, who supervised the removal of the body, confided in later years that he had seen only two *niftarim* whose bodies were still whole, after such a passage of time — Reb Shraga Feivel and the Stoliner Rebbe, Rabbi Yochanan Perlow.

Before the reburial, the *aron* was brought to Williamsburg where a eulogy was held before thousands of people on South Third Street. The Ponevezher Rav spoke movingly, saying that Reb Shraga Feivel's holy remains belonged in the holy soil of *Eretz Yisrael*, and that although he preferred to be known as "Mister," he was truly a *nistar*, someone who succeeded in keeping his greatness hidden. Among those accompanying Reb Shraga Feivel to his final resting place in the Shomrei Shabbos cemetery were the Chazon Ish, the Ponevezher Rav, and the Ponevezh *Mashgiach*, Rabbi Yechezkel Levenstein. At graveside, his dear friend from his first days in Scranton, Rabbi David Eisenberger, was so overcome with emotion that he threw himself prostrate on Reb Shraga Feivel's grave sobbing, "Reb Shraga Feivel, *gevalt*, pray for all your kosher *talmidim*."

Reb Shraga Feivel's matzeivah   *The matzeivah of Reb Shraga Feivel's wife*

A simple, unobtrusive gravestone marks Reb Shraga Feivel's grave. In death, as in life, he avoided calling any attention to himself. On it is inscribed:

HaChassid
R' Shraga Feivel
son of Moshe, זצ"ל,
Mendlowitz
He served Hashem with love and accepted
his suffering with serenity.
He spread Torah among the multitudes
and caused many to return from sin.
He passed away 3 Elul 5708 in America
and was brought to his final resting place 11 Av 5710.
תנצב"ה

At the end of *Daniel*, the *matzdikei harabbim* (those who return the multitudes to righteousness) are compared to stars. Because of the great distance between the stars and us, the light of a star goes on il-

The matzeivah of Rabbi Moshe Yitzchak Segal beside that of Reb Shraga Feivel. Both men devoted their lives to spreading Torah in their respective countries, England and America.

luminating the earth for thousands of years after the star itself is extinguished. So it is with *tzaddikim;* their light lives on long after they are gone.[23]

Such a star was Reb Shraga Feivel Mendlowitz.

---

23. This explanation is Rabbi Simchah Wasserman's.

Appendix

A Talmid Remembers

Reminiscences of Rabbi Nesanel Quinn

O N SHABBOS REB SHRAGA FEIVEL ELEVATED HIMSELF to rare spiritual loftiness. His countenance took on a
The Neshamah Yeseirah (The Added Soul) of Shabbos changed expression, an exalted expression that revealed the dominant presence of the *neshamah yeseirah* (the "added soul" that comes with Shabbos) within him. His features were a vivid representation of the expression of the Sages that "on Shabbos the faces radiate with a Heavenly glow."

On Fridays, Reb Shraga Feivel would leave the yeshivah at noontime and begin preparations to greet the Shabbos Queen. After having immersed himself in the *mikveh*, he immersed himself in the fountain of his favorite *sefarim*. He departed from the province of his numerous responsibilities and entered the sphere of Heavenly spirituality.

During these Erev Shabbos afternoons his comrades and mentors were *Likkutei Torah*, or *Sfas Emes*, or *Pri Tzaddik*. Reb Shraga Feivel would study a passage, then lift his eyes from the text to concentrate on what he had read, and meditate long enough to internalize the thought. His features betrayed his mental and emotional turbulence. At times intense emotion stirred him to tears, but these were tears of joy.

On Erev Shabbos Reb Shraga Feivel recited *Shir HaShirim* with reverent joy. With melodious tone, he articulated the love of the Jewish people for the A-mighty and the compensating love of the A-mighty for the Jewish people.

To some, Shabbos is a day of passive rest, but not so for Reb Shraga Feivel. To him, Shabbos was for intense spiritual advancement and an occasion to unite with the Divine Presence.

Although far from so high a level of spirituality, his *talmidim* were nonetheless profoundly influenced by just being in Reb Shraga Feivel's shadow.

It was a moving experience to daven Friday night and receive the Shabbos in Reb Shraga Feivel's company. Reb Shraga Feivel pronounced the six psalms of *Kabbalas Shabbos* with his eyes focused outward, as if addressing himself to the entire universe. He reached an emotional climax with the melodious singing of *Lecha Dodi*, which welcomes the Shabbos Queen and expresses a deep yearning for the universal acceptance of the Kingdom of the A-mighty. During these stirring moments the *talmidim* beheld Reb Shraga Feivel's gleaming face, his right hand raised and motioning as to an audience, and his entire body pulsating. In such a setting, the singing of the *talmidim* "pierced the roof."

In the words of one *talmid*, "this heavenly sight will accompany me throughout my lifetime."

After the *davening*, Reb Shraga Feivel left the *beis medrash* without waiting for the *Gut Shabbos* greetings. He was on his way to yet another *avodah* (service to the A-mighty), the Shabbos repast. It began with a joyous *Shalom Aleichem*, welcoming the two angels that accompany every Jew returning from shul on Friday night. Then he recited *Ribbon Kol HaOlamim* (Master of the Worlds). The words needed no translation; his passionate tone gave meaning to his words and deeply penetrated the hearts of all present.

The members of his family at the table refrained from ordinary conversation. The Shabbos table was for *zemiros* and Torah. His sons Moshe Yitzchak and Shmuel, like him, were greatly talented musically and their singing added to the blissful atmosphere.

Following the *seudah* came the song לְקֵל אֲשֶׁר שָׁבַת, *To the G–d Who rested*, with the melody composed by the chassidic Rebbe, Reb Naftali of Ropshitz. After this song Reb Shraga Feivel withdrew to study *Chumash* and *Ramban*.

He arose on Shabbos morning at about the same time as on other days. The day began with the *mikveh* after which he became engrossed in his *sefarim*. After thus having been inspired, he proceeded to the Mesivta. Usually he was among the first ten to arrive in shul.

The *shalosh seudos* that Reb Shraga Feivel conducted in the Mesivta was again an *avodah*, an intense *avodah*. The setting was an unlit room, long tables lined with *talmidim*. The repast — a matzah for each *talmid*. At the head sat Reb Shraga Feivel, unseen, but keenly felt.

Then began the *zemiros*, heartfelt, stirring *zemiros*. The lyrics were sentences or phrases from the Scriptures or the Talmud, repeated over and over until they were assimilated into the *neshamos* of the *talmidim*. Reb Shraga Feivel maintained that this type of *zemiros* is more penetrating than the spoken word; there were no *divrei Torah* at *shalosh seudos*.

Shalosh seudos was the culmination of all the Shabbos *avodah*, the *ne'ilah*, the climax of the Shabbos. With Reb Shraga Feivel the hour of *shalosh seudos* was an hour borrowed from Heaven. Even to an occasional visitor it left an indelible impression. As a genuine virtuoso, Reb Shraga Feivel chose the *niggunim* with a sequence, to produce the desired effect on the participants.

Rabbi Yitzchak Sheiner, the long time *Rosh Yeshivah* of Kamenitz-Jerusalem explained: "For us American-born boys, unfamiliar with chassidic customs and practice, the *shalosh seudos* was a revelation. We were introduced to a new Shabbos, a Shabbos of Heavenly substance. We felt lifted to higher spiritual strata, we were emotionally moved, our thoughts were focused on how to improve ourselves. We wished to retain this sublime joyous disposition. The *shalosh seudos* carried us through the week. To this day, remembering it moves us."

Rabbi Moshe Wolfson, *Mashgiach* of Mesivta Torah Vodaath, founder and *rav* of Congregation Emunas Yisrael, adds: "The dazzle of sublimity that overtook us in the company of our *rebbi* was because of the selected melodious *niggunim, niggunim* of yearning, an outpouring of the *neshamah, niggunim* selected by our *rebbi*."

He adds, "Reb Shraga Feivel had a brilliant mind, a joyful lively disposition and a symphonic *neshamah*, a Shabbos *neshamah*. His *neshamah* was a song for the glory of our Creator, a song for the marvels of Creation, and a song for the unique, distinctive status of the Jewish people in the history of mankind."

Reb Shraga Feivel was possessed with a Shabbos *neshamah*, because *Shabbos Shalom*, Shabbos represents peace and harmony. We absent ourselves from the conflicts of the week. We greet the Shabbos with Psalm 29, in which the word קוֹל, *sound*, is mentioned seven times, corresponding to the seven days of Creation. On Shabbos, Creation became complete, appropriate for song.

Reb Shraga Feivel's personality embodied the kaleidoscopic spectrum of Jewish thought and religious expression: His roots were in Hungary; he preferred Lithuanian *gedolim* as Talmudic teachers in the yeshivah; he insisted on the discipline and punctuality of Frankfurt; and he exuded the spirit of Chassidus, emphasizing deep-seated fervor, genuine humility, and ubiquitous joy. Reb Shraga Feivel personified a harmonious synthesis of all the multicolored trends in the Torah world.

This spirit of harmony he infused into his *talmidim,* and he taught them to have a positive regard for every sincere trend in the Torah world. He also impressed on them the need to accept the vicissitudes of life optimistically and stressed that life was a symphonic song with variations of rhapsody and sorrow, success and failure, all of which should be accepted in the spirit of "*Gam zu letovah* — This, too, is for the good."

That Reb Shraga Feivel himself was consistent in this attitude can be illustrated by the following episode: When the Old City of Jerusalem fell into the hands of the brutal Arabs, Reb Shraga Feivel burst into violent sobs that triggered a massive heart attack. He was confined to his bed for many weeks. After he was able to sit up in a chair a *talmid* visited him and found him learning Mishnayos. Reb Shraga Feivel looked up with a broad smile saying, "I am most fortunate that I am able to learn a *Perek* Mishnayos. But, I regret that I shall no longer be able to gladden and enliven the hearts of a *talmid* and his *kallah* by dancing at their wedding."

REB SHRAGA FEIVEL WAS AN EMINENTLY GREAT MAN. HIS WAS a restless uncompromising personality. He was careful not to hurt

Multiple Greatness the sensitivities of people, but he took extreme exception with religious leaders who, while professing allegiance to the Torah, rationalized their inconsistent views and practices. He fought like a lion for the honor of the A-mighty and His Torah. He did not entertain the slightest ambition for himself but, in sharp contrast, he dreamed magnificent plans for the Torah. Despite all his glorious visions, he was pragmatic in his pursuit to bring his plans to fruition. This talent is the secret of his extraordinary success.

With all his success Reb Shraga Feivel was the essence of humility. When he succeeded in fulfilling an extensive plan, he minimized his accomplishment to avoid any self-glorification, and forthwith he began dreaming another grand plan for the advancement of Torah and its observance.

His kaleidoscopic personality was a synthesis of mental genius, selfless humility, joyous disposition, love of people, loyalty to friends and *talmidim*, glorious vision, practical planning, dedication to absolute truth, and impeccable integrity — all motivated by firm *emunah* in Providence and the Torah.

Reb Shraga Feivel preferred to lead his life in obscurity and shun publicity. Because his heart burned with a glowing fire to serve the A-mighty and to advance the glory of the Torah, he was catapulted into the public domain, but the public viewed only his talents, his actions, his accomplishments; the greatness of his soul remained concealed, even from those close to him.

Reb Shraga Feivel possessed the unique ability to adapt his

disposition to the particular occasion. Here he was humorous, there he was stern; here insistent, there compliant. Reb Shraga Feivel was present at the wedding of Rabbi Mannes Mandel, a favorite *talmid.* It was during World War II and the tragedy of the Jewish people was evident on Reb Shraga Feivel's features. Reb Mannes respectfully reminded his *rebbi* that he once said, "At your wedding I will show great joy." At once Reb Shraga Feivel's countenance was transformed to exultation.

Reb Shraga Feivel was a pioneer. With trust in the A-mighty he ventured into uncharted territory. A learned skeptic once criticized, "Herr Mendlowitz, you are not of this century," to which Reb Shraga Feivel replied, "Correct, I am of the next century."

In 1926 Reb Shraga Feivel made known his intention to open Mesivta Torah Vodaath, to educate generations of American youth who would be uncompromising in the observance of the Torah, unyielding to the temptations of modern America, erudite in the Talmud, and learning Torah for its own sake, not for a career. The Jewish religious establishment viewed his efforts with pathetic skepticism. Some Jewish leaders actually opposed the introduction in America of a way of life incongruous with modern Orthodoxy.

But Reb Shraga Feivel forged ahead, and with the help of the A-mighty he triumphed. Having tasted the sweet words of the Talmud and the vigorous mental activity it demanded, American youths became enchanted with their learning. This, together with the *emunah* and *kedushah* (faith and holiness) inspired by Reb Shraga Feivel, produced genuine *talmidei chachamim* proud of our eternal heritage. The American establishment looked on with amazement. They saw youths who to all appearances were thoroughly American, yet they adopted completely the faith, attitudes, and undivided loyal devotion to Torah and mitzvos.

But more, Reb Shraga Feivel instilled in his *talmidim* a love for the Jewish people and a passionate drive to transmit our Jewish heritage to others who were not fortunate to receive a Torah education. And yet more. He instilled in them an ardent love for the Land of Israel and an ambition to live there. Every Yom Tov and wedding, Reb Shraga Feivel concluded by singing *Od Yishama*, Yeshayah's prophecy that the joy of young and old, of groom and bride, would return to the streets of Jerusalem. With a yearning, pining melody, with tears flowing from his closed eyes he sang, and his *talmidim* were swept along with him, in a scene that left an indelible impression on everyone present. When, in teaching *Tanach*, he came to passages describing the return of the Jewish people to Israel, his eyes became a fountain of tears, tears of joy.

REB SHRAGA FEIVEL EXPLAINED THAT ALL WORLD EVENTS LEAD to the era of Mashiach, when all nations will recognize and accept

Jewish Philosophy of World History

the rule of the A-mighty. To understand events that seemingly do not point in that direction, we will have to wait for enlightenment by Eliyahu and Mashiach.

Often we are stupefied by an immense national tragedy. We fail to see a "why." The reason for this perplexity is that our vision is limited. We are unaware of the "before" nor do we see the "after" of the event. It is without context, like tearing out a page from the middle of a novel. From that one page a reader might get the false impression that criminality succeeds while saintly conduct fails.

When Mashiach comes, we will see in hindsight how, like a jigsaw puzzle, every event fits in the right place. מִשְׁפְּטֵי ה' אֱמֶת צָדְקוּ יַחְדָּו, *the judgments of Hashem are just,* but only יַחְדָּו, when we view them all together, as an inseparable unit. On the superficial level we witness how all the nations of the world are becoming increasingly united economically and even politically. This is stage one in the process of the eventual perfection of mankind. We look forward to the culmination of that process in stage two — לַעֲשׂוֹת רְצוֹנֶךָ, *to do your will,* when the nations will submit to the commands of the Creator.

Our Holy Scriptures do not record mere events. Rather, they explain the cause of each occurrence in order for us to learn lessons for our proper conduct. The emphasis is on the "why," more than on the "what."

Secular historians also define the "whys" of events, but they see *immediate* causes; they do not recognize the hidden hand of the A-mighty.

They see the stone that broke the pane but fail to see the one who threw it. By now we know more than ever of the miraculous harmony that exists between all parts of the universe. Should we thoughtfully study history we would discern the same marvelous harmony and interaction of events.[1]

This view of history is manifest vividly in the history of the Jewish people. When a cataclysmic tragedy befell the nation, outside observers predicted its disappearance. But, these observers were astonished to see the Jews emerge from under their ruins with renewed vigor.

To illustrate: After the destruction of the First *Beis HaMikdash* the Jews were driven from their homeland into Babylonia. But, there, in that exile, grew up our greatest *Tannaim*, the Sages of the Mishnah.

After the destruction of the Second *Beis HaMikdash* the exiled Jews produced more great *Tannaim* and the *Amoraim*, the Sages of the Talmud.

After the Jews were brutally decimated by the Crusaders, there emerged our great *Rishonim*.

Following the tragic years of *Tach V'tat* (1648-1649) we were blessed with the great *Acharonim*.

This phenomenon of Jewish triumph over tragedy mystifies the prophets of Jewish doom.

The prophet Michah (7:8) exclaims: "אַל תִּשְׂמְחִי אֹיַבְתִּי לִי כִּי נָפַלְתִּי, *My enemy, do not rejoice over my fall, because,* קַמְתִּי, *I shall rise again.*"[2]

Our holy prophets recorded not only past happenings. They also articulated the ultimate Jewish future, in clear, definite terms. Yechezkel (20:32) exclaims, "I swear that should you decide to be like the other nations, I will rule over you with force and outpouring

---

1. The Blessings of the *Shema* explain how we can recognize the One and Only Creator: In the first blessing, it is from the marvels of nature; in the second, from the Torah; and in the third, from the vicissitudes of fortune manifest in Jewish history. This is the relation of the blessing with *Hashem Echad*, the One and Only G-d.

2. To compare to our days:

The Germans were positive that they had exterminated the "Talmud Jews." But, behold! In America, as well as in Israel, sprouted an army of Talmudic scholars, masses of Jews loyal to Torah, and a vast array of publications, including fresh commentaries on the Talmud.

wrath." Yeshayah prophesies about the days of the future Redemption (2:2).

This portrayal of our glorious future and future of the world provided us with fortitude, courage, and faith to outlast our mortal enemies.

One of the great tasks our Creator assigned to the Jewish people was for us to be a light for the nations. This was our responsibility as a free people in the Land of Israel. We failed and we were relegated to the status of exiles scattered among all the countries of the world. The purpose of the exile was for the nations to learn from us the Torah's lofty ideals of justice, morality, and faith.

We are sluggish in our performance and the nations are slow in embracing these idealistic persuasions, so our exile is prolonged and our eventual Redemption delayed.

Yet, with steadfast convictions we repeat daily, "I believe with perfect faith in the coming of Mashiach."

The Divine guiding hand in world events could be compared to a grand master playing chess with a novice. Every move the latter makes, the grand master uses to his own purpose. Sometimes he sets a trap for the novice, who ignorantly thinks he is making the next move by his own decision while in reality the grand master has lured him into deciding as he did.

Hashem, too, utilizes every move of the rulers for His ultimate goal for humanity. When the Mashiach and Eliyahu arrive, we will understand, and the pattern will be clear. Until then, we will continue to live with our faith. Such was our *rebbi* and his unforgettable example and teachings.

Index

Camp Ohr Shraga — Bais Medrash L'Torah, 276
camps, summer, 117,273,
carbon dating, 192,193
Carpathian Mountains, 31
Chassidim and *misnagdim*, melding of the two approaches, 248
Chanukas HaBayis of the Mesivta, 85*illus.*, 86*illus.*,213
Chasam Sofer, 29,33,201,202,224,235*fn.*
Chassidic stories, 241
chassidic thought, depths of, 246
Chassidismus, 191,192*fn.*
Chassidus, 39,95,98,103,154,191,241,342,350
Chavaidan, 91
Chayei Adam, 271*fn.*
Chazan, Rabbi Elya, 96,96*illus.*
Chazon Ish, 91,325,325*illus.*,342*fn.*,343
chazzan, 140
chesed, 252
Chida, 207
Chiddushei HaRim, 108*fn.*,246,
Chiddushei Reb Reuven, 151*fn.*
chillul Hashem, 234*fn.*
Chinn, "Ohr Shraga," 16*fn.*,25*fn.*,46*fn.*, 110*fn.*,112*fn.*,113*fn.*,114*fn.*,123*fn.*,127*fn.*,130*fn.*,140*fn.*,141*fn.*,159*fn.*,172*fn.*,173*fn.*,203*fn.*,208*fn.*,213*fn.*,231*fn.*,236*fn.*,239*fn.*,252*fn.* ,287*fn.*,288*fn.*,332*fn.*,339*fn.*
Chinn, Rabbi Yitzchak, 130,141
chinuch, a career in, 286
chinuch, separate classes for boys and girls, 308
chitzonius, 199
Chofetz Chaim, 65,93,105*fn.*,131*fn.*,149,220, 223,323,340
Chovos HaLevavos, 26,33,109,122,136
Chust, 29,30,34,175
Cohen, Feivel, 167*fn.*,168*fn.*
Cohen, Rabbi Shmuel Elya, 317
Cohen, Rabbi Zev, 167*fn.*,168*fn.*
college, 94,123,196,197,198,198*fn.*,218,295*fn.*
comparison between Noach and Avraham, 18
concerns about kashrus, 43
Confession (originally named Gottesvolk), 191,191*fn.*
Congregation Emunas Yisrael, 350
Conservative and Reform movements, 202
Conservative movement, 194,195*fn.*,309
Cordovero, Rabbi Moshe, 271*fn.*
Czechoslovakia, 48
Czechoslovakia, yeshivah in, 262
Daas Press, 271*fn.*

Daas Soferim, 121*fn.*
Daas Tevunos, 122,336
daas Torah, 308
daf shiur, 178
Daf Yomi, 154,155*fn.*
Delving Within, 238*fn.*,246*fn.*,252*fn.*
Derech Hashem, 122,125
Dershowitz, Leibel, 68
Der Weg, 191*fn.*
Dessler, Rabbi Eliyahu Eliezer, 127,127*illus.*, 128*fn.*,342*fn.*
Dessler, Rabbi Nochum Velvel, 260,260*illus.*
destiny in life, each Jew has a particular, 182
Detroit, transformation of, 316
Dicker, Abe, 170*fn.*
difference between a *rav* and professionals, 77*fn.*
Divrei Chaim of Sanz, 35,207,209,238
Doros HaRishonim, 38*fn.*,123
Dos Yiddishe Licht, 50,51,54,118*fn.*,207,210, 271,283
Drush V'Chiddush, 271*fn.*
earning a living, 185
educating children, the importance of, 287
Eiger, Rabbi Akiva, 155,159*fn.*,201*fn.*
Eiger, Rabbi Leibel, 201*fn.*
Eisemann, Rabbi Moshe, 261
Eisenberger, Rabbi David, 46,74,323,343
Elias, Rabbi Joseph, 298*fn.*,316
Eller, R' Mendel, 290*illus.*,311
emunah peshutah, 295*fn.*
Epstein, Rabbi Moshe Mordechai, 91*fn.*, 271*fn.*
Epstein, Rabbi Zelik, 96,173,194,198*fn.*, 257*fn.*,276,298*fn.*
Eretz Yisrael, 42,48,110,210*fn.*,220,221,225,226, 228,229,262,265,271,279*fn.*,289,321*ff.*
faith, questions of, 193
farmhouse in Mountaindale, 274
farmhouse in the Catskills, 117
Feigelstock, Rabbi Moshe, 301
Feiner, Yaakov, 327
Feinstein, Rabbi Moshe, 16,73*fn.*,102*fn.*, 276,294,308,
Felsenberg, Rabbi Binyamin, 34,34*fn.*
Feuerstein Foundation, 271*fn.*
Feuerstein, Moses, 164*fn.*,164*illus.*,306*fn.*
Feuerstein, Samuel, 164*fn.*,166,167*illus.*,306
Fink, Dr. Jerry, 130*fn.*,180*fn.*
Finkel, Rabbi Nosson Tzvi, (the Alter of Slabodka),81, 81*illus.*,173*fn.*
Finkelstein, Rabbi Mordechai Eliyahu, 72
Fink, Rabbi Anshel, 259*fn.*,306*fn.*330*illus.*
Flam brothers, 115

Hutner, Yaakov, 267*illus.*
Ikvesa d'Meshicha, 336
Imrei Emes, 279,279*fn.*
Inter-Yeshivah Student Council, 254
"Is Yiddish Back From the Dead?", 18*fn.*
Izhbitzer Rebbe, 154
Jacobs, Rabbi Yaakov Michoel, 203*fn.*,204*fn.*
Jewish belief, issues of, 124*fn.*
Jewish Education Committee, 298*fn.*
Jewish historians, secular, 195
Jewish history, 38,123,123*fn.*,194,283,283*fn.*, 295
Jewish Theological Seminary, 195*fn.*
Jewish thought, works of, 38
Jews, to be a light for the nations, 355
Joseph, Rabbi Jacob, (the first Chief Rabbi of New York), 65*illus.*, 65*fn.*
joy in life consists of being a better, more elevated Jew, 295
joy, the greatest, 21
Judaism, 271*fn.*
Jung, Rabbi Leo, 51,54*illus.*,60,196*fn.*264,315
Kahn, Rabbi Nachman, 318
Kalmanowitz, Rabbi Avraham, 218, 218*illus.*,264,265,276
Kalmanowitz, Rabbi Shraga Moshe, 301, 244,244*illus.*
Kamenetsky, Rabbi Yaakov, 23,96,97*fn.*,142*fn.*, 144*illus.*,143,151,151*fn.*,152,152*illus.*,153,153*fn*,154,167,173,173*fn.*,206*fn.*,210,212*fn.*,217,256,275,292*fn.*,308,330,330*illus.*,342,330*fn.*
Kamenitz Yeshivah in Europe, 151
Kaminetsky, Dr. Joseph, 311*illus.*,313,314*illus.*, 315
Kanarek, Rabbi Yisrael, 261
Kantrowitz, Rabbi Yaakov, 96,144,144*illus.*
Kaplan, Rabbi Baruch, 81,85,273
Kaplan, Rabbi Yisrael Chaim, 243*illus.*,244, 301,302
Kaplan, Rebbetzin Vichna, 81,272,273
Karlin Stolin institutions, 324*fn.*
Karp, Elias, 17,73*fn.*,74,79*fn.*,94*fn.*,116,123*fn.*, 125,126,126*fn.*,143,197*fn.*,231*fn.*,322*fn.*
Karpf, Rabbi Yitzchak, 37*fn.*,157*fn.*,204, 204*illus.*,205*illus.*
Karpf, Rivkah, 37*fn.*
kashrus, 56*ff.*
kashrus supervision, 54
Katz, Rabbi Avraham Shalom, 31*fn.*
Katz, Rabbi Mordechai, 308
Katz, Rabbi Mottel, 260,261
Kaufman, Freidel, 35*fn.*,48*fn.*
Kaufman, Rabbi Shmuel, 318

kedushah, quest for 242
Kesher Chizuk Hadas, 54
Kestenbaum, Lennie, 290*illus.*,293
Ketzos HaChoshen, 201*fn.*
kiruv (or outreach), 317
Kitzur Sefer Chareidim, 122,131,271*fn.*
klal work, 253
Klal Yisrael, in the service of, 184
Klal Yisrael, specific contribution to make to, 182
Klausenburger Rebbe, 19,217,242,242*illus.*, 247,256,263,264
Klausner, Jack, 101*fn.*,127*fn.*,170*fn.*,192,193, 193*fn.*,194*fn.*,195*fn.*,198*fn.*,199,200,266*fn.*, 298*fn.*,324*fn.*,325
Kletsk, 154,261
Knesses Beis Yitzchak, 149
kollel, 302
Kollel Kodashim, 82
Kook, Rabbi Avraham Yitzchak, 227
Kopitchinitzer Rebbe, 218,218*illus.*
Kotler, Rabbi Aharon, 16,90*illus.*,96,96*illus.*,97, 151*fn.*,154,159*fn.*,218,219,261,263,266*illus*.,266,273,278,299,306*illus.*,308,309*illus.*,331*fn.*
Kotzk, 201
Kotzker Rebbe, 140,201,202,224
Kovno, 77*fn.*
Kovno Kollel, 93
Kramer, Aryeh Leib, 135*fn.*,254
Kranzler, Gershon, 126*fn.*,280*fn.*
Kremenchug, 149
Ksav Sofer, 29,33
Kulefsky, Rabbi Yaakov Moshe, 301
Kushelewitz, Rabbi Shmuel, 161*fn.*,243*illus.*
Kuzari, 26,122,129,192,196
Kuznitzki, Shlomo, 267*illus.*
k'vod Shamayim, 268
Lag B'Omer, 175
Lampert, Reb Berish, 113*illus.*
Leff, Rabbi Zev, 284*fn.*
Lehmann, Rabbi Marcus, 271
Leibowitz, Rabbi Baruch Ber, 90,90*illus.*, 91,146*illus.*,149,151,218,301*fn.*
Leibowitz, Rabbi David, 79*fn.*,93,96, 142,143*illus.*,146,197*fn.*,148*fn.*,274
Leiman, Rabbi Hershel, 140*fn.*,176*fn.*, 194,194*illus.*,298*fn.*, Leiman, Rabbi Yehoshua, 44*fn.*,213*fn.*
Leshinsky, Rabbi Yaakov, ,33,99,128*fn.*, 165,177*fn.*,204*fn.*,206*fn.*,219,247*fn.*,277*fn.*, 300,322*fn.*,339*fn.*
Lessin, Rabbi Yaakov Meir, 308

his every action is l'shem Shamayim, 261
his goal to produce anshei ruach, 302
his goal was to produce soldiers, 300
his humility, 23,203
his intense yearning for Eretz Yisrael, 321ff.
his learning Mishnayos, 29fn.
his levayah, 16
his loathing of luxury, 203
his method of reproof, 132
his poetic soul, 274
his principle of no compromise, 90
his semichah, 44,
his sense of obligation to give of himself
    entirely to Hashem, 237
his tuberculosis, 20
"I don't understand," 283 Illus.: 42,85,113,
    151,165,176,187,213,233,243, 276,309,330.
joyful lively disposition, 350
kaleidoscopic personality, 351
learning Mishnayos, 339fn.
manufacture of kosher ice cream, 49
melamed from Mezo-Laboretz, 74
melamed in Scranton, 45
melamed with a beard and payos, 73
nepotism, 204
no compromise of halachah, 202
on aesthetic sensibility, 233
on atom bombs, 232
on boys and girls socializing, 132
on different paths to reach the A-mighty, 25
on not living up to one's creative potential,
    250
on pleasures of the physical world, 20
on proper decorum, 139
on seeing Hashem's hand in nature, 232
on sefarim chitzonim, 132
on simchah, 229
on the chassidic approach, 174fn.
on the task for which one was created, 183
rejoicing at a talmid's simchah, 187
Shabbos neshamah, 350
should he focus on his own spiritual
    development, 50
symphonic neshamah, 350
the nefesh klali, 22
to plant Torah in the United States, 41
wanted to create ambassadors for Torah, 299
Mendlowitz, Reuven, 48
Mendlowitz, Rivkah, 273
Mendlowitz, Sima Tcheba, 27
Mendlowitz, Toibe, 28,36
"Men of the Spirit," 196fn.
Merling, Berl, 184,311

Mesillas Yesharim, 122,271fn.
mesiras nefesh, 82,253,291
Mesivta library, 160illus.
Mesivta of Warsaw, 219
Mesivta Tifereth Jerusalem, 73fn.
Mesivta Torah Vodaath, 16,329
Mezo-Laboretz, 29,31
Mezo-Laboretz, Reb Aharon, dayan in, 29
middos, 109,114
Miller, Shimon, 267illus.
Mintz, Rabbi Moshe, 80,116,116fn.
Mirrer Yeshivah in Brooklyn, 264
Mirrer Yeshivah in Europe, 128fn.,178,182
mishmar, 78
Mishnah Berurah, 102
"Mister," 20,44,157,161fn.,211,212,221
mitzvah of welcoming guests, 27
Mizrachi,   70,70fn.,73fn.,84,225,226,227,228,
    314fn.,326
Modeh Ani, 136,136fn.
modern hair style, 34, 102, 218
Modzhitzer   Rebbe,
    115,115fn.,218,218illus.,236,236fn.
Moetzes Gedolei HaTorah, 152fn.
Monsey, 104,152
Moreh Nevuchim, 126,196
Morgenstern, Rabbi Menachem Mendel, 201fn.
Morning Journal, 77,84,304
Moseson, Rabbi Chaim Yechezkel, 65fn.,
    72,73fn.
Moskowitz, Y.M., 42fn.
mosquitos, as "enemies," 296
Motza'ei Shabbos, 122fn.
Munkaczer Rebbe, 122fn.
mussar, 203
mussar sefer, a walking, 153
mussar shmuessen, 33,44fn.,222
mussar works, 125
National Conference on Torah Education, 310
National Society for Hebrew Day Schools, 303
Navos HaCarmeli, 183
Nefesh HaChaim, 128,196
Ner Yisrael, 212
Nesivos HaMishpat, 201fn.
Nesivos Olam, 104
Netzach Press, 271
Neuschloss, Rabbi Moshe, 262
New Haven, Connecticut, 80
New Haven Yeshivah, 83,116fn.
Newman, Frank, 306fn.
Nezer HaKodesh, 91
Nimukei Ridbaz, 55,64
Nitra Rav, 279